THE ROLE OF THUNDER IN *FINNEGANS WAKE*

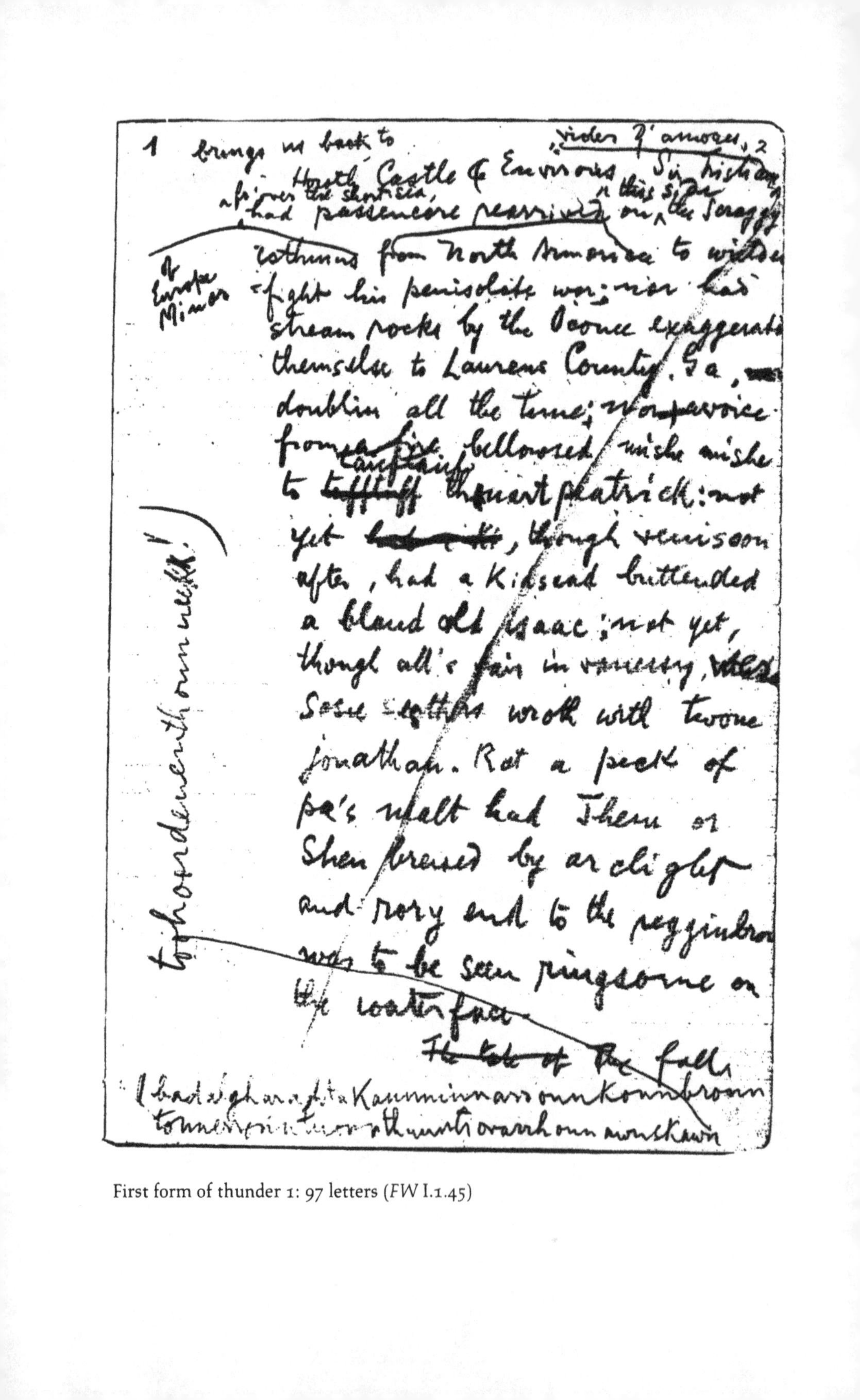

First form of thunder 1: 97 letters (*FW* I.1.45)

ERIC McLUHAN

The Role of Thunder in *Finnegans Wake*

UNIVERSITY OF TORONTO PRESS
Toronto Buffalo London

Published by University of Toronto Press 1997
Toronto Buffalo London

Reprinted 2014
ISBN 0-8020-0923-9

Canadian Cataloguing in Publication Data

McLuhan, Eric
    The role of thunder in Finnegans wake

Includes bibliographical references and index.
ISBN 0-8020-0923-9

1. Joyce, James, 1882–1941.   Finnegans wake.   I. Title.

PR6019.O9.F593613   823'.912   C96-931751-4

Material from works of James Joyce, © Estate of James Joyce, reproduced here by permission. Permission to reproduce images from the James Joyce Archive granted exceptionally, by the Estate of James Joyce.

Exceptional permission to reproduce images from the *James Joyce Archive* graciously granted by the Estate of James Joyce. The author wishes to thank especially the Trustee, Seán Sweeney, and Stephen Joyce.

University of Toronto Press acknowledges the financial assistance to its publishing program of the Canada Council and the Ontario Arts Council.

This book has been published with the help of a grant from the Humanities and Social Sciences Federation of Canada, using funds provided by the Social Sciences and Humanities Research Council of Canada.

Tout vue des choses qui n'est pas étrange est fausse.

Paul Valéry

Outragedy of poetscalds! Acomedy of letters!

Finnegans Wake, 425.24

Contents

Preface

The odd language of *Finnegans Wake* clearly marks it as belonging to a lively tradition of composition called Menippean satire and thereby relates it to serious cultural observation and poetic activity of a high order. To identify *Finnegans Wake* as an example of this particular species of satire requires looking at it in an unorthodox manner. Both of the conventional approaches to Menippism miss the mark. Classicists define it as involving 'a mixture of verse and prose' (the *Wake* does contain plenty of verse, overt as well as embedded in the text), but maintain that the practice of Menippizing died out either in antiquity or in the Middle Ages. Contemporary literary critics, particularly those basing their approach in the observations of Northrop Frye, classify works as Menippean using objective description of outward features and themes of known Menippean satires. But to approach Menippism objectively is to miss the essential character of the satire.

Of the three modes of satire – the other two are Horatian and Juvenalian – Menippism, following the practice of the Cynics, aims its attack at the reader. A Menippist will do anything necessary to reinvigorate the reader's numbed sensibilities, so the art blossoms with novelty in every age as well as with blatant plagiarism of other, earlier Menippists. Descriptive approaches cannot keep pace with novelty, and objective appraisal of the satires and their contents means ignoring their effect on the reader. The first part of this study, then, focuses on the nature and tradition of Menippism and the techniques needed to study a Menippean satire, especially Joyce's. Since rhetoric is the science of using words and images to produce a given effect in an audience (of hearers, viewers, or readers), classical rhetoric and principles of decorum are invoked as the ideal method of approach.

A great deal of the remainder of this study involves examining the language of *Finnegans Wake* and the reasons for its departures from the normal and the expected. Once we know that the *Wake* is a Menippean satire, we know two things, both crucial: we know what the *Wake* is (not simply a 'monstrous joke,' as one bewildered reader howled in frustration), and we know what it is for. As a Menippean satire it is far from alone, for it belongs to a vital tradition of writing that contains similar works and that extends from Homer (*Margites*) through Varro, Seneca, Plutarch, Lucian, Macrobius, Martianus Capella, Alan of Lille, Chaucer, Erasmus, Rabelais, Cervantes, Thomas Nashe, Burton, Swift, Sterne, Mark Twain, Byron, Flaubert, and Ezra Pound, and onward through Flann O'Brien, John Fowles, Don DeLillo, and Italo Calvino, to mention but a few.

Without a doubt, the most unusual, the most conspicuous, and the most Menippean feature of the curious verbal landscape of *Finnegans Wake* is the ten 'thunderclaps.' That each of them is one hundred letters long, and that each apparently contains words for 'thunder,' has been part of *Wake* lore since it first appeared. But although their exact length points to deliberate craft and precision on Joyce's part, hitherto there have been no serious studies of these concoctions. In fact, the tenth thunder contains an extra letter: the total of letters in all ten is 1,001 – a deliberate invoking of *The Arabian Nights, The Book of a Thousand Nights and a Night.* (Needless to say, that book too is a Menippean satire.) Long loosely associated with Viconian cycles and Vico's theory of history, these enigmatic thunders turn out to be carefully crafted words, macroscopic puns that include terms from all of the languages used in the *Wake.* Moreover, each of the thunders has an exact purpose, a specific role to play in the drama of the *Wake.* Each thunder, far from being a random collage of sounds, articulates words and themes from its context that echo and dramatize particular characters and events occurring in the wake of technological man. The thunders are statements, but without syntax. Although a multitude of features of *Finnegans Wake* mark it as a Menippean satire, its Menippean identity could be established on the basis of the thunders alone.

The thunders record and replay by means of human speech the most profound effects of our technologies on shaping our culture and sensibilities. The first thunder, for example, dramatizes the effects of the first palaeolithic and neolithic technologies: fire, building of walls (and with them various forms of architecture), weaponry, and even speech itself. Thunder 2 ushers in the Prankquean, mistress and matriarch of the eye; she rules by means of clothing and uses fashion as weaponry. Thunder 5 brings onto the stage another matriarchate: that of Belinda the Hen and the printing press – both modes of repetitive reproduction for the marketplace. (The prostitution of nature to the market is a major theme of thunder 4.) The last four thunders concern electric technologies, such as radio (7), film (8), and even television (10). Thunder 6, which brings down the curtain in the Phoenix Playhouse, constitutes a general reprise of the effects of electricity and encapsulates them in the theme of retrieval and rebirth, and renaissance. For this century, as Joyce saw clearly, is embroiled in the greatest renaissance the world has ever witnessed: rebirth and renewal in electric fire. It is a commonplace of primitive cultures that thunder is nature speaking, or is the speech of the gods, and they ask the shaman to interpret each clap – 'what did he say that time?' – as automatically as we say 'Gesundheit.' Performing the ancient role of *vates* and poet, Joyce listened to the rolling of technological thunders as they resound in human languages and replayed them for us in the words of the *Wake*, and the wake of human progress and innovation.

Reading and interpreting the thunders, the reader is able to discover a new rationale for the main characters and their mysterious relations to one another. They cast a new light on many of the episodes (such as the Prankquean, Persse O'Reilly, Belinda and the Letter, the Phoenix Playhouse, Kersse and the Captain, the Ondt and the Gracehoper), and link them together in the drama of human culture and technology. To assist, I also provide detailed exegesis of each thunder and show its relation to the text at large, to its proper context, and to specific characters, episodes, and themes.

Now I must acknowledge a profound defect. At every turn, in writing this study, I have regrettably been forced to pass over a great deal of the exegetical work that has been done on the text of the *Wake* during the past half-century. To incorporate into this essay even a representative amount of that vast erudition would have meant extending the manuscript many hundreds of pages more, with a result none but the most determined insomniac reader would willingly endure. At the same time, it would have risked losing track of our purpose: to show Menippus at work, to interpret the ten thunderclaps, and to demonstrate how they relate to the rest of the text. There are no other studies of *Finnegans Wake* as Menippean, or of Joyce's Menippism in his other major works; and there are no other studies of the ten thunders. So a fresh approach seemed called for. I will mine here only some of the strata of Joyce's language, and must leave to others better qualified the task of integrating what I have unearthed with the learned corpus of Joyce scholarship.

The present volume has its roots in studies undertaken about thirty years ago with another Joyce scholar, Marshall McLuhan. Many of the discoveries and insights that make up this essay are latent or were foreshadowed in his writings and observations about culture and technology. He was never reticent about the debt he owed to Joyce in particular, and frequently uttered and published such statements as this: 'Nobody could pretend serious interest in my work who is not completely familiar with all of the works of James Joyce and the French symbolists.' Such statements were intended to be taken quite literally: a full appreciation of McLuhan's work is impossible without the sort of perceptual training that such familiarity instils. Needless to say, that is not an attractive proposition, particularly to those from fields other than litera-ture. They often resent any imputation that the training afforded by their own studies is in some measure inadequate. Consequently, such statements have come to be regarded as simply provocative hyperbole. McLuhan, how-ever, like Joyce, demanded the highest scholarship and erudition of those who would take him seriously or who would attempt to share his vision. He once remarked to me, as I know he did to many others, that his work on media and culture was, in the main, 'applied Joyce.' Conversely, then, it might be fair to say that no one can claim a serious appreciation of Joyce's work without a complete familiarity with the full spectrum of McLuhan's work.

Joyce himself claimed that he was the greatest engineer who ever lived. Unquestionably, he is the towering figure in twentieth-century language and letters. McLuhan occupies much the same position *vis-à-vis* the study of communication in this century, having done for that field what Joyce did for expression in prose; yet he is the only scholar to maintain that he has taken up where Joyce left off and pressed on to explore new areas of experience and understanding. One objective of this book, then, is to disclose some of what McLuhan saw in the *Wake* and followed up in his work. Actually, that topic is large enough to deserve a separate study, for neither McLuhan nor Joyce worked in isolation from the mainstream of our intellectual tradition; rather, they were aware of that tradition in all of its complexity and working, and conscious of their roles in it.

It was, in fact, about 1966, a couple of years before the writing of *War and Peace in the Global Village*, when my father and I first tackled Joyce's ten thunders. We had been reading the *Wake* off and on together for a year or two, for sheer enjoyment and delight in playing with language, and as a way to whet our wits.

We had developed the habit of reading aloud together each day 'a page' of the *Wake*. The 'page' often extended to three or four, and our beginning point was usually chosen at random. 'A page' may not seem like a lot, but a page of the *Wake* is not like an ordinary page. It demands the closest atten-tion with all senses operating at once, or as many as one can muster. And with two minds alert for nuance and reference, even a few lines can occupy five or ten minutes of very hard work, what with probing back and forth in the text and making links with other passages in the book and entering marginal references. The *Wake* is not, like a novel, to be read all at one go, but sampled and sipped and relished in bits. And used.

Of course, now and then we would stumble across a thunder, and wonder what in blazes Joyce was doing there. Eventually, we grew sufficiently curious about these odd 'words' to compile a list of all ten. We spent several days reading the thunders and puzzling over them. Several years later, we used the basic identifications as three pages in *War and Peace in the Global Village: an inventory of some of the current spastic situations that could be eliminated by more feedforward.* The introduction begins with this paean to Joyce's prescience and his omnipresence in the text:

The frequent marginal quotes from *Finnegans Wake* serve a variety of functions. James Joyce's book is about the electrical retribalization of the West and the West's effect on the East:

The West shall shake the East awake ... while ye have the night for morn ...

Joyce's title refers directly to the Orientalization of the West by electric technology and to the meeting of East and West. The *Wake* has many meanings, among them the simple fact that in recoursing all of the human pasts our age has the distinction of doing it in increasing wakefulness.

Joyce was probably the only man ever to discover that all social changes are the effect of new technologies (self-amputations of our own being) on the order of our sensory lives. It is the shift in this order, altering the image that we make of ourselves and our world, that guarantees that every major technical innovation will so disturb our sensory lives that wars necessarily result as misbegotten efforts to recover the old images.

There are ten thunders in the *Wake*. Each is a cryptogram or codified explanation of the thundering and reverberating consequences of the major technological changes in all human history ...

Joyce was not only the greatest behavioural engineer who ever lived, he was one of the funniest men, rearranging the most commonplace items to produce hilarity and insight: 'where the hand of man never set foot.' (4–5)

War and Peace is festooned with marginalia taken from *Finnegans Wake*, by way of letting Joyce comment in person on the text from the sidelines. It also includes, on three pages (46–8), my adumbration of the themes (explored in this book) in the ten thunders of the *Wake*. Decades later, it took me a year or more of concentrated effort to begin to winkle out the thousands of words *in* the thunders; now, several of them have yielded thirty and more pages of words each. The lists presented hereunder have been kept to the clearest and the most persuasive selection.

A final note about Joyce and McLuhan: my father used Joyce as a colleague. Whenever he made a discovery about technology and culture, he would open the *Wake* and read for a bit, and there, sure enough, he would find that Joyce had already been over the ground, decades earlier. Joyce did it by following the lines of force in the language, reading and using what was registered there about the convolutions and disturbances of human experience and perception. Often, too, McLuhan would find a pregnant allusion or turn of phrase in the *Wake* that would trigger associations to some matter currently under discussion. He did not merely use Joyce to confirm an insight, but also used Joyce as the stimulus for fresh awareness of the present moment. In the same vein, Joyce recommended using Vico 'for all he was worth.' Even today, Joyce gladly performs the same service for anyone willing to rise to his level of play. (Some, including Joyce, would have it sink, not rise: he often avowed that his art did not set out to be highbrow: Shem, after all, 'was a sham and a low sham.') It is a commonplace that all great art has the same invigorative and illuminative power; in particular, that power is a defining characteristic of 'low and motley' Menippean satire.

Abbreviations

I Global

Annotations	Roland McHugh, *Annotations to 'Finnegans Wake.'* Baltimore, London: Johns Hopkins University Press 1980; rev. ed. 1991. Pagination is identical with *Finnegans Wake,* so is seldom cited separately. See 'McH' below for citation in thunder lists.
AWN	*A Wake Newslitter.* Colchester: University of Essex.
FW	James Joyce, *Finnegans Wake.* I use the eleventh printing (New York: Viking 1964), incorporating the author's corrections, made after publication of the first edition by Faber and Faber (1939). Conventions of textual citation by page and line number are observed; 'the bird in the case (111.05)' locates the quote on p. 111, l. 5. In contexts where it is not otherwise clear that *Finnegans Wake* is being referred to, citation is prefixed by 'FW': (e.g., *FW* 111.05).
JJ	Richard Ellmann, *James Joyce.* New York: Oxford University Press 1959.
JJII	*James Joyce.* New York: Oxford University Press 1982.
JJQ	*James Joyce Quarterly.* Tulsa, OK: University of Tulsa.
Korkowski	E.P. Korkowski, 'Menippus and His Imitators: A Conspectus, up to Sterne, for a Misunderstood Genre.' Diss. University of California, San Diego, 1973.
Letters I	*Letters of James Joyce,* ed. Stuart Gilbert. New York: Viking 1957. Reissued with corrections as *Letters of James Joyce,* vol. 1, 1966.

Letters II, III   *Letters of James Joyce*, vols. 2 and 3, ed. Richard Ellmann. New York: Viking 1966.

Loeb   Volumes in the series, Loeb Classical Library. Cambridge, MA: Harvard University Press; London: Heinemann.

Lucian   *The Works of Lucian*, ed. and trans. A.M. Harmon, K. Kilburn, and R.D. MacLeod. 8 vols. Loeb 1913–61.

OED   *The Oxford English Dictionary*. 12 vols. Oxford: Clarendon Press 1933–61.

Ulysses   James Joyce. *Ulysses*. New York: Random House (Modern Library) 1961. *Ulysses: The Corrected Text*, ed. Hans Walter Gabler with Wolfhard Steppe and Claus Melchior. New York: Random House 1986.

II Thunder Lists

The following abbreviations are used in citing sources and languages in the thunder word-lists at the end of chapters 3 to 13.

Sources

ClL   Brendan O'Hehir and John M. Dillon. *A Classical Lexicon for 'Finnegans Wake': A Glossary of the Greek and Latin in the Major Works of Joyce*. Berkeley, Los Angeles, London: University of California Press 1977.

Egy   *The Egyptian Book of the Dead*, trans. E.A.W. Budge. New York: Dover 1967.

Gaz   Louis O. Mink. *A 'Finnegans Wake' Gazetteer*. Bloomington, London: Indiana University Press 1978.

GaL   Brendan O'Hehir. *A Gaelic Lexicon for 'Finnegans Wake.'* Berkeley, Los Angeles: University of California Press 1967.

GeL   Helmut Bonheim. *A Lexicon of the German in 'Finnegans Wake.'* Berkeley, Los Angeles: University of California Press 1967.

Gla   Adaline Glasheen. 'Part of What the Thunder Said in *Finnegans Wake.'* Mimeographed as issue 23 of *The Analyst*, ed. Robert Mayo. Evanston IL: Dept. of English, Northwestern University 1964.

McH   Roland McHugh. *Annotations to 'Finnegans Wake.'* Baltimore, London: Johns Hopkins University Press 1980.

SE   Dounia Bunis Christiani. *Scandinavian Elements of 'Finne-gans Wake.'* Evanston IL: Northwestern University Press 1965.

Wig   L.A. Wiggin. 'The First Thunderbolt.' In *James Joyce Review,* II, nos. 1–2, 1959.

26L   Peter M. Bergman, ed. *The Concise Dictionary of Twenty-six Languages in Simultaneous Translations.* New York: Bergman Publishers (Polyglot Library) 1968.

Languages

Alb	Albanian	Ma	Malay
Ar	Arabic	ME	Middle English
AS	Anglo-Saxon	Nor	Norwegian
Bre	Breton	OE	Old English
BL	Bog Latin	ORum	Old Rumanian
Cz	Czech	OSw	Old Swedish
Dan	Danish	ON	Old Norse
Egy	Egyptian	Port	Portuguese
Fi	Finnish	Pol	Polish
Fr	French	Prov	Provençal
Gael	Gaelic	PS	Pan-Slavonic
Ger	German	R	Russian
Gr	Greek	Rum	Rumanian
Heb	Hebrew	Sa	Samoan
Hin	Hindustani	Sax	Saxon
Hu	Hungarian	S-C	Serbo-Croatian
Icel	Icelandic	Sh	Shelta
Indog	Indo-German	Skt	Sanskrit
Indon	Indonesian	Sl	Slang
Ital	Italian	Sp	Spanish
Jap	Japanese	Sw	Swedish
Ki	Kiswahili	Turk	Turkish
Lat	Latin	Vo	Volapük
Lett	Lettish	We	Welsh
Li	Lithuanian		

PART I

1

Cynic Satire

Like Shakespeare, who lent his name to a kind of sonnet that existed before him, Menippus gave his to a kind of writing that had been practised for centuries before his time. For Menippus set the basic tone and patterns of the form for subsequent writers. The first Menippean satire in the Western tradition antedates Menippus by several centuries: Homer's *Margites*. We can piece together a sense of the *Margites* from the few fragments that remain – remarks that Aristotle let slip in the *Poetics*, some lines in Clement of Alexandria's *Stromata*. Evidently, Margites was a Ulysses-in-reverse. Where wily Ulysses had ingenuity equal to any demand, Margites was a sort of jerk-of-all-trades who failed at everything to which he turned his hand. Flaubert used the idea in *Bouvard and Pecuchet*.

Menippus of Gadara, the Cynic philosopher, lived in the first half of the third century B.C. Diogenes Laertius, the main source of information about Menippus, remarks, 'there is no seriousness in him; but his books overflow with laughter, much the same as those of his contemporary, Meleager ...'[1] Menippus was a Cynic, a 'dog-philosopher' – the pun between Cynic and dog is possible only in Greek: a wry, self-conscious remark, it is oft-used in the satires as comment on their low nature. (Joyce, in the same vein, chuckles in the *Wake*, 'Shem was a sham and a low sham': that is, Shem, the penman, the writer, the artist.) Strabo, too, speaks of him as *spoudogeloios*, as mixing serious and comic, high sentence and low wit. This serio-comicality, one of the ways in which Cynicism informs Menippean satire, is a kind of shock tactic whereby elevated ('high') matters are treated in low style or trivialities examined scrupulously with all the pomp and erudition that decorum and scholarship can supply. Handy examples of the latter abound in the literature of paradoxical encomia: Gorgias' *Praise of Helen*, Erasmus' *Praise of Folly*, Swift's 'Digression in Praise of Madness' in *A Tale of a Tub*.

Classical scholars use the formula 'a mixture of verse and prose' to identify a Menippean satire and to define the genre, but this and all other descriptive approaches are inadequate. The 'mixture' formula serves well enough to include works such as Petronius' *Satyricon*, Apuleius' *Metamorphoses*, Martianus Capella's *De nuptiis*, Alan of Lille's *De planctu naturae*, or Dante's *La Vita Nuova*, but it also admits works that are clearly not Menippean (such as Boethius' *Consolatio*): at the same time, it excludes some writers who claim to be Menippean but who wrote only in prose or only in verse – such as Byron (*Don Juan*). Another problem is that of variety. Menippizing now embraces many dozens of techniques in addition to serio-comicality and prosimetrum form, and it has lately sprung up in newer media: for example, films such as Woody Allen's *Zelig*, *The Purple Rose of Cairo*, and *Mighty Aphrodite*.

Descriptive approaches – and there are many of them – however elaborate, can't get a grip on Menippism precisely because the satire does not work through the content or any set of surface characteristics listed in the description, but rather in the effect on the reader's sensibilities. Description, as a mode of criticism, has inherent limitations: it is valued because of the objectivity it apparently confers, but it is objective because it isolates the thing being defined from its ground of effects and its audience (including the critic). By its nature, description focuses attention on content and organization; consequently, while the commonplace topics and techniques used by Menippists proliferated, descriptive definitions of Menippean satire have become increasingly complex and unwieldy. In the end, these definitions not only divert attention from the fun and the satire, but more and more they have formed a system or philosophy of Menippism – the very kind of pedantry Menippus and his imitators routinely attacked. Thus Swift in his footnotes.

T.S. Eliot, in *Poetry and Drama*, was first in our time to point out the reason for mixing verse and prose. Such a mixture he wrote, 'in the same play is generally to be avoided: each transition makes the auditor aware, with a jolt, of the medium.' Neither of the other forms of satire, Horatian or Juvenalian, aim for this effect; in fact, they shun it. Rather, they attack the private vice or public hypocrite, the moral sham or civic scandal. Menippean satire goes after the reader instead. Urbanity (Horace) and moralism (Juvenal) each demand smooth consistency of attitude and tone if they are to be carried off convincingly. Evenness of style allows the writer to focus attention away from the writing and onto the evil or good; Cynic satire, perversely, wallows in the macaronic – the medley of prose and verse, of high and low style and subject – to focus attention on the satire as an artefact, on the medium, on the language, on the self-conscious reader. The content or 'meaning' in the ordinary sense is anything at all as long as it entices the reader into staying with the satire long enough for it to have its effect. And that is the crux of the matter.

A Cynic or Menippean satire – the terms are interchangeable – behaves as if it were a Cynic philosopher. It is the literary embodiment of a Cynic, a Diogenes or Menippus or Lucian turned by some mad Merlin into a book yet allowed to *act* as before. As an active form, a Menippean satire goes to any extreme necessary in order to frustrate objectivity or detachment on the part of the reader. So: *any work in any medium that produces the Cynic effect is thereby a Menippean/Cynic satire.* What, then, is the Cynic effect?

As one of Petronius' modern translators observes, 'a main characteristic of Menippean satire was the union of humour and philosophy'[2] – of the long face and the leer. Cynics, and Diogenes in particular (and, after him, Burton's Democritus Junior), were often referred to as 'laughing philosophers,' for they refused to take seriously any political, private, social, intellectual, or other kind of pretentiousness. The Cynics did not have a system of philosophy or found a school: they regarded such things as vanities too likely to become ends in themselves that would distract attention from serious matters – reality and one's human scale. I.G. Kidd gives a succinct account in *The Encyclopedia of Philosophy*:

The Cynic saw himself as 'scout and herald of Gods,' dedicating his own labours as a reconnaissance for others to follow: he was the 'watchdog of mankind' to bark at illusion, the 'surgeon' whose knife sliced the cancer of cant from the minds of others. Cynics deliberately adopted shamelessly shocking extremes of speech and action to jolt the attention and illustrate their attack on convention ...

The Cynics did not offer arguments to intellectuals, whose theories they despised as useless ... thus the more formal types of philosophical instruction were abandoned and three new literary genres fostered: the *chreia*, or short anecdotal quip with a pungent moral tang; the *diatribe*, or popular sermon in conversation; and Menippean satire.[3]

Cynics were called 'dog-philosophers' because they snarled at pretence, lived in the streets, emphasized the natural life, combining in various degrees bohemian indigence and antisocial individualism. Nor did they (for example, Antisthenes, Diogenes, Crates) attempt to build followings or show any special reverence for one another or for their Cynic predecessors. Lucian, a touchstone Menippist, frequently displays Diogenes and other Cynics as utter fools.

Cynic writers across the years have revelled in the 'dog' epithet. Rabelais recommends doggishness to the reader in typical Cynic fashion:

Have you ever uncorked a bottle of wine? God help us, do you remember the look on your face?

Or have you ever seen a dog fall on a marrow bone? (The dog, I may add, is, as Plato says in Book II of the *Republic*, the most philosophical beast in the world.) If you have seen my dog, you may recall how intently he scrutinizes his bone, how soliticously he guards it, how fervently he clutches it, how warily he bites his way into it, how passionately he breaks it, how diligently he sucks it. What force moves him to act so, what hope fosters such zealous pains, what recompense does he aspire to? Nothing but a little marrow. (To be sure this little is more toothsome than large quantities of any other meat, for – as Galen testifies in Chapter III of his *Concerning the Natural Faculties*, and Chapter XI of *Concerning the Uses of the Various Parts of the Human Body* – marrow is the most perfect food elaborated by nature.)

Modelling yourself upon the dog, you should be wise to scent, to feel and to prize these fine, full-flavoured volumes. You should be fleet in your pursuit of them, resolute in your attack. Then, by diligent reading and prolonged meditation, you should break the bone of my symbols to suck out the marrow of my meaning – for I make use of allegory as freely as Pythagoras did. As you read, you must confidently expect to become valiant and wise. For here you will find a novel savour, a most abstruse doctrine; here you will learn the deepest mysteries, the most agonizing problems of our religion, our body politic, our economic life.[4]

The most extensive expression of the Cynic/dog pun and trope is Leon Rooke's *Shakespeare's Dog*, a wondrous romp with a canine narrator whose perspective on humans and the world in general is decidedly Cynical: 'O sainted dog that is in Heaven, where's the dignity, where's the decorum, what tree trunk of poisoned hemlock have these fools eaten?'[5] And the barkers, as Lucian called them, are given pride of place (the last dozen lines) in Martianus. He calls the *Marriage* 'a melange sportively composed by Satire,' who 'has heaped learned doctrines upon unlearned, and crammed sacred matters into secular; she has commingled gods and the Muses and has had uncouth figures prating in a rustic fiction about the encyclopedic arts.' So Satire ends the work with this: 'I have been inspired by Felix Capella – whom ignorant generations have observed ranting as he passed judgment upon barking dogs, giving to the high office of proconsul a bumble bee long separated from his blossoms by the sickle, and in his declining years ...'[6] No one escapes.

Cynics were, on the whole, uncompromising in their antagonism to all forms of systematized living or learning, particularly to philosophical systems. Hence their own refusal to found a school or to canonize their Cynic forebears. All systems, they felt, dehumanized the adherents and rendered them robotic. The Cynics' constantly reiterated message stressed three things:

- To the great and powerful, remember you're human.
- To the proud, remember you're mortal.
- To the rest, discard all your pretences and illusions.

Can a continual 'Wake up, you numbskulls!' be called a philosophical system?

A more modern Cynic, the satirist Wyndham Lewis, wrote that 'the most virtuous and well-proportioned of men is only a shadow, after all, of some perfection; a shadow of an imperfect, and hence an "ugly," sort. And as to laughter, if you allow it in one place you must allow it in another. Laughter – humour and wit – has a function in relation to our tender consciousness; a function similar to that of art. It is the preserver much more than the destroyer. And, in a sense, everyone should be laughed at or else no one should be laughed at.'[7]

The Cynic's impulse was satiric, as his behaviour demonstrates: his aim, like that of the satires, was ever to correct the perceptions of the target – the public. Just as would a Cynic in person, the satire itself administers the therapy to the reader. So Rabelais claims that 'as you read, you must confidently expect to become valiant and wise.' Or, to illustrate from another quarter, Diogenes styled himself a 'Socrates gone mad.'

This 'madness' was Diogenes' habit of unconventional behaviour – reviling great men to their faces, fornicating in public, relieving his bowels in the middle of the market place, and breaking wind in polite gatherings – for he insisted that the beginning of human evil was the delusion that man was above the natural state, and he would go to any length to remind of what that state was. The Cynics, following Diogenes' example, took to wearing rough cloaks both winter and summer, and a life of wandering, carrying staves and wallets, eating only bread and lupines, and sleeping out of doors. For a time, Diogenes took to living in (actually, wearing) a tub from the temple of Cybele, and this tub appears often in the later Menippean landscape.[8]

Diogenes also likened himself to a choir master 'pitching the note too high, that the rest might get the right one.'

Eugene Kirk offers this summary of the outward characteristics of Menippean satires:

Those 'family resemblances' turn out to be fairly definite. The chief mark of Menippean style was unconventional diction. Neologisms, portmanteau words, macaronics, preciosity, coarse vulgarity, catalogues, bombast, mixed languages, and protracted sentences were typical of the genre, sometimes appearing all together in the same work. In outward structure, Menippean satire was a medley – usually a medley of alternating prose and verse, sometimes a jumble of flagrantly digressive narrative, or again a potpourri of tales, songs, dialogues, orations, letters, lists, and other brief forms, mixed together. Menippean topical elements included outlandish fictions (i.e., fantastic voyages, dreams, visions, talking beasts) and extreme distortions of argument (often, 'paradoxes'). In theme, Menippean satire was essentially concerned with right learning or right belief. That theme often called for ridicule or caricature of some sham-intellectual or -theological fraud. Yet sometimes the theme demanded exhortation to learning, when books and studies had fallen into disuse and neglect.[9]

Cynic satire constantly takes what Matthew Arnold might term the attitude of 'low seriousness': never so serious as when at riot of play, combining low sham with profound learning and the trite and trivial with the quadrivial.

In fact, Cynic satire has always frustrated purely descriptive approaches because the tradition is not so much detectable in the ploys or mannerisms of the writers – although the 'family resemblance' approach of Kirk and Korkowski serves better than any other yet proposed – as unerringly detectable in the effect produced on the reader. Kirk[10] and others have reviewed the problems inherent in trying to grasp Cynic satire by means of description. Cynicism, whether literary or personal, simply defeats systematizers. How, then, proceed?

By way of decorum. Kirk remarks that 'the Menippean writer expects one constant result: that humour, some fiction, coarseness, or the appeal to caricature, and resentment of some proud elite, or suspicion against pretenders to privileged knowledge, will help convey his message.'[11] The message, in a nutshell, is 'Wake up!' Eliot spoke of the 'jolt' produced by sudden shifts of register or decorum or verse/prose. It can quickly be seen that every technique in the descriptive catalogue aims at the same jolt or sudden flash of awareness by irrationally flinging the reader from one situation or mental posture to another.

Their simultaneous insistence on clear perception and distrust of theories and illusions signals the confluence of interests of Cynic satire and philology. Philosophy, part of dialectic in the trivium, is the home of theory. Interpretation of a text must always begin with the text, with reading and conning as clearly as possible what the letters (gramma) present: the 'literal level.' Consequently, philology – grammar in the trivium – is adamantly empirical. No theory or system of theories could substitute for exact reading: in this manner, philology has always held to practical empiricism and preserved its reservations about theory, even (or especially) about figurative levels of meaning.

Long before the alphabet, the world and the heavens were regarded as a text to be read and interpreted. The Old Testament, in Genesis, presents the creation as a divine speech, a rhetorical act by which every created thing or circumstance is a word, a *logos*, pregnant with signification. Then came further divine speech by way of the prophets and the Scriptures, old and new.

For centuries before Christianity, readers had practised multilevel interpretation of written texts. Anaxagoras (500–428 B.C.), says Diogenes Laertius, 'was the first to maintain that Homer in his poems treats of virtue and justice'; and he adds, 'Anaxagoras was the first to publish a book with diagrams.'[12] Edwin Hatch discussed Anaxagoras as founding a method of interpretation:

In Anaxagoras himself the allegory was probably ethical: he found in Homer a symbolical account of the movement of mental powers and moral virtues: Zeus was mind, Athene was art. But the method which, though it is found in germ among earlier or contemporary writers, seems to have been first formulated by his disciple Metrodorus, was not ethical but physical. By a remarkable anticipation of a modern science, possibly by a survival of memories of an earlier religion, the Homeric stories were treated as a symbolic representation of physical phenomena. The gods were the powers of nature: their gatherings, their movements, their loves, and their battles, were the play and interaction and apparent strife of natural forces. The method had for many centuries an enormous hold upon the Greek mind; it lay beneath the whole theology of the Stoic schools; it was largely current among the scholars and critics of the early empire.[13]

Anaxagoras and his school laid the foundation for the patristic (grammatical) tradition of fourfold exegesis of texts: he and his disciples employed the techniques of etymology and symbology.[14] From Anaxagoras, the development of the tradition passes through the Stoics (for example, Cornutus) and to the Romans (for example, Varro, Priscian, Donatus, Jerome, Augustine). 'Cornutus writes in vindication not so much of the piety of the ancients as of their knowledge: they knew as much as men of later times, but they expressed it at greater length and by means of symbols. He rests his interpretation of those symbols to a large extent upon etymology. The science of religion was to him, as it has been to some persons in modern days, an extension of the science of philology.'[15]

In the meantime, the pattern for science had been set by Empedocles, whose theory of the elements derived from an etymological approach to the governing/informing *logos*: 'His four elements Empedocles allegorically calls by the names of gods and goddesses of popular Greek religion: "First, therefore, let me tell you of all that there is in the four roots: Zeus the resplendent, the life-bearing Hera, and Aïdoneus, and Nestis who in her tears is spilling man's fountain of life."'[16] The Fathers of the Church brought together these two understandings in their Doctrine of the Logos. Here were two texts, the created universe and the Scriptures – two encyclopaedic texts, or revelations, or speeches, with a single author. It was inconceivable that they might contradict each other, so the patristic exegetes played them as parallel texts (the 'Two Books') subject to parallel techniques of interpretation.[17] Naturally, nothing must be allowed to interpose itself between reader and either text, no philosophy or theory of hermeneutics; however, one can (in fact, must) avail oneself of the help of all previous (reliable) exegetes. Thus accumulates that body of understanding and learned commentary, the Tradition.

Every reader of *Finnegans Wake* passes through similar portals. After the first baffling encounters with the text, theories about what it is and means look most beguiling. But in the long run they fail to satisfy: the book simply cannot be explained away (as, say, a novel, or poem, or even a Menippean satire) or dismissed as a failed experiment or the product of a diseased imagination. In fact, it continues to succeed admirably, by adamantly insisting that readers take it on its own terms: begin with the text itself; learn to read it. Learn; change.

While the Cynics were none of them camp-followers – their every effort pushed people into autonomy – their aims and activities coincided exactly with those of grammar. Both Cynics and grammarians begin by demanding clearsightedness and accuracy of perception so that nothing stands between the reader and the text – the world, especially including the reader. Cynic philosophers attacked their audiences in person: so do Cynic satires. Menippean satirists simply deploy the one text, the written book, to cleanse the Augean stables of their readers' sensibilities, and then set the readers to work on the other text, the Book of the World: in all, an intensely grammatical enterprise, and no less so because they do it with language. Of these two books, one, the satire, is an entirely human production, while the other, the world, has been remade and re-uttered by man in and by his own speech and technologies and culture. Civilized man is so enveloped by his own artefacts and technological whims that he has forgotten himself, has lost the ability to perceive and read them as 'signatures' or signs, has become subject to them and spends his days ignorant that he lives in a wild fairyland of his own making. Restoring awareness is a Herculean labour. As Joyce remarked: 'Yes, the viability of vicinals if invisible is invincible. And we are not trespassing on his corns either. Look at all the plotsch! Fluminian! If this was Hannibal's walk it was Hercules' work. And a hungried thousand of the unemancipated slaved the way' (81.01–04).

Numbing of sensibility and the interplay of technology and culture have long been central concerns of serious Menippean satire. The first has its roots in Cynicism and manifests itself through the tradition in the various tactics Menippists deploy to jolt the reader awake. The second has its roots in both Menippism and grammar, and may be dated from Varro or Apuleius or Martianus Capella. The latter two concentrated on the technology of language as an object of attention. Martianus in particular explored all of the available grammatical and rhetorical schemes and tropes, devices and puns as he presents Satire's account of the marriage of Mercury (rhetoric) and Philology (grammar, and the word). With its roots in Cicero, Quintilian, and St Augustine, the alliance between these two sciences of language remained the basis of medieval humanist culture until the next major technology arrived, the printing press. Martianus' *De nuptiis* was so thorough and so effective (and so popular) in illuminating both the technology and culture of literacy, and changes were so slow to develop, that many Menippists after him concerned themselves with more local and more limited concerns. Alan of Lille's *De planctu naturae* stands out as an exception, as a Menippean re-evaluation and rebalancing of its time's relation to language: the twelfth-century renaissance was a renaissance of grammar.

With Rabelais, a new kind of Menippean satire emerges, one that takes the new technology of print into account and shows overtly its relation to the heady and burgeoning renaissance culture. The mid-sixteenth century saw a sudden spate of Menippean responses to new forms of culture born of Ramism and the printing press. This includes, among many others, the satires of Thomas More, Erasmus, and the Obscure Epistolers at Erfurt. The latter were young humanists who posed 'as ignorant, lazy, anti-humanistic, debauched old professors – "obscurantists" – who wrote to each other about the nuisances of having to learn Greek and Hebrew, and about the threat that the new learning represents to their indigent, dullard's life.'[18] (Such were their affinities with Erasmus that he was frequently credited with authorship of their *Epistolae*.) Combined attacks on culture and the new technology are also registered during this period in a series of works leading to Swift and Sterne, though not as flamboyantly, perhaps, as in Rabelais: Henry Cornelius Agrippa's *De incertitudine*, the *Satyre Ménippée*, Bonaventure Desperières' *Cymbalum Mundi*, and a little later, Cervantes' *Don Quixote*.[19] In general, it appears that during periods when other technological development is slow or is lacking, Menippists focus on the prevailing culture, on the readers' ignorance of and assumptions about that culture, and on the technology of language as an up-to-date storehouse of the culture's experience and perception. The language is a main poetic and grammatical concern.

In periods of more rapid innovation and change, such as our own, both language and culture are extensively modified as side-effects of the new technologies. At such times, Menippean attention expands to embrace directly or indirectly the new technologies while continuing to satirize their side-effects on language, culture, and the readers' sensibilities. Rabelais' exuberant language is born of the printing press; Flaubert's of the popular newspaper press and journals. Sterne was born too late to be a Scriblerian, but his *Tristram Shandy* has, with equal wit, a figurative side in which the midwife and Dr Slop figure as old- and new-style publisher-printers. Dr Slop (sloppy) exerts such pressure and haste in yanking the newborn infant (the book/Tristram) into the world with his high-powered new technology (forceps/the new presses) that he quite disfigures the infant's face.[20] Sterne uses his five main characters to personify the divisions of rhetoric: Walter Shandy = *inventio*; Uncle Toby (indisposed, and given to whims) = *dispositio*; Corporal Trim = *elocutio* (style and ornament); Parson Yorick = *memoria* (all of the *Sermons of Yorick* were stolen); Dr Slop = *pronuntiatio*/Delivery.[21] With a light but incisive touch, Sterne dissects the fads and follies of the new rationalist culture and its mores and theories of language, particularly those of Locke, as they proceed from the latest innovations in printing.

Swift and Sterne are particularly important as regards Joyce and the *Wake*, where they most frequently occur as a pair, as in 'one yeastyday he sternely struxk his tete in a tub ... but ere he swiftly stook it out again ...' (04.22–3), or in 'your wildeshaweshowe moves swiftly sterneward: For here the holy language' (256.13-14). It was above all Swift's and Sterne's Menippean playfulness with language to satirize the cultural ground that attracted Joyce. Swift had served his grammatical apprenticeship under a defender of the Ancients, Temple. His rhetorical inventiveness has been the subject of a study by Martin Price,[22] as has Sterne's in a study by Richard Lanham.[23] Swift's *A Tale of a Tub* is a more condensed Menippean satire than the rambling *Gulliver's Travels* because of its closely integrated concern with language. In its original version, each of the five chapters of the *Tale* was assigned one of the five divisions of rhetoric as a means of dissecting the prevailing abuses of religion and of learning (the 'ancient' or traditional was seen bastardized in various modern modes).[24] These abuses were variously dramatized as the brothers Peter, Martin, and Jack (St Peter, Martin Luther, Jack Calvin) fell prey to the whims of fashion. This structure was blended, by way of the digression chapters, with a second satire concerning intellectual and popular culture: thereby the whole of the *Tale* constitutes a double plot. Though Swift does not tackle print directly, he does so indirectly, both by playing with the form and conventions of the printed book and by satirizing (in his comments and in the person of the 'hack' narrator) the 'modern' abuses of culture and learning that print gives rise to. He puts on Puritan, scientific, and Papist languages and uses them to explore the new rationalist entries in the Book of Nature.[25]

Cynic philosophers behaved outrageously and scandalously not to satisfy some merely private whim or need but to use street theatre to satirize their public, to so jolt the sensibilities of the crowd or passers-by as to freshen awareness and thereby to restore balance in private life as well as in society. They were sworn enemies to pretence and numbskull systematization, adamant about preserving a sense of proportion and human scale. They had no theory to advance or defend, no system of philosophy, as did the Epicureans, for example, or the Stoics. Yet for all their clowning and iconoclasm they remained steadfastly traditional in their aims. By their behaviour, the original Cynics made themselves into walking satires; their literary successors have made satires into Cynics. Now it is the satire that attacks the crowd or the passing reader, the satire that administers the corrective directly. The new medium vastly enlarged the audience. Using the ordinary literary approach, a poet might lament the passing of this or that tradition or affect horror at then-current worldliness, and invite the reader to ponder, assess, remedy. Thus, a Wordsworth might moan: 'The world is too much with us; late and soon, / Getting and spending, we lay waste our powers; / Little we see in Nature that is ours; / We have given our hearts away, a sordid boon!' etc., tugging respectfully at the thinking apparatus. Instead, a Cynic would promptly stand you on your head and force you to see your world aright; your ground, anew, and long enough for the fresh awareness to settle into habit. In so doing, the Cynic writers simply bring up-to-date centuries- or millenia-old techniques for reading the Book of the World.

Does *Finnegans Wake* concern itself with the Book of the World? Richard Ellmann reports Joyce as remarking: 'I might easily have written this story in the traditional manner. Every novelist knows the recipe. It is not difficult to follow a simple, chronological scheme which the critics will understand. But I, after all, am trying to tell the story of this Chapelizod family in a new way. Time and the river and the mountain are the real heroes of my book.'[26]

2

Finnegans Wake as Cynic Satire: An Ancient Attack on Modern Culture

– Why have you written the book this way?
– To keep the critics busy for three hundred years.

Mimesis informs the Menippean tradition in two ways. The works that compose the backbone of the tradition mime each other quite consciously and deliberately even while they vigorously assert their individuality.[1] The reader performs the other mimesis while reading: it is crucial both to how the satires work and to the radical difference between Menippism and the rest of satire. The other two strains of satire – Horatian and Juvenalian – rail at or castigate licence, wickedness, perfidy, hypocrisy, stupidity, and weakness, or they exhort the reader or the target to reform. They assume a fundamental separation of reader, writer, and work. By using mimesis, which means the involvement of the reader, Cynic satires have their effect directly, via play, via the 'jolt' T.S. Eliot mentioned. The satire forms a participatory environment for the reader. Other satires work on the readers' concepts; Menippean satires, on their percepts. Hence, the Menippists' cavalier attitude about the reader's getting the meaning, while (paradoxically) insisting on prolonged study of the satire: the *Wake* is a 'tobecontinued's tale that while blubles blows there'll still be sealskers' (626.18–19). Hence, too, the riot, the fun, and the laughter, the play of senses and styles and genres and wit.[2]

The musical aspect of [*Finnegans Wake*] was one of its justifications. 'Heaven knows what my prose means,' Joyce wrote his daughter. 'But it's pleasing to the ear. And your designs are pleasing to the eye. That's enough, it seems to me.' Another visitor ... asked him if the book were a blending of literature and music, and Joyce replied flatly, 'No, it's pure music.' 'But are there not levels of meaning to be explored?' 'No, no,' said Joyce, 'it's meant to make you laugh.' Of course, laughter and levels of meaning were not mutually exclusive, and to someone else, a drinking companion, Joyce corrected '*In vino veritas*' to '*In risu veritas*.' 'Why have you written the book this way?' someone else demanded. 'To keep the critics busy for three hundred years.' 'The demand that I make of my reader,' he said with a disarming smile to Max Eastman, 'is that he should devote his whole life to reading my works.' In *Finnegans Wake* he gave his humorous approval to 'that ideal reader suffering from an ideal insomnia.'[3]

The language of *Finnegans Wake* makes uncompromising demands of the reader. The reader has to put on its style, its way of seeing, or be denied access to the book: that is, the reader has to adapt, to change. As with so many other Menippean satires, this mimesis is attained by playfulness, by enticing or seducing the reader into joining in the fun: 'It is their segnall for old Champelysied to seek the shades of his retirement and for young Chappielassies to tear a round and tease their partners lovesoftfun at Finnegan's Wake' (607.14–16). Lots of fun, indeed, at *Finnegans Wake*. But in this wise, Joyce was playing the thoroughly conventional and traditional Irish poet. As Vivian Mercier points out, '... Gaelic satire, both early and late, retains the stamp of its origins. For one thing, it abounds in word play: the quantity of synonyms and nonce-words which it employs makes it the despair of editors and translators; I also get the impression that alliteration is an ornament particularly prized in satiric verse. Verbal virtuosity, always greatly cultivated in Gaelic prose and verse, reaches its peak in satire.'[4] The demand to perform the text aloud, to involve and attune both eye and ear, both left and right hemisphere in conning the text, assists the satire in attaining its effect: 'harmonize your abecedeed responses' (140.14). In making such demands, so extremely, and so adamantly, the *Wake* is unique in English prose.

The question of whether *Finnegans Wake* is a Cynic satire then becomes simply, does it have the Cynic effect? Does the *Wake* attack and retune the dulled sensibilities of its users?

Most readers find the language and style of the *Wake*, the ways in which Joyce used words, utterly foreign and disconcerting: they perhaps expect to encounter a more literary or more mandarin prose in a work reputed to be of the first rank. Well, its language *is* the most striking feature of the work, and founds its Menippean identity. Joyce's choice of decorum was deliberate, as his careful reworking of passages attests; therefore, he designed the *Wake* to produce a particular range of effects.[5] Cynic fun and horseplay abound on every page; nearly every word is a pun.

One of the ground rules for reading the book, one that has been assimilated into the mystique surrounding it, is that it must be read aloud, preferably *to* someone: 'here keen again and begin again to make soundsense and sensesound kin again' (124.14–16). The reader is told to expect that 'every word will be bound over to carry three score and ten toptypsical readings throughout the book of Doublends Jined' (20.14–15). With silent reading, much of the book's texture and structure submerges, and you lose touch with puns and devices that permit much interweaving of themes. Joyce's puns are as much visual as auditory, and, as Derek Attridge has noted, the *Wake* can turn the most ordinary word into a pun. Joyce carefully planted enough hints with friends for the necessity of reading aloud to become well known. On one occasion, he wrote to his patroness, Harriet Shaw Weaver: 'If I ever try to explain to people now what I am supposed to be writing, I see stupefaction freezing them into silence. For instance Shaun, after a long absurd and rather incestuous Lenten lecture to Izzy, his sister, takes leave of her "with half a glance of Irish frisky from under the shag of his parallel brows." These are the words the reader will see but not those he will hear. He also alludes to Shem as my 'soamheis' brother; he means Siamese.'[6] This information spotlights several matters, all concerning the Menippean nature of the *Wake*. For one, the reader participates in the work as its performer and co-creator. Second, as the reader is performer and simultaneously listener and observer of the text, his senses are engaged and retuned. Here is another means of administering the basic Menippean 'jolt': the reader-cum-performer is forced to shift (irrationally) from one posture of sensibility to another, without any one of them being allowed to dominate.[7] Everyone who has tried it will tell you that, after reading aloud passages or sections of *Finnegans Wake*, one's relation to words, to their music and rhythms and multiple meanings, is vastly invigorated. For example, Roland McHugh describes his first encounter with the *Wake*, after reading through *Ulysses*, as follows: 'Opening the book, I read slowly and mechanically as far as page 18, where I reached the lines '(Stoop) ... to this claybook ... Can you rede (since We and Thou had it out already) its world?' I closed it. I felt that I had made a respectable attempt and that I could not read its world. Or at least, the results of so doing were paltry compared with the cascade of illumination pouring out of *Ulysses*, so I returned to the earlier work.'[8] An unpromising start, but later he returned and found that play was central: 'FW must always mean many things at once. In the piece just considered there is a battlefield which is also a bottlefield – a table with food and bottles on it. Is the "compositor" trying to explain some point of strategy by moving the butter, cheese, etc. about to represent parties in conflict? Only on one level. Unfortunately, the balancing act of keeping one's attention fluid between all the levels defeats most readers, who trust one level and pay lip-service to the others.'[9] Here, in what

McHugh calls the balancing act, we find the Cynic awakening and limbering up the reader's sensibilities. Language itself, its nature, condition, uses, and changing properties, form a principal subject of this satire.

T.S. Eliot wrote his celebrated grammatical essay 'Tradition and the Individual Talent' to make two major points. One concerned the irrelevance of chronology to an artist (or for that matter to the arts); the other, the 'impersonality' of the serious artist. The first is germane to the *translatio studii* of grammar, to mimetic Menippism, and to *Finnegans Wake*, which uses the continuous present.[10] The second is confirmed in an unexpected manner in the case of the *Wake*, as evinced in Joyce's remarks about his authorship.

Eliot's doctrine of impersonality rests upon a number of implicit premises. One, that poetry is made with words, not ideas: the ideas may indeed be the private possession or production of one writer, but the language belongs to all who use it and have used it. To that extent, no one can claim ownership either of the language or of the shape in which it is put. Another premise: the poet's main business as poet is to refurbish the language, constantly to make it new, to bring it up-to-date and cleanse the Augean stables.[11]

Joyce remarked at a party: 'Really, it is not I who am writing this crazy book. It is you, and you, and that girl at the next table.'[12] This retort echoes the common Menippean pose that the satire is writing itself, or that the pen is doing it, or the readers, etc. (the Menippists' 'autonomous pen' conceit). The same notion found expression in each of the moderns: Lewis put it one way; Pound called it the 'serious artist'; Eliot, the notion of impersonality (borrowed from Keats): the artist has '... not a "personality" to express, but rather a particular medium, which is only a medium and not a personality, in which impressions and experiences combine in peculiar and unexpected ways ... the business of the poet is not to find new emotions, but to use the ordinary ones ...'[13] The whole point is to counter lingering romantic notions of poetics as self-expression. Eliot argues that the serious artist has a role and a set of attendant responsibilities. Both place him in direct relation to his time and his culture and its sensibilities through the common ground of language, and not off in a private corner of his own imaginings. In 'Tradition and the Individual Talent,' Eliot discussed the 'historical sense' as an awareness of the past, the past efforts as forming a simultaneous order, such that everybody is your contemporary – precisely the grammarian's idea of tradition. In a later essay, by way of illustrating his doctrine of 'impersonality,' he asserted that one who works with that 'historical sense' works mimetically, through masks and the putting-on of styles.

The historical method is, of course, the one which suits Mr Pound's temperament: it is also a conscious and consistent application of a procedure suggested by Browning, which Mr Pound applies more consciously and consistently than Browning did. Most poets grasp their own time, the life of the world as it stirs before their eyes, at one convulsion or not at all. But they have no method for closing in upon it. Mr Pound's method is indirect and extremely difficult to pursue. As the present is no more than the present existence, the present significance, of the entire past, Mr Pound proceeds by acquiring the entire past: And when the entire past is acquired, the constituents fall into place and the present is revealed. Such a method involves immense capacities of learning and of dominating one's learning, and the peculiarity of expressing oneself through historical masks. Mr Pound has a unique gift for expression through some phase of past life. This is not archaeology or pedantry, but one method, and a very high method, of poetry. It is a method which allows of no arrest, for the poet imposes upon himself, necessarily, the condition of continually changing his mask; *hic et ubique*, then we'll shift our ground.[14]

Those who know the tradition will recognize in Eliot's ideal poet, Mr Pound, Cicero's ideal orator. The *doctus orator* was a man of encyclopaedic wisdom and eloquence, a master of both grammar (encyclopaedism – the full tradition) and rhetoric (skill with every style). Mimesis of the inventory of styles is mask-wearing and a technique of 'impersonality': by this passage, Eliot shows that as a consequence of the 'historical sense' and the 'historical method' the tradition of literature becomes, like the Menippean tradition, a mimetic one. Joyce simply tightened the circle of impersonality and participation with the *Wake*, so that it comes as a shock to our literate sensibilities to find ourselves simultaneously the readers, writers, and performers of an endless work. He wryly commented on this procedure, perhaps alluding to Eliot's remarks: 'If there is a future in every past that is present *Quis est qui non novit quinnigan* and *Qui quae quot at Quinnigan's Quake!* Stump! His producers are they not his consumers? Your exagmination round his factification for incamination of a warping process. Declaim!' (496.35–497.03).

It is a commonplace among anthropologists that 'anonymous' equals 'unanimous': in preliterate cultures, anything not ascribable to a particular individual is regarded as the work of the culture at large. So it is with our own oral tradition, whether of ballad, or of jokes, or of neologisms and the language as a whole. And, it would appear, Joyce was working similarly when writing down the *Wake*. A related problem is that of authorship in a mimetic tradition, as exemplified in those areas of satire outlined by Korkowski. It is not simply a matter of plagiarism or originality: Menippism is essentially a corporate undertaking of a sort that is neither conspiratorial nor ideal. Rather, it expresses one of those larger modes of thought that can emerge in various forms – oral, literary, cinematic, or whatever is at hand and most likely to serve the turn.

In writing *Finnegans Wake* as he did, Joyce adopted a particular configuration of stylistic techniques and tactics quite different from those he used in his other, more 'literary' Menippean satires, *Ulysses* and *Dubliners*. These tactics were not chosen in a haphazard quest for novelty but carefully patterned after the new sensibility his generation had learned from the new electric media. The language of the *Wake* puts on those sensibilities, declaiming and staging them simultaneously. It puts them on display, in a dramatic vivisection of the alterations of mind and culture they embody. In his essay 'The Metaphysical Poets' T.S. Eliot remarked on the occurrence, evident from the poetry of the seventeenth century onward, of a dissociation of sensibility.[15] (The same splitting-apart of the senses appears thematically in the *Wake* as the royal divorce and in the shattering of Humpty Dumpty.)

But Joyce noted something Eliot did not mention, a reintegration of the senses in the twentieth century. Based on this perception, fully explored and enacted in the *Wake*, he decided upon a style for it that would activate and exercise more than just his readers' eyes. This ploy is both an artistic device for putting on and tuning up the new posture of the senses, and a Menippean tactic for drawing attention to the text itself.

The reader of *Finnegans Wake*, like that of Martianus' *De nuptiis*, is forced to wrestle with words and eventually to let them have their way with him. 'Harmonize your abecedeed responses' (140.14). Like the themes, the language is labyrinthine. The many Menippean precedents for such complexity include Apuleius, Martianus Capella, Alan of Lille, and, to a lesser extent, Cervantes and Rabelais. There is no single 'right' reading or pronunciation of most of the words, or of any passage, of the *Wake*: some work and others don't, although something of an Irish accent is popularly supposed to help. Every reader, therefore, makes his own *Wake*. Even the title includes puns: 'wake' also means after-effect, and awakening.[16] The book serves Joyce as stage, workshop, and labyrinth, for enacting, forging, tracing, and retracing the processes of cognition and experience. As a teaching machine, then, the *Wake* functions as a Menippean satire.

Joyce's emblem for the book, untitled for years, was □, which brings to mind Swift's analogy of satire and a mirror. On sending an early draft of 'The Mookse and the Gripes' section to Harriet Shaw Weaver, Joyce commented: 'I am glad you liked my punctuality as an engine driver. I have taken this up because I am really one of the greatest engineers, if not the greatest, in the world besides being a musicmaker, philosophist and heaps of other things. All the engines I know are wrong. Simplicity. I am making an engine with only one wheel. No spokes of course. The wheel is a perfect square. You see what I am driving at, don't you? I am awfully solemn about it, mind you, so you must not think it is a silly story about the mouse and the grapes. No, it's a wheel, I tell the world. And it's all square.'[17] It has occurred to more than one commentator that an open book presents a square, more or less, and that Joyce's book of 'Doublends Jined' is a wheel or circle because it ends and begins in the middle of the same sentence.[18] But Joyce added, in his next letter to Miss Weaver, that his 'remarks about the engine were not meant as a hint at the title.' Rather, 'I meant that I wanted to take up several other arts and crafts and teach everybody how to do everything properly so as to be in the fashion.'[19] Besides confirming that he intends this encyclopaedic work to initiate an updating process, his remark also helps us to see it as principally grammatical. Menippism is the extension, and as far as I can ascertain the only extension, into satire of traditional *grammatica*.[20]

Several writers have noted that the *Wake* is to be understood in terms of grammar. The most succinct observations are those of H.M. McLuhan:

...grammatica or philology ... involves speech itself, which has been properly named as the main protagonist of every work of Joyce. 'Our speech is, as it were,' says Julius Caesar Scaliger in his Poetics, 'the postman of the mind, through the services of whom civil gatherings are announced, the arts are cultivated and the claims of wisdom intercede with men for man.' Joyce employs this image of speech as letter in the Belinda episode of the *Wake* as well as in the section on Shaun the Post cycling back through the night of history and collective consciousness. Words as a network of tentacular roots linking all human culture, and 'reaching down into the deepest terrors and desires,' as Mr Eliot says, were the study of ancient grammatica. So that it is easy to see how a Quintilian could say that in a certain sense grammar embraces all other studies, and why Varro's *De Lingua Latina* is an encyclopedic work. There was a 'nominalist' school in antiquity but the main tradition was via the Stoics or analogists for whom speech was a specific level of communication in the divine Logos which distinguished men from brutes. From this point of view it followed naturally that the cultivation of eloquence and verbal precision was the principal means of achieving human excellence. 'Every letter is a godsend,' wrote Joyce. And, much more, every word is an avatar, a revelation, an epiphany. For every word is the product of a complex mental act with a complete learning process involved in it. In this respect words can be regarded not as signs but as existent things, alive with a physical and mental life which is both individual and collective. The conventional meanings of words can thus be used or disregarded by Joyce, who is concentrating on the submerged metaphysical drama which these meanings often tend to overlay. His puns in the *Wake* are a technique for revealing this submerged drama of language, and Joyce relied on the quirks, 'slips,' and freaks of ordinary discourse to evoke the fullness of existence in speech. All his life he played the sleuth with words, shadowing them and waiting confidently for some unexpected situation to reveal their hidden signatures and powers. For his view of the poet was that he should read, not forge, the signatures of things. As he explains in *Stephen Hero*, this involves the poet in a perpetual activity of retracing and reconstructing the ways of human apprehension. A poem is a vivisection of the mind and senses in action, an anagenesis or retracing, begetting anagnorosis or recognition. This is the key to the theme of memory and history embodied in Anna Livia of the *Wake*. She runs forward but 'ana' is Greek for backwards, and spells the same both ways. Anna Livia is also the Liffey nourishing the Guinnesses (anagenesis) of all things. It is the business of grammarian and poet to see this cyclic process of emanation and return as the origin and term of all words and creatures.[21]

The concerns of grammar are naturally encyclopaedic, for the grammarian reads and interprets two parallel texts, those of the written book and the Book of Nature. The Cynic Menippist does the same and expects no less from the reader of his satire, who, with sensibilities freshtuned by the satire, will then be able to turn to the texts of himself and his world and read them aright. Such activity is ongoing, a lifetime occupation; and some Menippists insist, only half-jokingly, that their readers spend their lives exclusively on the satire. Rabelais, for example, tells his reader that he may 'confidently expect to become valiant and wise ...' as it works its therapies.[22] And Joyce, as we noted at the beginning of this chapter, said, 'The demand that I make of my reader is that he should devote his whole life to reading my works.' Rabelais also remarks: 'I intend each and every reader to lay aside his business, to abandon his trade, to relinquish his profession, and to concentrate wholly upon my work.'[23] Joyce included, in a section about exegesis of manuscripts as well as of individual letters of the alphabet, these directions to his 'ideal reader': '... look at this prepronominal *funferal*, engraved and retouched and edgewiped and puddenpadded, very like a whale's egg farced with pemmican as were it sentenced to be nuzzled over a full trillion times for ever and a night till his noddle sink or swim by that ideal reader suffering from an ideal insomnia ...' (120.09–14).

Joyce's concern in the *Wake* with media and technology and their reconfigurations of culture was integral with his grammatical concern with language. Hugh Kenner has commented[24] on Joyce's habit of regarding figures of speech as objects: Joyce equally regarded objects as figures of speech in traditional grammatical fashion. He wrote Miss Weaver of finding a flat 'in the Paris jungle, stampede of omnibuses and trumpets of taxi-elephants etc and in this caravanserai peopled by American loudspeakers I compose ridiculous prose ...'[25] Later he wrote: 'It is a bewildering business ... Complications to right of me, complications to left of me, complex on the page before me, perplex in the pen beside me, duplex in the meandering eyes of me, stuplex on the face that reads me. And from time to time I lie back and listen to my hair growing white ...'[26] In a similar vein, Shem the Penman, lives surrounded by midden-hordes of words as storehouse of experience, and of objects 'stinksome' in nature, both trash heaps, both full of treasures: his lair is

persianly literatured with burst loveletters, telltale stories, stickyback snaps, doubtful eggshells, bouchers, flints, borers, puffers, amygdaloid almonds, rindless raisins, alphybettyformed verbage, vivlical viasses, ompiter dictas, visus umbique, ahems and ahahs, imeffable tries at speech unasyllabled, you owe mes, eyoldhyms, fluefoul smut, fallen lucifers, vestas which had served, showered ornaments, borrowed brogues, reversibles jackets, blackeye lenses, family jars, falsehair shirts, Godforsaken scapulars, neverworn breeches, cutthroat ties, counterfeit franks, best intentions, curried notes, upset latten tintacks, unused mill and stumpling stones, twisted quills, painful digests, magnifying wineglasses, solid objects cast at goblins, once current puns, quashed quotatoes, messes of mottage, unquestionable issue papers, seedy ejaculations, limerick damns, crocodile tears, spilt ink, blasphematory spits, stale shestnuts, schoolgirls', young ladies', milkmaids', washerwomen's, shopkeepers' wives, merry widows', ex nuns', vice abbess's, pro virgins', super whores', silent sisters', Charleys' aunts', grandmothers', mothers'-in-laws', fostermothers', godmothers' garters, tress clippings from right, lift and cintrum, worms of snot, toothsome pickings, cans of Swiss condensed bilk, highbrow lotions, kisses from the antipodes, presents from pickpockets, borrowed plumes, relaxable handgrips, princess promises, lees of whine, deoxodised carbons, convertible collars, diviliouker doffers, broken wafers, unloosed shoe latchets, crooked strait waistcoats, fresh horrors from Hades, globules of mercury, undeleted glete, glass eyes for an eye, gloss teeth for a tooth, war moans, special sighs, longsufferings of longstanding, ahs ohs ouis sis jas jos gias neys thaws sos, yeses and yeses and yeses, to which, if one has the stomach to add the breakages, upheavals distortions, inversions of all this chambermade music one stands, given a grain of goodwill, a fair chance of actually seeing the whirling dervish, Tumult, son of Thunder, self exiled in upon his ego, a nightlong a shaking betwixtween white or reddr hawrors, noondayterrorised to skin and bone by an ineluctable phantom (may the Shaper have mercery on him!) writing the mystery of himsel in furniture. (183.10–184.10)

To a grammarian reading the Book of Nature, Johann Huizinga has explained, 'Every event, every case, fictitious or historic, tends to crystallize, to become a parable, an example, a proof, in order to be applied as a standing instance of a general moral truth. In the same way, every utterance becomes a dictum, a maxim, a text. For every question of conduct, Scripture, legends, history, literature, furnish a crowd of examples or of types, together making up a sort of moral clan ...'[27] Huizinga acknowledges that the unity of the *logos* comprises both word and deeds; only God speaks with events, a mode of verbal gesticulation beyond man's capacities of utterance. Joyce tells us repeatedly that his ability to write *Finnegans Wake* depends upon having learned to read the Book of Nature. For example: 'The prouts who will invent a writing there ultimately is the poeta, still more learned, who discovered the raiding there originally. That's the point of eschatology our book of kills reaches for now in soandso many counterpoint words. What can't be coded can be decorded if an ear aye sieze what no eye ere grieved for. Now, the doctrine obtains, we have occasioning cause causing effects and affects occasionally recausing altereffects' (482.31–483.01). Hugh Kenner expounds further:

Furthermore, the traditional Two Scriptures are explicitly incorporated into [*Finnegans Wake*]. They are the letter and the barrow of rubbish, the Word and the World. The wheelbarrow turns up constantly as a creation-symbol: 'he dumptied the wholebarrow of rubbages on to soil here,' F17. This is not only the refuse of Earwicker's house, it is Dublin itself and it is the world created by God in time (left 'to soil' and requiring to be refreshed by Grace). It is also the barrowload of rubbish (equated with the 'barrow' of Finn's entombment – Christ allegorically entombed till the Last Day, significance locked up in material opacity since the Fall) from which the hen retrieved the letter (pp. 80, 110–11). As is made plain on p. 19, reading the letter is equivalent to reading, like an archaeologist slicing through a kitchen-midden, or a stratified city, the contents of the barrow itself: '(Stoop) if you are abced-minded, to this claybrook, what curios of signs (please stoop), in this allaphbed!' The 'middenhide hoard of objects' contains 'Olives, beets, kimmells, dollies, alfrids, beatties, cormacks, and daltons' (=aleph, beth, gimel, daleth, alpha, beta, gamma, delta.) The letter and the barrow, that is, are the two scriptures, to which identical exegetical techniques are applicable. Both, furthermore, are analogous with *Finnegans Wake* itself. 'The world, mind, is, was and will be writing its own wrunes for ever, man, on all matters that fall under the ban of our infrarational senses ...' (19.35–20.01)[28]

Joyce went much further than any previous Menippist or grammarian in exploiting language as the storehouse or midden-heap of cultural experience. He made explicit the ways in which language codifies the effects of technology on culture and on the ratio among the senses bodily as well as exegetical. 'The war is in words and the wood is the world ... Elsewere there here no concern of the Guinnesses. But only the ruining of the rain has heard ... A human pest cycling (pist!) and recycling (past!) about the sledgy streets, here he was (pust!) again! Morse nuisance noised.' (98.34–99.06)

'The war is in words' at once relates to Joyce's grammatical and Menippean concerns with language as the storehouse of experience, and to his concern 'inwards' with the senses. The 'wood is the world' resonates with another of his concerns, the effects of unbridled technological development: 'For a burning would is come to dance inane' (250.16). However, neither was *Finnegans Wake* the first expression Joyce gave to his exploration of the senses, nor was Joyce the first grammarian to have that interest. Vico has much to say about the senses that is relevant to the *Wake*, and in *Ulysses* Joyce made, as it were, some preliminary explorations of the sensory modalities of the eye and the ear.

In the chapter of *Ulysses* devoted to metamorphosis, the 'Proteus' chapter, Stephen Dedalus finds himself poised for exploring on the border between several pairs of worlds. He paces meditatively along Sandymount strand, a border between water and land. He limns, opening and closing his eyes, the borders between inner experience and outer, between vision and hearing, and between sleeping and waking. He reflects:

Ineluctable modality of the visible: at least that if no more, thought through my eyes. Signatures of all things I am here to read, seaspawn and seawrack, the nearing tide, that rusty boot. Snotgreen, bluesilver, rust: coloured signs. Limits of the diaphane. But he adds: in bodies. Then he was aware of them bodies before of them coloured. How? By knocking his sconce against them, sure ... Limit of the diaphane in. Why in? Diaphane, adiaphane. If you can put your five fingers through it, it is a gate, if not a door. Shut your eyes and see.

Stephen closed his eyes to hear his boots ... A very short space of time through very short times of space. Five, six: the *nacheinander*. Exactly: and that is the ineluctable modality of the audible. Open your eyes. No. Jesus! If I ... fell through the *nebeneinander* ineluctably. I am getting on nicely in the dark. My ash sword hangs at my side. Tap with it: they do. My two feet in his boots are at the end of his legs, *nebeneinander*. Sounds solid: made by the mallet of *Los Demiurgos*. Am I walking into eternity along Sandymount strand? ... Rhythm begins, you see. I hear.[29]

Here is no passive meditation, no 'emotion recollected in tranquillity.' He is active, probing, exploring. His borderline stance gives him the ability to perceive, to explore, and to pass back and forth between worlds. That this activity is grounded in grammatical exegesis of the Book of Nature is signalled by a reminder: 'Signatures of all things I am here to read ...' He turns to the grammar of perception.

This passage is the vestibule to the chapter, an interior monologue governed by the art of philology (as Joyce noted in his chart for *Ulysses*[30]). The key terms are 'ineluctable' and 'through' or 'diaphane.' The two senses, visual and auditory, are 'ineluctable' in isolation but, poised on the border between the two, each may be conned through or in terms of the other: in this manner, Stephen 'reads' the two modalities. He reports his readings directly to the reader, with enough glossing from the sidelines that the reader can make his own interpretation. So each sense reports on itself while appearing to report on the other. When one of them is isolated for observation, the other provides the *way* of seeing it; hence, each is ineluctable. Stephen observes that the visual is not 'diaphanous' ('limits of the diaphane') and that it makes outer experience available in a sequential and static and abstract manner: 'he was aware of them bodies before of them coloured.' When he closes his eyes, he moves directly into the 'diaphane' or transformative mode of one-thing-through-another: 'A very short space of time through very short times of space.' Spaces and times coalesce: 'Am I walking into eternity ... ?' The 'audible' mode, then, is constituted by flux, by simultaneity, and by intervals of resonance and rhythm, *nacheinander*: recall Eliot's remarks concerning 'the auditory imagination' (see below, 30). The complementary mode, *nebeneinander*, is constituted by connectedness and continuity: it does not present intervals and hence is 'limited' as a 'diaphane.' So Stephen plays with the contradiction of falling 'through the *nebeneinander* ineluctably.' Meanwhile, Joyce tinkers away backstage, lightly sending up German philosophizing (then still all the rage) by using German terms in the meditation where English ones might have served quite as well, and sending scores of readers off to consult the word-hoard.

This is as far as Joyce presented an analysis in *Ulysses*. But if one 'reads' his book *qua* artefact, as a 'signature,' it appears in the light of these remarks to be structured acoustically rather than visually, that is, rather than sequentially, in normal novelistic form. This acoustical presentation is evident in the two-book structure (Odysseus and Bloom) and in the interpenetration of interior and exterior worlds, made explicit in the stream-of-consciousness style of the work. At this point, it may be observed that (Menippean) two-situation structures and tactics are basically acoustic and resonant in nature, including the Milesian tale ('frame tale') and all the two-book or double-plot forms, as well as some of the wrenchings of decorum that require that the reader operate on two or more levels simultaneously. All of them work, structurally, in the mode of the pun. *Finnegans Wake* moves much further from the strictly visual than did *Ulysses* to explore the multisensory and worldly dimensions of language. Peter Myers demonstrates that Joyce has pushed the verbal pun to the point where it shades off into the catalogue, not only of words and meanings but of media, and in so doing he 'has devised what is practically a new form of art. He has made his single literary medium create the impression of a multimedia event. If an audience hears the hymn to Chuff performed it is at once in the worlds of music, story, drama, wassailing and popular song, together with the world of children singing on the street.'[31] As an example, he selects this passage:

The Fomor's in his Fin, the Momor's her and hin. A paaralone! A paaralone! And Dublin's all adin. We'll sing a song of Singlemonth and you'll too and you'll. Here are notes. There's the key. One two three. Chours! So come on, ye wealthy gentrymen wibfrufrocksfull of fun! Thin thin! Thin thin! Thej olly and thel ively, thou billy with thee coo, for to jog a jig of a crispness nice and sing a missal too. Hip champouree! Hiphip champouree! O you longtailed blackman, polk it up behind me! Hip champouree! Hiphip champouree! And, jessies, push the pumkik round, Anneliuia! (236.09–18)

Myers calls this 'one of the most performable moments of the *Wake*, with children's games, songs, nursery rhymes and carols pieced together into a vigorous medley. Most of it has a definite accompanying tune, the rhythms of the original are retained and ... it forms a satisfying musical whole that would admit of no reorganisation.'[32] He comments:

In his second symphony Charles Ives creates a medley of songs, folk-tunes and marches, to mingle traditional sentiments and associations. What Joyce is doing is akin to this *in a way that is not merely analogical.* For when the above is sung we really do *hear* the original tunes in a new arrangement. What the writer has created is a musical work in the strictest, narrowest sense of the word. Existing music has been cut and arranged and spliced to produce a new composition.

Thomas Moore wrote new words to old airs, and Joyce of course does this throughout the *Wake*. That is a poetic achievement. But the musical achievement is the forming of a collage which has been pieced together from fragments of old songs. In this instance the final rhythmic and melodic composition can even be considered as more significant than the question of how and where the score is written out in verbal notes instead of crotchets.

There is, then, one purely musical plane in this piece. But above this musical plane there are Joyce's words; and below it there are the words to the original songs. If we ignore Joyce's *words* we find a work which depends on the particular characteristics and associations of the songs and chants employed. In the case of Ives's work American sentiments and traditions are explored and commented upon; in the case of the hymn to Chuff the world of childhood is reawakened. Religion and infancy merge in the mixture of carols and nursery rhymes. The mixture inevitably debunks the carols, and the transformation of 'Christmas night' to 'crispness nice' emphasises this; but even in that phrase there is an appealingly felicitous evocation of the wintriness of Christmas, with 'crispness' applying to both the air and the snow. Joyce does not transform only in order to satirically destroy; but to explore, expose and *include*.

The piece is a collection as well as an arrangement. There is an assortment of appropriate objects: holly, ivy and mistletoe ('olly,' 'ively' and 'a missal too') within the piece; oatcake, snow and blackbirds outside it. The objects may not be part of the music but they are part of the total experience and are within the control of the artist.

We can take the piece as a microcosm of the *Wake* and can visualise it as comprising spheres within spheres. In the inner sphere are the rhythms and sounds of the text: whatever enters the ear when the piece is read aloud. In the next sphere, which surrounds it, are the elements of the songs or chants, whether musical or verbal, which are not sounded by the text, but which may be momentarily heard in the imagination ... The remoter spheres are the objects present in the songs or chants alluded to and the feelings, moods and general associations which they may evoke.[33]

Joyce constantly teased his earnest readers and explicators with remarks such as the one concerning Vico and Bruno, that you should not pay much attention to them 'beyond using them for all they are worth'; for, he added, 'they have gradually forced themselves on me through circumstances of my own life.'[34] Given that the *Wake* is a Menippean and grammatical work, however, this remark suggests that while their theories may or may not be pertinent, their perceptions as grammarians are of fundamental relevance. Hugh Kenner was the first writer to discuss at any length the grammatical relation between Vico and the *Wake*.[35] He has noted that Vico could manipulate the parallels between the Two Books: 'In describing Philology as "the doctrine of everything that depends on the human will," Vico registers his understanding of language as a social product whose morphologies simultaneously link and harmonize the mind itself, the external world as perceived by the mind, the human community of minds and wills, and the artifacts and deeds of all peoples.'[36] These last are also Joyce's principal concerns in *Finnegans Wake*. It is clear from a reading of *The New Science* that Vico regarded language as a cultural storehouse of experience and perception. He recognized that causal processes of cultural changes would be embedded in the strata of words' etymologies and uses, and he described three etymological stages of perception through language: phatic, oral, and written.

These three stages present, respectively, thing (or experience), word-as-thing (not yet divorced from experience), and word alone (divorceable from thing or experience). The sensory progression implied here is from tactile/ kinetic to auditory/kinetic, to visual (written words). Joyce meticulously traced these and other progressions, in the thunders and fables and set-pieces (such as Mutt and Jute, and the Prankquean) of the *Wake*, as will appear in subsequent chapters. Vico used philology and etymology to backtrack the stages of language in the hope of compiling a 'mental dictionary' that he deduced to lie at the root of all human speech. He regarded communication by thing or gest (pre-articulate) as a form of 'real words' that 'people must have used before they came to vocal words and finally to written ones' (*The New Science*, 45). Vico's training in etymology provoked the notion that 'there must in the nature of human things be a mental language common to all nations, which uniformly grasps the substance of things feasible in human social life' (60).[37] This supposition complements the notion of a real 'mental vocabulary of human social things, which are the same in substance as felt by all nations but diversely expressed in language according to their diverse manifestations' (94).[38] Stephen's philological labour in *Ulysses* is similarly to 'read' the substantive forms in the Book of Nature.

Vico argues that the index to his 'mental dictionary' is evidently the human sensorium; that, though the things perceived remain the same, both the perceptual stance of a knower and his relation to the thing known affect the cognitive process and are reflected differently in a language at different times. Aware that the most environmental (and therefore invisible) aspect of human consciousness is the bodily or sensory perceptions, he points out that the mind 'is naturally inclined by the senses to see itself externally in the body, and only with great difficulty does it come to attend to itself by means of reflection'(70). He adds that 'this axiom gives us the universal principle of etymology in all languages' (ibid).

Vico's fullest expression of these principles comes as a restatement of the axioms:

But in the night of thick darkness enveloping the earliest antiquity, so remote from ourselves, there shines the eternal and never-failing light of a truth beyond all question: that the world of civil society has been made by men, and that its principles are to be found within the modifications of our own human mind. Whoever reflects on this cannot but marvel that the philosophers should have bent all their energies to the study of the world of nature, which, since God made it, He alone knows; and that they should have neglected the study of the world of nations or civil world, which, since men had made it, men could hope to know. This aberration was a consequence of that infirmity of the human mind ... by which, immersed and buried in the body it naturally inclines to take notice of bodily things, and finds the effort to attend to itself too laborious; just as the bodily eye sees all objects outside itself but needs a mirror to see itself (85).

These mental modifications, he asserts time and again, are perceptual shifts related to the technologies of speech and writing:

But the nature of our civilized minds is so detached from our senses, even in the vulgar, by abstractions corresponding to all the abstract terms our languages abound in, and so refined by the art of writing ... and as it were spiritualized by the art of numbers ... It is equally beyond our power to enter into the vast imagination of those first men whose minds were not in the least abstract, refined, or spiritualized, because they were entirely immersed in the senses, buffeted by the passions, buried in the body. (106)

And it may be said that in the fables the nations have in a rough way and in the language of the human senses described the beginnings of this world of sciences, which the specialized studies of scholars have since clarified for us by reasoning and generalization. From all this we may conclude what we set out to show in this [second] book: that the theological poets were the sense and the philosophers the intellect of human wisdom. (265)

By the very nature of poetry it is impossible for anyone to be at the same time a sublime poet and a sublime metaphysician, for metaphysics abstracts the mind from the senses, and the poetic faculty must submerge the whole mind in the senses; metaphysics soars up to universals, and the poetic faculty must plunge deep into particulars. (281)

For Vico, the poet's erudition and perceptual orientation are not at all visual; rather, entirely mythic and auditory. He notes that many of the ancient poets were blind: 'Homer himself describes as blind the poets who sing at the banquets of the great, such as the one who sings at the banquet of Alcinous for Ulysses, and the one who sings at the feast of the suitors ... It is a property of human nature that the blind have marvellously retentive memories' (288). The ancient seer, too, was blind: deprived of outward visual stress he gained inward vision – insight – as well as the ability to read clearly signs and portents of the times.

The debt *Finnegans Wake* owes to Vico, I suggest, must be reckoned largely in terms of these matters. Both works are grammatical, both entirely concerned with language and the effects on it and the senses of human technologies and artefacts. But whereas Vico propounded theories and reported the results of his studies, Joyce forges the language directly to probe sensibility and awaken and retune the senses of his readers. Vico wrote a report, as it were; Joyce, a satire that makes us do the exploring.

The chief bodily senses that concern Joyce in the *Wake* are those of sight, hearing, and touch. He is also concerned to show how our technologies rearrange them and make one or another king or queen of the sensorium. Language is always the technology of first concern to him; of the senses, eye and ear are singled out for particular attention in the text. 'Ear! Ear! Not ay! Eye! Eye!' he exclaims (409.03). Or 'Television kills telephony in brothers' broil. Our eyes demand their turn. Let them be seen!' (52.18–19). Above all, ear and eye are engaged and 'harmonized' in and by the *Wake* language itself.[39]

Eliot's observations about the nature of the 'auditory imagination' are apposite:

What I call the 'auditory imagination' is the feeling for syllable and rhythm, penetrating far below the conscious levels of thought and feeling, invigorating every word: sinking to the most primitive and forgotten, returning to the origin, and bringing something back, seeking the beginning and end. It works through meanings, certainly, or not without meanings in the ordinary sense, and fuses the old and obliterated, and the trite, the current, and the new and the surprising, the most ancient and the most civilized mentality.[40]

Eliot might have been describing *Finnegans Wake*. The keynote here, as in Stephen's meditation in *Ulysses*, is simultaneity in cyclicity, a restatement of ideas presented in 'Tradition and the Individual Talent.' In the auditory mode, the merely diachronic or sequential is suspended in favour of simultaneity of all things and aspects, past and present: the 'supervention of novelty' retrieves old and forgotten dimensions as apposite to or latent in the new, in language and culture alike.

For Joyce decided that, in the *Wake* (awakening plus aftereffect – one that churns and heaves up things from below), the language had to be 'put to sleep.'[41] Else, the 'conscious levels' would obtrude upon or obliterate all the others. Ellmann notes how Joyce implies, through the very form of language used in the *Wake*, 'that there is no present and no past, that there are no dates, that time – and language, which is time's expression – is a series of coincidences which are general all over humanity. Words move into words, people into people, incidents into incidents like the ambiguities of a pun, or a dream.'[42] Ellmann goes on to observe of the nightworld: 'Sleep is the great democratizer: in their dreams people become one, and everything about them becomes one. Nationalities lose their borders, levels of discourse and society are no longer separable, time and space surrender their demarcations. All human activities begin to fuse into all other human activities, printing a book into bearing a baby, fighting a war into courting a woman. By day we attempt originality; by night plagiarism is forced upon us.'[43] One might add, 'and by night, author and reader fuse, and all human artefacts, material and intellectual, fuse and are processed through the language.' For Joyce regards all of our artefacts as extensions or expressions or utterances of the body or mind that reflexively modify our sensibilities and our experience. 'Language for Joyce is not simply a transparent medium of reality but that reality itself. It is also its own world, consciously foregrounded by word-play, syntactic deviations, leitmotifs, symbolism and ambiguity. Those readers of *Ulysses* and *Finnegans Wake* who look for the 'real world' beyond the complex words and structural technicalities of the texts will continually be thwarted.'[44]

Derek Attridge points out that the *Wake* digresses from the 'central path of the novel' in our conventional expectation of that form, 'because it fails to conform to the expectation that novels reflect a pre-existing reality, foregrounding instead the properties of language, its instability and shiftiness, its material patterns and coincidences, its intertextual slidings, its freedom from determining sources or goals, its independence from its referents, even its refusal to be bound by a single language system.'[45] Since our language is a midden-heap of our collective experience, it faithfully stores all of these modifications.[46] It is therefore with the language and style of *Finnegans Wake*, its most distinctive and most controversial features, that any Menippean assessment or interpretation of that work must begin.

Even at the literal level, nearly every word in the *Wake* is a pun. Yet the *Wake* does have a unifying voice, one that contains hundreds of characters and utters many thousands of wisecracks. It 'reflects a distinct brand of humour that is revealed partially through technique; for the continual use of puns tends to create an air of jocularity even after the pun has ceased to seem a joke. We are aware throughout of a more or less straightforwardly comic voice characterised by unremitting double talk.'[47] Joyce's inventiveness comes from using all of the schemes and tropes of both grammar and rhetoric not just in amplification and exposition but also as a means of releasing, of freeing for our contemplation the simultaneous history of our experience that language represents. The 'collideorscape' of puns uses all the traditional modes, of antanaclasis,[48] paranomasia,[49] syllepsis,[50] and the rest, as well as new ones suggested by the language and forged by Joyce. Our conventional wisdom has it that 'the pun is the lowest form of humour but the highest form of wit'; G.K. Chesterton put a spin on the idea by observing that, if it is the 'lowest' form, it must constitute the very foundation. Puns are for the connoisseur of words, not the snob. The coincidence of lowest and highest is completely in keeping with the joco-serious decorum of Menippean satire. Once asked whether some of his puns weren't rather trivial, Joyce retorted that yes, they were, and that some of them were quadrivial too.

By far the majority of Joyce's puns rely on the music, rhythm, and texture of words and phrases: reading aloud restores their full availability. Often his puns are multilingual; almost always they involve the complementarity of the reader's eye and ear, for each sense carries one or more levels of meaning. Additional meanings often result from the interactions. When used alone, the eye can numb our awareness of the other senses. To illustrate: the silent reader of

the teatimestained terminal ... is a cosy little brown study all to oneself and, whether it be thumbprint, mademark or just a poor trait of the artless, its importance in establishing the identities in the writer complexus ... will be best appreciated by never forgetting that both before and after the battle of the Boyne it was a habit not to sign letters always. Tip.' (114.29–115.01)

will almost certainly miss the reference to *A Portrait of the Artist as a Young Man* embedded, with an irony that is entirely apposite, in these remarks on authorship, ownership, and the writer's quest for identity.

One further illustration. A crucial character, and episode, early in the text concerns a seductress who enchants via the sense of sight, and who thrice taunts her quarry with variants on the riddle, 'Why do I am alook alike a poss of porterpease?' (21.18–19) By rhythmic and textural echoes of the question, Joyce marks her seductive presence in the ground of a dozen and more other occurrences. Here are a few examples.

How do you do that lack a lock and pass the poker, please? (224.14–15)

And howelse do we hook our hike to find that pint of porter place? (260.05–06)

And she had to seek a pond's apeace to salve her suiterkins. (301.n1)

Hwere can a ketch or hook alive a suit and sowterkins? (311.22–3)

– Nohow did he kersse or hoot alike the suit and solder skins ... (317.22–3)

And ere he could catch or hook or line to suit their saussyskins ... (324.12)

Moke the Wanst, whye doe we aime alike a pose of poeter peaced? (372.04–05)

... wondering wheer would his aluck alight or boss of both appease ... (417.07)

For why do you lack a link of luck to poise a pont of perfect, peace? (493.29–30)

What'll you take to link to light a pike on porpoise, plaise? (623.14–15)

As Patrick McCarthy points out, this technique allows Joyce not only to map one theme onto another but also to overlay whole sections of the book: 'By retaining the basic rhythm of the riddle while changing not only the words but even, at times, the major consonant sounds and the syntax, Joyce is able to adapt his riddle to almost any situation and – more importantly – any theme he desires. It is the rhythm of the sentence that established correspondences between parts of the book (e.g., the structural parallels between the stories of the Prankquean and the Norwegian Captain).'[51] Another example, mentioned above, is 'a poor trait of the artless' for *A Portrait of the Artist*. This mode of language play adapts the French figure, the holorime. Properly, a holorime is a two-line poem: each line uses the same music, the same pronunciation, but different words. For example, 'Par le bois du Djinn, ou s'entasse de l'éffroi, / Parle! Bois du gin, ou cent tasses de lait froid.' As Bryson comments, in *The Mother Tongue*,

It translates roughly as 'When going through the Djinn's woods, surrounded by so much fear, keep talking. Drink gin or a hundred cups of cold milk.' We have the capacity to do this in English – 'I love you' and 'isle of view' are holorimic phrases and there must be an infinity of others. William Safire cites the American grandmother who thought that the line in the Beatles' song about 'the girl with kaleidoscope eyes' was 'the girl with colitis goes by,' which would seem to offer rich potential to budding holorimistes. A rare attempt to compose an English holorime was made by the British humorist Miles Kingston (from whom the previous example is quoted) in 1988 when he offered the world this poem, called *A Lowlands Holiday Ends in Enjoyable Inactivity*: 'In Ayrshire hill areas, a cruise, eh, lass? / Inertia, hilarious, accrues, hélas.'[52]

While Joyce used puns as a means to compress statements, he would string together words and syllables that as they collided released new meanings, more puns. This practice is no novelty in the Menippean tradition of language experimentation. Dorothy Coleman, for example, devotes much of her chapter 'Poetic Prose,' to this aspect of Rabelais, for example, his 'Antiperica-tametanapareugedamphicribationesmerdicantium.' Joyce carried that excess to new lengths (101 letters, at full stretch) and added to the horseplay a serious poetic (and satyric) dimension. His vehicle is the famous 'thunderclaps': the hundred-lettered words, not spoken by any character but environmental utterances made by the language itself.[53] Any word that draws attention to itself independently of its meaning, whether by inappropriateness or by density or richness of meaning or texture or any other feature (such as unusual spelling), becomes a thing, an object of scrutiny as an artefact. Joyce routinely pushed words to this point in the *Wake*, and not only words themselves: he even meditates, at one point, upon the writer as alchemist, magically transforming events with literacy and writing on his own skin (reversing the usual process of making parchment from hides: the page as extension of skin): '... this Esuan Menschavik and the first till last alshemist wrote over every square inch of the only foolscap available, his own body, till by its corrosive sublimation one continuous present tense integument slowly unfolded all marryvoising moodmoulded cyclewheeling history (thereby, he said, reflecting from his own individual person life unlivable, transaccidentated through the slow fires of consciousness into a dividual chaos, perilous, potent, common to allflesh, human only, mortal) but with each word that would not pass away the squidself which he had squirtscreened from the crystalline world waned chagreenold and doriangrayer in its dudhud' (*FW*, 185.34–186.08).

The word is become a thing with properties ('corrosiveness') and motion ('continuous present tense'). In similar Menippean fashion, he even has us dwell on the letters (in a manuscript) themselves as things: '... the pees with their caps awry are quite as often as not taken for kews with their tails in their or are quite as often as not taken for pews with their tails in their mouths, thence your pristopher polombos, hence our Kat Kresbyterians; the curt witty wotty dashes never quite just right at the trim trite truth letter; the sudden spluttered petulance of some capItallsed mIddle; a word as cunningly hidden in its maze of coufused drapery as a fieldmouse in a nest of coloured ribbons ... those superciliouslooking crisscrossed Greek ees awkwardlike perched there and here out of date like sick owls hawked back to Athens' (*FW*, 119.35–120.20). The ten thunders are conspicuously *things* in the text, more than just words undergoing mutation by pun or portmanteau.

The next chapters attempt a reading of *Finnegans Wake* as a Menippean and grammatical satire, based on an examination of the verbal landscape and in particular on the oddest features of that landscape, the ten thunderclaps. Joyce intended them to figure prominently in the reader's attention: he placed the first one directly in the reader's path – a few lines down on the first page of the book. Yet to date there is not one study of the thunders. As shown earlier, language and style, directed towards a particular satiric effect, are what make a work a Cynic satire. In the *Wake*, language and style are particularly concentrated in the thunders, and hence it is with an examination of the thunders that a reading of *Finnegans Wake* should begin.

PART II

WHAT THE THUNDER SAID

3

Introduction to Part II

... in *Finnegans Wake*, the multilingual combinations are intended towards a richer, more cunning public medium. They do not aim at creating a new language. Such invention may well be the most paradoxical, revolutionary step of which the human intellect is capable.

George Steiner, *After Babel*, 190.

Finnegans Wake presents ten thunderclaps. The tenth has an extra letter: the total number of letters, then, is 1,001, and so refers deliberately (if obliquely) to that other book of night tales, *The Thousand and One Nights*. This allusion is appropriate because, as will be seen in chapter 12, the figure of Aladdin with his glowing magic lamp serves as an image for television, the subject of the final thunder. In terms of the Viconian progression from things to written words, the thunders operate both at the level of things (experiences) and at that of words-as-things. They are simultaneously words to be studied and interpreted, and – as speech of the gods – inarticulate gestures, constitutive utterances that both are, and are the formal cause of, the things or situations or changes they utter.[1] The thunders themselves have no syntax. Each is the metamorphic *logos* of a condition or order of human culture: it condenses into a single utterance an entire making process. Put another way, all of the thunders in the *Wake* are accompanied by a technological reign (thunder and rain) and an en-lightening of the attentive reader.

The traditional grammatical theory of words is that they are the sounds made by things – God's artefacts or human ones – as they 'play upon' or interact with the sensibilities of different groups of people. This assumption lies behind Vico's quest for a 'mental dictionary' as much as it informs the grammarian's attitude to etymology. (They usually point out that Adam's first job was the naming of creatures.)[2] So, a door registers as 'door' in English (and similarly in Dutch, Swedish, Danish, and Norwegian – respectively *deur, dörr, dør,* and *dør*), as *Tur* in German, as *porte* in French, as *ovi* in Finnish, *kapi* in Turkish, *dver* in Russian, and *bab* in Arabic. Similarly, as words, the ten thunderclaps are the sounds made by cultural changes as the process of change is registered in human language (and noted and orchestrated by Joyce). Exegesis of any of the thunders reveals that more than one human language is present, but the mixture is carefully controlled. The first thunder is the only one with a considerable portion of Arabic; others abound in Romance languages; others in Scandinavian words.

Joyce's ten thunders can be arranged in two groups of five. The first group deals with five stages in the dissolution of oral, corporate society and the establishment of culture based on visual values and individualism. His images for the breaking-up of the integral sensorium include the smashing of Humpty Dumpty when he falls off the wall, and the theme of the 'royal divorce' of the senses when vision becomes matriarch. The condition of corporate or private identity is dramatized by a group of characters: Finnegan personifies the corporate or tribal mode of culture; the HCE family of five, who together are Finnegan, personifies aspects of the civilized and individualized mode. During the course of the first three thunders (cultural revolutions) old Finnegan 'dies' and members of the civilized family emerge, as it were, from the Humpty-Dumpty egg. The second group of five thunders puts on display the complementary process as, under the influence of various electric technologies (telephone, radio, movies, television), Finnegan, dormant rather than outright dead, gradually revives and resumes his position. This action in turn renders the HCE family obsolete, and Humpty Dumpty goes back together again.

The role of the thunders in *Finnegans Wake* resembles that of a divine 'fiat!' On the one hand they both proclaim and are a cultural transition; on the other, they function as a linguistic door ('diaphane') through which the culture passes. To reinforce this sense, each thunder carries words for 'door.' Thus, the thunders occur at moments of change, and are both the sound of the change and the word – the *logos* – of the change. The kind of change in each case is not one of total metamorphosis: it is rather like the alterations in perception that occur when one stands on one's head. Elements that make up the *ground* of a situation are suddenly thrust into prominence, as formerly prominent elements are relegated to ground. A parallel process is described by St Thomas Aquinas:

The succession of opposites in the same subject must be looked at differently in the things that are subject to time and in those that are above time. For, in those that are in time, there is no last instant in which the previous form inheres in the subject but there is the last time, and the first instant when the subsequent form inheres in the matter or subject; and this for the reason, that in time we are not to consider one instant as immediately preceding another instant, since neither do instants succeed each other immediately in time, nor points in a line, as is proved in *Physics* vi.1. But time is terminated by an instant. Hence in the whole of the previous time wherein anything is moviong towards its form, it is under the opposite form; but in the last instant of this time, which is the first instant of the subsequent time, it has the form which is the term of the movement.[3]

This adequately describes the action of thunders in their contexts in the *Wake*. A situation is presented, developed, subjected to increasing stress until, with the thunder, a collapse, and suddenly a complementary situation that was latent in the first is seen to be in place. In the *Wake*, a result of each of these changes is that the displaced former situation – or at least some of its components and technologies – is absorbed by the new situation as its content and is eventually converted into an art form as the result of modifications of sensibility that enable the 'old thing' to be seen in a new way. Thus, in the context of thunders 1 and 2, after the introduction of architecture, clothing becomes an art form, and fashion (and its uses as weaponry in a battle of the sexes) is born. At the same time, new arts of language appear after the introduction of writing.

My procedure in part 2 is to examine both the ten thunders and their contexts. In some cases the thunder is obviously the crux of the set-piece or episode – as with the Prankquean tale, for example. In two cases, the thunder begins the dénouement of a chapter, all or most of which must be considered its context (thunders 3 and 6). More usually, however, the thunder comes as a Menippean digression from a longer passage of straight text and no set-piece is provided: in these cases I have examined the ten or twenty pages on either side of the thunder that serve as its context. Each context forms a situation, a before and after, and is shot through with a set of themes that are explicitly echoed in the thunder word, so that the choice of context pages for those thunders not directly involved with a set-piece or chapter is controlled rather than arbitrary.

Just as primitives, when they hear a thunderclap, ask their shaman, 'What did the god say just then?' so exegesis of one of Joyce's thunders begins with an oral performance.[4] There is no 'one right way' to pronounce a thunder either in whole or in part. Each letter- and syllable-group should be pronounced and mimed in as many ways as the letters themselves allow until it produces the intelligible, that is, with the ears alive to words and puns in as many languages as possible. An inventory of the words heard (and their translations) can then be compiled.

For example, the second thunder begins 'Perkodhuskurunbarggruauyagok ...' On occasion, entire phrases can be heard in a thunder: but not here, so exegesis begins with the first syllable. *Pe* yields pea. *Per*, per (through), pair, pare, and peer (look or lordship). *Perk* gives perk, and park. *Perkod* yields pea-pod, per quod, Pequod, and, by stretching things a bit, perkons (Lettish, thunder). The length of a letter-group listened to gradually grows longer until it ceases to render new intelligible meaning. Then one begins with the second letter, and expands a syllable at a time. Then the third letter, and then the fourth, and so on to the end of the thunder. This is the first stage.

The second stage involves relating the inventory of words from the thunder, both those of which one is certain and those one suspects are present, to the themes provided by the context of the thunder. The first stage requires great playfulness and receptivity of suggestion; the second brings one down to earth again. In the latter, words or phrases that bear no evident relation to themes or actions in the context are set aside (for future reference, if they are not too unlikely: no one can claim to have exhausted the themes in any section of the *Wake*). The words that remain fall into two groups: those related to that particular context and theme-group, and those – such as words for thunder and door – that are present in all of the thunders.

A word-list for the thunder is given at the end of each of the ten chapters that follow. Throughout these chapters, I have tried to keep in mind Edmund Wilson's riposte in 1940 to Thornton Wilder, concerning Wilder's interpretation of *Finnegans Wake*: 'Nor does it seem to me quite legitimate to get arse out of heart. Have you read any of those books about Baconian ciphers in Shakespeare? Those theories can sometimes be made to seem quite plausible.'[5]

4

The First Thunderclap: The First Technologies (*FW* 3–18.36)

First we feel. Then we fall. (627.11)

By his magmasine fall. Lumps, lavas and all. *Bene!* But, thunder and turf, it's not alover yet. One recalls Byzantium. (294.25–7)

What then agentlike brought about that tragoady thundersday this municipal sin business? (05.13–14)

Most of the thunder contexts follow a definite pattern: for some pages prior to the thunder word, the scene is set. Relevant themes are interwoven so as to indicate the environmental, cultural, and sensory state prevailing before the thunder metamorphosis. Then, as a new technology is introduced, aspects of this prior situation begin to assume a gradient rise in their intensity of operation. When this rise reaches a peak, the thunderword is 'spoken' and a new technological environment is seen to be in place by means of its effects on the initial components (the closure process). At this point, in most cases, the text dissolves again into a sort of general discussion.

When a thunder is associated with a specific episode, such as the Prankquean's or Belinda's, this pattern or progression becomes better defined and, as a consequence, is more easily discernible. Most of the thunders assemble their structural components from themes and metaphors developed elsewhere in the *Wake*, and though resulting patterns of structure are more difficult to unravel, they are no less precise.

In the case of the first thunderclap, the problems of recognizing thematic structures in a thunder not specifically associated with an episode are multiplied because the primary themes of the initial gradient are compressed into

run
rivers brings us back to
Howth Castle & Environs. Sir Tristram, violer
d'amores, fr'over the short sea, had passencore
rearrived from North Armorica on this side
the scraggy isthmus of Europe Minor to
wielderfight his penisolate war; nor had
stream rocks, by the stream Oconee exaggerated
themselse to Laurens County's gorgios,
while they went doubling their mumper all the time:
nor avoice from afire bellowsed mishe
mishe to tauftauf thuartpeatrick: not
yet, though venisoon after, had a kidscad
buttended a bland old isaac: not yet
though all's fair in vanessy, were sosie
sosie sesthers wroth with twone nathandjoe.
Rot a peck of pa's malt had Jhem or
Shen brewed by aaclight and rory end
to the regginbrow was to be seen ringsome
on the waterface.
    The fall (bababadalgharaghtakamminn-
arronnkonnbronntonnerronntuonnthunn-
trovarrhounawnskawntoohoohoordenenthurnuk!)
of a once wallstrait oldparr is retaled
early in bed and later on life down
through all christian minstrelsy. The great
fall of the offwall entailed at such short
notice the schute of Finnigan, erse solid
man, that the humptyhillhead of humself
prumptly sends an unquiring one well to
the west in quest of his tumptytumtoes:
and their upturnpikepointandplace is
at the knock out in the park where oranges
have been laid to rust upon the green
since devlins first loved livvy.
    What clashes here of wills

Thunder 1 revised: 94 letters

the fourteen lines preceding the thunder. These begin: 'riverrun, past Eve and Adam's, from swerve of shore to bend of bay, brings us by a commodius vicus of recirculation back to Howth Castle and Environs.' Perhaps the most important sentence (or part sentence) in the book, this opening immediately establishes themes of matriarchy, language, and the cognitive labyrinth. The river personifies the flow of speech and of experience and limns the lines of force of the language as we trace its course from the garden of Eden to modern times and back again. Matriarchy is signalled by placing Eve before Adam, and the domesticated HCE is fore-echoed in 'Howth Castle and Environs.' The mode is active; the river runs. The next phrase, 'past Eve and Adam's,' sets the scene as Edenic, yet it is an Eden of lost innocence, penetrated by the sinuous serpentine river. (The 'snaky' temptress is a key figure in the next thunder episode.) 'Past' suggests a sense of historical time and separating of experience into 'past' and 'present.' The transition effected by this thunder is from Edenic palaeolithic to neolithic by means of the first technologies: speech, fire, weapons.

'Commodius vicus' combines a reference to the Roman emperor, Commodus (the themes of city and empire, and of weaponry: sword tip or spear tip cutting the earth), with two further forms of snaky 'recirculation': as the river recirculates rain to the sea, the commode returns water to the river. 'Vicus' includes the Vico Road (Dalkey) and the *ricorsi storici* of Vico. The references to recirculation serve at least two purposes: first, they are scene setting – 'let us return to Eden ...'; second, they refer to the circular 'square wheel without spokes,' the paradoxical nature of this Menippean satire. The reference to Howth Castle is to a Dublin landmark. Campbell and Robinson describe it:

a high headland crowned by a castle and guarding Dublin Bay. It is particularly regarded as the cranium of a recumbent giant whose belly is the city of Dublin and whose feet turn up amidst the hillocks of Phoenix Park. If the river Liffey is the heroine, this sleeping landscape giant is the hero. Historical associations crowd around his recumbent form. On this headland the sentinels of Finn MacCool stood guard against the invaders from the sea. Centuries later, when the Anglo-Norman king Henry II subjugated the island, the present castle was founded by one of the invading company, Sir Almeric Tristram. That was in the century of the flowering of the Arthurian romances, with which are inseparably woven the names of Tristram and Iseult.[1]

In the *Wake*, Finnegan is an image or icon of integral, corporate, tribal man. His demise occurs as the integral body is exaggerated and distorted by the first technologies – speech, fire, weapons, clothing, architecture – each of which constitutes a 'fall' or 'sin' of self-knowing and self-love and gives rise to aggression. The figure of Humpty Dumpty also symbolizes the integral body and, more important, the integrity of the sensorium that is shattered by falls in this and subsequent thunders. The exaggerations and extensions pile up in the forms of both a magazine (storehouse) and a wall until Humpty Dumpty and Finnegan fall – from vertigo or drunkenness. This 'magazine wall' is made up of all of man's accumulated specialist extensions and innovations; as they accumulate, it stretches upward higher and higher, teeters ... and Humpty plunges down. Thereafter Finnegan, or perhaps only the memory of him, lingers awhile as a deformed man, a hunchback. We see him in silhouette, a man carrying on his back a hod laden with bricks – for building walls and houses. Now, bricks are uniform and repeatable, so he is characterized as 'Bygmester Finnegan, of the Stuttering Hand' (04.18). Stuttering or 'stutterance' introduces several themes: speech, compared to song, is a mode of stuttering, and technological innovation and repetition is also a form of stutter. This loss of primal, Edenic integrity through speech and innovation constitutes a kind of 'original sin' (*ab origine*) – a theme that, as 'the sin in the park,' will later assume import for HCE and thunder 3. At this point, in effect, integral Finnegan ('solid man' as he will shortly be called) has 'died' and been interred in both exterior and interior landscapes. The interior 'interment': Finnegan tribalism remains dormant in the human psyche until resurrected by later thunders. In comparison to other cultures of the West, Irish tribalism has never submerged far below the surface, so perhaps the chthonic Finnegan is an apt figure for it. The *Wake* is about what occurs both at and in his wake.

The demise of Finnegan proceeds apace in the remaining lines before the thunder:

Sir Tristram, violer d'amores, fr'over the short sea, had passencore rearrived from North Armorica on this side the scraggy isthmus of Europe Minor to wielderfight his penisolate war: nor had topsawyer's rocks by the stream Oconee exaggerated themselse to Laurens County's gorgios while they went doublin their mumper all the time: nor avoice from afire bellowsed mishe mishe to tauftauf thuartpeatrick: not yet, though venissoon after, had a kidscad buttended a bland old isaac: not yet, though all's fair in vanessy, were sosie sesthers wroth with twone nathandjoe. Rot a peck of pa's malt had Jhem or Shen brewed by arclight and rory end to the regginbrow was to be seen ringsome on the aquaface. (03.16–26)

This is particularly dense text. Joyce wrote it as a piece especially for Harriet Shaw Weaver and sent it to her with a gloss (in his letter of 15 November

1926). Where the previous paragraph indicates an awareness of historical past and present, this one, by prescience, distinguishes future and present. Of the two sentences that comprise it, the first proceeds by negatives, presaging actions and events that follow the thunder but that cast their shadows here before them. Sir Amory Tristram, the first earl of Howth, was born in Brittany (North Armorica) and later changed his name to St Lawrence. Sir Tristram was also one of the knights of the Round Table. The references together bring in allusions to sentimentalism and courtly love, to warfare, to armour (clothing), and to weaponry.[2] The 'round table' and various circlings and recyclings constitute an allusion to another neolithic technology, the wheel. 'Violer' is a French verb meaning 'break, violate, invade, profane,' which relates to loss of innocence, expulsion from the sacred presence into the secular world, bellicosity, and shattering of the integral. (I know that's a lot, but in his gloss, Joyce says to take the word in all senses.) He is come to 'wielderfight his penisolate war' – a war of erections (military, architectural, and sexual) and of extensions of man. (Howth is a sort of peninsula, joined to the mainland by a 'scraggy isthmus': a peninsula is an extension or jutting of the land into the sea.) The closure for the thunder makes this more explicit: the paragraph after the thunder ends with 'Phall if you but will, rise you must: and none so soon either shall the pharce for the nunce come to a setdown secular phoenish.' (04.15–17)

In the next stage of the episode, 'avoice from afire bellowsed mishe mishe to tauftauf thuartpeatrick: not yet, though venissoon after ... though all's fair in vanessy ...' Anna Livia is, severally, the serpentine 'riverrun,' the temptress in the garden of innocence, and the flow of utterance, language (an outering of thought), and experience. In this section of the book, Joyce casts her as the instigator of the 'burning would' of innovation. As he remarks in the closure section,

And we all like a marriedann because she is mercenary. Though the length of the land lies under liquidation (floote!) and there's nare a hairbrow nor an eyebush on this glaubrous phace of Herrschuft Whatarwelter she'll loan a vesta and hire some peat and sarch the shores her cockles to heat and she'll do all a turfwoman can to piff the business on. Paff. To puff the blaziness on. Poffpoff. And even if Humpty shell fall frumpty times as awkward again in the beardsboosoloom of all our grand remonstrancers there'll be iggs for the brekkers come to mournhim, sunny side up with care. (12.06–15)

Here, the voice from the 'bellowsed' fire bellows 'mische mische' (Gael, I am I am), emphasizing private awareness and identity and further dissolving

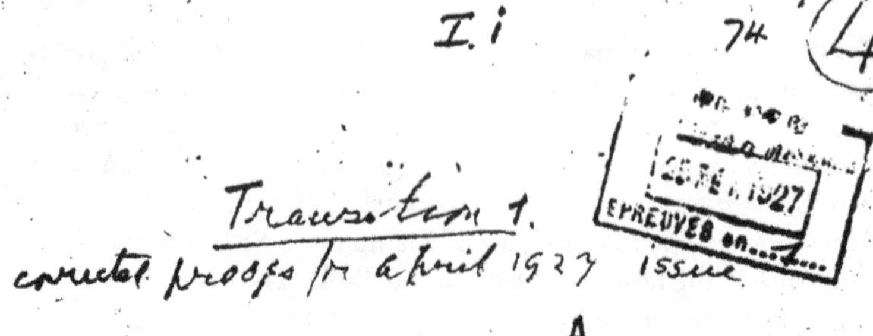

A

OPENING PAGES OF WORK
IN PROGRESS

by JAMES JOYCE

riverrun brings us back to Howth Castlo & Environs. Sir Tristram, violer d'amores, fr' over the short sea, had passencore rearrived from North Armorica on this side the scraggy isthmus of Europe Minor to wielderfight his penisolate war: nor had topsawyer's rocks by the stream Oconee exaggerated themselse to Laurens County's gorgios, while they went doublin their mumper all the time; nor avoice from afire bellowsed mishe mishe to tauftauf thuartpeatrick: not yet, though venissoon after, had a kidsced buttended a bland old isaac; not yet, though all's fair in vanessy, were sosie sesthers wroth with twone nathandjoe. Rot a peck of pa's malt had Jhem or Shen brewed by arclight and rory end to the reggimbrow was to be seen ringsome on the waterface.

The fall (badalgharaghtakamminarronnkonnbronntonnerronntuonnthunntrovarrhounawnskawntoohooho-ordenenthurnuckl) of a once wallstrait oldparr is retaled early in bed and later on life down through all christian minstrelsy. The great fall of the offwall entailed at such short notice the schute of Finnigan, erse solid man, that the humptyhillhead of humself prumptly sends an unquiring one well to the west in quest of his tumptytumtoes: and their upturnpikepointandplace is at the knock out in the park where oranges have been

Thunder 1: galleys

corporate awareness (Finnegan). 'Tauftauf' (Ger, *taufen*, baptize) sounds again the Edenic Fall motif and that of individualism and private awareness (forgiveness and salvation are individual). Individualism or self-awareness are further echoed in the two subsequent references to vanity: the first of these (an oblique reference to Swift's Vanessa) also contains a reference to hunting (that is, of venison – hart and deer, so perhaps also 'hearts and dears' or mate-hunting and the battle of the sexes), while the second extends the first reference to include the 'love and war' theme.

The second and final sentence refers principally to the first technologizations of nature through cultivation and (appropriate to Finnegan themes from the ballad[3]) various brews. Among the included references: 'Noah planted the vine and was drunk'; the song, 'Willie Brewed a Peck o' Malt!'; 'John Jameson [Jhem or Shen] is the greatest Dublin brewer.'[4] The final references, to rainbows, link with the Noah/brewing themes. Joyce's glosses include that 'rory' is 'red' in Irish and 'dewy' (*roridus*) in Latin, that 'at the rainbow's end are dew and the colour red ...' and that 'when all vegetation is covered by the flood there are no eyebrows on the face of the waterworld.' The river of utterance and innovation is in full flood. In addition, the whole paragraph, which begins with violet ('violer'), has yellow fire in the middle ('afire bellow ...') and ends with red (Irish 'rory'), mirrors the rainbow-spectrum of seven colours with its structure of seven clauses. The rainbow is another form of fragmentation of the integral, of white light.

The next paragraph, the third of the book, opens with two words, 'The fall,' then hands you the first thunderclap (in parentheses, suggesting that it functions both as onomatopoeic illustration and as transformative digression):

The fall (bababadalgharaghtakamminaronnonnbronntonnerronnuonnthunntrovarr-
hounawnskawntoohoohoordenenthurnuk!) of a once wallstrait oldparr is retaled
early in bed and later on life down through all christian minstrelsy. The great fall of
the offwall entailed at such short notice the pftjschute of Finnegan, erse solid man,
that the humptyhillhead of humself prumptly sends an unquiring one well to the
west in quest of his tumptytumtoes: and their upturnpikepointandplace is at the
knock out in the park where oranges have been laid to rust upon the green since
devlinsfirst loved livvy. (03.27–36)

Having tasted the first fruits of technological utterance, Adam/Finnegan/Humpty Dumpty falls from integrity, grace, and garden. Two 'minor rumbles' come after the thunder, one of twenty-three letters and one of thirty. The first, 'upturnpikepointandplace' (above), suggests the plough's tooth erect both as a weapon and as a picket in a fence. The second, 'hierarchitectitiptitoploftical' (05.01–02), includes social and intellectual hierarchies as well as architectural erections – towers and skyscrapers.[5] This second rumble follows a complex reference to Finnegan as a mason and master builder who spans the ages from pre-biblical times to the developed oral world of Arab culture and 'bulbous dome' architecture:

> Bygmester Finnegan, of the Stuttering Hand, freemen's maurer, lived in the broadest way immarginable in his rushlit toofarback for messuages before joshuan judges had given us numbers or Helviticus committed deuteronomy ... and during mighty odd years this man of hod, cement and edifices in Toper's Thorp piled buildung supra buildung pon the banks ... Oftwhile balbulous, mithre ahead, with goodly trowel in grasp ... like Haroun Childeric Eggeberth he would caligulate by multiplicables the alltitude and malltitude until he seesaw by neatlight of the liquor wheretwin 'twas born, his roundhead staple of other days to rise in undress maisonry upstanded (joygrantit!), a waalworth of a skyerscape of most eyeful hoyth entowerly ... baubletop ... (04.18–05.02)

Here Joyce weaves in the themes of architecture and commerce announced in the fourth word following the thunder (waalstrait).

The thunder paragraph is followed by one (4) that develops the themes of sins, weaponry and battles, love and war, and expulsion from the garden of innocence; and, punning on a type of sword (a badelaire), it introduces Baudelaire, suggesting thereby these effects of the thunder and fall are more 'flowers of evil.'

The rest of the closure section can be reviewed quickly. Following the second rumble comes a paragraph replete with Arabic words and references, including one to *The Arabian Nights*: 'There extend by now one thousand and one stories, all told, of the same.' This is appropriate since both the *Thousand and One Nights* and the *Wake* are frame tales, and since all of the thunders together run for 1,001 letters. Every letter is a story (and letters themselves are another story), and by now there are, all told, a thousand and more extensions (innovations), and all pretty much the same story so let the thunders show them all. The paragraph begins: 'What then agentlike brought about that tragoady thundersday this municipal sin business? Our cubehouse still rocks as earwitness to the thunder ...' (05.13–15). McHugh (*Annotations*) glosses cubehouse as 'literal translation of Ka'aba, centre of Islam.' The paragraph ends with a parody of the ballad, 'Tim Finnegan's Wake,' and presents him as interred in Egyptian mastaba tombs: '... (There was a wall of course in erection) Dimb! He stottered from the latter. Damb! he was dud. Dumb! Mastabatoom, mastabadtomm, ...' (06.09–11)

Two episodes round out the closure section. The first is the famous set-piece, the Willingdone Museyroom (pages 8–10), which displays all manner of weapon and warrior, particularly those associated with Napoleon's campaigns. (It is noteworthy that Wellingtons, Bluchers, and Napoleons are types of boots – the clothing motif.) Additionally, it parodies the life cycle. It opens: 'This way to the museyroom. Mind your hats goan in!' (08.09: we enter the world head first); and it ends: 'This way the museyroom. Mind your boots goan out.' (10.22–3: we leave the world feet first). The second episode dramatizes the birth of speech and language as a brief dialogue between two cavemen, Mutt and Jute (pages 16–18: they are also mute and jut), as an aspect of this first thunder. It ends,

> Mutt. – Ore you astoneaged, jute you?
> Jute. – Oye am thonthorstruck, thing mud.

The thunder itself (in parentheses, so delivered *sotto voce*) –

(bababadalgharaghtakamminarronnkonnbronntonnerronntu-
onnthunntrovarrhounawnskawntoohoohoordenenthurnuk!) (3.27–9)

– resounds with allusions to all of the themes woven into its context. This particular thunder contains a large number of Arabic words that, by their very presence, signal the closure theme of transition from a palaeolithic garden to the ear-culture of the Arab world and its resonant architecture. Today, as we close the twentieth century, we are far from unfamiliar with domed stadia; but these lines were written sixty or seventy years ago, when such structures were rare in the West. Thunder 2 is the only other thunder to contain an appreciable amount of Arabic (yet much less than thunder 1) for it carries forward themes and action from the Arab-world milieu to that of medieval European romance.

The following list is representative of the thunder allusions to themes treated in this chapter. Abbreviations for sources and languages are listed and expanded on xvi–xvii.

Thunder	Interpretation	Theme Sounded
ba	Egy, *Ba*, shining form, soul	armour (shining form), weaponry; the fall
bab	Ar, *bab*, door	doors

Thunder	Interpretation	Theme Sounded
	Indog, *bha, bhabh*, to tremble (Wig)	fall (vertigo, etc.)
baba	baby	HCEggebirth, birth of civilization; innovations
	[Ali] Baba	Arab world, 1,001
	Papa	Adam, Finnegan
	R, woman	ALP, Eve, matriarch
	Ar, *barbar*, language	Mutt and Jute, birth of language
	Turk, *babur*, lion	Mutt and Jute
bababa or baba	Ka'aba	The Ka'aba, centre of Islam; cubehouse
bababada	sound of child learning to speak	Birth of language, Mutt and Jute
	stuttering sound	Birth of language, Mutt and Jute; Bygmester Finnegan
ab	Ar, *ab*, father	Adam, Finnegan
	Egy, *Ab*, heart, 'seat of good and evil thoughts'	the fall
aba	(biblical), *abba*, father (e.g., Romans 8:15)	Adam, Finnegan
abada	Ar, to cause a separation	Humpty Dumpty, fragmenting of corporate, uttering/outering
bad	Dan, *bad*, boat	Noah, commerce
	Ger, *rad*, wheel	Wheel, recirculation; knights (round table)
	Ar, *bad*, after	chronological time
bada	Ar, *bayda*, egg (26L)	Humpty Dumpty
badal	battle	battle, Willingdone Museyroom

Thunder	Interpretation	Theme Sounded
	Ar, change	neolithic revolution; thunder change
	[Indian/Hindu], *badal*, revenge, vendetta, blood feud	battle, revolution
badalghar	battle scar	battle, Willingdone Museyroom
	Trafalgar	battle, Willingdone Museyroom
	Baudelaire	Flowers of Evil, Eden
	Fr, *badelaire*, a short broad sword with a curved blade	battle, weaponry
	Ar, *baad al-zuhr*, afternoon (26L)	'day' of Finnegan ends
dal	Sw, *tal*, number	fragmentation
algha	Gr, *algia*, pain	battle (wound), loss of Eden
alghara	The Al-Koran, 'that which is to be read aloud'	Arab world, ear
ghar	Ar, cave	Mutt, Jute, cavemen
	Ar, *gar*, neighbour	architecture, cities
	Indog, devour (Wig)	eggs for breakfast, new day
	AS, spear	weaponry, penisolate war, Willingdone Museyroom
ghara	Heb, *kara*, call	language, ear
	Ar, *garya*, village	civil; architecture
	Hin, a wheeled cart	wheel
gharag	Hin, *karak*, thunder (McH)	thunder, change
	Ger, *grab*, grave	sleeping giant, tomb
gharaghtak	Gael, *gaireachtach*, boisterous (GaL)	battle; 'lots of fun at Finnegan's wake'
arag	Fr, *orage*, storm	thunderstorm, battle
ra	Egy, *Ra*, sun god: conqueror of darkness, responsible	demise of Finnegan; expulsion from

Thunder	Interpretation	Theme Sounded
	for the destruction of humanity	Garden of Eden; dissolution of tribe
rag	rag	clothing
	rage	storm; battle; innovation
	to break up with a hammer	fragmentation
	Ar, *raad*, thunder	thunder
aghtakammin	Tutankhamun	East/ear-world, 'mastabatomb'
tak	talk	speech
	Sw, Nor, *tak*, roof	architecture
taka	OSw, Icel, seize	battle
ka	Egy, *Ka*, double	drunken double-vision, echo world, repeatable
kam	Ar, *qamh*, wheat	agriculture
kamm	Ger, *Kamm*, comb (GeL)	self-awareness
kammin	Ar, ambush	battle
	Ger, *Kamin*, chimney	architecture, fire, erection
kammina	Lat, *camera*, a small room	architecture
	Fi, *komiina*, stove	fire
kamminarro	Jap, *kaminari*, thunder (McH)	thunder
amm	Ar, *umm*, mother	Eve, matriarchy
ammi	Ar, *aama*, blind	sense battle, ear world
min	mine	neolithic technology (mining); possessiveness, individualism
mina	a Greek coin	commerce, repeatability
	Lat, *minae*, battlements	architecture, battles
minar	Ar, lighthouse, minaret	architecture, erection, Arab world

Thunder	Interpretation	Theme Sounded
	Fr, *miner*, consume, weaken	demise of Finnegan
narr	Ger, *Narr*, fool (GeL)	the fall
	Ar, *nar*, fire	fire
narro	Lat, tell, report	speech, the ear
arro	arrow	weaponry, battle
	Lat, plough	agriculture
arronn	Haroun [Childeric Eggebirth] [H. al Raschid – Caliph of Baghdad]	Humpty Dumpty, HCE 1,001; Arab world
	around	recirculation, wall
	Ger, *geronnen*, flowed (GeL)	river: speech innovation
arronnko	Sp, *arado*, plough	agriculture
konn	Gael, *can*, sing	ballad of Finn's wake
bronn	bronze	mining, commerce, weaponry
	prone	sleeping giant
bronnto	Gr, *bronte*, thunder	thunder
	Sp, *pronto*, abruptly	thunder changes
bronnton	Gr, *Brontôn*, Lat. *Bronton*, 'Thunderer': epithet of Zeus (ClL)	thunder
ton	tone	ear
	Lat, *tono* (ClL)	thunder
tonner	Fr, *tonnerre*, thunder	thunder
	Lat, *tonare*, to thunder	thunder
	Ger, *Donner*, thunder	thunder
	Ger, *tonen*, resound	thunder; ear/echo; recirculation
onnerro	Lat, *onus, oneris*, burden	hod-carrier Finnegan
err	err	the fall (Eden)
	ear	ear
erro	arrow	weaponry, etc.

Thunder	Interpretation	Theme Sounded
erronn	Erin	Eden
	around	recirculation, wall
	hearing	ear
tuonn	Ital, *tuono*, thunder	thunder
	two-one	
	twin	
	tone	ear
uonn	you won	battle
	you-one	individualism
thunntr	thunder	thunder
	ME, *thuner*, thunder	thunder
hun	Hun (warlike tribe)	tribal; battle
hunnt	hunt (venison; dears and hearts)	hunting, weaponry; sexes
trova	Port, *trovao*, thunder (26L)	thunder
trovarr	Prov, *trobar*, troubador, cavalryman	speech, ear (no stutter) battle, weaponry
var	Ar, *phar*, lighthouse	erection, Arab world
varrho	Ar, *zahra*, flower	flowers of evil, the Garden of Eden, the fall
arrhoun	Haroun (etc. as above)	Humpty, 1,001, etc.
	around	recirculation, wall
houn	Ger, *Hune*, giant	Finnegan, Howth
oun	Ar, *oum*, mother	Eve, matriarchy
ounawn	Onan (-ism)	self-knowledge as sin
awnska	Sw, *äska*, thunder (26L)	thunder
	onslaught	battles
skawn	Gael, *scan*, crack (26L)	thunder, Humpty, fragmentation
	skein	clothing (weaving, etc.)
tooh	Ar, *toub*, brick	wall, hod carrier

Thunder	Interpretation	Theme Sounded
toohoohoo	sound of crying	exit from Eden
	stuttering	stutter
	sound of first speech	speech
ohoorde	Dan, *ophøre*, expire	demise of Finnegan
hoor	whore	Eve
	hour	chronological time
	houri	Arab world
	Ger, *Hören*, to hear	ear
	Dan, Nor, *hør*, to hear (26L)	ear
	Dan, *hør*, flax	clothing
hoorden	Ger, hordes	tribes; battles
hoordenen	Dan, *tordenen*, thunder (McH)	thunder
oor	Du, *oor*, ear	ear world
orde	Erde (earth-mother)	Eve (ur-mother)
orden	Dan, Nor, *torden*, thunder (26L)	thunder
	Ger, *Orden*, medal	battle, minting
odenenth	ordnance	weaponry
den	den (i.e. cave)	caveman
	Ar, *denn*, cave	caveman
enthur	inter	sleeping giant interred
thur	Ar, revolution	wheel, cycle, battle, recirculation, thunder changes
	Ger, *Tür*, door	doors
thurnuk	Gael, *tornach*, thunder (GaL)	thunder
hurnu	Sl. horny	penisolate war
nuk	Indog, *nak*, to perish (Wig)	demise of Finnegan, Humpty, the tribe
	Dan, night	day of Finnegan over
	Ger, *Nacht*, night	day of Finnegan over.

5

The Second Thunderclap: The Prankquean: She (Stoops) to Conjure – Courtship by Piracy (*FW* 18.17–24.14)

... what the mischievmiss made a man do. (20.31)

This thunder comes at the end of one of the *Wake*'s more enchanting set-pieces, a fairy tale concerning the legendary piratess, Grace O'Malley, and her altercation with the lord of Howth Castle. Adaline Glasheen's entry in her *Third Census of 'Finnegans Wake'* may serve as a summary: 'Irish legend says Grace sailed to Howth castle and demanded entrance. The earl of Howth refused her because he was at dinner. Angry, she kidnapped his young heir ... and did not return him until the earl promised that his doors would always stand open at mealtime.' The tale is told through twice; it is begun a third time and interrupted in mid-flight by the thunder, which serves as the resolution and coda for the whole.[1] The three times suggest a traditional charm: at the thunder the spell is cast and the earl (here a Scandinavian Jarl) is transformed from a feudal aristocrat into a middle-aged, middle-class burgher. The build-up to this set-piece, however, includes the dramatized after-effects of the first thunder, in particular the developments of neolithic technology, of language (Mutt and Jute) and writing, and of architecture, which allows clothing to become an art form – fashionable weaponry for use in the ongoing battle of the sexes. The clothing-as-ornament metaphor extends as well to ornamentation of language. The piece begins, at one level, in the 'old stone age' ('in an auldstane eld' 21.05).

The Persona of the Prankquean

The Prankquean and her activities are accorded a thunder (or two: she has much to do with thunder 7), marking her as having signal import to whatever drama the thunders are involved in.[2] Furthermore, this section yields explicit information about the meaning of the rain that accompanies some – but not all – of the thunders. PQ is the arch-temptress of the book. She is no Eve – rather, as Grace Eckley has argued,[3] a retrieval of Lilith – but she does combine the piratess Grace O'Malley, Grania the consort of Diarmuid, the witch Isolde (and therefore Issy or Izzy, the daughter of HCE and ALP), and other bewitching females, including Cleopatra – another piratess (who stole Mark Antony). She it is who seduces by and of the eye, which 'charms' the other senses into submissive sleep. She is a little girl, a vain movie star, a queen, a quean (whore), a piratess, a tyrant sexually and sensually. Her role in the *Wake* is always connected with the dissociation of sensibility and the reign/rain of tyrrany of the visual over the other senses. Joyce presents her as diminutive, a 'cutletsized consort, foundling filly of fortyshilling fostertailor and shipman's shophoyden, weighing ten pebble ten, scaling five footsy five and spanning thirtyseven inchettes round the good companions, twentynine ditties round the wishful waistress, thirtyseven alsos round the answer to everything, twentythree of the same round each of the quis separabits, fourteen round the beginning of happiness and nicely nine round her shoed for slender' (255.29–36).

PQ's relation to Anna Livia is complex, to say the least, but so is everything at this wake. At one level, that of the family, she is the capricious sexpot daughter. In the Book of Nature, ALP the river flows down to 'Old Father Ocean,' while PQ is the rain (distilled, that is, abstract, water) whose clothing is the clouds. As a queen, she reigns; and from the cloud, she rains, often thunderously. Her dream castle is in the sky.

In the house of breathings lies that word, all fairness. The walls are of rubinen and the glittergates of elfinbone. The roof herof is of massicious jasper and a canopy of Tyrian awning rises and still descends to it. A grape cluster of lights hangs there beneath and all the house is filled with the breathings of her fairness, the fairness of fondance and the fairness of milk and rhubarb and the fairness of roasted meats and uniomargrits and the fairness of promise with consonantia and avowals. There lies her word, you reder! The height herup exalts it and the lowness her down abaseth it ... Her reverence. (249.06–32)

At another level, PQ and ALP are related as aspects of language. ALP is the river of speech, of natural, unadorned eloquence (prior to writing); PQ, her daughter, flaunts all the styles and decoration, the ornaments, or 'flowers' of rhetoric (the art of speech after writing).[4] Caveat: her word lies, we are twice

made her wittest in front of the arkway
of trihump, asking: Mark the Tris,
why do I am alook alike three poss [28]
of porterpease? But that was how
the skirtmisshes endupped. For like
the campbells acoming with a fork lance
of lightning, Jarl van Hoother
Boanerges himself, the old terror of the dames,
came hip hop handihap out through
the pike opened arkway of his three
Shuttoned castles, in his broadginger
hat and his civic chollar and his
allabuff hemmed like a rudd yellan
gruebleen orangeman in his violet
indigonation to the whole longth
of the strongth of his bowman's
bill. And he clopped his rude hand
to his eacy hitch and he ordered
and his thick spoke for
her to shut up shop, dammy.
And the dummy shot the shutter
up. And they all drank free. And
that was the first peace of illiteratu
porthery in all the flaminid, floody,
flatuous world. The prankquean
was to hold her dummyship and
the jiminies was to keep the
peacewave and van Hoother
was to git the wind up. Thus the
hearsomeness of the burger
felicitates the whole of the
polis.

O fænix culpri! Ex nickylow
mickel vialo comes bonum. Hill, rill, ones in
company, billeted, less be proud
of. Bresst high and bestride!
Only for that these will not breethe

Thunder 2: first version: 76 letters

told: all is not what it seems. Her locus, her house, resonates with the 'fairness of promise with consonantia and avowals,' the word adorned for the eye, on the page – a white cloud.

If you nude her in her prime, make sure you find her complementary or, on your very first occasion ... she'll prick you where you're proudest with her unsatt speagle eye. Look sharp, she's signalling from among the asters. (248.03–07)

'Asters' combines flowers (called 'bloomers' a few lines on) and 'stars,' the latter alluding to the movie-queen aspect and to PQ's home in the sky. The Prankquean's rain/reign, the matriarchy of the eye over the rest of the family of senses, nourishes the flowers – of rhetoric as much as those of technological innovation, the Flowers of Evil – and brings in its wake (the wake of Grace O'Malley's pirate ship) other forms of dissociation, including the breakup of white sunlight into the colours of the rainbow. Joyce links the flowers and the PQ tale in many ways, including this:

Aghatharept they fleurelly to Nebnos will and Rosocale. Twice is he gone to quest of her, thrice is she now to him. So see we so as seed we sow. And their prunktqueen kilt her kirtles up and set out. And her troup came heeling, O. And what do you think that pride was drest in! Voolykins' diamondinah's vestin. For ever they scent where air she went. While all the fauns' flares widens wild to see a floral's school
(250.27–33)

As regards the Prankquean episode, however, PQ's most important identification is with the innovation of letters (consonantia and avowals) and the resulting manuscript culture in which all editions are what we would call pirate editions. She is depicted as the heroine of a novelette romance, *as* the novelette, as letters (novel letters), and as the rain coursing to meet her mother, the river Liffey (Missisliffi). As it rains, the cloud dissipates.

Then Nuvoletta reflected for the last time in her little long life and she made up all her myriads of drifting minds in one. She cancelled all her engauzements. She climbed over the bannistars; she gave a childy cloudy cry: *Nuée! Nuée!* A lightdress fluttered. She was gone. And into the river that had been a stream (for a thousand of tears had gone eon her and come on her and she was stout and struck on dancing and her muddied name was Missisliffi) there fell a tear, a singult tear, the loveliest of all tears (I mean for those crylove fables fans who are 'keen' on the prettypretty commonface sort of thing you meet by hopeharrods) for it was a leaptear. But the river tripped on her by and by, lapping as though her heart was brook ... (159.06–17)

The Prankquean Episode

Preparation for the fairy tale begins three pages before and immediately follows the Mutt and Jute dialogue. It opens with an invitation, extended to literates schooled in exegesis, to read the Book of Nature:

(Stoop) if you are abcedminded, to this claybook, what curios of signs (please stoop), in this allaphbed! Can you rede (since We and Thou had it out already) its world? ... A hatch, a celt, an earshare the pourquose of which was to cassay the earthcrust at all of hours, furrowards, bagawards, like yoxen at the turnpaht. Here say figurines billycoose arming and mounting. Mounting and arming bellicose figurines see here ... When a part so ptee does duty for the holos we soon grow to use for an allforabit. Here (please to stoop) are selveran cued peteet peas of quite a pecuniar interest inaslittle as they are the pellets that make the tomtummy's pay roll ... A middenhide hoard of objects! Olives, beets, kimmells, dollies, alfrids, beatties, cormacks and daltons. Owlets' eegs (O stoop to please!) are here, creakish from age ... Sss! See the snake wurrums everyside! Our durlbin is sworming in sneaks. (18.17–19.13)

Much of the difficulty in interpreting a passage of *Finnegans Wake* arises from the fact that each, besides having a local significance in the text, is a microcosm of the entire book. Every passage anticipates future developments, recapitulates earlier ones, and elaborates present ones. In language, all periods and layers of experience are simultaneous and each is visible through the others: the text is a diaphane. In true Menippean fashion, Joyce warns the reader that such is the case. 'So you need hardly spell me how every word will be bound over to carry three score and ten toptypical readings throughout the book of Doublends Jined' (20.13–16). In the passage above, the gradation '(Stoop)' to '(O stoop to please!)' announces a new posture or trope for literate (abcedminded) attention, while at the same time it signals an increasing intensity of operation in and of the text, building up to the tale and the thunder. The new trope is the Two Books of grammar, implying that manuscript culture has already developed to sufficient degree; each is subject to multilevel exegesis. HCE is embedded in each book: 'hatch ... celt ... earshare ... cassay ... earthcrust ... hours,' each written in its own 'allaphbed.' Early boustrophedon writing in both books is described next and then illustrated in a manner indicating that at this stage eye and ear still mingle ('Here say ... see here [hear] ...'). Following this, a clever synecdoche (part for whole and vice versa) relates abstraction to the use of the alphabet, with 'all-forabit.' After the next step in the gradation we find a direct reference to PQ's riddle, itself concerned with abstract repetition and uniformity as they relate to problems of identity, that connects her activities to minting of uniform coins, 'alike as peas in a pod.' Next is a restatement of the two scriptures, the letter and the midden, both, as Hugh Kenner has pointed out, analogous to the *Wake* itself. The barrow is the wake of a settlement; a text, that of a scribe; a language, the stored experience or wake of its users: 'But the world, mind, is, was, and will be writing its own wrunes for ever, man, on all matters that fall under the ban of our infrarational senses ...' (19.35–20.01). The final step in the gradation precedes another reference to PQ under the guises of the Gorgon and of Cleopatra. As the Gorgon, she stuns her male opponents; as Cleopatra or Isolde, she bewitches them. As Cleopatra, she brings into play the Eastern ear-world that formed part of the resolution of thunder 1 – 'fore the last milchcamel ... has still to moor before the tomb of his cousin charmian where his date is tethered by the palm that's hers' (20.01–04). Charmian (a 'charmer') was the maidservant who supplied Cleopatra with the fatal asp.[5]

After mention of Charmian, a sorceress's charm (PQ's/witch's potion) is brewed for the forthcoming battle. The brew foreshadows print as the culmination of neolithic technology, but points directly at PQ's identification with manuscript culture (mss [that is, misses]: bones, stones, and skins are all early media of writing):

A bone, a pebble, a ramskin; chip them, chap them, cut them up allways; leave them to terracook in the muttheringpot: and Gutenmorg with his cromagnom charter, tintingfast and great primer must once for omniboss step rubrickredd out of the wordpress else is there no virtue more in alcohoran. For that (the rapt one warns) is what papyr is meed of, made of, hides and hints and misses in prints. Till ye finally (though not yet endlike) meet with the acquaintance of Mister Typus, Mistress Tope and all the little typtopies. Fillstup. (20.05–13)

The final prelude to the tale echoes the themes of fashion, matriarchy, reversals (for example, of sexual roles), sneakiness and snakiness, piracy, whoring, and flirting:

For then was the age when hoops ran high. Of a noarch and a chopwife; of a pomme full grave and a fammy of levity; or of golden youths that wanted gelding; or of what the mischievmiss made a man do. Malmarriedad he was reversogassed by the frisque of her frasques and her prytty pyrrhique. Maye faye, she's la gaye

this snaky woman! From that trippiery toe expectungpelick! Veil, volantine, valen-
tine eyes. She's the very besch Winnie blows Nay on good. Flou inn, flow ann.
Hohore! (20.28–36)

The tale of the Prankquean is formed as a single paragraph of eighty-three
lines. It is mythic allegory and romance in one. The action occurs allegorically on several levels at once. PQ's legendary pirate is a bewitching seductress *and* the visual influence of manuscript culture. The Jarl is a coarse and
comparatively uncivilized ear-man, a sort of Mutt-and-Jute-stage neolithic
hunter-aristocrat. The romance aspect derives from PQ's identification with
Isolde and from the themes of the battles of the sexes and the senses. There
are other parallels: for example, the pirate ship is the tub of Swift's tale (both
stories concern Scripture – manuscript exegesis – and ornamentation) and,
by association with the clothing theme, the tub of Diogenes.

As all three themes that normally call for rhetorical high style (love, war,
and religion) are present, the tale as a whole uses high style.[6] The contents
appear to follow a gradation from low (pastoral) to middle (Georgics) to high
(thunder). It is helpful to scan the first cycle of the tale before relating it to
the variations and to the thunder:

It was of a night, late, lang time agone, in an auldstane eld, when Adam was delvin
and his madameen spinning watersilts, when mulk mountynotty man was everybully
and the first leal ribberrobber that ever had her ainway everybuddy to his lovesaking
eyes and everybilly lived alove with everybiddy else, and Jarl van Hoother had his
burnt head high up in his lamphouse, laying cold hands on himself. And his two little
jiminies, cousins of ourn, Tristopher and Hilary, were kickaheeling their dummy on
the oil cloth flure of his homerigh, castle and earthenhouse. And, be dermot, who
come to the keep of his inn only the niece-of-his-in-law, the prankquean. And the
prankquean pulled a rosy one and made her wit foreninst the dour. And she lit up
and fireland was ablaze. And spoke she to the dour in her petty perusienne: Mark
the Wans, why do I am alook alike a poss of porterpease? And that was how the
skirtmisshes began. But the dour handworded her grace in dootch nossow: Shut! So
her grace o'malice kidsnapped up the jiminy Tristopher and into the shandy wester-
ness she rain, rain, rain. And Jarl van Hoother warlessed after her with soft
dovesgall: Stop deef stop come back to my earin stop. But she swaradid to him:
Unlikelihud. And there was a brannewail that same sabboath night of falling angles
somewhere in Erio. And the prankquean went for her forty years' walk in Tourle-
monde and she washed the blessings of the love-spots off the jiminy with soap
sulliver suddles and she had her four owlers masters to tauch him his tickles and she
convorted him to the onesure allgood and he became a luderman. So then she started

to rain and to rain and, be redtom, she was back again at Jarl van Hoother's in a brace of samers and the jiminy with her in her pinafrond, lace at night, at another time. (21.05–33)

The last two phrases, 'lace at night, at another time,' are the opening words of the second time through the tale. The announced setting of the above passage is pastoral, the Garden of Eden, indicating usage of low style, but 'at another time' is followed by a middle-class setting: 'And where did she come but to the bar of his bristolry,' indicating middle style. For the third telling, Joyce gives the transition, 'by the ward of his mansionhome of another nice lace for the third charm,' the mansion suggesting high style. It is not so much that each telling uses a different style as that the several tellings contain markers to indicate which mode serves as undercurrent: a gradation of styles is mounting here. PQ uses the full force of rhetoric in her verbal assaults; the Jarl is only gradually drawn from semi-articulate fury to full eloquence as the tale progresses and escalates.

The tale charts the progress of language and its users through a number of cognitive labyrinths, elemental, textual, sensual, psychological, sexual, and rhetorical. While PQ's aggression, and the questions and replies, press forward the action of tracing the labyrinth, the four elements are evenly apportioned between her and the Jarl. Her milieux as pirate are the labyrinths of air and water; his, with 'his burnt head ... in his lamphouse,' those of earth (stone) and fire. An alchemical transmutation occurs at the thunder whereby his 'element of fire is quite put out' by her 'rain, rain, rain,' reign, and pranks (jests/clothes), symbolic of his sexual subversion and submission. Still a landsman, he 'gets the wind up,' and is demoted from the aristocracy to a bourgeois burgher. Although every thunder concerns transformation, the concern with alchemy in the PQ section is further heightened by references to Giordano Bruno. In Bruno's time, alchemy was a part of the curriculum of grammar, and all of the great grammarians were also alchemists. On the title page of Bruno's mocking comedy *Il Candelaio*, he wrote under his name the motto 'Hilaris in tristia, tristis in hilaritate.' Joyce used this motto in naming the twin 'jiminies' (gemini), Hilary and Tristopher.[7] In the tale, these two undergo, like the Jarl, transmutation from 'base elements' (crude and savage) into civilized, refined mettle, via PQ's clothing. All are washed and bathed and taught manners and made respectable. The Scandinavian van Hoother is also a sort of Cain: according to the Sigurd legend, Loki arranged for Hother to murder his glorious and adulated brother, Balder. But that is not as significant as the fact that Hother was the dark, blind brother: in our tale, van Hoother is described first as cold and dour, then warm and wicked as his metamorphosis progresses. In his earlier aspect, he is a feudal lord, his 'blindness' a function of his acoustic rather than visual orientation.

As the tale unfolds, the gemini are playing on the floor of the castle with their 'dummy.' The 'dummy' is both the donkey of Jean Buridan's pons asinorum[8] (the will – unable to act, or inarticulate – caught between two balanced, equal motives) and the donkey of 'the four' – the four gospellers and the four levels of exegesis. The four, in the *Wake*, 'ride on the back' of the donkey, like the *logos* of Scripture. The castle is the Jarl's 'homerigh, castle and earthenhouse,' which brings in Swift through his girlfriend, Vanessa van Homerigh: vanessa/vanity is quite appropriate to PQ; Swift's *A Tale of a Tub* allegorized excesses of fashionable trends in scriptural exegesis as forms of clothing and ornamentation. As PQ snatches first one and then another of the twins, the dilemma of Buridan's donkey is resolved, and as she returns them from her finishing school, they live their new specialisms. For example, the first twin is 'turned' to the 'onesure allgood,' to single-level clear meaning, and becomes a 'luderman' (Lutheran; but also Ger. 'scoundrel,' Ir. 'lazy idler,' and Lat. 'playful').

As she arrives at the door of the castle (of Scripture), in the first telling (above), PQ 'lit up and fireland was ablaze'; in the second version, she 'lit up again.' This is both her deployment of fiery eloquence and her illumination-from-without of the text. In the medieval tradition, the light of understanding of the manuscript shone *from* the page with its glosses and illuminations as *from* the tradition of learned commentary: this light was completely reversed by the Reformation, when illumination passed to the intellect of the private and individual reader with his visual, single-level bias.

PQ is the quean of wit rather than that of kenning and of cunning. Joyce is particular about this. Most languages have at least two words for forms of knowing: one holistic, multisensory, and profound; the other incisive and particularized. French, for example, gives *connaître* and *savoir*; German, *kennen* and *wissen*; English (at root), cunnan/kennan or cunning and conning and kenning and kin, and witan/wit or reason (by extension, logic). PQ is given as the Jarl's 'niece-of-his-in-law,' that is, not genuine kin but merely related by legalism. Not kin, she does not ken or con him, but outwits and outfits him: in the first round of the tale, he 'made her wit foreninst the dour'; in the second and third, as action and pressure escalate, 'she made her witter before the wicked' and 'she made her wittest in front ...' As a tribal and feudal lord, Van Hoother is immersed in the flux of conning and kenning and kinfolk: he has no defences against her sharp wit. PQ penetrates and unravels the labyrinths with probes – questions:

Mark the Wans, why do I am alook alike a poss of porterpease? And that was how the skirtmisshes began.

Mark the Twy, why do I am alook alike two poss of porterpease?

Mark the Tris, why do I am alook alike three poss of porter pease? But that was how the skirtmishes endupped.

The usual interpretation of the questions (by Campbell and Robinson, and subsequently others) is that she demands of the Jarl/innkeeper a pint (poss/posset) of porter (beer).[9] Aside from the escalation of numbers, triple statement for a charm, and the use of emphatic form (why *do* I am), the most interesting points of the question/riddle concern 'I am,' 'alook alike,' 'poss of ... peas' and the commentary, 'skirtmis(s)hes.' PQ's labyrinthine quest is a quest for identity. The Jarl embodies the maze of corporate loyalties and identifications that charactize ear-culture. Her battle is 'to isolate i from my multiple Mes,' to split off the individual from the group mess, the pea-queue alike as peas in a pod, by means of visual stress; hence the stress on number, on 'I am' and 'alook alike.' Before she went to work on the twins, they were ill-defined, indistinguishable gemini. In much the same manner, she engages the Jarl in a battle royal of the sexes and senses – a 'skirtmisshe': this word includes, besides skirmish, skirt, miss and mss, mishe (Gael, 'I am': emphatic for 'I' and 'me'), she/shes and he/hes – all of which compress kaleidoscopically the themes of battle, clothing/weaponry, identity, and sexual roles.

In response to the first riddle and kidnapping, the Jarl declines to be drawn into open conflict and tries a peaceful plea: so he 'warlessed after her with soft dovesgall.' The last word compresses 'doves call,' and 'love call' and, in Gaelic, *Dubh-gall*, a Dane. His message includes a plea that she not interfere with his hearing, which she is trying to steal from him: 'Stop deef [deaf and thief: Du., *dief*, thief] stop come back to my earin stop.' In response to her second assault, he begins bleating and blithering but soon puts on some of her weather imagery: he 'bleethered atter her with a loud finegale.' His mode is still somewhat tribal, however, as 'finegale' includes Fine Gaedhil (Gael, a tribe of the Irish: Fine Gael is a political party), Fine-Gall (Gael, 'foreign tribe'; N. Co. Dublin district, anglic., Fingal), and Fionn-gall (Gael, 'fair foreigner,' that is, Norwegian).[10] His message this time, 'Stop domb stop come back with my earring stop,' nearly repeats the first iteration, but now emphasizes her piracy of his hearing plus an indication that he has succumbed to ornamentation by wearing earrings.

The third assault and statement of the riddle sees the resolution of the bat-

Tris, why do I am allook alike three poss of porter pease?
But that was how the skirtmishes endupped.   For like the
campbells acoming with fork lance of lightning, Jarl van Hoother
Boanerages himself, the old terror of the dames, came hip hop
handihap out through the pika-opened arkway of his three shuttoned castles, in his broadginger hat and his civic chollar and
his allabuff hemmed like a rudd yellan gruebleen orangeman
in his violet indigonation, to the whole length of the strongth
of his bowman's bill.   And he clopped his rude hand to his eacy
hitch and he ordered and his thick spch spck for her to shut
up shop, dappy.   And the dumby shot the shutter up (gokgor-
:layorgromgremmitghundhurthrumathunaradidillifaititillibum-
:ullmakkunin!)   And they all drank free.   For one man in
his armour was a fat match always for any girls under shurts.
And that was the first peace of illiteratise porthery in all
the flamand, floody, flatuous world.   The prnakquean was to
hold her dummyship and the jimminies was to keep the peacewave and van Hoother was to git the wind up.   Thus the hearsomeness of the burger felicitates the whole of the polis.

     O foenix culprit! Ex nickylow malo comes
bonum.   Hill, rill, ones in company, billeted, less be proud
of.   Breast high and bestride!   Only for that these will not
breethe upon Norsönesen or Irenean the secrest of their soor-
celossness.   Quarry silex, Homfrie Noanswa!   Undy gentian fles-
tyknees, Livia Noanswa?   Wolkencap is on him, frowned; auditu-
rient, he would evesdrip, were it mouseat hand, were it dinn
of bottles in the far ear.   Murk, his vales are darkling.

Thunder 2: a few weeks later: 75 letters

tles. The Jarl is en-duped and transformed while PQ reigns/rains as matriarch, a position she will hold until the seventh thunder reverses the entire process. Suddenly the Jarl appears 'like the campbells acoming with a fork lance of lightning,' hopping unceremoniously out of the castle, sporting a wild assortment of clothes and the entire spectrum of colours of rhetoric:

... in his broadginger hat and his civic chollar and his allabuff hemmed and his bullbraggin soxangloves and his ladbroke breeks and his cattegut bandolair and his furframed panuncular cumbottes like a rudd yellan gruebleen orangeman in his violet indigonation ... (22.34–23.03)

The terms of this inventory, the spectrum, suggest that he is now subject to the full force of visual fragmentation.[11] (An inventory of the Jarl-PQ pair in various modes is given on 576.23–577.18: for example, 'lame of his ear and gape of her leg ... guide them through the labyrinth of their samilikes and the alteregoases of their pseudoselves ... basal curse yet grace abunda,' etc. The tale is retold analogically, in Darwinian terms on 504–5, culminating with 'the form masculine. The gender feminine. I see ... And remounts to the sense arrest ...')

Subsequent to the inventory of his clothes, above, the Jarl's speech thickens suddenly, and the castle door is slammed a final time, creating an onomatopoeic thunderword. The crash ('with a fork lance of lightning' – this is one of the few illuminated thunders) is followed by the traditional ending to Irish fairy tales, 'they put on the kettle and they all drank tea':[12]

And they all drank free. For one man in his armour was a fat match always for any girls under shurts. And that was the first peace of illiterative porthery in all the flamend floody flatuous world. How kirssy the tiler made a sweet unclose to the Narwhealian captol. Saw fore shalt thou sea. Betoun ye and be. The prankquean was to hold her dummyship and the jimminies was to keep the peacewave and van Hoother was to git the wind up. Thus the hearsomeness of the burger felicitates the whole of the polis. (23.07–15)

PQ's pirate ships are beached and the process of civilization enters the second stage of urban/rural development: her sailors turn from the handling of ships' tillers to become tillers of the soil. The demise of the old Jarl signals the archetypalization of the oral by the written and by the new scribes who furrow the page.

In this closure section for the thunder, 'one man' is presented, an individual and not a (tribal) group: he has 'matched' the quean's prankings and is wearing her cast-off 'armour.' 'Fat match' derisively translates as 'not much of a match,' like our 'fat chance' for 'slim chance.' The tale is retrospectively regarded as 'illiterative porthery' and as an 'illustrative' example of preliterate poetry (a mode now made archetypal and quaint by writing and the PQ's visual stress). The Jarl now minds his P's and Q's, and has turned 'abcedminded.'[13]

Part of the closure for the first thunder, which contributed to the developing commerce undercurrents in this section of *Finnegans Wake*, was that of fishing. With the fishing theme, an unexplored aspect of the HCE-to-come is provided: he has appeared (in the area following the first thunder) as a whale, a 'groot hwide Whallfisk' (also, variously, a salmon or codfish) – a modern Leviathan. Swift's preface to *A Tale of a Tub* links Hobbes' work to his and Joyce's with these comments:

... seamen have a custom, when they meet a whale, to fling him out an empty tub by way of amusement, to divert him from laying violent hands upon the ship. This parable was immediately mythologised; the whale was Hobbe's Leviathan, which tosses and plays with all schemes of religion and government, whereof a great many are hollow, and dry, and empty, and noisy, and wooden, and given to rotation: this is the Leviathan, whence the terrible wits of our age are said to borrow their weapons. The ship in danger is easily understood to be its old antitype, the commonwealth. But how to analyze the tub, was a matter of difficulty: when, after long enquiry and debate, the literal meaning was preserved; and it was decreed, that in order to prevent these Leviathans from tossing and sporting with the commonwealth, which of itself is too apt to fluctuate, they should be diverted from that game by a Tale of a Tub.

Of additional note to both Tales, Joyce's and Swift's, is the practice (discontinued shortly before the writing of *A Tale of a Tub*) whereby the gallery shops over the piazzas in the Royal Exchange were administered by women. Appropriately to the themes of commerce and sex/sense reversal, they were called 'Exchange-women' and were deemed the first ministers of fashion.[14]

When she wears her 'coat of male,' PQ assumes another temporary identity related to the conflict between the individual and the tribal, the 'one and the many' – that of Kerse, the tailor. Kerse is also a type of cloth, and Joyce's rendering here of the word anticipates the Persse of the next thunder. The anecdote, which Joyce's father is reputed to have found hilarious, is recounted by Richard Ellmann as concerning '... a hunchbacked Norwegian captain who ordered a suit from a Dublin tailor, J. H. Kerse of 34 Upper Sackville Street. The finished suit did not fit him, and the captain berated the tailor for being unable to sew, whereupon the tailor denounced him for being impossible to fit.'[15] The hunchbacked captain is obviously the diminished Finnegan carrying his hod (the 'hunch'), and the reference to him here as the 'Narwhealian captol' resounds with many of the closure themes. 'Narwhealian' includes part of this thunder's development in the earlier neolithic wheel and the HCE-narwhale or Leviathan, while 'captol' involves money (capital), nationalism, and urbanization (capitol). The latter is further alluded to with be-town ('Betoun'), 'burger,' and 'polis.' The admonition 'Betoun ye and be' supplies a partial reply to PQ's earlier identity questions.

Evidently, the old pirate ships have not been totally abandoned but rather have been converted to use in commerce and fishing – for Leviathans. Another such switch appears in a pun. Shakespeare's Antony comments, 'O, then we bring forth weeds / When our quick minds lie still, and our ills told us / Is as our earing ... (I.ii.113–15). Most editors gloss 'earing' as an old term for 'ploughing.' Thus 'earing' links the Jarl's feudal telegram with the closure themes of agriculture.

Although the effects of the visual stresses PQ applies are great, the auditory mode has not yet been totally discarded: rather, it has become an art form. The Jarl-now-burgher's old orientation serves some present purpose for his 'hearsomeness' benefits the city. The next thunder follows the demise of the last acoustic champion, Persse O'Reilly: that thunder will complete the de-tribalization process and provide the still-germinal HCE and ALP with an environment in which they can emerge and reign.

As did the first, the second thunder 'sounds' all of the themes and structural metaphors involved in this episode:

(Perkodhuskurunbarggruauyagokgorlayorgromgremmitghundhurthrumat-hunaradidillifaititillibumullunukkunun!) (23.05–07)

Thunder	Interpretation	Theme Sounded
Pe	pea	PQ: peas in a pod: identity quest;
	pay	commerce; 'royalties'
Per	pair	jiminies, alook alike
	pier	ship, piratess
	peer	visual; aristocracy
Perkod	Pequod (ship in *Moby Dick*)	ships, Leviathan
	pea-pod	pea-queue, identity

Thunder	Interpretation	Theme Sounded
	Per Quod (Cf. 'P/K split,' GaL, pages 402–5)	uses PQ's initials
	Lett, *perkons*, thunder (McH)	thunder
er	ear	ear, earring, earing,
	Eire	ear-ring
rko	RKO film studios	love goddess, (movie) quean
kod	cod (fish)	Leviathan
	cold	JvH
	hod	JvH/Finnegan/Norwegian Captain
	code	telegram; thunderword, labyrinth
kodhus	cold house	JvH castle
	goddess	PQ/Venus/love goddess
	codex	PQ-mss
odhus	(Cornelia) Otis (Skinner): actress who threw her clothes off Notre Dame cathedral in Paris	PQ, clothes
dhus	Dis (goddess of the underworld)	PQ, (under)clothes
	(Eleanora) Duse, actress	PQ
hus	house	JvH castle; cities
husk	husk: corn	agriculture
	pea-pod	PQ, identity
	clothing	PQ clothing
uskur	Istar	PQ goddess; asianism
	a star	PQ, stellar navigation (reading Book of Nature), Swift's Stella
	Esther (Swift's girlfriends, Stella and Vanessa, were both named Esther)	Swift, PQ
usk	ask	PQ question

Thunder	Interpretation	Theme Sounded
	asp	PQ/Cleopatra/Charmian
usku	a skow	Cleopatra's barge, ships, Grace O'Malley
skurun	stern	JvH's demeanor; ships, wakes
	Ger, *Sterne*, star	PQ, navigation (Book of Nature)
	Sterne	*Tristram Shandy*, 'shandy westerness'
	schooner	ships, Grace O'Malley
kur	cure	charm, witchcraft
	Ger, *Kur*, a malignant spirit	witchcraft, visual stress (PQ)
kuru	Egy, *Kharu*, sailor	ships, piracy, Cleopatra
kurun	the Koran	ear, Arab architecture
	Bre, *kurun*, thunder (McH)	thunder
urun	Erin	Eden, pastoral
	earin/eraring/earring	JvH, agriculture
	herring	fishing
	Orion	PQ/Istar/Stella; navigation
unbar	un-bar (the door)	Grace at the door
unbarg	embark	ships
	umbrage	Grace's ire, JvH's ire
unbarggru	embargo	Cleopatra, piracy, kidnapping
barg	barge	Cleopatra's; piracy
	burg	cities, burgher (citizen)
	Heb, *baraq*, lightning	thunder, rain; private enlightenment
barggru	burgoo (sailors' stew)	ships, etc
arg	ark	ships, etc.
arggru	argue	PQ/JvH battles
	our crew	ships, etc.
	Argo (Jason's ship)	ships, etc.
grua	Sp, *bruja*, witch	PQ, charm

Thunder	Interpretation	Theme Sounded
gruauya	Graunya (Grace O'Malley)	Grace O'Malley, PQ
	Li, *griauja*, it thunders (McH)	thunder
gruauyagok	Gael, *gruagach*, hairy, ugly	JvH; cavemen
	wizard (GaL)	charm, transformation
ago	Lat, *ego*, I am	identity
	Egy, *aga*, ship's rudder	ships, plough, wake
gokgorlayor	Turk, *gök gürliyor*, thundering	
	sky (McH)	thunder; change, rain
gorl	girl	PQ
	Jarl	JvH
orl	oral/aural	ear
orlayor	o'er layer	clothes, ornamentation
layor	layer	clothes
	lay her	seduction
	lyre	ear
	leer	eye, seduction
orgr	ogre	JvH
grom	Gr. O'M	Grace O'Malley
	Ar, love	battles; seduction
gromgremmit	R, *grom gremit*, thunder(s) (McH)	thunder
omgremmi	enemy	PQ, battles
	Gr, *ennumi*, to clothe	PQ, clothing
	to put on	PQ, style, ornaments
grem	Grimm	fairy tale
	grim	JvH
remmi	Egy, goddess of the harvest,	agriculture
	fish god	Leviathan, fishing
mit	mitt, mitten	clothes
ghund	ME, *cund*, to direct a ship	ships, navigation
ghundhur	Ma, *guntur*, thunder (McH)	thunder
	Indon, *guntur*, thunder (McH)	thunder
hundhur	thunder	thunder

Thunder	Interpretation	Theme Sounded
dhu	dhow (ship)	ships
dhur	door	doors: castle; perception; thunder
	dour	JvH, 'the dour'
hurth	hearth	homes, cities
hurthrum	hearthroom	
urth	(name of Wagnerian norn)	Tristan and Isolde (PQ)
thrum	OE, waste threads, loose ends	clothes
	Naut. for hemp, yarn	ships (ropes), clothes
thruma	ON, *thruma*, thunder (McH)	thunder
	Icel, *thruma*, thunder (McH)	thunder
rum	Ar, Roman, Byzantine	Cleopatra, Arab world
mat	mat	clothes
	mate	court ship (PQ)
athu	Egy, fish god	Leviathan, fishing
athuna	Athena	PQ; rhetoric
thuna	Rum, *thuna*, thunder (McH)	thunder
thunar	thunder	thunder
	ME, *thuner*, thunder	thunder
nar	Turk, *nahr*, river (26L)	rain, rain; eloquence
nara	Hindu, *Mara*, goddess of death	PQ
	Morogh, son of Grace O'Malley	PQ, jiminies
ara	Aran, isle where cloth is woven and ships built	clothing, ships
rad	Ar, *raad*, thunder (26L)	thunder
radi	Ki, *radi*, thunder (McH)	thunder
radidi	raided it	PQ/Grace O'Malley, the castle
didill	diddle (slang, cheat)	PQ, deception
	diddle (slang, intercourse)	seduction
dil	Deal castle	castle, JvH

Thunder	Interpretation	Theme Sounded
dill	Ar, *dill*, thunder (McH)	thunder
illifa	Sp, *lluvia*, rain	rain, reign
illifait	Lilliput illicit	Swift, ship travel piracy, cheat/deception
lifait	[Jean] Lafitte, pirate	piracy
fait	Lat, *fiat*, let there be (ClL)	thunderer/cause
faititilli	Sa, *failitily*, thunder (McH)	thunder
illi	Lat, *illi*, yonder, in that place (ClL)	JvH's castle
ait	Lat, said an 'eight,' rowing shell/galley	oral ships

ibu	Fr, *hibou*, owl: the O'Malleys
	    were the Lords of Owles
		Grace O'Malley;
		    'Owler's masters'

bum	boom Ar, *bum*, owl	ship's boom; sound of thunder Grace O'Malley; 'Owler's masters'
bumul	tumult	battle
bumullu	Alb, *bumulloj*, thunder (McH)	thunder
mul	Naut., type of sail mule	ships donkey (*logos*)
ullu	Ger, *Ullu*, good luck charm	magic, charms
unuk	eunuch	matriarchy, sex reversals
nukku	Egy, a serpent	temptress, Cleopatra Charmian, 'snaky woman'
ukkunun	Finn, *ukkonen*, thunder (26L)	thunder
kun	Ar, *kun*, be, exist	PQuestion, identity; 'Betoun ye and be'
kunun	cannon canon (law)	weaponry, battles, ships religion (Swift)
unun	onan(ism)	narcissism, weak (sexual) identity
nun	nun: Elizabethan sl, a whore	PQ

6

The Third Thunderclap: HCE, The 'New Womanly Man' (*FW* 30–47)

Earwicker, that patternmind, that paradigmatic ear ... bruskly put out his langwedge and quite quit the paleologic scene ... his feminisible name of multitude ... (70.35–73.05)

But the whacker his word the weaker our ears for auracles who parles parses orileys. (467.28–9)

So all rogues lean to rhyme. (96.03)

(we are back in the presurnames prodomarith period, of course just when enos chalked halltraps). (30.03–04)

Humptydump Dublin squeaks through his norse,
Humptydump Dublin hath a horriple vorse
And with all his kinks english
Plus his Irismanx brogues
Humptydump Dublin's grandada of all rogues.
(Dustjacket blurb for Faber and Faber's issue of the booklet *Haveth Childers Every-where*, 1930, 1931: later, *FW* 532–54)[1]

The context for the third thunder is the entirety of I.2 (book I, chapter 2) of the *Wake*. It traces the genesis of HCE – Here Comes Everybody – and raises him to the position of prominence he will occupy throughout the 'civilized' portion of the thunder cycle. 'An imposing everybody he always indeed looked, constantly the same as and equal to himself and magnificently well worthy of any and all such universalization.' (32.19–21)

down to a few good old souls evidently
under the spell of liquor, a fair girl, a
jolly postboy thinking off three flagons and
one who clings and clings and clings to
her cloudhued pittycoat as child, as
curiolater, as Caoch O'Leary. Word went round,
so it did, and the ballad, printed on a slip
flancovidf ~~their spite~~ ~~and~~ headed by a rough and red
woodcut, soon fluttered to on white highway
and brown byway to the rose of the winds
and the blew of the gaels, from archway to
lattice and from black hand to pink ear, village
crying to village, through the five perssyfours
green of the united states of Scotia Picta. To
the added strains of his majesty the flute
which Delaney, anticipating a perfect
downpour of plaudits among the rapsods,
drew out of his decentsoort hat, looking
still more like his namesake as men noted
the snowycrested curl amoist his wild
and moulting hair Hitchcock hoisted
his fezzy fezz at bludgeon's height
for silentium in curia! and the cairo was
chanted there by the old tollgate. And around
the lawn the raun it rain and this is
the raun that Hosty made. Arrah, leve
it to Hosty, frosty Hosty, leave it to Hosty
for he's the mann to rhyme the raun, the
raun, the raun, the king of all rauns.
Have you heard? Have we where? Have you
heard? Have we whered? It's cumming!
It's brumming! the clip, the dop! The (klatsche
battacreppycrottygraddagh semmihsammih-
nouithappluddyappladdypkonjsk os!)
Ballad of Persse O'Reilley
(as sung by Phoblacht)

Thunder 3: first cut: 58 letters

The Persona of HCE

The defunct, integral, tribal Finnegan is replaced by the nuclear, civilized HCE family. It numbers five: HCE and ALP, the twin brothers, Shem and Shaun, and the daughter, Issy or Izzy (Isolde/PQ). In terms of language, whereas Finnegan is the integral *logos*, each of the HCE family members is one of the five divisions of rhetoric (Shaun the Postman, for example, is delivery), and each also enacts one of the five bodily senses. Roland McHugh remarks:

FW frequently mentions ⵍ's ears and in the notebooks such generalizations as the following occur:

VI.B.5.122:	ⵍ his good ear			
VI.B.15.113	ⵍ deaf as Taub			
VI.B.15.153	ⵍ ear	Δ smell	[?]	
	Λ taste	⊏ touch	⊣ sight	

But the appropriation of senses to sigla [the shorthand symbols used above] is only partly allowed in FQ for, as we shall see, a critical difference between ⊏ and Λ is the good hearing and bad eyesight of the former, and the reverse attributes of the latter. These two systems of correlation may function independently: it is often asserted that ⵍ is deaf, and this links with his speech impediment. VI.B.36.306 states 'ⵍ is earweak.' Perhaps an earwig has entered his auditory meatus: 059.22 mentions 'what they took out of his ear.' But when ⊏ is telling Λ that he is mad, he begins 'Come here, Herr Studiosus, till I tell you a wig in your ear' (193.12–13). It is frequently imputed that ⵍ is mad too.[2]

Joyce used the 'sigla' for structural (character) elements of the *Wake*: ⵍ includes HCE and almost every other male personage in the book; Δ includes ALP; Λ includes Shaun; ⊏ includes Shem; and ⊣ includes Izzy (the Prankquean).[3] His seeming ambivalence about identifying HCE with the ear is easily explained.

In the first place, Earwicker's name in German, *ihre Wecker*, means 'alarm clock,' an identification closely related to overall themes of dreaming and waking that also juxtaposes two principal methods of timekeeping: by the bell (discontinuous intervals) and by the watch or clock (continuous, linear, and visual). Following the events of the first two thunders and the battles therein of the sexes and the senses, HCE comes on stage as the type of civilized man, matriarchally dominated, the ear dominated by the eye. Ear-wicker's main occupation in the present chapter of *FW* seems to be not piracy but trapping earwigs (30.10–11): by extension, an earwigger is himself an earwig or ear-piercer (perce-oreille). Malcolm Burr says that earwigs 'inspire dread in the minds of the superstitious, and it is this instrument [a pair of forceps] at the end of their sinuous body and their habit of bolting into dark holes and crevices that has led to the widespread notion that they are apt to enter the human ear with fatal results. From this belief arose our familiar name, which appears first in Anglo-Saxon as earewicga, the second half of which is an old verb which survives in the words wiggle, waggle, wriggle, meaning quick movement.'[4] In fine, HCE embodies the battle of the senses (the royal divorce of ear and eye, suit brought by the Prankquean) as won by the eye. As a visual man he has a private identity, but as the corporate type of all such men, he doesn't. The dominated or suppressed ear is expressed in this corporate dimension, as well as in his archetypal ('paradigmatic') alter ego, Persse O'Reilly (perce-oreille). He has another *alter ego* (or altar ego?) in this chapter, that of Hosty, the host or group, the Everybody of HCE that constitutes his 'mystical body' and that figures in HCE's-Persse's-Perseus's-Parsifal's grail quest. The 'grail' is two things: the mug of beer lifted in HCE's public house, and the object of his identity quest. The latter begins or ends – it is not clear which – with the mysterious incident in the park. In all likeli-hood, the encounter with the cad in the park, which has spurred considerable scholarly wrangling, is just a Menippean red herring, the sort of thing Alfred Hitchcock called 'the McGuffin' in his movies.[5]

The first chapter of the *Wake* contains the first two thunders; the second chapter concerns HCE and ends with the third thunder. It reprises a number of themes from chapter 4, but in a new mode: 'the seim anew.' It is both a re-enactment and a new development. The trio of thunders does not perform in the pattern of syllogism or that of Hegelian triad (thesis-antithesis-synthesis: there is no antithesis of the first thunder by the second) but rather enacts a set of Viconian cycles. These are the only thunders to do so. Richard Ellmann relates that, as Joyce began work on the *Wake*, he was particularly drawn to the Neapolitan grammarian's 'use of etymology and mythology to uncover the significance of events, as if events were the most superficial manifestations of underlying energies. He admired also Vico's positive division of human his-tory into recurring cycles, each set off by a thunderclap, of theocratic, aristo-cratic, and democratic ages, followed by a *ricorso* or return. Joyce did not share Vico's interest in these as literal chronological divisions of "eternal idea his-tory," but as psychological ones, ingredients which kept combining and recombining in ways which seemed always to be *déjà vus*. "I use his cycles as a trellis," he told Padraic Colum later.[6] The first thunder is 'theocratic' in that it is concerned with the expulsion from the Garden and with the god-like Finnegan; the second thunder (aristocratic) presents the battle of a queen and an earl; the third thunder ushers in the *demos*: here comes everybody.

Accordingly, and in contrast with the first chapter where the style is coarse and explosive and uneven, here the style is civilized and stilted. As McHugh points out:

it insists on vulgarity with Victorian squeamishness and abounds in Latin constructions and euphemisms. For example: 'royalty was announced by runner to have been please to have halted itself,' 'the literal sense of which decency can scarcely hint,' 'a respectable prominently connected fellow of Iro-European ascendances with well-dressed ideas who know the correct thing,' 'to be exquisitely punctilious about them.' It is fairly easy reading in comparison with the rest of *FW*.

The chapter begins in the afternoon of a golden age, 'just when enos chalked hall-traps' (030.05). Enos, son of Seth, was regarded by the Kabbalists as a greater magician than any before him: presumably he is chalking circles to compel the spirits. The Phoenix Park appears in a more urbane aspect, with gardening and human artifacts in evidence. Eventually we attain the city centre, thronged by diverse ramifications of humanity.[7]

The surface outlines of the chapter are simple: it begins with an overture, the genesis of the name and person of Earwicker, mention of the encounter in the park, and his defence. Then the encounter itself is described: HCE meets the cad who asks him the time and HCE unnecessarily defends himself. The puzzled cad goes off home, 'with a flea in his ear,' as it were (as do others: see 38.23), tells his wife, who tells her priest, who tells everybody else. Gossip about HCE and his 'sin' inspires a procession through the city and the composition and (thunder!) recitation of a ballad that, exposing HCE, reviews most of the themes of the chapter.[8]

The HCE Episode

While the mood of the chapter remains festive, the procedures are purely grammatical. The narrator opens with and frequently returns to the 'voice of scholarship': 'Now concerning the genesis of Harold or Humphrey Chimpden's occupational agnomen ... and discarding once for all those theories from older sources which would link him back with ...' HCE is examined first by means of etymology: his name and then his initials are scrutinized for clues to their sources and to his nature and significance. Two solutions are proposed: one from a recorded encounter with a royal hunting party (30.23–32.12); the other a trope, 'a pleasant turn of the populace ...' (32.17; 32.14–33.13). Attention then turns to oral traditions, showing that his influence has penetrated every level of society. The narrative moves on through the incident with 'the cad in the park' to the thunder and the ballad, which is structured by digressions in the pattern of four-level exegesis.

Themes drawn from the first two thunders that are recapitulated, redeveloped, and interrelated, include the fall, sin in the garden (here, Phoenix Park), the quest for identity, hunting, gathering/agriculture, language and technological innovation, stuttering, weaponry and clothing, Humpty Dumpty, and commerce and social classes. In view of the length of the chapter (eighteen pages) and the density of the material, the following discussion will focus on these and related themes rather than proceeding through page-by-page demonstration.

Broadly speaking, the entire chapter is a quest for the identity of HCE, at once the one and the many. The central, most enigmatic, catalytic event is the encounter in the park with the cad: it balances PQ's encounters with the Jarl. As HCE strolls in the park (his clothes – PQ's influence – are detailed, 35.08-10), he meets 'a cad with a pipe.'[9] The cad greets HCE in Gaelic, 'to ask could he tell him how much a clock it was that the clock struck had he any idea by cock's luck as his watch was bradys' (35.18–20). As much as PQ challenged the Jarl's identity with her quest/questions, the cad has challenged HCE's (whose name means alarm clock – *ihre Wecker*) by asking if he knows the time. Immediately HCE, alarmed, fears for his existence (his very being is now open to question): the scene parodies the American western 'shootout':

The Earwicker of that spurring instant, realising on fundamental liberal principles the supreme importance, nexally and noxally, of physical life ... and unwishful as he felt of being hurled into eternity right then, plugged by a softnosed bullet from the sap, halted, quick on the draw ... (35.21–6)

He produces one or more watches (a Jurgensen, a Waterbury): 'prodooced from his gunpocket his Jurgensen's shrapnel waterbury (35.27–8). He hears a church bell strike ten (or stutter, as an alarm clock stutters), pub-closing time: 'hearing ... the bellmaster ... at work upon the ten ton tonuant thunderous tenor toller in the speckled church' (35.29–32). He mistakenly reports the time as twelve, the moment of transformation: 'told the inquiring kidder, by Jehova, it was twelve of em sidereal and tankard time (35.32–4). And then he begins to stutter about some 'hakusay accusation' that he feels had been made. As a clock, HCE's problem is to utter the time, or an alarm, but in any case to utter or to speak *himself*. He fails to do so in this case, whether because he was flustered or because he was lying, and in relying on other forms (extensions, outerings) of himself – watches and bells – he errs. Since this act occurs in a park, it parallels Adam's mistake in the Garden (cf. verses 1 and 2 of the ballad at the end). His stuttering recalls Finnegan 'of the Stuttering Hand.'

The themes of technology, language, stuttering, identity, and self-expression (and self-knowledge, which presumes a self to know) are brought together in this chapter. 'Ive mies outs ide Bourn' (31.32–3) begins the process early in the chapter by relating identity (I, me, I'd) to externalizing or uttering (outside born). Articulate speech is itself a form of stuttering; consonants interrupt the song of vowels. The chapter is replete with stutterances, verbal and technological. After mentioning the 'hakusay accusation,' HCE utters a group ('Shsh shake co-comeraid' 36.20), a reference to the need for 'our ruru redemption' (36.25) following the fall, and another to his 'woowoo willing'[ness] (36.23–4) to disprove any rumours as the 'purest of fibfib fabrications' (36.34). Additional forms of stuttering occur, for example, as the cad relates (the encounter) 'in his secondmouth language as many of the bigtimer's verbaten words which he could balbly call to memory' (37.15–16: cf., Ital, *balbo*, 'stutter,' and Fr, *balbutier*, 'stutter'), and later the balladeers are 'flushed with their firestuffostered friendship' (42.07),[10] and HCE is called 'the vilest bogeyer' (42.15: cf., Fr, *bégayeur*, 'stutterer'). Stuttering is woven into three of the verses of the ballad and figures prominently in the sounds of the thunder as well. Verse 5 begins, 'We had chaw chaw chops ...' and the verse is prefaced by the aside, *'Balbaccio, balbuccio!'* (Ital, *balbo*, 'stuttering,' -*accio*, a pejorative suffix, and -*uccio* a diminutive suffix). Verse 11 concerns urban transport and roads, and shows 'our rotorious hipppopopotamuns / When some bugger let down the backtrap of the omnibus ...' Verses 3 and 5 link him as a Prometheus 'capable of any and every enormity in the calendar' (33.23) to all manner of innovation.[11] Verse 3:

He was fafafather of all schemes for to bother us
Slow coaches and immaculate contraceptives for the populace
Mare's milk for the sick, seven dry Sundays a week,
Openair love and religion's reform,
    (Chorus) And religion's reform,
        Hideous in form.   (*FW* 45)

HCE's 'fall' or indiscretion (see verses 1 and 2) adds a few new dimensions to the 'fall' motif already established. It is variously displayed as self-knowledge, onanism, exhibitionism (perhaps of his extensions, to a pair of PQ-ettes in the park: 34.18–19), or a bodily ('social') disease (33.17–18, and verse 4) – the bodily disease is the deformity (or hump: verse 1) caused by extending the body with technologies – which causes him to fall from social grace (O'Malley? but see verse 2: from aristocrat to common convict). But as he is the civil group personified – Here Comes Everybody – HCE's extensions by technology have this difference from those encountered earlier: they include group artefacts and services, roads and transportation, agriculture and kitchen gardens and dairy-farming, legal systems, writing and publishing, pubs, small businesses, and social class structures.[12] Even the ballad serves as a mirror, a means for the group to know itself. Another link between technological extension or 'utterance' and verbal utterance is given by the use of Volapük in the chapter. Volapük is, like Esperanto, an *ersatz* language: in using it, Joyce seems to be saying that technological utterance is also an artificial language, and is therefore of grammatical interest when, in the Volapük cluster on *FW* 34 he remarks: 'zessid's our kadem, villapleach, vollapluck' (34.31–2), 'necessity's our academy,' that is, the mother of the urge to invent.[13]

Invention surfaces as a theme in several ways. As the word means 'finding' it relates to the hunting and questing themes. The grammarian/narrator is hunting for HCE who in turn is trying to find (invent) himself. As Persse/Parsifal, HCE quests for the grail of group identity, the host where companionship is 'glued' by cups of Guinness and singing (of the ballad) in the pub. So, for example, we meet 'Our sailor king, who was draining a gugglet of obvious adamale' early in the chapter (31.11–12), who, by chapter's end, is become 'still more like his purseyful namesake' (43.35–6), and who, in the pub, 'hoisted his fezzy fuzz at bludgeon's height signum to his companions of the chalice for the Loud Fellow ... and the canto was chantied there chorussed and christened ...' (44.02–05). It is Hosty the composer who lifts his voice in song and lifts the cup and the spirits of the group (host or secular mass). He is abjured to 'lift it, ye devil ye! up with the rann, the rhyming rann' (Ballad, second digression, *FW* 46) – an example of HCE's 'religious reform / Hideous in form' (verse 3).

The other related theme is that of actual hunting and weaponry. In the civilized context, hunting is both aesthetic social ritual (in which the quest involves tradition) and an art form. As Joyce noted, all such 'pastimes are past times' (263.17). Here, the hunting theme is in turn related to themes of roads, horse racing, and social classes. In the first anecdote concerning the genesis of HCE's name that the scholar-narrator considers, the vassal HCE unexpectedly appears amid a medieval royal hunting party that has paused on the high road, 'jingling his turnpike keys and bearing aloft amid the fixed pikes of the hunting party a high perch' (31.01–02). It is the night before the feast of Chevy Chase: 'Hag Chivychas Eve' (30.26; *hag* is Heb, 'feast'). They have been fox-hunting (30.30–1 and 31.28–9; but see 34.25 reference to the law of 1455, 'a first offence of vert or venison,' as well as the tipsters hunting for game at 39.21, and 'snipehitting and mallardmissing on Rutland heath' at 42.35–6). Hunting entails weapons, and a good assortment of them figure in this chapter, but with no particular changes in significance until we come to the ballad used as a weapon.

The old theme of 'recirculation' is reprised in this chapter with several new twists, as rumours that 'go around' about HCE, as the Baldoyle racetrack (39.01ff: another go-around), which functions as a rumour mill, as the pub where the customers drink round after round, and as the roads that run 'round the town and along which urban transport traces its circular routes. There are also various social circles to which HCE, 'more mob than man,' is related, and finally, there is the round of applause in the pub that greets the singing of the ballad, and that is the thunder.

The Prankquean also figures in this chapter and in the formation of HCE's person, but more as circumstance than as character. Reference is made (73.04) to HCE's 'feminizable name of multitude,' and, as noted above, he is the ear matriarchally dominated by the eye. Early in the chapter he is presented, both as man and mob, in attendance at her palace, a theatre, viewing another performance (or recirculation) of the 'royal divorce' (of the senses):

from good start to happy finish the truly catholic assemblage gathered together in that king's treat house of satin alustrelike above floats and footlights from their assbawlveldts and oxgangs unanimously to clapplaud (the inspiration of his lifetime and the hits of their careers) Mr Wallenstein Washington Semperkelly's immergreen tourers in a command performance by special request with the courteous permission for pious purposes the homedromed and enliventh performance of the problem passion play of the millentury, running strong since creation, *A Royal Divorce*, then near the approach towards the summit of its climax, with ambitious interval band selections from *The Bo' Girl* and *The Lily* on all horserie show command nights from his viceregal booth ... our worldstage's practical jokepiece and retired cecelticocomediant in his own wise, this folksforefather all of the time sat, having the entirety of his house about him ... (32.24–33.05)

The applause in the theatre merges with that in the pub later on. PQ's 'rain' now becomes the 'rann,' the scurrilous ballad.

the lawn the rann it raun and this is the rann that Hosty
made. Arrah, leave it to Hosty, frosty Hosty, leave it to
Hosty for he's the mann to rhyme the rann, the rann,
the rann, the king of all ranns. Have you here? Have we
where? Have you hered? Have we whered? It's cumming
It's brumming! The clip, the clop! The (klikkaklakka
klaska klopatz klatschabattacreppycrottygraddagh sem-
mih sammihnouihpkonpkor!)

BALLAD OF PERSSE O'REILLEY
(as sung by Phoblacht)

Have you heard of one Humpty Dumpty
How he fell with a roll and a rumble
And curled up like Lord Olofa Crumple
By the butt of the Magazine Wall,
   Of the Magazine Wall,
    Hump, helmet and all?

Thunder 3: second cut: 83 letters

The ballad 'recirculates' in several senses. It recapitulates the chapter, it goes around countryside and town, and the music is repeated with each verse.[14] The melodic score is printed immediately following the thunder in true Menippean fashion: as music, it serves no narrative or logical purpose. It is composed by Hosty (that passage, 41–2.16, is replete with references to writers and poets, e.g., Shelley, Swinburne, Shaw, Yeats, Wilde, Byron), and evidently has the potency of traditional Irish satiric verse, even in the printed form that gives it its widest circulation:

The wararrow went round, so it did, (a nation wants a gaze) and the ballad, in the felibrine trancoped metre affectioned by Taiocebo in his *Casudas de Poulichinello Artahut*, stumpstampaded on to a slip of blancovide and headed by an excessively rough and red woodcut, privately printed at the rimepress of Delville, soon fluttered its secret on white highway and brown byway to the rose of the winds and the blew of the gaels, from archway to lattice and from black hand to pink ear, village crying to village ... anticipating a perfect downpour of plaudits among the rapsods ... (43.21–34)

If the Prankquean is the queen of all rains, Hosty is the king of all ranns:

And around the lawn the rann it rann and this is the rann that Hosty made. Spoken. (44.07–08)

Arrah, leave it to Hosty, frosty Hosty, leave it to Hosty for he's the mann to rhyme the rann, the rann, the rann, the king of all ranns. (44.15–17)

This ties in the horse-race around the park (the king of all 'rans,' around the lawn it ran) with circulation of the ballad and of rumours, with satiric and poetic activity, and with one further theme. As 'the rann, the rann, the king of all ranns' suggests, the ballad also serves as a parody of a rite of passage, the ritualistic 'hunting of the wren' which, Sir James Frazer has remarked,

still takes place in parts of Leinster and Connaught. On Christmas Dat or St. Stephen's Day, the boys hunt and kill the wren, fasten it in the middle of a mass of holly and ivy on the top of a broomstick, and on St. Stephen's Day go about with it from house to house singing:
The wren, the wren, the king of all birds,
St. Stephen's Day was caught in the furze,
Although he is little, his family's great,
I pray you good landlady, give us a treat.

Money or food (bread, butter, eggs, etc.) were given them, upon which they feasted in the evening.[15]

Bread, butter, and eggs link to the established themes of agriculture and dairy-farming (see verse 4), while the rann Frazer quotes is related to the Persse/cad/Prometheus themes by means of a variant found in the legend of another bird, Robin Hood. (Joyce scholars sometimes regard the cad as a thief or hold-up man.) Robert Graves points out: '"hood" (or Hod or Hud) meant "log" – the log put at the back of the fire – and it was in this log cut from the sacred oak that Robin had once been believed to reside ... In the popular superstition Robin himself escaped up the chimney in the form of a robin and when Yule ended, went out as Belin against his rival, Bran, or Saturn – who had been 'Lord of Misrule' at the Yule-tide revels. Bran hid from pursuit in the ivy-bush disguised as a Gold Crest Wren; but Robin always caught and hanged him. Hence the song: "Who'll hunt the Wren?" cries Robin the Bobbin.'[16]

Hood and hod easily evoke the figures of PQ and Finnegan, but more crucial to developments in the HCE chapter is the relation of the wren tradition to technology and the large theme of recirculation. Graves suggests that 'the most ancient wren tradition is quoted by Pausanius in his *Description of Greece*: he says that Triptolemus, the Eleusinian counterpart of Egyptian Osiris, was an Argive priest of mysteries named Trochilus who fled from Argos to Attica when Agenor seized the city. Trochilus means 'wren' and it also means 'of the wheel,' presumably because the wren is hunted when the wheel of the year has gone full circle The connexion of the wren with the wheel was retained until recently in Somersetshire.'[17]

Allied to the wheel theme is the Roman ritual of running a 'horse-race' to establish the perimeter of a city. Joyce links Hosty, Roman roads (in Britain: Watling Street, Icknild Street, Erning Street, and Foss Way) and newspaper/press-circulation with 'mention of the mainland minority and such as had wayfared *via* Watling, Ernin, Icknild and Stane, in chief a halted cockney car with its quotal of Hardmuth's hacks, a northern tory, a southern whig, an eastanglian chronicler and a landwester guardian' (42.25–9).

The fourteen verses of *The Ballad of Persse O'Reilly* (45–7) are interrupted by three digression that group the verses according to the four grammatical levels of exegesis. Of these, the first two digressive interruptions or stutters in the song are the crowd crying encouragement to Hosty. The third, presumably provided by the narrator, is: 'Suffoclose! Shikespower! Seudodanto! Anonymoses!' As Finnegan and HCE epitomize modes of culture and society in the *Wake*, each of these four stands at the peak of his respective culture: Dante (medieval) and Moses (pastoral) each stand on the border between two worlds, while Sophocles' age was the first age of writing and Shakespeare's the first age of print. The first group of four verses (the literal level) rehashes themes from the first two thunders: (1) Humpty Dumpty, the magazine wall, and the 'fall'; (2) the Jarl's 'fall' through the social classes, and retribution (legal); (3) technological and social innovation; and (4) agriculture, domestication of animals (and men), and HCE's 'disease.' The second group of four verses (the figurative or allegorical level) presents HCE through various aspects of the crowd that composes him: a stuttering salesman, a small-businessman, and a social ape, a pub-keeper, a sailor king (Viking invader), and a constable. The third group of four verses (the tropological level) discloses several immoral escapades of HCE and his shirking of his (moral) duty to his wife and family. The last group of two verses (the eschatological level) concerns his death and burial. The ballad, too, comes full circle: having begun, 'Have you heard of one Humpty Dumpty'; it ends 'And not all the king's men nor his horses / Will resurrect his corpus ...' (verse 14).

The third thunder –

the   (klikkaklakkaklaskaklopatzklatschabattacreppycrottygraddaghsemmihsammihnouithappluddyappladdypkonpkot!) (44.20–1)

– contains allusions to all of the themes in the HCE chapter, as follows.

Thunder	Interpretation	Theme Sounded
klik	clique	group, class
klikkaklakka	Sw, *kackerlacka*, cockroach (26L)	earwig, subdued ear
klikkaklakka- klaskaklopat- zklatschabatta	(onomatopoeia) stutter: horseshoes watch ticking railway cars eggs breaking presses running applause	stutterance hunting, horserace watch/alarm clock HCE metro/urban transport Humpty Dumpty printed ballad applause, thunder
akla	Lat, *aqua*, water	PQ, rain
klak	Fr, *claque*, clap	applause, thunder

Thunder	Interpretation	Theme Sounded
	Du, *klok*; Dan, Nor, *klokke*, clock (26L)	alarm clock/HCE
	Sl, *clack*, swindle	thief (cad); HCE's 'schemes for to bother us'
klakka	Sw, *klocka*, Dan, Nor, *klokke*, bell (26L)	alarm clock/HCE, church bell
akka	Egy, *akar*, ship's hold	sailor king, Viking, commerce
	Egy, *paka*, chief man	HCE
kak-kak-kak	Gr, *kak*, letter k (ClL)	print
	Gr, *kakos*, bad (ClL)	incident in the park
klas	class	classes
	glass	grail, beer, pub
aklaska	Gr, *akleistos*, nameless	mob; identity quest
klaska	Skt, *kalasa*, chalice	grail, beer/pub
	Gr, *klazo*, to shut	door
	to make a loud noise	applause, thunder
las	lace	PQ, clothing
	lass	PQ-ettes
	laws	legal codes
	Fi, *lasi*, glass (26L)	chalice, beer/pub
aska	Sw, *äska*, thunder (26L)	thunder
skak	Sw, Nor, *skatt*, tax (26L)	cities, commerce
aklo	Lat, *oculo*, eye	HCE, eye; 'royal divorce'
aklopatz	Gr, *aklopos*, not furtively concealed	Ballad-exposé of HCE
klopa	Nor, *kjøpe*, buy	commerce
	Gr, *klopaios*, secret	rumours, the park ...
	Gr, *klopaios*, stolen, fraudulent (ClL), Gr, *klopa*, to steal	thief, the cad, HCE's 'schemes for to bother us'; Robin Hood wren/rann

Thunder	Interpretation	Theme Sounded
klopat	Rum, *clopot*, bell	alarm clock
	Pol, *klopot*, trouble (26L)	rumors of HCE's indiscretion, 'fall'
	R, *khlopat*, clap (26L)	applause, thunder
lopa	low pay	HCE vassal; commerce
klatsch	klatsch (e.g., of apes)	mob, social classes
	Ger, *Klatsch*, gossip (GeL)	rumors
	clap (McH)	applause
klatscha	Indon, *katja*, glass	chalice, beer/pub
schaba	Ger, *Schabe*, cockroach	earwig
abatta	Egy, your father	HCE, Finnegan
bat	bought	commerce
	Sw, Nor, *bat*, boat	PQ, Viking, sailor king, commerce
	Fr, *botte*, boot	clothing
	Fr, *botte*, bunch	HCE mob, Hosty, customers
batta	Ar, *batta*, duck (26L)	dairy
	Fr, *battaille*, battle	weaponry
	Ger, butter	dairy, HCE disease (verse 4), wren gift
	Ital, *battere*, to clap (McH)	applause
battacr	baedecker (raincoat)	clothes, shield from PQ
battacre	Gr, *battarízo*, to stutter	stutterance
attacr	attacker	cad; hunters
rep	reap	agriculture
eppy	epée (foil)	weaponry
pyc	pike	weaponry; turnpike; hunting
	Fr, *pique*, spade	agriculture
crot	carrot	agriculture
	crotch	HCE exhibitionist
rot	wrote	the ballad (Hosty)
	rote (memory)	rumors, ballad

Thunder	Interpretation	Theme Sounded
ottygradda	integrity	Finnegan; Humpty Dumpty; cad questions HCE's
tyg	Scand, cloth, clothes Dan, *byg*, Nor, *bygg*, barley (26L)	clothing agriculture, beer
grad	S-C, *grad*, town Gael, *gradh*, love; *cradh*, misery	cities, village-to-village 'royal divorce'
gradda	Sw, *grädde*, cream Sw, *skada*, damage	dairy farm; domesticated animals HCE's reputation, the 'fall,' rumours
graddagh	Gael, *greadadh*, clapping (GaL) driving rapidly	applause, thunder horse-race, urban transport
rad	Ar, *rad*, thunder (26L) Ger, *Rad*, wheel Du, *raad*, Sw, Dan, Nor, *rad*, advice	thunder wheel, recirculation cad's request
addagh	Ardagh (chalice)	grail, beer
dag	dog Sw, *tag*, train	hunting hounds, John Peel (31.28–9) urban transport, metro (41.20–1), recirculation
daghsem	dachshund (badger hound)	hunting
agh	egg	Humpty Dumpty; dairy farm
aghsem	awesome	HCE
sem ... sam	Shem, Shaun	HCE family
semmihsam-mihnouithapp-pluddyapp-ladd	see me say 'mine' with that bloody applause	Hosty's pride about his ownership/authorship of the ballad, its reception; (pride – a deadly sin); 'the fall'
	or	

Thunder	Interpretation	Theme Sounded
	see me say 'me' with that bloody applause	HCE/group finds its identity in the pub
mihsa	Gael, *mishe*, I am Egy, *masa*, infantryman	identity quest weaponry, fusiliers (verse 11)
ihsa	Izzy/Issy	PQ, HCE daughter
ihsamm	Ar, *assam*, deaf (26L)	ear dominated by eye
sammihn	Du, *samen*, Dan, Nor, *sammen*, together (26L)	HCE as host; audience in theatre, pub
sammihnoui-thappluddyappl	'say "mine" with that/the bloody apple' (var: see 'luddyappl' below)	'fall' as discovery of self
mihnouit	Fr, *minuit*, midnight	HCE/cad: the time, clock theme
nou	Fr, *nous*, we Du, *nieuw*, new	mob, group Prometheus, invent
ouit	wheat	agriculture
thappl	Egy, *tapal*, companies	group; commerce
appluddyap-pladdy	applause	applause, thunder
plud	Dan, *klud*, rag	clothing, paper (press)
luddyappl	Fr, *le diable*, the devil	the 'fall'; Hosty (digression 2); HCE's (hideous) religious reforms
uddyappl	Pol, *obywater*, citizen (26L)	HCE; cities
pla	ALP	HCE family
plad	plaid (cloth) ploughed	clothing agriculture
laddy	laddie lady Dan, *lade*, Sw, *lada*, barn (26L)	cad (younger son) ALP, PQ agriculture
dypkonpkot	Fi, *pääkaupunki*, capital (of cities) (26L)	cities, civilized man

Thunder	Interpretation	Theme Sounded
	Fi, *kaupunki*, town (26L)	village-to-village
ko	Sw, Dan, *ko*, cow	dairy farm
kot	Indon, *kota*, town (26L)	village-to-village
	Ger, *Kot*, dirt, excrement (GeL)	agriculture (fertilizer)
	coat	clothing
ot	oat	agriculture

7

The Fourth Thunderclap: The Fall of the Garden Itself (*FW* 81–93.22)

The Market Garden and the Railroad – an Eireann Whores' Race
or
Prostituta in Herba – 'the crack that bruck the bank in Multifarnham' (90.24; cf. 115.13–21).

Yes, the viability of vicinals if invisible is invincible. And we are not trespassing on his corns either. Look at all the plotsch! (81.01–02)

And it is as though where Agni araflammed and Mithra monished and Shiva slew as mayamutras the obluvial waters of our noarchic memory withdrew, windingly goharksome, to some hastyswasty timberman torchpriest, flamenfan, the ward of the wind that lightened the fire that lay in the wood that Jove bolt, at his rude word. (80.23–8)

Thunder 4 occurs two-thirds of the way through chapter 4 of the *Wake* (pages 75–103 of book I). Most of the themes in the chapter are already familiar. The chapter may be divided into three sections; the middle one contains the thunder and takes the form of a courtroom hearing at which HCE's and the cad's enigmatic alleged indiscretion in the park is discussed.[1] Although questions are posed, answers given, and evidence presented, this is a Menippean court in which nothing really happens. The court, and the palaver, are the point. The hearing serves to put on display some of HCE's 'Environs' and to develop their ramifications. Of the ten, this thunder is perhaps the 'weakest'; that is, it does less work than do the other nine in developing themes of 'characters' and in exploring the effects of major Western technologies on shaping the course of civilization and sensibility. A Menippean sub-

*Exactly what he meant by a pederast prig?
Just a gentleman who prayed his lent.*

I.

ambush was laid (roughly speaking around halftime twixt dusk in

dawn near (the only abfalltree in auld the land) there was

not as much light from the widowed moon as would dim a child's

altar.   The mixer, accordingly, was bluntly broached as to

whether he was one of those lucky cocks for whom the audible-

visible- gnosible- edible world existed.   That he was only

too sure of it.   Whether he was sure too of his names in this

King and countryman business?   That he was particularly so?

It was O'Somebody?   Quite.   And how did he arrive at the B. A?

That it was like his poll.   A crossgrained trapper with odd eyes,

projecting ears, inquiline nose and a twitcherous mouth?   He

would be.   Not unintoxicated, fair witness?   Drunk as a fishup.

The grazing rights expired with the expiry of the goat's sire,

if they were not mistaken?   That he could not exactly tell the

worshipsfuls but his mother had the receipt for the price of the

coffin and she could tell them.   Quare hircum?   No answer.

Unde gentium fe....?   No ah.   As to the pugnacities evinced

during the affray how they appealed to him then?   That it

was wildfires night Mickmichael's soords shricking shrieks

through the wilkinses, and neckanicholas' toastingforks pricking

prongs up the tunnybladders?   Briefly, how it all finally struck

him now?   Like the crack that bruck the bank in Multifarnham.

Whether he knew what they meant?   That he supposed he did.

If it was a bad clap?   Oo!   Bloody awful?   Shocking!

Whurawhorascortastrumpaporna------------strippuckputtanach...

eh?   You have it all right.

Thunder 4: 46 letters, with the middle left blank

plot involves the fortunes of the character, Festy King. This character combines the festival or carnival king or mock-king that figures so large in Bakhtin's sense of the Menippea, with the fisher king of traditional legend, whose private and corporate (that of his kingdom) health are intertwined:

Critics have never fully understood the Festy King section of *Finnegans Wake* (85.20–93.22), and with good reason. Joyce's technique in this passage is to present the details of a court proceeding in such a way that the reader is left with only confusion. The witness does not understand the prosecutor; the prosecutor does not understand the witness; the defendant does not understand the prosecutor or the witness; the judges understand little of the proceedings, and the reader is hard pressed to understand anything. Through a series of misunderstandings, the narrative becomes a parody of blind (and deaf)justice.[2]

In short, a typically Menippean court.

Simply put, thunder 4 presents the development of modes of transportation, represented by the road and the railroad, and their effect on accelerating agricultural and rural economy. The pattern of small-scale dairy-orchards amid kitchen gardens, calculated to serve small village communities and individual families, is completely re-formed by the high-speed railroad. Those communities have a human, 'family-like' dimension, whereas the large and distant markets the railroad makes accessible to the countryside are detached and impersonal. The land that surrounded and was ploughed by the community (symbolic intercourse) is now rutted and ploughed impersonally and by complete strangers. This process is dramatized as prostitution. Large-scale animal breeding (prostitution) and slaughter (murder) occur equally impersonally. The whole is presented as a blight or social disease – a thundering dose of clap – that has infected the more human-scale village pattern. The 'horse-race' of thunder 3 is extended here to accommodate the iron horse, or Eireann horse, running on a track of its own. At the same time, competition among the several prostitutes in and for the attentions of the stock-market-place becomes a whores' race.

PQ and the Court

The enveloping action for the thunder is a curious hearing and inquest, held, apparently, at a papal court – perhaps in hope a bull may result, to fit with the agriculture theme. Dramatis personae are evidently few: there are the narrator, the court (the four old men as judges: cf. 94.24), 'the prisoner' who seems to be the cad (a highwayman or combination of thief and businessman, in keeping with the roads theme), the four senses summoned as witnesses (personified as 'an eye, ear, nose and throat witness' 86.32–3), and, finally, the counsel, 'two disappainted solicitresses' (whores, 90.16: cf., 'a pair of sycopanties with amygdaleine eyes' 94.16, given to merging, or to splitting into a quartet of spectrum girls as the phases of the moon: 'all the two-fromthirty advocatesses within echo, pulling up their briefs' – of the legal variety, of course: 93.11–12). These ladies are, naturally, PQs: 'And both as like as a duel of lentils? Peacisely' (89.04), as like as peas in a pod.

The court is formally convened on 85 (with 'Oyeh! Oyeh!' 85.31). After preliminary remarks, the eye-ear-nose-throat witness is introduced (86.32) and a question/answer session follows (88–90) with the thunder as the final question (90.31–3). The narrator provides a further page of description (91) at the end of which a courtroom brawl occurs, and he subsequently devotes a paragraph to each of Shem and Shaun as affected by PQ. Then the court adjourns to cries of 'shame ... shames' (93.21: James/Jim the Penman/Shem/ 'Shun the Punman') in seven languages, recalling the spectrum. After cross-examination of the four senses (bodily *and* scriptural, as always) in court, the aftermath is decidedly literal: the close of court is followed by an account (93.24–94.23ff) of The Letter (the first of the four senses: literal, figurative/ allegorical, tropological/moral, final/spiritual) that is so crucial to thunder 5.

PQ is much more in this chapter than advocatess, or a pair of them. Her rain/reign provides nourishment essential for the farm crops (the crop – throat – of the witness as well), and her reins supply the whore theme (and involve the nose – slang for penis – of the witness). As both crops and farm animals are raised and bred systematically for the stock market (references to goats, pigs, horses, bulls – even the papal variety – geese, etc. stud the pages), PQ-whoring is related to all aspects of the process. We read of 'off-dealings which were welholden of ladykants te huur [Du, bed ... for hire] out such as the Breeders' Union, the Guild of Merchants of the Staple' etc. (77.21–3), and that 'Venuses were gigglibly temptatrix, vulcans guffawably eruptious and the whole wives' world frockful of fickles' (79.18–19; forficula is an earwig). In her more traditional role as garb, she clothes the prisoner, the cad, and uses all the flowers of speech and rhetoric ('fluors of sparse') in a deposition to secure his release. It is ultimately effective. He appears in the [dry] dock,

appatently ambrosiaurealised, like Kersse's Korduroy Karikature, wearing, besides stains, rents and patches, his fight shirt, straw braces, souwester and a policeman's corkscrew trowswers, all out of the true (as he had purposely torn up all his cymtry-manx bespokes in the mamertime), deposing for his exution with all the fluors of sparse in the royal Irish vocabulary how the whole padderjagmartin [cf Peter, Jack,

and Martin – St Peter, Jack Calvin, and Martin Luther – in Swift's *A Tale of a Tub*]
tripiezite suet and all the sulfeit of copperas had fallen off him quatz unaccountably ...
(in feacht he was dripping as he found upon stripping for a pipkin ofmalt as he feared
the coold raine) (85.32–86.06)

Her clothing, especially her underclothing, is much in evidence throughout
the chapter, but her most conspicuous activities here are as 'Rainmaker'
(87.06), as quean (whore), and as giver of impetus to the action. The litigants,
including 'kings of mud and tory, even the goat king of Killorglin, were
egged on by their supporters in the shape of betterwomen with bowstrung
hair of Carrothagenuine ruddiness, waving crimson petties and screaming
from Isod's towertop' (87.26–9).
  PQ's pranksome whoring was developed at length in the previous chapter
(I.3), as:

finding one day while dodging chores that she stripped teasily for binocular man and
that her jambs were jimpjoyed to see each other, the nautchy girly soo found her
fruitful hat too small for her and rapidly taking time, look, she rapidly took to neck-
ing, partying and selling her spare favours in the haymow or in lumber closets or in
the greenawn *ad huck* ... serving whom in fine that same hot coney *a la Zingara*
which our own little Graunya of the chilired cheeks dished up to the greatsire of
Oscar, that son of a Coole. Houri of the coast of emerald, arrah of the lacessive poghue
... A reine of the shee, a shebeen quean, a queen of pranks. (67.36–68.22: but see the
entire passage).

In the present chapter, PQ is identified variously with the farm animals – presumably as comment upon whoring as a reducing of humans to animal level
– as well as with vehicular technologies (omnibus, bicycle, trams, railroad),
which, through association with her, become another mode of whoring.
  Chief among her animal identifications is the pig; the chapter contains
more references to pigs than to any other animal. She hovered over the altercation in the park dressed figuratively as a pig: 'did the imnage of Girl Cloud
Pensive flout above them light young charm, in ribbons and pigtail' (82.19–
21). In keeping with PQ-matriarchy, this chapter shows sex with roles
reversed (woman on top: she 'flouts' above them; for example, also, 92.04,
92.28), or debased (by whoring), or perverse (cf. 81.29, 79.23), or diseased (as
at the thunder 'clap'), or all of these at once. The pig was such an intimate
part of Irish peasant household economy that it was affectionately referred to
as 'the gentleman' or 'the little man who pays the rent.' It appears thus several times in the section, and is related to PQ. For example, the 'gentleman

ratepayer' of 86.27 two lines later becomes 'what a whore!' (86.29, *Qui Sta Troia* – Ital, *questa troia*). The reference to 'Cliopatrick (the sow) princess of parked porkers' (91.06) is a complex synthesis of themes. She is the pig (slang for whore) in or of the park, she is parked (as a vehicle), she is PQ in her Cleopatra guise and as 'princess'; as PQ she wears a print (-patrick: Dan, *paa tryk*, in print), and she is promiscuous (Cli-: *clith* – pron. kli – is a Gaelic term for 'sexual heat in swine' [GaL, gloss to this word, 62]). The allusion to Clio, the muse of history, relates her to other fires in the chapter besides those of lust and lightning. There is the 'memory's fire rekindling' (83.04), as well as the Promethean fires of innovation, and the fire under the boiler of the (locomotive) steam engine. At the end of the courtroom session, Shaun, now thoroughly civilized, the darling of the 'maidies of the bar' and a man of many extensions (he is complimented by the girls, 'the captivating youth, on his having all his senses about him' 92.16), is nominated by them for 'the swiney prize' (92.15). He is a paradigm of PQ's effects. Finally, immediately surrounding the thunderclap, the whorish developments of agriculture are described as a pox ('suppoxed' 90.25), as an 'ach bad clap' (90.28),[3] and as 'Meirdreach an Oincuish' (90.34). The latter phrase is a compressed statement of 'Murder and Anguish,' 'Shite and Onions' (*merde* plus *drökh*), and 'Whore the Giddy Woman' (Gael, *meirdreach*, whore; *an*, the; *oinseach*, harlot or giddy woman).

PQ is identified with various modes of transport (ridden or used for a fee). Mention is made of 'circulating ... alongst one of our umphrohibited semitary thrufahrts, open to buggy and bike' (85.07–10), and therefore we are told 'that herself was the velocipede that could tell them kitcat' (89.24). The tram or locomotive race is also depicted, at its outset, as a scampering group of PQs (see below). The remaining themes, of roads, the Book of Nature, bridges, the papal court, sacrilege, the witness of the senses, and levelling, are closely intertwined.

The Role of the Railroad

The rail race begins ten pages before the thunder, in a setting where 'there being no macadamised sidetracks on those old nekropolitan nights in, barring a footbatter, Bryant's Causeway, bordered with speedwell ...' (80.01–03), and one 'that would be lust on Ma, than then when ructions ended, than here where race began' (80.15–16) ... and they're off!

The mausoleum lies behind us (O Adgigasta, *multipopulipater!*) and there are milestones in their cheadmilias faultering along the tramestrack by Brahm and Anton

Hermes! Per omnibus secular seekalarum. Amain. But the past has made us this present of a rhedarhoad. (81.05–09)

It was hard by the howe's there, plainly on this disoluded and a buchan cold spot, rupestric then, resurfaced that now is, that Luttrell sold if Lautrill bought, in the saddle of the Brennan's (now Malpasplace?) pass, versts and versts from true civilisation ... (Beneathere! Benathere!) (81.12–17)

Woowoo (82.31: train whistle, and wolf whistle)

... turning his fez menialstrait in the direction of Moscas, he first got rid of a few mitsmillers and hurooshoos and levanted off with tubular jurbulance at a bull's run over the assback bridge ... picked up to keep some crowplucking appointment with some rival rialtos anywheres between Pearidge and the Littlehorn (83.36–84.08)

... wurming along gradually for our savings backtowards motherwaters so many miles from bank and Dublin stone (olympiading even till the eleventh dynasty to reach that thuddysickend Hamlaugh) ... obtaining a pierced paraflamme and claptrap fireguard there crops out the still more salient point of the politish leanings and town pursuits of our forebeer, El Don De Dunelli [Venetian dialect, *el don de dunelle*, the gift of women, that is, a Don Juan, a womanizer] ... who ... was ... circulating ... alongst one of our umphrohibited semitary thrufahrts, open to buggy and bike, to walk, Wellington Park road, with the curb ... (84.30–85.10)

... Even while he was trying for to stick fire to himcell ... (86.04–05)

Ballera jobbera. Some majar bore too? Iguines. And with tumblerous legs ... (88.19–20)

A stoker temptated by evesdripping aginst the driver who was a witness as well? Sacred avatar ... (89.01–02)

Askt to whether she minded whither he smuked? Not if he barkst into phlegms. Anent his ajaciulations to his Crosscan Lorne, cossa? It was corso in cursu on coarser again. (89.08–11)

This Menippean race has no finish. It can just be glimpsed through the hedgerows of the text from time to time as the trams or trains endlessly circulate, creating a vortex of influence, a 'vicinal' that when 'invisible is invincible' (81.01). An apotheosis of sorts appears to have occurred after the thunder, for, the narrator remarks, 'the inexousthausthible wassailhorn tot of iskybaush the hailth up the wailth of the endknown abgod of the fire of the moving way of the hawks with his heroes in Warhorror' (91.27–30).

As the race gets under way, roads pop up everywhere in the text: for example, 'Fluminian! If this was Hannibal's walk it was Hercules' work. And a would say Not unintoxicated, fair witness? Drunk as a fishup. The gracious miss was no doubt sensible how he was altered? That she generally was. As to his religion, if any? It was the see-you-Sunday sort. Exactly what he meant by a pederast-prig? Just a gent who prayed his lent. And of middleclassed portavorous was a usual beast? Bynight as useful as a vomit to a horn man. The grazing rights (Mrs Magistra Martinetta) expired with the expiry of the goat's sire, if they were not mistaken? That he exactly could not tell the worshipfuls but his mother-in-waders had the recipis for the price of the coffin and that he was there to tell them that herself was the velocipede that could tell them kitcat. *Quare hircum?* No answer. *Unde gentium fe...?* No ah. And, changing the venders, as to the pugnaxities evinxed during the effrays round fatherthyme's beckside and the regents in the plantsown raining they appealed to him then? That it was wildfires night on all the bettygallaghers, Mickmichael's soords shrieking shreck through the wilkinses and neckanicholas' toastingforks, pricking prongs up the tunnybladders. Let there be light? And there was. Foght. The devoted couple was or were only two disappa'not'o' ainted solicitresses on the job of the unfortunate class on Saturn's mountain fort? That was about it, jah! And if it was all about that, egregious sir? About that and the other. Briefly, how such beginall finally struck him now? Like the crack that bruck the bank in Multifarnham. Whether he fell in with what they meant? Cursed that he suppoxed he did. If it was, in yappanoise language, ach bad clap? Oo! Bloody awful? Shocking! Whirawho-rascortastrumpapornanennykocksapastippatappatupper-strippuckputtanach, eh? You have it all right.

But a new complexion was put upon the matter when to the perplexedly uncondemnatory bench the senior king of all, Pegger Festy, as soon as the outer layer of stucckomuck had been removed at the request of a few live jurors, declared in a loudburst of poesy, through his Brythonic interpreter on his oath, whereas take notice be the relics of the bones of the story honchah

Thunder 4: second and final version: page proof

hungried thousand of the unemancipated slaved the way' (81.03–04). But references to both roads and bridges become less frequent and less direct as matters progress.⁴ Railroads, and to a lesser extent railroading in general, require a great amount of levelling of land for the way in addition to bridge-building (part of the same levelling activity). Joyce relates his themes of bridging and levelling roads to levelling in the secular Book of Nature and bridging in the spiritual: a papal court involves a *pontiff*, a bridge. Levelling extends to the four senses in each of the books, both bodily and exegetical.

At least one of the matters under consideration by the court concerns the cad's attack on HCE: 'On a pontiff's order as ture as there's an ital on atac' (89.35). HCE's 'sin' and 'fall' had resulted in 'religion's reform ... Hideous in form,' a levelling down or degradation. In this chapter, all sorts of perverse secular idolatries are practised, involving each of the themes:

Fact, any human inyon you liked any erenoon or efter would take her bare godkin out, or an even pair of hem, (lugod! lugodoo!) and prettily pray with him (or with em even) everyhe to her taste, long for luck, tapette and tape petter and take pettest of all. (Tip!) (79.19–23)

Per omnibus secular seekalarum. (81.07–08)

(*tout est sacré pour un sacreur, femme à barbe ou homme nourrice*) (81.28–9)

... the endknown abgod of the fire of the moving way (91.29)

In general, missionary zeal (cf. 80.20–1, 82.03–04) has become perverted to mercenary zeal and fire, as represented by PQ and the agricultural themes:

And it is as though where Agni araflammed and Mithra monished and Shiva slew as mayamutras the obluvial waters of our noarchic memory withdrew, windingly goharksome, to some hastyswasty timberman torchpriest, flamenfan, the ward of the wind that lightened the fire that lay in the wood that Jove bolt, at his rude word ... What are you doing your dirty minx and his big treeblock way up your path? Slip around, you, by the rare of the ministers'! (80.23–31)

In the end, the prisoner is released and retorts roadishly to a Latin parody of the cad's question of HCE:

To the Switz bobbyguard's curial but courtlike: Commodore valley O hairy, Arthre jennyrosy?: the firewaterloover returted with such a vine-smelling fortytudor ages rawdownhams tanyouhide as would turn the latten stomach even of a tumass equinous ... (93.06–09: *Quomodo vales hodie, Arator generose? ... fortitudo eius Rhodanum tenuit.*)

The Book of Nature theme includes all of the aspects of agriculture, commerce, roads, and technology mentioned thus far. It is first explicitly evoked as the race begins:

that dangerfield circling butcherswood where fireworker oh flaherty engaged a nutter of castlemallards and ah for archer stunned's turk, all over which fossil footprints, bootmarks, fingersigns, elbowdints, breechbowls, a. s. o. were all successively traced of a most envolving description. (80.08–12)

The trope also appears as the 'lexicon of life' (83.25) and as a comment on the phrase 'a chip off the old Flint' – 'in the Nichtian glossery ... this is nat language at any sinse of the world' (83.10–12). It is entirely appropriate for Joyce to insert references to reading 'signatires' in Nature into a section of the *Wake* devoted to the degradation of the natural environment that results from marketing it as a technology of reproduction. As a final example of writing and 'signatires' in the *liber natura*, Joyce weaves the names of a number of ogham ciphers into part of the courtroom questioning just prior to the thunder, ending with the letters, a-b-c-d-e-f:

Which was meant in a shirt of two shifts macoghamade or up Finn, threehatted ladder? That a head in thighs under a bush at the sunface would bait a serpent to a millrace through the heather. Arm bird colour defdum ethnic fort perharps? (89.29–33)[5]

The prisoner at court wounded someone in a tussle in the park so that he bled 'in self defiense' (the 'I' defended) 'from the nostrils, lips, pavilion and palate' (84.21–2), and so an eyewitness, or rather 'an eye, ear, nose and throat witness' (86.32–3) is called to testify. The pretext may be thin and what the witness says may or may not be pertinent or even intelligible, but as is generally the case in the *Wake*, the significance of a 'character' lies for the most part in what it personifies, in its presence, nature, and fortunes. This 'character' affirms the truth in the thunder question (the first thunder of the book given directly and not in parentheses as an editorial aside or illustration). The fourfold judges are paralleled by his fourfold expertise, which is reviewed in the penultimate question (prior to the thunder): 'Augs and ohrs with Rhian O'kehley to put it tertianly, we wrong? Shocking!' (90.28–9).[6] His credentials are established at the outset of the question/answer session:

The mixer, accordingly, was bluntly broached, and in the best basel to boot, as to whether he was one of those lusty cocks for whom the audible-visible-gnosible-edible world existed. That he was only too cognitively conatively cogitabundantly sure of it because, living, loving, breathing and sleeping morphomelosophopancreates, as he most significantly did ... (88.04–09; see also .09–20)

The minor rumble serves to underline his competence with thunder and the language of forms, while at the same time his description as a 'lusty cock' suggests that he could become susceptible to PQ's machinations and allurements.

His four modes of knowing operate on two levels, as already suggested. Their integrity and decorum are precarious because the witness is presented as already fragmented and specialized (an eye-ear-nose-throat specialist). The correspondences are eye – literal sense (as established in thunders 2 and 3); ear – the echo of allegory; nose – the stink of moral turpitude and depravity; throat – the breath of spirit. His patristic (exegetical) dimension is confirmed both by his presence and acceptance at a papal court, and by the narrator's observation that 'he was patrified to see, hear, taste and smell' (87.11–12). After the thunder, which enacts the abstract, impersonal, and commercialized environment dramatized in the section, the witness is abused as 'that eyebold earbig noseknaving gutthroat' (91.11); his testimony is contradicted as useless in the new circumstances, and, as the brawl ensues, he gives in to PQ's influence: 'the testifighter, reluctingly, but with ever so ladylike indecorum, joined. (Ha! Ha!)' (92.04–05). His ultimate fate is mirrored in Shaun's response to a matriarchal seductress, a 'lovelooking leapgirl' – 'he, wan and pale in his unmixed admiration, innamorate with heruponhim in shining aminglement' (92.26–8). Once more the eye has seduced and subdued the interplay of the other senses. The literal level, the Letter, follows.

The fourth thunder –

Bladyughfoulmoecklenburgwhurawhorascortastrumpapornanennykocksapastippatappatupperstrippuckputtanach, eh? (90. 31–3)

– reverberates with echoes of each of the themes present in its context.

Thunder	Interpretation	Theme Sounded
Bla	Fr, *blé*, wheat	agriculture

Thunder	Interpretation	Theme Sounded
Blad	blade (young man) (of a plough) Pol, *blad*, mistake (26L) Du, Sw, Dan, Nor, *blad*, leaf (26L)	cad; Shem or Shaun agriculture, 'rutting' the fall agriculture, clothing
Blady	bloody R, *blyad*, whore (McH)	slaughter of animals whoring
Bladyugh	Gael, *bladaireacht*, flattery (GaL)	womanizing, whoring
Bladyughfoul-moecklen-burgwhura-whorascort-astrumpa	bloody awful, Mecklenburg, you're a whore, a skirt, a strumpet	moral judgment (papal court), prostitution of nature, degra-dation, etc.
la	lay (eggs, etc.)	whoring
lad	lad laid (had intercourse) Fr, *laide*, ugly	cad; Shem or Shaun whoring thunder changes, whoring, degradation
lady	lady	PQ 'maidies at the bar'
ladyu	Fr, *l'adieu*, the goodbye	prisoner released
ugh	(expression of disgust) Gael, *ugh*, egg	degradation, levelling farm
fou	Fr, *fou*, crazy Fr, *feu*, fire	degradation, sexual infatuation lust, steam engine fires
foul	foul Ar, beans	'ach bad clap' disease, degradation, whoring agriculture, farming
moeck	Gael, *muc*, pig (GaL)	PQ/pig/whore
moecklenburg	Mecklenberg (agricultural territory on the Baltic) (GeL and Gaz)	agriculture

Thunder	Interpretation	Theme Sounded
	Mecklenburgh Street, Dublin (heart of nighttown: cf. *Ulysses*) (Gaz)	whoring
len	Fr, *laine*, wool	farm, sheep, whoring
lenburghwhur	Limburger (smelly cheese)	the nose witness
bur	Fr, *beurre*, butter	farm
burg	city	railroad, tram, etc.
burgwhur	burg-whore/town-whore	whoring
urg	Ger, terrible, awful	thunder/disease/ degradation
whurawhor	whore, a whore; you're a whore	whoring
whurawhora	Gael, *Mhuire, Mhuire*, Mary, Mary (generally B.V.M. only; here, Mary Magdalene)	the integral/sacred degraded; whoring
whur	Du, *huur*, rent	pig (little man who pays the rent)
hura	houri	PQ whore, temptress
	Sw, *höra*, to hear (26L)	the witness (eye-ear-nose-throat)
	Ger, *Hure*, whore	whoring
awhora	Dan, *ophøre*, expire (26L)	slaughter; integrity (of countryside, of Nature, of the witness, of four senses)
awhoras	a horse-race, a whore race	whoring, railroad
awhorascor-tastrumpa	a whore's court of strumpets	whoring, the court, degradation, PQ
awhorascort	a whore's escort	Don Juan
whorascorta	Swiss Sl, a syphilitic whore	whoring, 'ach bad clap'
hora	Sw, *höra*, to hear	the witness
horasco	Fr, *haricots*, beans	agriculture

Thunder	Interpretation	Theme Sounded
oras	Rum, *oras*, town (26L)	railroad, tram, etc.
asco	Sw, *äska*, thunder	thunder
ascorta	Cf. 'Immaculacy, give but to drink to his shirt and all skirtaskortas must change her tunics' (247.28–9)	PQ, whoring, temptress
scor	score (obtain intercourse) Nor, *skjor*, fragile	whoring integrity of ecology, morals, witness
scort	skirt (clothes) skirt (circle around) Sw, *skord*, harvest	PQ roads, racetrack agriculture, whoring
scorta	Sw, *skjorta*, shirt (26L) Lat, *scorta*, whores Gael, *scartadh*, shouting	clothes, PQ whoring courtroom 'brawl'; 'shame'
cor	Fr, *cours*, course, run	race (whores, etc.)
cort	court (verb) (noun) Du, *gort*, barley (26L)	Don Juan, whoring, etc. papal court, witness agriculture
corta	Gael, *corta*, right, proper (GaL) Sp, Port, *carta*, letter (26L)	decorum, integrity the Letter/literal sense
tast	taste Ger, touch	decorum; the witness the witness
astr	aster (flower)	PQ's 'fluors of sparse'
strumpa	strumpet	whoring
trumpa	Fr, *tromper*, be wrong	the fall (error); clap; the witness discredited
rump	rump	court; pederasty (sex perversion – PQ theme)
papo	papal	court; bull (slaughter)
aporn	acorn	agriculture

Thunder	Interpretation	Theme Sounded
porn	corn	agriculture
porna	Gr, *pornê*, harlot (ClL)	whore
nenny	nanny (goat)	farm
nennykocksapas	Hu, *mennyköcsapás*, lightning stroke	thunder, fires (engine, sex, etc.)
ennykocksa-pasti	'any cock's your pasta'	'Qui Sta Troia' (questa troia): what a whore
ko	Sw, Dan, *ko*, cow	farm, whoring
kock	cock (rooster) (phallus)	farm, whoring whoring
kocks	pox	disease (venereal)
kocksa	Li, *kekse*, whore (McH)	whoring
ksapasti	Pol, *kapusta*, cabbage	agriculture
sti	sty	PQ/pig, etc.
stippata	Gr, *styppeion*, *stippeion*, pl. of *styppeia*, *stippeia*, coarse fibre of flax or hemp, tow, oakum ClL)	farming, agriculture
tip	Sl, overthrow, cause to fall	the fall; discredit witness
tippatappa	Pippa Passes	destruction and levelling, thunderclap
tappat	Fr, *tapette*, homosexual	PQ perverse sex (cf. 79.22–3)
patappa	potato	agriculture
tap	Nor, *tap*, loss (26L)	decorum, integrity, levelling
	Sl, seduce burglarize, steal	PQ whore PQ – crack that broke 'the bank in Multifarnham' (90.24)
tup	dupe: fool	seduce

Thunder	Interpretation	Theme Sounded
	duplicate	whoring (reproduction for cash), 'maidies at the bar' 2, 7, 28.
	Sl, a young bullock	whoring, slaughter
	a man questing for a woman	whoring, fires
	to have intercourse	whoring
tupper	one who has intercourse	whoring
pers	pears	agriculture
	purse	economy, whoring
strip	strip (clothing)	PQ, whoring
	(farming)	agriculture
	peel away	levelling
strippu	Nor, Sw, throat (26L)	witness
	Shelta, *stripu*, whore	whoring
trip	(travel)	vehicles, race
	(stumble)	the fall, degradation
	tripe	slaughter
rip	reap	agriculture
	ripe, Du, *rijp*, ripe (26L)	agriculture; maidies/whores
	R.I.P.	slaughter
puck	Sl, intercourse	whoring
	Gael, *poc*, he-goat	farm
	sudden blow	thunder; brawl
puckputta	(sound of motor)	railroad
putt	Ger, *putt*, vagina	whoring
putta	Sp, whore	whoring
	Ger, *Pute*, turkey-hen	farm
	conceited woman	PQ, whore
puttan	Fr, *putain*, whore	whoring
puttana	pudenda	reproduction, whoring
	It, *puttana*, whore (McH)	whoring

Thunder	Interpretation	Theme Sounded
anach	Gael, *anach*, path, pass (GaL)	roads, levelling, railway
nach	Ar, *naqd*, cash	economy, whoring
ach	'ach bad clap'	disease, whoring, thunder

8

The Fifth Thunderclap: Belinda the Hen (*FW* 107.08–125)

The Poule, the Press, and the Photograph
or
Belleslettristics and the Technologies of Reproduction

No, assuredly, they are not justified, those gloompourers who grouse that letters have never been quite their old selves again since that weird weekday in bleak Janiveer (yet how palmy date in a waste's oasis!) when to the shock of both, Biddy Doran looked at literature. (112.23–7)

Stamp out bad eggs. (437.21)

Cockalooralooraloomenos, when cup, platter and pot come piping hot, as sure as herself pits hen to paper and there's scribings scrawled on eggs. (615.08–10)

... while the ear, be we mikealls or nicholists, may sometimes be inclined to believe others the eye, whether browned or nolensed, find it devilish hard now and again even to believe itself. *Habes aures et num videbis? Habes oculos ac mannepalpabuat?* Tip! (113.27–30)

[Jymes wishes to hear from wearers of abandoned female costumes, gratefully received, wadmel jumper, rather full pair of culottes and onthergarmenteries, to start city life together. His jymes is out of job, would sit and write. He has lately commited one of the then commandments but she will now assist. Superior built, domestic, regular layer. Also got the boot. He appreciates it. Copies. ABORTISEMENT.] (181.27–33)

The fifth thunderclap occurs about halfway through chapter 5 (104–25) of book I of the *Wake*. The main subject is language and the printing press, while the photograph, another mode of visual reproduction, supplies a technological subplot in the thunder context. One of the most overtly grammatical chapters of the book (the other is II.2, 'Triv and Quad,' as Campbell and Robinson have dubbed it), this one appears to have been constructed in two sections, later joined by a bridge that contains the thunder.[1]

This narrated chapter is entirely Menippean. The narrator never interposes himself between the reader and the events presented, but, prior to the thunder, does provide extensive instructions for reading the chapter, instructions that apply equally to the other thunders as well as to the *Wake* as a whole, and that most readers to date have passed over. In so doing they enjoy the same fortunes as the learned critics and palaeographers whose researches are sent up in the chapter.

The Structure of the Episode

The chapter begins with a brief invocation to the governing muse – ALP in this case – composed as a smooth blend of formulas of the East (ear) and West (eye). The blend is a moment of equipoise before the reader is plunged into the typographic contrasts and riot of thematic disorder (disguised as scrupulous order) that follow:

In the name of Annah the Allmaziful, the Everliving, the Bringer of Plurabilities, haloed be her eve, her singtime sung, her rill be rung, unhemmed as it is uneven!
Her untitled mamafesta memorialising the Mosthighest has gone by many names at disjointed times. (104.13–17)[2]

The next ninety-nine lines, in italics ('feminine,' contrasted with the 'masculine' Roman typeface of the rest of the chapter), serve up a catalogue or inventory, a carnival feast or hodgepodge, in no evident sequence, of the names used for ALP's 'mamafesta.' Among other things, the catalogue includes passing references to each of the other thunders and ends with this allusion to events and themes from thunders 3 and 4.

... First and Last Only True Account all about the Honorary Mirsu Earwicker, L.S.D., and the Snake (Nuggets!) by a Woman of the World who only can Tell Naked Truths about a Dear Man and all his Conspirators how they all Tried to Fall him Putting it all around Lucalizod about Privates Earwicker and a pair of Sloppy Sluts plainly Showing all the Unmentionability falsely Accusing about the Rain-coats. (107.01–07)

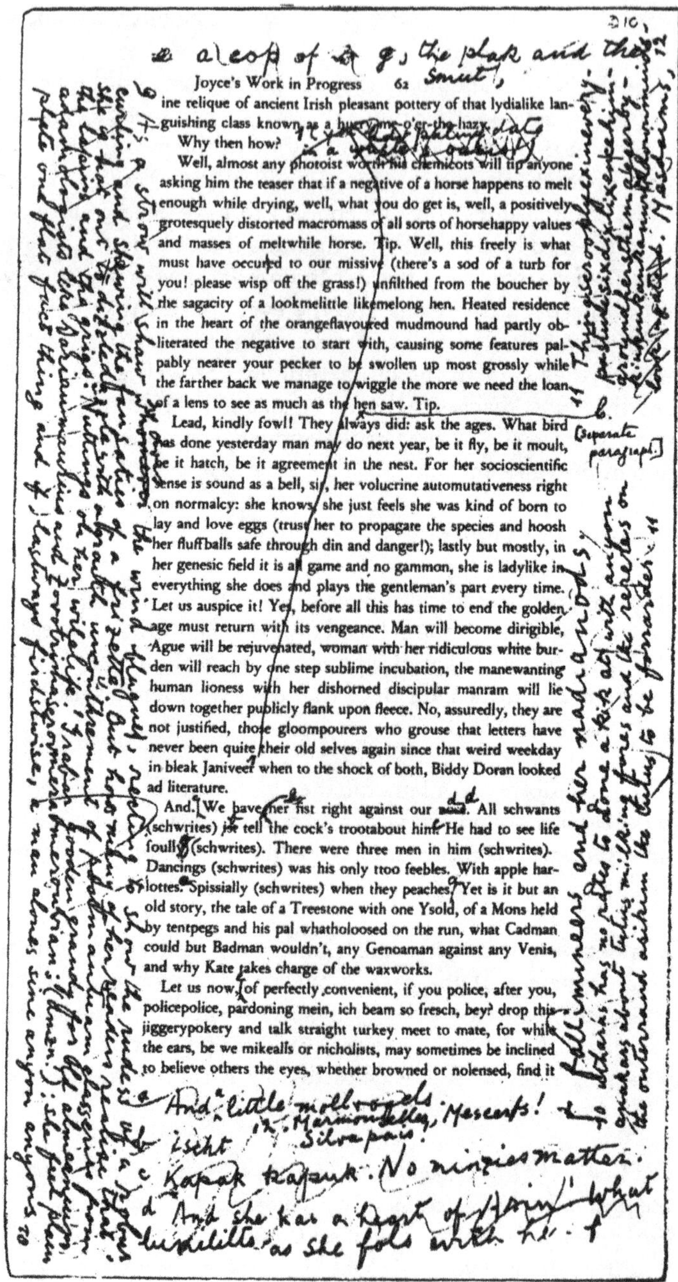

ine relique of ancient Irish pleasant pottery of that lydialike languishing class known as a huecome o'er-the-hazy.

Why then how?

Well, almost any photoist worth his chemicots will tip anyone asking him the teaser that if a negative of a horse happens to melt enough while drying, well, what you do get is, well, a positively grotesquely distorted macromass of all sorts of horsehappy values and masses of meltwhile horse. Tip. Well, this freely is what must have occured to our missive (there's a sod of a turb for you! please wisp off the grass!) unfilthed from the boucher by the sagacity of a lookmelittle likemelong hen. Heated residence in the heart of the orangeflavoured mudmound had partly obliterated the negative to start with, causing some features palpably nearer your pecker to be swollen up most grossly while the farther back we manage to wiggle the more we need the loan of a lens to see as much as the hen saw. Tip.

Lead, kindly fowl! They always did: ask the ages. What bird has done yesterday man may do next year, be it fly, be it moult, be it hatch, be it agreement in the nest. For her socioscientific sense is sound as a bell, sir, her volucrine automutativeness right on normalcy: she knows she just feels she was kind of born to lay and love eggs (trust her to propagate the species and hoosh her fluffballs safe through din and danger!); lastly but mostly, in her genesic field it is all game and no gammon, she is ladylike in everything she does and plays the gentleman's part every time. Let us auspice it! Yes, before all this has time to end the golden age must return with its vengeance. Man will become dirigible, Ague will be rejuvenated, woman with her ridiculous white burden will reach by one step sublime incubation, the manewanting human lioness with her dishorned discipular manram will lie down together publicly flank upon fleece. No, assuredly, they are not justified, those gloompourers who grouse that letters have never been quite their old selves again since that weird weekday in bleak Janiveer when to the shock of both, Biddy Doran looked ad literature.

And. We have her fist right against our nose. All schwants (schwrites) to tell the cock's trootabout him. He had to see life foully (schwrites). There were three men in him (schwrites). Dancings (schwrites) was his only ttoo feebles. With apple harlottes. Spissially (schwrites) when they peaches. Yet is it but an old story, the tale of a Treestone with one Ysold, of a Mons held by tentpegs and his pal whatholoosed on the run, what Cadman could but Badman wouldn't, any Genoaman against any Venis, and why Kate takes charge of the waxworks.

Let us now, of perfectly convenient, if you police, after you, policepolice, pardoning mein, ich beam so fresch, bey? drop this jiggerypokery and talk straight turkey meet to mate, for while the ears, be we mikealls or nicholists, may sometimes be inclined to believe others the eyes, whether browned or nolensed, find it

Thunder 5: final cut on galleys

Perhaps the catalogue of nicknames should be regarded as a large Menippean riddle: 'I have been called this, and this, and this ... What am I?' If so, the answer must be: an exhibition or 'mamafestation' of ALP's domain.

The rest of the chapter consists of a deadly satire on the *philosophus gloriosus* at work on exegesis and palaeography: in this respect, the chapter is Joyce's 'Dunciad.' In the balance of the first half of the chapter the narrator presents the 'learned investigation of the Letter's sources,'[3] which serves to describe the document in question and sets forth the rules for examining it (107–09). The narrator also produces Belinda the Hen (110–13: these include the bridge between halves) and the Letter upon which the chapter focuses.

The Letter is many things in the *Wake*. Since the Hen disinters it from the cultural midden-heap, it represents Scripture (the manuscript word) dragged up from integral interrelation with the Book of Nature. (In tradition, the Letter *per se* – the literal level – regardless of its content, is the central concern of all grammatical enterprise: 'gramma' is Greek for letters; 'grammar,' literature.) Other versions of the Letter, long and short, appear in different parts of the *Wake*, as do other letters tenuously related to this one (for example, those on 308 and 337), parodies of the Letter, histories of the Letter and its travels, etc. Clive Hart views the Letter as being itself a cultural dump or midden, a microcosm of *Finnegans Wake*:

the wonderfully rich and expressive motif-complex which makes up the Letter must rank first among the many 'expanding symbols' in *Finnegans Wake*. Significantly, it begins with the word 'Reverend' (615.12) – pronounced in popular Irish speech almost exactly like 'riverrun' – and goes on to treat every theme in *Finnegans Wake*, so that it very quickly comes to stand for the book itself. Detailed correspondences proliferate in all directions as the Letter is developed in every conceivable context: it is a french letter which the lewd Shaun introduces into the hermaphroditic pillar-box ('a herm, a pillarbox,' 66.26); 'Every letter is a hard...' (623.33), says Anna, and she is obviously making an allusion to Earwicker's virility as well as to the obscurity of his means of expression; it is any and every letter of the alphabet, which forms yet another cyclic microcosm; interpreted as the agent from the verb 'to let,' it is both a charter of liberty and a source of inhibition for HCE and for all who may read it; it is the 'leader' and the 'latter' – the first and last, Genesis and Revelation; it is the sea itself, source of all: 'The Letter! The Letter!'[4]

While this effusion may seem a bit excessive, nevertheless the significance of the Letter to the grammatical nature of the *Wake* was evident from the earliest drafts in 1923. Hayman points out that 'the most significant single theme of the *Wake* was then the concept of the Word as suggested through the treatment of the "Letter."[5]

There are in fact two principal letters in the *Wake*, linked yet distinct. The much longer one in book IV (615.12–619.19) was composed earlier and, it may be argued, is the one to which most of the *Wake* references (to its genesis, odyssey, etc.) allude. Yet there are sufficient points of contact, references in the Reverend Letter to the one in I.5, to suggest that the earlier letter serves as it were general purposes in the texture of the book and that Belinda's Letter was composed and designed more specifically for the satire of the exegetes and scholars. It is as if Joyce, having settled on a context for the Reverend Letter (which turned out to be book IV of the *Wake*), composed an extension of it for use in I.5. If so, that would explain why he makes no particular effort to differentiate between the two in any of the references to a 'letter.' For example:

The letter! The litter! And the soother the bitther! Of eyebrow pencilled, by lipstipple penned. Borrowing a word and begging the question and stealing tinder and slipping like soap. From dark Rosa Lane a sigh and a weep, from Lesbia Looshe the beam in her eye, from lone Coogan Barry his arrow of song, from Sean Kelly's anagrim a blush at the name, from I am the Sullivan that trumpeting tramp, from Suffering Dufferin the Sit of her Style, from Kathleen May Vernon her Mebbe fair efforts, from Fillthepot Curran his scotchlove machreether, from hymn Op. 2 Phil Adolphos the weary O, the leery, O, from Samyouwill Leaver or Damyouwell Lover thatjolly old molly bit or that bored saunter by, from Timm Finn again's weak tribes loss of strenghth to his sowheel, from the wedding on the greene, agirlies, the gretnass of joyboys ... The solid man saved by his sillied woman. Crackajolking away like a hearse on fire. The elm that whimpers at the top told the stone that moans when stricken. Wind broke it. Wave bore it. Reed wrote of it. Syce ran with it. Hand tore it and wild went war. Hen trieved it and plight pledged peace. It was folded with cunning, sealed with crime, uptied by a harlot, undone by a child. It was life but was it fair? It was free but was it art? The old hunks on the hill read it to perlection. It made ma make merry and sissy so shy and rubbed some shine off Shem and put some shame into Shaun. (93.24–94.12)

In this account of the genesis of the Letter, the Two Books are intertwined and mingle with references to both 'Letters,' Belinda's and ALP's. Additional references occur in the paragraph of PQ's chitchat about the contents of the Letter (457.25–461.32) and in the cryptically abbreviated account of the Letter's travels during Shaun's botched attempts to deliver it (419.21–421.14).

Finally, a few pages following the Reverend Letter in book IV, ALP recollects a brief account of the Letter (either or both principal versions) in terms that suggest an identity of her and Belinda:

And watch would the letter you're wanting be coming may be. And cast ashore. That I prays for be mains of me draims. Scratching it and patching at with a prompt from a primer. And what scrips of nutsnolleges I pecked up me meself. Every letter is a hard but yours sure is the hardest crux ever. Hack an axe, hook an oxe, hath an an, heth hith ences. But once done, dealt and delivered, tattat, you're on the map. Rased on traumscrapt from Maston, Boss. After rounding his world of ancient days. Carried in a caddy or screwed and corked. On his mugisstosst surface. With a bob, bob, bottledby. Blob. When the waves give up yours the soil may for me. Sometime then, somewhere there, I wrote me hopes and buried the page when I heard Thy voice, ruddery dunner, so loud that none but, and left it to lie till a kissmiss coming. (623.29–624.06)

On the whole, ALP's relation to Belinda is mysterious. Like PQ, ALP's specialist *alter ego*, Belinda is an exuberant and relentless matriarch; yet it appears to be ALP's motherhood, always feminine and gentle, that is echoed perversely in the egg-laying, whorish hen (recall that the French word for hen, *poule*, also means whore).

Belinda's Letter takes up less than half of a page of the chapter. It is followed by a paragraph on the photograph and then by material that bridges the two halves. The last of these bridges contains the thunder.

The second half of the chapter presents the exegetes at work. They examine, in turn, the organization of lines (of words) on the page, the type of paper and the various stains on it, the calligraphy, and the signature (or lack of it). Then attention shifts to individual words, and farfetched interpretations (mostly allegorical) ranging from the Freudian to the historical (115–16). Phonetics are considered, as also various artificial languages (Volapük, Universal, etc.), as the exegetes grapple with the Letter's contents. Next (118) they tackle it in terms of grammar and syntax, and, when that yields no profit, they turn (119) to calligraphic cues and thence to the studying individual letters of the alphabet (119–23). All the while, they keep up a steady stream of commentary and conjecture until they finally seize on the ultimate minutiae, the punctuation marks. True to Menippism, few of those examined actually appear in the Letter, so the passage ends up being a sort of philosophy of punctuation with the Letter as the catalyst. The text at this point mimes the learned idiocy of the exegetes in characteristic Cynic fashion. The Letter, it is found,

... was but pierced butnot punctured (in the university sense of the term) by numerous stabs and foliated gashes made by a pronged instrument. These paper wounds, four in type, were gradually and correctly understood to mean stop, please stop, do please stop, and O do please stop respectively, and following up their one true clue, the circumflexuous wall of a singleminded men's asylum, accentuated by bi tso fb rok engl a ssan dspl itch ina, – Yard inquiries pointed out → that they ad bîn 'provoked' ay ∧ fork, of à grave Brofèsor; àth é's Brèak – fast – table; ;acùtelŷ profèššionally *piquéd*, to=introdùce a notion of time [ùpon à plane (?) sù ' ' fàç'e'] by pùnct! ingh oles (sic) in iSpace?! (124.01–12)

Joyce here stops just short of Swift, whose 'hack' narrator in *A Tale of a Tub* drivels on to writing about nothing. However, Joyce lends the satire in this second half of the chapter a gentle touch of authenticity through a second plot.

Like Belinda's Letter, *The Book of Kells* was once retrieved from burial in the earth.[6] Also, like Belinda's Letter, the Irish *Book of Kells* was the object of intense scholarly scrutiny – or 'maddened pedantry,' depending upon one's point of view. Joyce lifted, transplanted, and paraphrased or parodied in the present chapter a great deal of Sir Edward Sullivan's 'introduction' to *The Book of Kells*. As Atherton shows, this part of the chapter is a tapestry of manuscript references.[7] Both his *Books at the 'Wake'* and McHugh's *Annotations* provide sufficient references to manuscripts (and to forgeries: I.5 ends with 'Shem the Penman') to make the point: they also provide references to Joyce's uses of Sullivan's 'introduction' in this chapter.

What made Sullivan's piece attractive to Joyce? In part, it is composed in that vapid and treacly sort of prose that we associate with popular coffee-table books for the masses rather than with serious literature and commentary – the sort written by an overearnest Shaun-the-Post, or by a Shem with tongue in cheek. For the rest, Sullivan's 'introduction' examines its subject as an aesthetic object rather than in terms of its content or its significance for serious art or for perception. Since one effect of the printed book was to divert attention to the manuscript book of the preceding era as a newly envisioned aesthetic object, Sullivan's prose serves Joyce's purposes by providing a ready example of aesthetics masquerading as scholarship.

Menippean Advice to the Reader

Joyce's advice and instruction to the reader in the first part of the chapter are precise and are given in what, at times, lapses into the plainest prose in the *Wake*. Following the inventory of names of ALP's mamafesta, the narrator begins by warning the reader to expect – or to have to provide – multilevel exegesis: 'the proteiform graph itself is a polyhedron of scripture' (107.08). This will call for manuscript-age performance. Immediately, Joyce begins to rally themes:

To the hardily curiosing entomophilust then it has shown a very sexmosaic of nymphosis in which the eternal chimerahunter Oriolopos, now frond of sugars, then lief of saults, the sensory crowd in his belly coupled with an eye for the goods trooth bewilderblissed by their night effluvia with guns like drums and fondlers like forceps persequestellates his vanessas from flore to flore. (107.12–18)

This is perhaps less satire than direct statement about the silliness of approaching a text and its details in the wrong manner. Those who select only the minutiae are like textual entomologists, caught up in, say, the moral behaviour of their subject but missing the general point entirely. Although the interplay of senses bodily and exegetical is of consequence, the necessary 'play' disappears soon under the specialist gaze of a lust-lover ('-philust') to whom 'it has shown a very sexmosaic of nymphosis.' The integral body is turned by the eye into a consumer product ('the goods trooth').

All writing, in this manner, turns into whoring or pornography. This point is important to the theme of the chapter as Belinda the Hen is a 'poule' (Fr slang, whore) involved in reproduction (of manuscripts) as a commodity.[8] Further discussion of the manuscript page, glossed by other 'personalities,' brings back into focus the motifs of the bodily senses and of print/reproduction:

Closer inspection of the *bordereau* would reveal a multiplicity of personalities inflicted on the documents or document and some prevision of virtual crime or crimes might be made by anyone unwary enough before any suitable occasion for it or them had so far managed to happen along. In fact, under the closed eyes of the inspectors the traits featuring the *chiaroscuro* coalesce, their contrarieties eliminated, in one stable somebody similarly as by the providential warring of heartshaker with housebreaker and of dramdrinker against freethinker our social something bowls along bumpily, experiencing a jolting series of prearranged disappointments, down the long lane of (it's as semper as oxhousehumper!) generations, more generations and still more generations. (107.23–35)

The fracturing of exegetical senses results from or mimes that of the senses bodily. Play down the visual sense, thereby letting ear and hand back into play, and the splintered components will reunite. Otherwise, both culture and society will become fragmented by the new thrust of printed, alphabetic, mechanical reproduction. Joyce glosses his text by noting that this sort of thing has happened often: since ox, house, and camel are the meanings of Aleph, Beth, and Gimel, 'it's as semper as oxhousehumper' means 'it's as simple as ABC' and 'it's as common as ABC.' Again, the reader's gaze is directed to the alphabet.

Joyce's next point of attack, the familiar theme of the quest – 'Luckily there is another cant to the questy' (109.01) – is followed by a consideration of the traditional four levels of exegesis. Along the way, he lampoons 'the twelve':

Has any fellow, of the dime a dozen type ... has any usual sort of ornery josser, flatchested fortyish, faintly flatulent and given to ratiocination by syncopation in the elucidation of complications, of his greatest Fung Yang dynasdescendanced, only another the son of, in fact, ever looked sufficiently longly at a quite everydaylooking stamped addressed envelope? Admittedly it is an outer husk: its face, in all its featureful perfection of imperfection, is its fortune: it exhibits only the civil or military clothing of whatever passionpallid nudity or plaguepurple nakedness may happen to tuck itself under its flap. (109.01–12)

The jury of pedant/exegetes, as they are now, is hypnotized by the content of print or printed manuscripts and therefore ignores the several levels of media, whether of alphabet, of paper supplies, or other enveloping facts or services. That this kind of media study calls for grammatical training of critical awareness and for the ability to perform multilevel exegesis, Joyce shows as follows.

The proper 'tuning' or orchestrating of these levels demands a balance of acoustic faculties with visual ones; but the latter, hypnotically intensified, have anaesthetized the jury's other senses. Print gave ascendancy to dialectic and to the Protestant reformers' insistence on literal interpretation. Joyce runs through the senses as he continues: 'Yet to concentrate solely on the literal sense or even the psychological content of any document to the sore neglect of the enveloping facts themselves circumstantiating it is just as hurtful to sound sense (and let it be added to the truest taste) as were some fellow ...' (109.12–15). The literal is seen under two aspects in this passage, an inner one and an outer one: both are parallel. The inner senses are the exegetical ones; outer or bodily vision suppresses attention to hearing (sound sense), taste (*elocutio* and decorum), et al. The figurative sense is commented upon through an analogy of an analogy: '... as were some fellow in the act of perhaps getting an intro from another fellow turning out to be a friend in need of his, say, to a lady of the latter's acquaintance, engaged in performing the elaborative antecistral ceremony of upstheres, straightaway to run off ...' (109.15–19). Visions of the female anatomy provide the moral paradigm while keeping the pervasive themes of whoring and seduction in the background: '... straightaway to run off and vision her plump and plain in her natural altogether, preferring to close his blinkhard's eyes to the ethiquethical fact that she was, after all, wearing for the space of the time being some definite articles of evolutionary clothing, inharmonious creations, a captious critic might describe them as, or not strictly necessary or a trifle irritating here and there, but for all that ...' (109.19–25). The weaving is complex: the nude figure is plain or unadorned in both style and non-literal levels. The spiritual or final level, which transcends the physical text and the physical world in providing 'so very much more,' is here alluded to in the metaphor of clothing: '... but for all that suddenly full of local colour and personal perfume and suggestive, too, of so very much more and capable of being stretched, filled out, if need or wish were, of having their surprisingly like coincidental parts separated don't they now, for better survey by the deft hand of an expert, don't you know?' (109.25–30).

The point being made in this passage is that attending solely to the content of a situation moves the subliminal or unconscious impact of the 'clothing' (the enveloping facts or whole situation) to a peak. As Joyce remarked in an earlier section, 'Yes, the viability of vicinals if invisible is invincible' (81.01). While the pedant/exegete is progressively hypnotized by minutiae, his senses are benumbed and retuned by the clothing of letters (typography and mail), presses, and reproduction ('generations'). Joyce concludes this paragraph by reiterating these concerns in the most straightforward English in the *Wake*: 'Who in his heart doubts either that the facts of feminine clothiering are there all the time, or that the feminine fiction, stranger than the facts, is there also at the same time, only a little to the rere? Or that one may be separated from the other? Or that both may then be contemplated simultaneously? Or that each may be taken up and considered in turn apart from the other?' (109.30–6). In terms of the chapter at hand, the 'clothiering' or 'enveloping facts' of the Letter – the object of attention of Joyce's critics – is composed of Belinda, the fifth thunder, and ALP's feminine influence (evident as the chapter begins). The Letter has hitherto been regarded by commentators merely in terms of its contents, and not *as* letter(s).

The Letter proper is a Menippean production of the first rank. It is, literally, a throwaway – the hen retrieved it from a (kitchen) midden, where it had been blotched by a tea stain. The contents are the wholly banal, innocuous, snobbish chitchat of a society woman. So banal and ambiguous are the contents that some scholars have suggested that the Letter is a microcosm of the *Wake*, or of life in general. They function exactly as a Menippean red herring should: they attract and hold the attention of critics and steer them away from the 'enveloping facts.' They do all this in a chapter that both discusses and displays (via the pedant/exegetes) just that susceptibility.[9] Menippean wit has seldom flown higher.

The Themes of Print and the Photograph

Exegesis of the Letter is withheld until after the thunder. Before it, the Letter is just another cliché manuscript production, abandoned as trash. After the thunder (and the establishment of the printing press), it gets full aesthetic scrutiny and treatment as an *objet d'art* like *The Book of Kells* – a parallel to the condition of manuscript culture before and after print. The tea stain, prophetically, 'marked it off on the spout of the moment as a genuine relique of ancient Irish pleasant pottery of that lydialike languishing class known as a hurry-me-o'er-the-hazy' (111.21–4).[10]

Here, Joyce resumes some older themes related to the wars of the senses and of the sexes, with minor modifications. 'Belinda of the Dorans' (111.05) personifies the printing press (Doubleday and Doran) and a certain mode of reproductiveness or of whorish activity.[11] She is a *poule* – French for hen and for whore. But her reproductivity is specialized, confined to an assembly line of eggs (few of which are allowed to hatch) that become a consumer commodity.

The eggs she lays and the terms on which she lays them serve as oblique comment on the condition of Humpty Dumpty at this stage of cultural development. Humpty Dumpty embodies the integral bodily sensorium and perhaps the exegetical senses as well. He is now completely presided over by the *poule*, mother and matriarch, and he is translated into visual terms – uniform, repeatable, linear assembly-line 'automutativeness.' He lives in an abstract, automated world 'where the hand of man never set foot' (203.15–16). Belinda's excesses make her the supreme matriarch who 'dishorns' (castrates), domesticates, and usurps the formerly male mode of the 'word.' She 'plays the gentleman's part every time':

Lead, kindly fowl! They always did: ask the ages. What bird has done yesterday man may do next year, be it fly, be it moult, be it hatch, be it agreement in the nest. For her socioscientific sense is sound as a bell, sir, her volucrine automutativeness right on normalcy: she knows, she just feels she was kind of born to lay and love eggs (trust her to propagate the species and hoosh her fluffballs safe through din and danger!);

Corrections for galley 62

a. Honeys wore camelia paints. Yours very truthful.
   Add dapple inn.

[N.P.] b. You is feeling like you was lost in the bush, boy ?
        You says : It is a puling sample jungle of
        woods. You most shouts out : Bethicket me
        for a stump of a beech if I have the poul-
        triest notions what the farest he all means.
        Gee up, girly ! The quad gospellers may own
        the targum but any of the Zingari shoolerijm
        may pink a peck of kindlings yet from the
        sack of auld hensyne.

c. She may be a mere marcella, this midget madgetcy,
   Misthress of Arths. B ut. It is not a hear
   or say of some anomorous letter, signed Toga Gi
   rilis, (teasy dear).

d. nosibos. We note the paper with her jotty young
        watermark : Notre Dame du Bon Marché. And
   she has a heart of Arin ! What humililts as she
   ~~~~~~
   fols with her fallimineers and her nadianods. l

e. y weather, health, dangers, public orders and
   other circumstances permitting,

f. a cop of ~~~~~~~~~~~~~~~~~~~~~~~~~~

g. iacht

h. Kapak kapuk. No minzies matter.

i. the plak and the smut,

k. And a little mollvogels.

l. As a strow will shaw she does the wind blague,
   recting to show the rudess of a robur curling and
   shewing the fansaties of a frisette. But how many
   of her readers realise that she is not out to
   dizzledazzle with a graith uncouthrement of post-
   mantuam glasseries from the lapins and the grigs.
   Nuttings on her wilelife ! Grabar gooden grandy,
   for old almeanium adamologists like Dariaumaurius
   and Zovotrimaserovmeravmerouvian; (dmzn !); she fee
   plain plate one flat fact thing and if, lastways
   firdstwise, a man alones sine anyom anyoms utharas
   has no rates to done a kik at with anyon anakars
   about tutus milking fores and the rereres on the
   outerrand asikim the tutus to be forrarder.
   Thingscrooklyexineverypasturesixdixlixencehimaround-
   ~hersthemaggerbykinkinkankanwithdownminds lookingated
   Mesdaims, Marmouselles, Mescerfs ! Silvapais !

m. (yet how palmy date in a waste's oasis !)

Thunder 5
   ~~~~~~

lastly but mostly, in her genesic field it is all game and no gammon; she is ladylike in everything she does and plays the gentleman's part every time. Let us auspice it! Yes, before all this has time to end the golden age must return with its vengeance. Man will become dirigible, Ague will be rejuvenated, woman with her ridiculous white burden will reach by one step sublime incubation, the manewanting human lioness with her dishorned discipular manram will lie down together publicly flank upon fleece. No, assuredly, they are not justified, those gloompourers who grouse that letters have never been quite their old selves again since that weird weekday in bleak Janiveer (yet how palmy date in a waste's oasis!) when to the shock of both, Biddy Doran looked at literature. (112.09–27)

It is not clear whether this language reflects the narrator's irony or is a pandering palaeographer's puff. Chief among the effects of Belinda's insatiable, whorish appetite is her retrieval of old things: she retrieves the manuscript (Letter) and all of 'golden age' culture from obscure burial in the midden, but the terms of retrieval are that the old items have lost their original potency and significance and are now aesthetic objects, museum pieces in a matriarchal 'waxworks' or wax museum.

The thunder bridge between halves of the chapter concludes with a reprise of matriarchy themes: 'Yet is it but an old story, the tale of a Treestone with one Ysold, of a Mons held by tentpegs and his pal whatholoosed on the run, what Cadman could but Badman wouldn't, any Genoaman against any Venis, and why Kate takes charge of the waxworks' (113.18–22).[12] In the 'Triv and Quad' chapter (II.2), Joyce embedded the following verse in the prose:

> And it's time that all paid tribute
>   to this massive mortiality,
>   the pink of punk perfection
>   as photography in mud.[13]
> Some may seek to dodge the gobbet
>   for its quantity of quality
>   but who wants to cheat the choker's
>   got to learn to chew the cud.

(277.33–278.03)

McHugh interprets this verse as equating **m** (for the most part HCE) 'with the horsepicture' in I.5.[14] The photograph is presented immediately after the Letter: it parallels in mechanical-chemical fashion the abstract machine process of the press[15] and also separates the eye from the other senses. The hand-drawn portrait or scene has the same analogical relation to the photo as does the manuscript to the printed book.

Accordingly, Joyce presents the photograph as a subplot that should 'tip' the reader off to what is going on:

Well, almost any photoist worth his chemicots will tip anyone asking him the teaser that if a negative of a horse happens to melt enough while drying, well, what you do get is, well, a positively grotesquely distorted macromass of all sorts of horsehappy values and masses of meltwhile horse. Tip. Well, this freely is what must have occurred to our missive (there's a sod of a turb for you! please wisp off the grass!) unfilthed from the boucher by the sagacity of a lookmelittle likemelong hen. Heated residence in the heart of the orangeflavoured mudmound had partly obliterated the negative to start with, causing some features palpably nearer your pecker to be swollen up most grossly while the farther back we manage to wiggle the more we need the loan of a lens to see as much as the hen saw. Tip. (111.26–112.02)

Letter and photo both serve as a sort of 'photo finish' to the horse/whores race of the last thunder. Both have now been cast up by the mud-mound or dump by the butt of the magazine wall and onto which Humpty Dumpty crashed. Both photo and Letter are litter, and both create and give birth to litter as they process the previous modes (manuscript and painting) and dump them onto the market as goods. Both inject a new aesthetic into reproduction and re-presentation, and both intensify the visual and literal, 'sterilized' of the other senses:

Love through the usual channels, cisternbrothelly, when properly disinfected and taken neat in the generable way upon retiring to roost in the company of a husband-in-law or other respectable relative of an apposite sex, not love that leads by the nose as I foresmellt but canalised love, you understand, does a felon good, suspiciously if he has a slugger's liver but I cannot belabour the point too ardently ... (436.14–20)

The new bias of stress and sense with its new myopic (foreshortened) perspective brings with it a new identity crisis and quest. This time the quest surfaces as a problem of authorship vs. plagiarism. In manuscript culture, authorship is very fluid and lacking in the formal copyright rigidities of the press and of private identity. Before the thunder, Joyce raises the matter:

To conclude purely negatively from the positive absence of political odia and monetary requests that its page cannot ever have been a penproduct of a man or woman of that period or those parts is only one more unlookedfor conclusion leaped at, being tantamount to inferring from the nonpresence of inverted commas (sometimes called quotation marks) on any page that its author was always constitutionally incapable of misappropriating the spoken words of others.

   Luckily there is another cant to the questy. (108.29–109.01)

After the thunder, with the ear firmly suppressed, the palaeographers confront the problem on different terms. The tea stain on the Letter is ambiguously regarded as either a signature or a watermark.

The teatimestained terminal ... is a cosy little brown study all to oneself and, whether it be thumbprint, mademark or just a poor trait of the artless, its importance in establishing the identities in the writer complexus (for if the hand was one, the minds of active and agitated were more than so) will be best appreciated by never forgetting that both before and after the battle of the Boyne it was a habit not to sign letters always. Tip ... So why, pray, sign anything as long as every word, letter, penstroke, paperspace is a perfect signature of its own? A true friend is known much more easily, and better into the bargain, by his personal touch, habits of full or undress, movements, response to appeals for charity than by his footwear, say. (114.29–115.11)

The latter remark seems to be one of the rare asides by the narrator. Joyce confronted the problem in a new way when he first began to experiment with the technique of 'continuous parallels.' Was the result Homer's? What exactly was his obligation to Homer? When he began letting his ear guide his pen, as he did with the *Wake*, the 'problem' evaporated; the audience, the 'man at that table over there' supplied words and rhythms. The writer's job then turned into one of orchestration. Similarly, the 'problem' exists outside but not inside the mimetic Menippean tradition, which tacitly exercises the principle of 'eminent domain' over other Menippists and over all other writers.[16]

   In the continuation of the passage quoted just above, Joyce proceeds to some exegesis of the Letter after dwelling on one of the oldest of Menippean topics, the correspondence of sexual and grammatical terms and interactions. At root is the understanding of speech as a form of oral intercourse (which writing and print have perverted), with the speaker or orator in the dominant position and the audience in a role that is relatively passive, open, and receptive. There are also available a variety of terminological double entendres, for example, 'copular verbs' (verbs are mutable and feminine) and 'conjugation.'[17] In languages that preserve noun genders and inflections, other possibilities are available.[18] Joyce's passage is too rich for paraphrase or descriptive reduction:

... his footwear, say. And, speaking anent Tiberias and other incestuish salacities among gerontophils, a word of warning about the tenderloined passion hinted at. Some softnosed peruser might mayhem take it up erogenously as the usual case of spoons, *prostituta in herba* plus dinky pinks deliberatively summersaulting off her bisexycle, at the main entrance of curate's perpetual soutane suit with her one to see and awoh! who picks her up as gingerly as any balmbearer would to feel whereupon the virgin was most hurt and nicely asking: whyre have you been so grace a mauling and where were you chaste me child? Be who, farther potential? and so wider but we grisly old Sykos who have done our unsmiling bit on 'alices, when they were yung and easily freudened, in the penumbra of the procuring room and what oracular comepression we have had apply to them! could (did we care to sell our feebought silence *in camera*) tell our very moistnostrilled one that *father* in such virgated contexts is not always that undemonstrative relative (often held up to our contumacy) who settles our hashbill for us and what an innocent allabroad's adverb such as Michaelly looks like can be suggestive of under the pudendascope and, finally, what a neurasthene nympholept, endocrine-pineal typus, of inverted parentage with a prepossessing drauma present in her past and a priapic urge for congress with agnates before cognates fundamentally is feeling for under her lubricitous meiosis when she refers with liking to some feeler she fancie's face. And Mm. We could. Yet what need to say? 'Tis as human a little story as paper could well carry ... (115.11–36)

The end of this passage presents the final development of the theme of sterilized reproductivity as humanly perverse: the camera is caricatured as a 'pudendascope.'[19]

Finally, the Letter itself, 'trouved by a poule in the parco' (201.01–02) carries overtones of social revolution and class snobbery. That it is stained by tea and originates from Boston (Mass.) suggests that a tea party of sorts has been in progress:

a goodishsized sheet of letterpaper originating by transhipt from Boston (Mass.) of the last of the first to Dear whom it proceded to mention Maggy well & allathome's health well only the hate turned the mild on *the van* Houtens and the general's elections with a *lovely* face of some born gentleman with a beautiful present of wedding cakes for dear thankyou Chriesty and with grand funferall of poor Father Michael don't forget unto life's & Muggy well how are you Maggy & hopes soon to hear well & must now close it with fondest to the twoinns with four crosskisses for holy paul holey corner holipoli whollyisland pee ess from (locust may eat all but this sign shall they never) affectionate largelooking tache of tch. (111.08–20)

That is the much-debated letter. In the '*van* Houtens' with their 'twoinns' we can discern JvH and PQ and the jiminies, now social upper-crust. The italics give the matriarch's tone a snobbish emphasis. Perhaps thinking of the character in the comic strip 'Bringing up Father,' Joyce nicknamed such ladies 'Maggies' as a diminutive for Margaret, for majesty (she is also a PQ), and for magistrate: they preside over drawing room, house, husband, and 'society,' and lay down the law.[20]

Joyce's helpful exegesis is this: 'that Father Michael about this red time of the white terror equals the old regime and Margaret is the social revolution while cakes mean the party funds and dear thank you signifies national gratitude' (116.07–10). The funeral – or funferall – for the 'old regime' is an aesthetic celebration (for Finnegan as well: this is his wake after all) and retrieval; the same Father Michael performed a *sortes virginianae* fourteen lines earlier 'under the pudendascope': the new regime, involving party politics and civilized matriarchy, has displaced entirely masculine royalty and decorum.

The fifth thunderclap –

Thingcrooklyexineverypasturesixdixlikencehimaroundhersthemaggerbykinkinkankanwithdownmindlookingated (113.09–11)

– resounds with allusions to all of the themes in the chapter, as follows.

Thunder	Interpretation	Theme Sounded
Thi	tea (-stain, -party)	authorship, plagiarism, identity, ownership; snobbery
	thy	individual ownership
	thigh	sex motif
Thin	thine	individual ownership
	tin (-type)	print/photo reproduction
Thing	Nor, tribal council	'old regime' obsolete
Thingcrooklyexineverypasture	think rooks lay eggs in every pasture; or, think quickly, eggs in (or egg-sin) every pasture; or ... eggs in every repast	eggs; published books/ photos; reproduction motif, printed book vs. Book of Nature, machine in the garden, etc.

Thunder	Interpretation	Theme Sounded
hin	hen Gr, *'en*, the one	Belinda: whore/reproduction individualism
ingcr	Fr, *encre*, ink	writing, print
ingcro	in-grow	midden, incest
crook	crook, thief	plagiarism; the cad; 'Stop deef stop…'
	Scottish, *crock*, old sheep a shepherd's staff	'manram' domestication
crookly	Sw, *trycka*, Dan, Nor, *trykke*, print (26L)	print
rook	rook	Belinda (fowl)
ooklya	Ger, *Kuchlein*, chicken (26L)	Belinda, hen, eggs, etc.
klyex	cliques	classes, snobbery, etc.
lyexin	Ger, *lesen*, to read	literacy, visual stress
yex	Fr, *yeux*, eyes	visual stress
exi	essay Lat, *esse*, to be	writing, print identity
exin	Lat, *exin*, from there, thence (ClL)	
xin	sin sign	prostitution/reproduction tea stain, authorship, levels of interpretation
	Du, *zien*, see (26L) Ger, *Sein*, to be	visual stress identity
eve	Eve Sp, *ave*, bird	matriarchy Belinda, et al.

everypast	every past	print retrieval of
		  ancient manuscript
		  culture; midden

	Eve repast (the apple)	the fall, matriarchy,
		  prostitution (cf.
		  'apple harlottes'
		  113.16), reproduction

Thunder	Interpretation	Theme Sounded
er	err	sin, the fall; erring exegetes-palaeographers
	ear	old regime
	Ger, *Eier*, eggs	publishing, Humpty Dumpty
ryp	reap	harvest of old mss
rypa	repay	commercial reproduction
past	past	old regime, retrieval
	post	mail, Letter
pastu	Ger, *Pute*, turkey-hen, conceited woman	Belinda, etc. Boston matriarch-snobs ('culture-vultures')
	Fr Sl, Sp Sl, whore	Belinda whore/reproduction
pastur	pastor	Fr. Michael, old regime
pasture	pasture	midden (fertilizer), machine in the garden
ures	whores	whores
res	raze	destruction of oral, single-level exegesis
resixdi	Sp, *revista*, magazine (26L)	midden (foot of magazine wall); print, photo
six	Sikhs (Indian sect, believes in abolishment of caste system)	oral replaced by class system
sixdix	six dicks (phalluses)	prostitution, reproduction
sixdixl	There are several references to numbers in this thunder, in English and French, and in Roman numerals. They probably allude to the reproduction motif. This particular letter-group contains: sixdix = 6, 10; IX-D-IX-L = 9-500-9-50. There are also several Greek letters, as *rho* and *xi* in -crooklyexin-, and -emagge- (*omega*), which presumably relate to the themes of the Letter, of literacy, of retrieval of ancient mss, and of the palaeographer's concern with letter-minutiae.	

Thunder	Interpretation	Theme Sounded
ixdi	Lat, *iste*, that, of yours	individual ownership/ authorship
dixlik	(fellatio)	whoring, reproduction equipment
ixdix	Lat, *extexo*, to cheat	plagiarism
liken	(similar appearance) Ger, corpses	repetition, waxworks waxworks, funeral (of Fr Michael), old regime
iken	eye-ken (kenning by eye) Gr, *ikon*, image	visual stress photo
ikencehima- roundhers- them	I can see him around her stem (or ... her seam)	whore; visual; pudendascope
enc	ink (Fr, *encre*)	writing, print
ceh	HCE, anagram; see	'womanly man' etc.
cehim	Shem (penman, forger)	Letter, forgery, mss
cehima	camera, cinema	photo, assembly line
cehimaro	chimera: vain/idle fancy	Boston matriarchs, Lydia Languishers (111.22)
	chimera: shade	photo image
mar	mar (damage)	effect of midden on Letter; effect of retrieval; effect of print on senses bodily/exegetical
	mare Fr, *mère*, mother	horse photo, whores... matrix, reproduction
arou	a roué (rogue) Ar, *arous*, bride	debauchery, whoring Eve, matriarchy, PQ
oun	own Ger, *Huhn*, chicken (26L)	authorship/plagiarism Belinda, etc.
undher	under	matriarch (on top); burial (midden, funeral); social classes

Thunder	Interpretation	Theme Sounded
hers	hears	ear
	hers	matriarch, ownership
	hearse	funeral
hersthemagge	her steam engine	whores race; steam presses (printing)
herst	Hearst (William Randolph)	print, presses, reproduction
sthem	Shem	penman, forger, etc.
sthemagger	stem-egger or steam-egger (encourager)	reproduction, presses, eggs
themagger-bykin	the 'magger' Viking	Belinda, matriarch
hem	hen	Belinda
hema	Ger, *Henne*, hen	Belinda
emagge	image	photograph, reproduction
	Gr, *omega*	the last Letter, alphabet, palaeography, etc.
mag	mag(azine)	print, wall/dump
magge	Magi	
magger	major	officer rank (classes)
	Magger: Margaret	'social revolution'
	majesty	matriarch, PQ.
	magistrates	jury of exegetes, palaeographers
agg	egg	Belinda, Humpty Dumpty
gerbyk	garbage	midden-heap
erbyk	her beak	Belinda's retrieval of the Letter
byk	beak: Sl, magistrate	jury of exegetes, palaeographers
	beak: Belinda's 'pecker'	reproduction photo, distortion
bykin	beacon (see Mary Baker Eddy's lighthouse)	Boston matriarchs
	bacon	

Thunder	Interpretation	Theme Sounded
kin	kin (-folk)	reproduction
	Gael, *cinn*, of a head, heads, principal (GaL)	old regime, matriarchy Boston society, etc.
kink	kink	distortion; cf. 'kink in his arts over sense'
kinkinkankan	kin-kin can-can	reproduction, whoring, copulation, 'generation,' publishing; dance of incest/eye feeds on itself
inkinkan	ink in [the] can	presses ready to roll
kank	Ger, *krank*, sick	sex/sense perversion
kankan	[Indian/Hindu], *khan*, affix to a name to indicate superior social status, often that of a village or tribal chief	old regime, Boston society snobbery, matriarchy
anka	Sw, *anka*, duck (26L)	Belinda
an	Ger, *Hahn*, rooster	old regime; fowl
	Ar, *ayn*, eye	visual stress
kanwi	Fi, *kana*, chicken (26L)	Belinda
withdown	Sax, *wittan*, know (specialist)	specialized knowing: senses bodily and exegetical
withdown-mindlookin-gated.	with down-mind	featherbrain exegetes, palaeographers
	mind-looking	visual dominance of senses, ignorant of 'feminine clothiering' environments or 'enveloping facts'
	looking at it	examining minutiae and missing the point, because hypnotized by kin/kin

Thunder	Interpretation	Theme Sounded
		can-can under the 'pudendascope,' i.e., attracted to reproductive technology and careless of its side-effects
dow	Dan, Nor, *due*, pigeon (26L)	Belinda
down	down: feathers	clothing (Belinda's)
ownmi	Gr, *ennumi*, clothing	'clothiering'
ownmind	[one's] own mind	private ego, authorship
indl	Ger dial., *Hendl*, hen, chicken	Belinda
dlookin	Ger, *drücken*, print	print, etc.
loo	Fr, *lu*, read	print, literacy
looki	Fi, *lukea*, read (26L)	print, literacy
lookin	Ger, to peep, to lure	camera voyeur, whore
looking	looking	visual stress
lookingate	look in gate, looking-gate	eyelids: visual stress camera lens, viewfinder, shutter (shutter as gate has to be open to view through a reflex camera); pudendascope
ook	Du, *oog*, eye (26L)	visual stress
king	king	old regime, patriarchy
gate	Fr, *gâteau*, cake	'wedding cakes' (116.09: 'party funds'): politics
ated	ate it edit	(the cake?) consumers publishing

9

The Sixth Thunderclap: The Phoenix Playhouse (*FW* 219–59): Retrieval and Revolution: Exits and Entrancings

And vamp, vamp, vamp, the girls are merchand. The horseshow magnete draws his field and don't the fillyings fly? (246.22–4)

Go in for scribenery with the satiety of arthurs in S.P.Q.R.ish and inform to the old sniggering publicking press and its nation of sheepcopers about the whole plighty troth between them, malady of milady made melodi of malodi, she, the lalage of lyonesses, and him, her knave arrant. (229.07–11)

For a burning would is come to dance inane. Glamours hath moidered's lieb and herefore Coldours must leap no more. Lack breath must leap no more.
… For ever they scent where air she went. While all the fauns' flares widens wild to see a floral's school. (250.16–33)

… we are recurrently meeting em … in cycloannalism, from space to space, time after time, in various phases of scripture as in various poses of sepulture. (254.25–8)

Loud, heap miseries upon us yet entwine our arts with laughters low! (259.07–08)

Material for thunder 6 embraces the first chapter of book II of *Finnegans Wake*. Book I contains eight chapters and the first five thunders; book II, four chapters and thunders 6, 7, and 8. Book III also contains four chapters, and the last pair of thunders. Book IV is but a single chapter. As will be discussed later, the four books follow the pattern of the four grammatical levels of exegesis.

wruch up in a hurly wurly
where he huddly could wruddle
to wallow his wey tilbay of the
bager's booth to beg of ill
widdiddy Itchin the price of a
prate of bakin for wold Forrester
Farley who was found of the sound
of the round of the round of the bound of the
Bang!
    Lukkedoerendunandurraschindi
looshoofermoyportertooryzooy
sphalnabortansporthaokansakroidverjkapakkapuk
Rutrwazybunkeros...

Thunder 6: first cut: 114 letters

The Prelude to Thunder 6

Most of the chapters of book I deal with a character: chapter 1 presents the demise of Finnegan and the pranks of PQ (the daughter, Izzy), and also the dialogue between Mutt and Jute. Chapter 2 presents HCE. The chapter that follows Belinda and thunder 5 is structured as a classic epyllion. It is formed as a catechism of twelve questions and answers (cf. the jury of twelve), and the penultimate answer is interrupted by an extended digression – eighteen or more pages – or rather a cluster of digressions. They include remarks by an anthropologist, Professor Loewy-Brueller (Lévy Bruehl), the fable of 'The Mookse and The Gripes' (152–8: satiric riposte to Wyndham Lewis's remarks on *Ulysses* in *Time and Western Man*), a novelette personified as Nuvoletta (yet another facet of PQ), and a butter-and-cheese version of Shem and Shaun as Burrus and Caseous.

The seventh chapter of book I is devoted entirely to the most Menippean member of the HCE family, Shem the Penman. Whatever their surface differences – and they were legion – this personage shows how Joyce's and Lewis's theories of the convergence of serious art and satire parallel each other. Among others, R.C. Elliott has pointed out (225ff.) how Lewis saw serious art as essentially satiric and therapeutic: Lewis's idea was also essentially Menippean. Shem the Penman is in part a persona for Joyce; Shaun, for Joyce's 'well-behaved' brother Stanislaus (cf. 'Stainusless,' 237.11). As he is a figure of The Artist in the *Wake*, Shem may be seen as embodying Joyce's theory of art.

Shem is a forger in both senses: he 'forges in the smithy' of his soul his works of art, and they are all forgeries and fakes (things made). And Shem, a gifted mime, as a successful forger must be, has a Menippean taste for the low and motley. He, 'Vulgariano[,] did but study with stolen fruit how cutely to copy all their various styles of signature so as one day to utter an epical forged cheque on the public ...' (181.15–16). This could easily be a reference to the epic *Ulysses* with its *tours-de-force* of 'stolen' styles. In any case, one large dimension of the Menippean 'tradition,' as Korkowski has shown in detail, is mimetic forging and reforging and updating of others' works. At the same time, Menippean digressiveness accords with the *olio* of a *satura lanx* heaped with an indecorous volume and variety of foods:

Shem was a sham and a low sham and his lowness creeped out first via foodstuffs. So low was he that he preferred Gibsen's teatime salmon tinned, as inexpensive as pleasing, to the plumpest roeheavy lax or the friskiest parr or smolt troutlet that ever was gaffed between Leixlip and Island Bridge and many was the time he repeated in his botulism that no junglegrown pineapple ever smacked like the whoppers you shook out of Ananias' cans, Findlater and Gladstone's, Corner House, Englend. None of your inchthick blueblooded Balaclava fried-at-belief-stakes or juicejelly legs of the Grex's molten mutton or greasilygristly grunters' goupons or slice upon slab of luscious goosebosom with lump after load of plumpudding stuffing all aswim in a ... (170.25–36)

The Rabelaisian inventory of Shem's food continues for most of the next page and smacks of Trimalchio's banquet in *Satyricon*. Shem's celebrated lowness – 'Talk abut lowness! Any dog's quantity of it visibly oozed out thickly from this dirty little blacking beetle' (171.29–31) – is due to his Cynic, doggish sense of indecorum. This, his Menippean sense of decorum, most often shows up in his wit as a punster: 'Shun the Punman!' (93.13). Artistic forging (and Menippean mimesis) is, of course, a form of pun.

The last chapter of book I is the famous ALP chapter. She appears, hendiadys-fashion, from the interchange of the 'washers at the ford,' two washerwomen on opposite banks of the Liffey scrub and wring out clothes (PQ!). The riverflow of their speech across and about the literal river is adorned by thousands of references to water, flow, and banks, and names many hundreds of the world's rivers. As both chapter and book I end, dusk, the moment of metamorphosis, arrives. The women themselves, who have been scrubbing and airing HCE's and ALP's laundry in public, fade and turn into an elm tree and a stone, straddling the river (clothes: PQ/Izzy/Isolde; tree/stone: Tristan).

Three of the four chapters of book II are constructed as epyllia, that is, with some sort of major plot interrupted by one or more large digressions. Chapter 2, 'Triv. and Quad.,' uses left and right marginalia and footnotes, except for a six-page digression on Shem. Chapter 3, with the seventh and eighth thunders, is a series of allegories of electricity, or tales and episodes amid interludes, all of them digressions. It ends with an account of King Roderick O'Conor, 'the last pre-electric king of Ireland' (380.12–13). Chapter 4 is about 'mamalujo,' the four (MAtthew, MArk, LUke, JOhn) gospellers, masters, senses or levels, and elements; it too contains a digression, on Tristan and Isolde.

Book II, chapter 1, 'The Phoenix Playhouse,' was long in production from its planning in 1926[1] to its publication in June 1934.[2] The bulk of the chapter was written from 1930 to 1932, and caused Joyce the greatest difficulty, 'partly due to a desire to write a stylistically advanced first draft.'[3] This section comprises roughly pages 222–46; the balance was 'added late,'[4] and was composed as Joyce revised the central section for publication. This 'balance' consists of the closing pages (which include thunder 6: 246–59) and the *dramatis personae* of the opening pages (219–22), which evoke the theatrical ground of 'The Mime of Mick, Nick and the Maggies' performed in the Playhouse. The nature of these two groups of material, the core and the end-pieces, suggests that Joyce, having written the former with one purpose in mind, decided to co-opt it as thunder material shortly before publication.[5] Our attention in the following discussion will, therefore, focus more on the end-pieces than on the core section.

The Context of Thunder 6

The ten thunders of the *Wake* can be arranged into two groups of five. The first group deals with the dissociation of sensibilities and the matriarchal reign of the eye over the other, subjugated, senses. The reciprocal movement is enacted in thunders 6 to 10. Unlike the other nine thunders, which have a focus in a particular character or technology, the sixth is a general reprise of the theme of retrieval and reawakening. The Phoenix does not itself participate in the action or 'play' in the Playhouse but simply stands as a symbol of Playhouse activity, the nightly coming-to-life of the stage and mummers and their consummation in the 'fire' of the footlights. Now, the night is the night of the *Wake*, the night of the senses subdued by the queenly eye, the night of the sleeping giant; but the Playhouse turns night into day so that various of these elements can rise again, foreshadowing on the stage their resurrection and reunification in the four thunders to come. The mythical phoenix was consumed and revivified every five or six hundred years; the Playhouse begins following Belinda's thunder (500 letters in the first five thunders) and ends after the sixth thunder (a total of 600 letters).

The play presented in the Phoenix Playhouse is 'The Mime of Mick, Nick and the Maggies'; that is, the mode of action is mime, participatory mimesis. The title characters are an angelic Shaun (as Mick: St Michael), a devilish Shem (as Nick, 'Old Nick': the devil), and the 'majesties' or matriarchs: PQ and her lunar entourage of colours (of the rainbow: 4 x 7) or flowers of rhetorical ornamentation.[6] The action played on the stage is the dance of seduction, the battle-royal of the sexes and senses as the twenty-eight attempt to entice first Glugg[7] and then Chuff (Shaun). Of course, they fail with the former and succeed with the latter. This action occupies the central portion of the chapter (the part written first: pages 222–45), and it ends with a moon-rise. (The significance of the moon will be discussed in chapter 11 in the remarks on thunder 8.) But as the action of this passage is mime, the senses involved are phatic, tactile, and kinetic; the sense reborn by the thunder 6 is the ear, with overtones of participation by the other senses. This reversal is implicit in the mime form itself; hitherto, thundering environmental pressure has increasingly intensified the visual sense, with the other senses (suppressed, reordered, controlled) as aesthetic content.

The front-piece that Joyce wrote to convert the central portion to Playhouse use has three components, all of which form a playbill of sorts. First (219.13–33, below) is an introduction to the Playhouse and to the mime; second is an annotated list of the characters (219.34–21.16), followed by a curious passage that is partly introduction to the chapter and partly synopsis of it (221.1–2.21). The chapter opens thus:

Every evening at lighting up o'clock sharp and until further notice in Feenichts Playhouse. (Bar and conveniences always open, Diddlem Club douncestears.) Entrancings: gads, a scrab; the quality, one large shilling. Newly billed for each wickeday perfumance. Somndoze massinees. By arraignment, childream's hours, expercatered. Jampots, rinsed porters, taken in token. With nightly redistribution of parts and players by the puppetry producer and daily dubbing of ghosters, with the benediction of the Holy Genesius Archimimus and under the distinguished patronage of their Elderships the Oldens from the four coroners of ... [catalogue of names] ... while the Caesar-in-Chief looks. On. Sennet. As played to the Adelphi by the Brothers Bratislavoff (Hyrcan and Haristobulus), after humpteen dumpteen revivals. Before all the King's Hoarsers with all the Queen's Mum. And wordloosed over seven seas crowdblast in cellelleneteutoslavzendlatinsoundscript. In four tubbloids. While fern may cald us until firn make cold. *The Mime of Mick, Nick and the Maggies*, adopted from the Ballymooney Bloodriddon Murther by Bluechin Blackdillain (authorways 'Big Storey'), featuring: ... (219.13–33: the last word introduces the cast of characters).

Elements of the next thunders are presented here, from the reference to Mack Sennett (silent movies) to the Babel of languages that is radio in the compressed 'minor thunder' of Celtic-Hellenic-Teutonic-Slavic-Zend-Latin-Sanskrit. The Playhouse as such provides several themes. It links the theme of the phoenix to the diurnal cycle, to the 'lighting up' of the phoenix fire as well as the street lamps outside at dusk (a borderline time of transition between states of day and dark) and to the 'burning would' of innovation. The Playhouse itself is the mind of man, seduced in his sleep (ignorance) by bewitching and entrancing dream girls. Exits and entrances – entrancings – are a key to this play-within-a-play chapter.[8]

The cast of characters includes, naturally, all of the principal figures of the *Wake*. In addition to Glugg and Chuff (Shem and Shaun),[9] PQ and her twenty-eight are recast as

(b) (The nurse'll give it you, stickypots!
And you wait, my lasso, feckseug the
twine!)
(a) (You'll catch it, oon't fret, Mrs Themmy
Lapstin! Come indoor, scoffynosey, and shed your
swank!)
of a morning arley and he met
with a plattonem blondes named
Hips and Haws and fell in with a
fellows of Trinity some header Skowood Shaws like auld Daddy Deacon
who could stow well his place of
beacon but he never could hold
his kerosene's candle to bold Farmer
Burleigh who wuck up in a hurlywurly where he huddly could
wuddle to wallow his weg tillbag
of the baker's booth to beg of illed
Diddiddy Achin for the prize of a
pease of bakin for Wold Forrester
Farley who was found of the round
of the sound of the lound of the
Lukkedoerendunandurraskewdy-
looshoofermoyportertooryzooysph-
alnabortansakroidverjkapakkapuk.
Byfall.
Upploud!
The play thou schouwburgst,
Game, here endeth. The curtain
drops by deep request. [A]

(d) (Ah, crabeyes, I have you, shsuring off
to the world with that gapse in your
stocking!)
(c) (You're well held now, Missy Cheekspeer,
and your panto's off! Fie, for shame,
Ruth Wheatacre, after all the boox
said!)

[a] with a pinch of the paunch of the pouch
in jurys

[b] , in dispenation of deispiration at the
diaspipration of his diasperation,

THE FLORAS (Girl Scouts from St. Bride's Finishing Establishment, demand acidulateds), a month's bunch of pretty maidens who, while they pick on her, their pet peeve, form with valkyrienne licence the guard for

IZOD (Miss Butys Pott, ask the attendantess for a leaflet), a bewitching blonde who dimples delightfully and is approached in loveliness only by her grateful sister reflection in a mirror, the cloud of the opal ... (220.03–10)

ALP is cast, in a role redolent of PQ, as Ann Corio,[10] the famous stripper:

ANN (Miss Corrie Corriendo, Grischun scoula, bring the babes, Pieder, Poder and Turtey, she mistributes mandamus monies, after perdunamento, hendrud aloven entrees, pulcinellis must not miss our national rooster's rag), their poor little old mother-in-lieu, who is woman of the house playing opposite to

HUMP (Mr Makeall Gone, read the sayings from Laxdalesaga in the programme about King Ericus of Schweden and the spirit's whispers in his magical helmet), cap-a-pipe with watch and topper, coat, crest and supporters, the cause of all our grievances, the whirl, the flash and the trouble, who, having partially recovered from a recent impeachment due to egg everlasting, but throughandthoroughly proconverted, propounded for cyclological, is, studding sail once more, jibsheets and royals ... (220.19–31)

As HUMP, HCE is cast in his early role as the hunchbacked transitional Finnegan, still more civil than tribal perhaps, but with the tribal element once more becoming prominent in his makeup. The remaining dramatis personae include Kate (the maid/made of all work) and the jury of twelve, who here parallel the FLORAS: 'THE CUSTOMERS (Components of the Afterhour Courses at St. Patricius' Academy for Grownup Gentlemen, consult the annuary, coldporters sibsuction), a bundle of a dozen of representative locomotive civics, each inn quest of outings' (221.01–04). They are the bureaucratic mob as customers in HCE's public house, robotized ('locomotive') and questing for technological novelties – 'inn quest of outings,' that is, new extensions.

Concluding the front piece is a developmental paragraph that, while it discusses miscellaneous credits and phoenix-like themes, has little to do with the chapter's central section. It begins:

Time: the pressant.
With futurist onehorse balletbattle pictures and the Pageant of Past History

worked up with animal variations amid everglaning mangrovemazes and beorb-tracktors by Messrs Thud and Blunder. Shadows by the film folk, masses by the good people. Promptings by Elanio Vitale. (221.17–22)

Joyce saw in Bergson's irrationalist philosophy a revival of the previsual acoustic awareness both of time as structured by interval (duration) and of being.[11] Certainly, it is the ear that at the conclusion of this chapter rises anew. The paragraph ends:

The whole thugogmagog, including the portions understood to be oddmitted as the results of the respective titulars neglecting to produce themselves, to be wound up for an afterenactment by a Magnificent Transformation Scene showing the Radium Wedding of Neid and Moorning and the Dawn of Peace, Pure, Perfect and Perpetual, Waking the Weary of the World. (222.14–20)

Much of what is promised here will not occur in the 'Mime' so much as in the last thunders taken together, except in so far as the Playhouse is emblematic of the resurrection motif.

Of the end-piece written just before first publication, the first pages continue the action of the central portion – the game of 'colours' or 'angels and devils.' At 248, PQ is reintroduced surrounded by the FLORAS, and she holds the stage for several pages. Then (253ff.) Finnegan begins to rise again, setting off a welter of retrievals and revivals:

... Finnfinn the Faineant ... and we are recurrently meeting em, par Mahun Mesme, in cycloannalism, from space to space, time after time, in various phases of scripture as in various poses of sepulture. Greets Godd, Groceries! Merodach! Defend the King! Hoet of the rough throat attack but whose say is soft but whose ee has a cute angle, he whose hut is a hissarlik even as her hennin's aspire. And insodaintily she's a quine of selm ashaker while as a murder of corpse when his magot's up he's the best berrathon sanger in all the aisles of Skaldignavia. As who shall hear. (254.20–34)

Grammatical retrievals are included:

... peel your peeps! And try to saviourise the nights of labour to the order of our blooding worold! While Pliny the Younger writes to Pliny the Elder his calamolumen of contumellas, what Aulus Gellius picked on Micmacrobius and what Vitruvius pocketed from Cassiodorus. Like we larnt from that Buke of Lukan in Dublin's capital, Kongdam Coombe. (255.17–22)

With 'cycloannalism' and the last reference, to 'kingdom come,' as well as with the time reversals involved in the plagiarism above, it appears that the new world being ushered in is one of cyclic simultaneity, one free of the strait-jacket of sequence. Immediately, Vico, 'the producer (Mr John Baptister Vickar)' (255.27), tries to create a diversion by putting 'the cutletsized consort' PQ on stage again, but the ploy fails and the pace quickens as the 'Mime' moves towards its dénouement, thunderous applause:

Home all go. Halome. Blare no more ramsblares, oddmund barkes! And cease your fumings, kindalled bushies! And sherrigoldies yeassymgnays; your wildeshaweshowe moves swiftly sterneward! For here the holy language. Soons to come. To pausse. (256.11–15)

The 'burning would' of 'kindalled bushies' is put out, now replaced by a phoenix-fire of rebirth, retrieval, and renewal. *Exeunt omnes* of the visual while the burgeoning ear-world crowds onstage from the wings:

For they are now tearing, that is, teartoretorning. Too soon are coming tasbooks and goody, hominy bread and bible bee, with jaggery-yo to juju-jaw, Fine's French phrases from the Grandmère des Grammaires and bothered parsenaps from the Four Massores, Mattatias, Marusias, Lucanias, Jokinias, and what happened to our eleven in thirtytwo antepostdating the Valgur Eire and why is limbo where is he and what are the sound waves saying ceased ere they all wayed wrong and Amnist anguished axes Collis and where fishngaman fetched the mongafesh from and whatfor paddybird notplease rancoon and why was Sindat sitthing on him sitbom like a saildior, with what the doc did in the doil, not to mention define the hydraulics of common salt and, its denier crid of old provaunce ... (256.17–29)

As the new mode is established, the frenetic exits and entrances begin to assume a definite geometry or pattern:

While, running about their ways, going and coming, now at rhimba rhomba, now in trippiza trappaza, pleating a pattern Gran Geamatron showed them of gracehoppers, auntskippers and coneyfarm leppers, they jerrilied along ... (257.03–06)

There follow five exempla of the new pattern; the third, for example, begins thus:

... bold Farmer Burleigh who wuck up in a hurlywurly where he huddly could wuddle to wallow his weg tillbag of the baker's booth to beg of (You're well held now, Missy

cap, lou Dariou beside la Matieto, all boy more all girl singout-
feller longa house blong store Huddy, whilest nin nin nin nin that
Boorman's clock a winny on the tinny side ninned nin nin nin
nin, about old Father Barley how he got up of a morning arley
and he met with a plattonem blondes named Hips and Haws and
fell in with a fellows of Trinity some header Skowood Shaws like
(You'll catch it, don't fret, Mrs Tummy Lupton! Come indoor,
Scoffynosey, and shed your swank!) auld Daddy Deacon who
could stow well his place of beacon but he never could hold his
kerosene's candle to (The nurse'll give it you, stickypots! And you
wait, my lasso, fecking the twine!) bold Farmer Burleigh who
wuck up in a hurlywurly where he huddly could wuddle to wallow his weg tillbag of the baker's booth to beg of (You're well
held now, Missy Cheekspeer, and your panto's off! Fie, for shame,
Ruth Wheatacre, after all the booz said!) illed Diddiddy Achin
for the prize of a pease of bakin with a pinch of the panch of the
ponch in jurys for (Ah, crabeyes, I have you, showing off to the
world with that gape in your stocking!) Wold Forrester Farley
who, in deesperation of deispiration at the diasporation of his
diesparation, was found of the round of the sound of the lound
of the Lukkedoerendunandurraskewdylooshoofermoyportertoo-
ryboysphalnabortansaktroidverjkapakkapuk.
Byfall.
    Upploud!
The play thou schouwburgst, Game, here endeth. The curtain
drops by deep request.
    Uplouderamain!
Gonn the gawds, Gunnar's gustspells. Fionia is fed up with
Fidge Fudgesons. Sealand snorres. Rendningrocks roguesreck-
ning reigns. Gwds with gurs are gttrdmmrng. Hlls vlls. The timid
hearts of words all exeomnosunt. Mannagad, lammalelouh, how
do that come? By Dad, youd not heed that fert! Fulgitudes ejist
rowdownan tonuout. Quoq! And buncskleydoodle! Kidoosh!
Of their fear they broke, they ate wind, they fled; where they
ate there they fled; of their fear they fled, they broke away.
Go to, let us extol Azrael with our harks, by our brews, on
our jambses, in his gaits. To Mezouzalem with the Dephilim,

Thunder 6: galleys, 1938, last insertion: 89 letters brought up to 100

Cheekspeer, and your panto's off! Fie, for shame, Ruth Wheatacre, after all the booz said!) ... (257.17–21)

All five present a bucolic male figure who becomes entangled with a PQ and who seems now to have returned to his senses. The fifth culminates in the thunder:

Wold Forrester Farley who, in deesperation of deispiration at the diasporation of his diesparation, was found of the round of the sound of the lound of the. Lukkedoeren ... [thunder] ... kkapuk. (257.24–8)

Peter Myers shows how the sounds in this section begin to spiral towards a climax reached by the thunder:

In terms of mimesis 'pinch of the panch of the ponch' suggests a revolving towards the climactic 'found of the round of the sound of the lound of the.' (257.26–7) which is cut off by the thunderclap. This may well be heard as the ringing of a bell before a door shuts out the sound. In musical terms there is a strong feeling of accelerando, which results from a replacing of the Ferris-wheel-slow recurrence of the 'Father Barley/Daddy Deacon' rhymes by the rapidly recurring 'found/round/ sound' rhymes. The slamming of the door is the final stuttering chord of a musical piece.

Sound is working in context to heighten meaning and to become an auditory illustration of it. But because the auditory suggestion of the cyclical is so strong the sound becomes bound up with the meaning, and becomes an essential subject for interpretation.[12]

The thunder is a 'round of sound' of applause, of the curtain crashing down, of the patrons from 'the gods' (gallery) exiting from the Playhouse, and of the closing of the Playhouse doors. More particularly, as a Playhouse that presents nightly (cyclic) performances and mimetic revivals, it 'shuts the door' on the visual era of strict sequence. The thunder is followed by more applause (Ger, *Byfall*) and the raising up-loud of the ear:

Byfall.
Upploud!
The play thou schouwburgst, Game, here endeth. The curtain drops by deep request.
Uplouderamain! (257.29–33)

'Loud' is also 'Lord,' a respectful address to a god. The epithet occurs frequently in the page and a half remaining of the chapter:

I hear, O Ismael, how they laud is only as my loud is one. (258.13)

Uplouderamainagain! (258.19)

Loud, hear us!

Loud, graciously hear us! (258.25–26)

O Loud, hear the wee beseech of thees of each of these thy unlitten ones! Grant sleep in hour's time, O Loud! (259.03–04)

Loud, heap miseries upon us yet entwine our arts with laughters low! (259.07–08)

With the desacralizing influence of the visual and rational displaced, the way is clear for the age of the gods – Finnegan included – to return. This last section, following the thunder, is replete with parodies of and paraphrases from the Old Testament, with Hebrew words and phrases, and with references and allusions to *The Egyptian Book of the Dead*, to Teutonic and Scandinavian mythology among other things, and even to Masonic rituals.[13] Because of its orality, even the telephone is mentioned, with a Carrollian fillip:

For the Clearer of the Air from on high has spoken in tumbuldum tambaldam to his tembledim tombaldoom worrild and, moguphonoised by that phonemanon, the unhappitents of the earth have terrerumbled from fimament unto fundament and from tweedledeedums down to twiddledeedees. (258.20–4)

We also hear in this passage a number of after-rumbles of the thunder. Peter Myers remarks that the 'effect of hearing a particular instrument dominate a passage of orchestral music is genuinely akin to the effect of hearing a predominance of one phoneme in a passage of literature. And sometimes Joyce sets, as it were, a particular paragraph for a particular group of instruments.'[14] In the last paragraph quoted, the instruments are nasals. Myers comments:

There are eighteen 'm's (I am assuming that in this case a double 'm' indicates a sustained /m/) and sixteen 'n's in this passage from the Mime, these giving it a continuous background drone to suggest the rumbling. The main presence is Tem; but the use of the nasals is rather like the Tibetan mystic formula *Om mani padme hum*.

There, the nasals are to be sustained, and I believe Joyce's passage invites the reader to dwell longer than usual on them, thereby creating a definite musical accompaniment in the background. The piece certainly benefits from such a rendition. It may sound artificial when a human imitates a musical instrument, but it really ought to be the other way round. In performance the artificiality has, in any case, an appropriate humorous effect; for since the whole of the Mime is, from one angle, a piece of amateur theatricals the human production of sound effects is precisely what an audience should expect.

The use of the nasals as phonemic instruments is, in the above, both musical and mimetic. The highly selective use of phonemes is of orchestral interest; but the 'orchestra' is clearly used to suggest a background rumbling of thunder.[15]

The sixth thunder –

Lukkedoerendunandurraskewdylooshoofermoyportertooryzooysphalnabortansporthaokansakroidverjkapakkapuk (257.27–8)

– sounds all of the themes and structural metaphors involved in the Phoenix Playhouse chapter.

Thunder	Interpretation	Theme Sounded
Luk	look	visual waning (content of 'mime')
Lukke	Loki	tribal gods return
	Dan, *lykke*, good fortune	tribal gods return
	Dan, *lukket*, closed (26L)	door; entrance/exit; doors of perception close on the visual, open for ear
	Dan, Nor, *ulykke*, accident (26L)	thunder/cataclysm
	Fi, *leikkia*, to play (26L)	Playhouse, mime, mummers
Lukkedoer	lock the door	doors, etc.
	Dan, *luk døren*, shut the door (SE)	shut the door
doe	Dan, Nor, *due*, pigeon (26L)	phoenix

Thunder	Interpretation	Theme Sounded
doeren	Dorans (Belinda of the)	matriarchy
oere	Ar, *houri*	PQ and the 28 temptresses
oerend	era end	waning of visual; phoenix
eren	Erin, erring, ear-ring	return of oral (with overtones of PQ tale)
rendunan–durrass	rending of the rocks (Ragnarok)	twilight/dawn of the gods
endunan–durrass	Ger, ending others	waning of visual
duna	It, woman	ALP, PQ and 28
unan	inane	'Tor a burning would is come to dance inane' (250.16)
dunandurrass	Gael, *dun an doras*, shut the door (GaL)	doors, etc.
nan	Nan/Ann	ALP/Ann Corio (Corio is here a PQ-temptress: her strip dance and parade are a 'horseshow' (cf. 246.22–4) or whore-show; the horse-race over, the rest is for show, for aesthetic retrieval
dur	Du, *duur*, Sw, *dörr*, Dan, Nor, *dør*, door (26L)	doors, etc.
urras	Eros houris	temptresses temptresses
aske	Sw, *äska*, thunder (26L) Aske: in Norse myth, the first man (McH, 320)	thunder Finnegan (on the rise)
askew	askew	old order (visual)
kew	cue	stage, Playhouse
kewd	cute	PQ/IZOD (beauty spot)

Thunder	Interpretation	Theme Sounded
	Fr, *coudre*, to sew	clothes, matriarchy
kewdy	cutie	PQ, Corio, the FLORAS
kewdyloosho	Ital, *chiudi l'uscio*, shut the door	doors, etc.
loos	Anita Loos (wrote *Gentlemen Prefer Blondes*)	PQ/IZOD – 'a bewitching blonde' (220.07–08); the first of the five exempla of the new pattern, 'Old Father Barley ... met with a plattonem blondes' (257.10–11)
looshoofer	Lucifer ('Old Nick')	Shem as the devil; the 'mime'
hoofer	(Stage slang) dancer	Playhouse, mummer
oofer	Ar, *asfour*, bird	phoenix
ofermo	inferno	phoenix-fire, burning would, regeneration
fermoyporte	Fr, (*fermes la porte*) close the door	doors, etc.
moy	Fr, *mois*, month	FLORAS: 'a month's bunch'
moypor	Fr, *mon père*	HUMP
oy	Fr, *oeil*, eye Fr, *oie*, goose	waning of visual phoenix
porte	Sp, *puerta*, Port, Ital, *porta*, Gr, *porta*, door	doors, etc.
porter	kind of beer, served to the porter (carrier) porter: doorkeeper	CUSTOMERS (in the pub) Finnegan, with hod doors, etc.
or	whore Ger, *Ohr*, ear	PQ and the 28 ear again

Thunder	Interpretation	Theme Sounded
tert	tart (whore)	PQ and the 28
toor	Ger, *Tur*, door tour	doors, etc. 'recirculation': revival of ear-mode, of phoenix
ooryz	houris	FLORAS, the 28
oryzo	orisons (prayer)	return of gods-age
ryz	Ger, giant rise	Finn again, sleeping giant return of gods
yzooys	Jesus (Gla)	return of gods
zoo	Gr, *zôon*, animal, living being (ClL)	
zooy	Gr, *zoe*, life	phoenix regeneration; revival of ear
zooys	Zeus (Gla)	return of gods
oysphal	eyes fail	waning of visual

ysphalnabort	he's following a bird	the sleeping giant revives,
		    after the manner of the
		    phoenix (or post-Belinda)

sphal	spell	bewitching IZOD; entrancings
sphalna	Gr, *sphalma*, a stumble, false step; failure (ClL)	waning of visual
sphalnabortan	MGr, *sphalna portan*, shut the door (McH)	doors, etc.
phalnabort	alphabet (Gla)	waning of visual
phalnabortans	fallen importance failed abortion	waning of visual phoenix revives
abor	a bore a boor	Shaun Shem
abortans	abortions	Belinda's mode (sterile reproduction), waning

Thunder	Interpretation	Theme Sounded
borta	Fr, Ital, Port, Gr, door porter	doors, etc. HUMP; beer
tans	Ger, *Tanz*, dance	'dance inane'; see hoofer, above
ansportha	Ital, *ancora*, again	renewal, retrieval, phoenix
sport	sport, game	angels and devils
sporthaok	Sl, *sport the oak*, shut the door	doors, etc.
portha	porter	HUMP; beer
orthao	Gr, *ortho–*, right, correct	renewal; end of imbalance
haok	Ger, *Haut*, skin	Corio, stripper; temptress
aokan	Ger, *Augen*, eyes Ger, *oben*, above, on high	waning of visual return of gods
kansakroid	consecrate	return of gods
ansak	Ger, *Ansicht*, opinion	private consciousness (waning)
sakroidver	R, *zakroi dver*, shut the door (McH)	doors, etc.
sakroidverj	Fr, *sacre Vierge*, Holy Virgin	return of gods, of sacred
akro	Gr, *akros*, extreme	reversal of eye/ear
kro	crow	birds: Belinda/phoenix
roi	Fr, *roi*, king	return of patriarchal
oid	Ar, *youid*, repeat	phoenix cycle, various recirculations
oidver	Dan, *uvejr*, storm, rough weather	thunder
dver	R, *dver*, Cz, *dvere*, dor (26L)	doors, etc.
verj	verge (edge)	transition/border between states (ear/eye)
kapakka	Fi, *kapakka*, tavern (McH)	HUMP/HCE is 'engaged in entertaining in his pilgrimst customhouse' (220.34–5) the

Thunder	Interpretation	Theme Sounded
		twelve CUSTOMERS; the pilgrimage is a quest (for grail/ beer/identity – another reading for the references to Porter in the thunder) and the movement back to the oral mode (to visit the sleeping giant).
kapakkapuk	[onomatopoeia] clapping, applause 'upplouds' Turk, *kapiyi kapat*, shut the door (McH)	Playhouse, applause expels the old from the stage; thunder doors, etc.
kapuk	Lat, *caput*, head, leader Ger, *Kaput*, over, finished	Finn again; return of gods end of visual reign
puk	Gael, *púca*, hobgoblin Gael, *poc*, sharp blow Dan, *pukkel*, hump	giant (sleeping) thunderclap HUMP

The Seventh Thunderclap: Radio: tribalbalbutience: Hams and Eggs (*FW* 305–15ff)

A talor would adapt his caulking trudgers on to any shape at see. Address deceitfold of wovens weard. (375.34–5)

In the buginning is the woid, in the muddle is the sounddance and thereinofter you're in the unbewised again, vund vulsyvolsy. You talker dunsker's brogue men we our souls speech obstruct hostery. Silence in thought! Spreach! Wear anartful of outer nocense! Pawpaw, wowow! (378.29–33)

… the ear of Fionn Earwicker aforetime was the trademark of a broadcaster with wicker local jargon for an ace's patent (Hear! Calls! Everywhair!) then as to this radiooscillating epiepistle to which, cotton, silk or samite, kohol, gall or brickdust, we must ceaselessly return … (108.21–5)

Hams, circuitise! Shemites, retrace! (552.08–09)

– All ears did wag, old Eire wake as Piers Aurell was flappergangsted. (496.15–16)

In general outline, thunder 7 and its context are an uncomplicated matter: they simply reverse the action of thunder 2 and its dominant theme, PQ. However, there are considerable differences between the two thunders and episodes. To begin with, whereas the tale of the Prankquean took only two and a half pages to recount, the reverse tale covers some twenty-two pages; and whereas thunder 2 is placed near the end of the PQ episode, thunder 7 occurs just over a quarter of the way through the reversed tale and during a passage that could be regarded as an inserted digression from the main narrative. (In any case the thunder, as heralding and causing transformation, is a cataclysmic digression.) The problem of exegesis is further complicated both

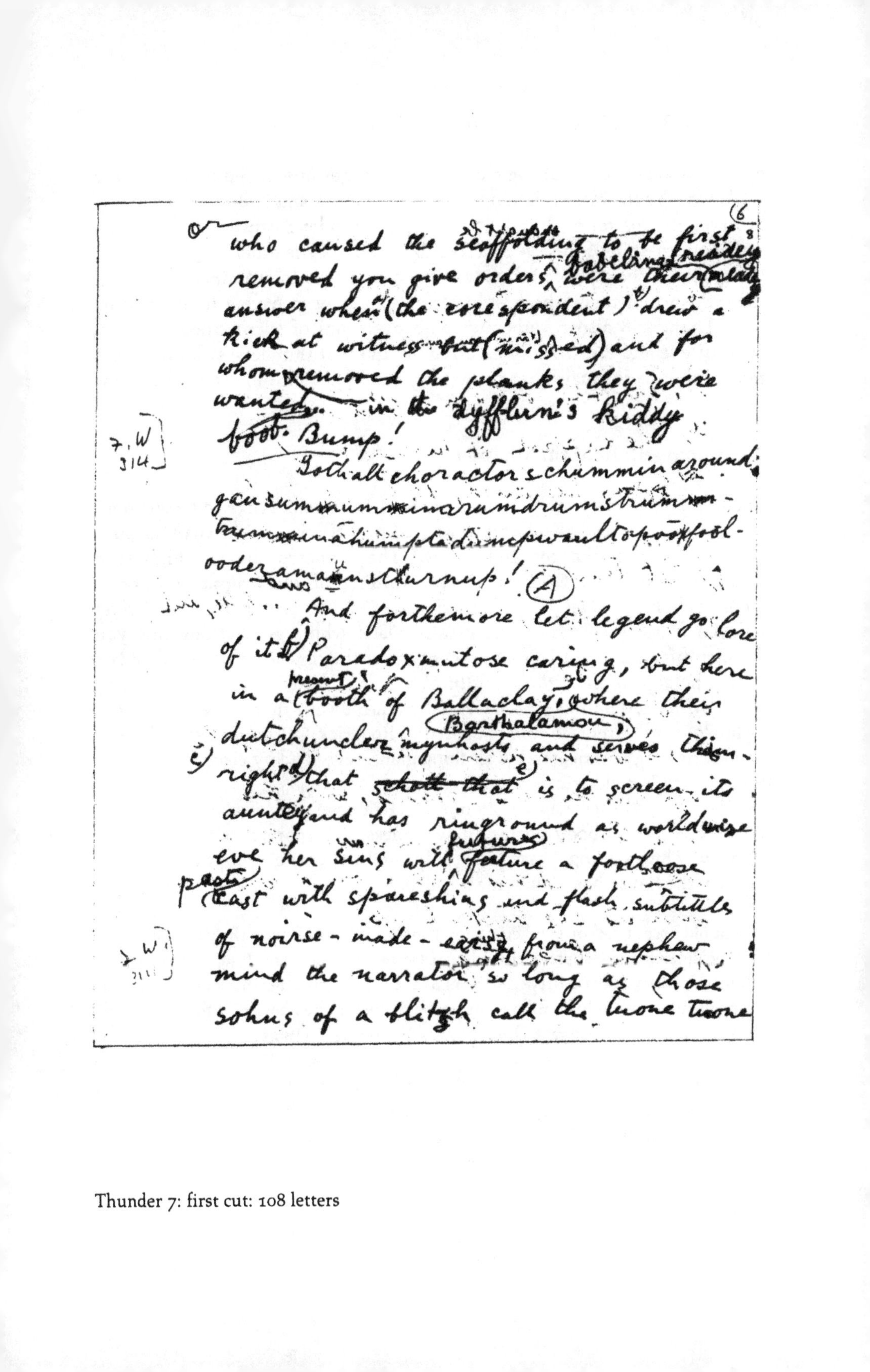

Thunder 7: first cut: 108 letters

by the episodic nature of the chapter (at 73 pages one of the longest in the *Wake*) and by the close relation between thunders 7 and 8. Broadly speaking, however, the matter of thunder 7 is simple. Thunder 2 concerned the matriarchal queen-ship of the eye and its subjugation of the other senses through the agency of the alphabet; thunder 7 restores the ear to prominence through the influence of radio, the first electric technology to have a thunder of its own. Thunder 8 also reverberates with overtones of silent cinema: consequently, eye and ear, 'royally divorced' by the first thunders, will now stand more or less as coequals, preparing the ground for their remarriage by thunder 8.

The Composition of the Chapter

The last pages of II.3 were the first pages of *Finnegans Wake* to be written.[1] First drafted in 1923, they were reworked into '*Wake*-ese' in 1938, as publication of the *Wake* got under way.[2] They concern the last high king of Ireland, Roderick O'Connor.[3] The wording of the original version – 'poor old *hospitable* King Roderick O'Connor the *paramount chief polemarch* last preelectric King of all Ireland who was anything like you between fiftyfour and fiftyfive years of age at the time after the socalled last supper he *greatly* gave *those maltnights & beerchurls in his (umbrageous) house of the 100 bottles –*'[4] shows that from the very first Joyce saw electric technology as corporate and monarchic. Roderick O'Connor was 'the last preelectric king': Finnegan, the sleeping giant, revivified by electricity, will be the first and last electric or post-electric king.

More correctly, perhaps, I should say Finnegan will awaken, for 'he' is resurrected not in body but as an awareness of corporate, tribal unity and identity. The opening passage is only slightly changed in the *Wake* as printed: the house has a radio mast added.

... poor old hospitable corn and eggfactor, King Roderick O'Conor, the paramount chief polemarch and last preelectric king of Ireland, who was anything you say yourself between fiftyodd and fiftyeven years of age at the time after the socalled last supper he greatly gave in his umbrageous house of the hundred bottles with the radio beamer tower and its hangars, chimbneys and equilines ... (380.11–17)

Aside from this passage, the rest of the chapter was evidently written smoothly in the years (1935 to 1938) just before publication of the *Wake*, episode and interlude following each other in sequence.

The chapter has five main pieces:

- *The first episode* The tale of Kersse and the Norwegian Captain, 309–332.09: it includes the seventh and eighth thunders.
- *The first interlude* (332.10–337.06), with a transition (337.07–338.03).
- *The second episode* The Butt and Taff dialogue and mimed reenactment of 'How Buckley Shot the Russian General' (338.07–355.20).
- *The second interlude* (355.21–370.29, written in three stages).
- *The last two episodes* (370.30–380.06, and Roderick O'Conor, 380.07–382).

By itself, the first episode is composed of an introduction (309–311.04), the tale (311.05–330.19) and a tail-piece containing thunder 8 (330.20–332.09) that blends smoothly into what Hayman has called the 'first interlude.'

The Themes of Radio and Ear

Book II.2, 'Triv. and Quad.,' ends (308) with a parodic letter, the telegraphic NIGHTLITTER, featuring a descent into or a contact with the elders in the underworld – a Menippean commonplace. By way of transition, the present chapter opens similarly (309), invoking the wisdom of the ancestors or beginnings ('Guinnesses' is 'genesis' or beginnings; 'stammpunct' is, on the surface, 'stand-point,' but it is also hybrid Danish/German, 'point of origin'):

> It may not or maybe a no concern of the Guinnesses but.
> That the fright of his light in tribalbalbutience hides aback in the doom of the balk of the deaf but that the height of his life from a bride's eye stammpunct is when a man that means a mountain barring his distance wades a lymph that plays the lazy winning she likes yet that pride that bogs the party begs the glory of a wake while the scheme is like your rumba round me garden, allatheses, with perhelps the prop of a prompt to them, was now or never in Etheria Deserta, as in Grander Suburbia, with Finnfannfawners ... (309.13–22)

'A man that means a mountain' is the sleeping giant of tribal awareness figured as one of HCE's initials reclining, ⼭, which Joyce learned to be a Chinese character: 'It means "mountain" and is called "Chin," the common people's way of pronouncing Hin or Fin.'[5] 'Tribalbalbutience' brings back into play stammering or stuttering and suggests that the tribe is now beginning to reassert itself, however hesitantly. In fact, this opening passage gathers together quite an array of thematic energies from the earliest thunders: the visual temptress (bride's eye), the dour and deafened Jarl van Hoother (doom of the balk of the deaf), HCE and his transitional relation to Finnegan, the wake, worshipping strange gods (technology: allotheism is the worship of strange gods), ricorso (the rhythm of rumba is a counterpoint of three beats against four: more likely, the rumba is the dance of the intellect in the garden of the senses 'mid the flowers of rhetoric).[6]

The reason that these energies are rallied here, as the next paragraph shows, is that the radio set has been introduced and the ear is once more dominant. The radio is, rather like Harington's jakes, a purely Menippean production:

... and as for Ibdullin what of Himana, that their *tolvtubular high fidelity* dail*dialler,* as modern as tomorrow afternoon and in appearance up to the minute, (hearing that anybody in that ruad duchy of Wollinstown schemed to halve the wrong type of date) equipped with *supershielded umbrella antennas* for *distance getting* and *connected* by the *magnetic links* of a *Bellini-Tosti coupling system* with a *vitaltone speaker, capable of capturing skybuddies, harbour craft emittences, key clickings, vaticum cleaners,* due to woman formed *mobile* or *man made static* and bawling the whowle *hamshack* and *wobble* down in an eliminium *sounds* pound so as to serve him up a melegoturny marygoraumd, *eclectrically filtered* for allirish *earths* and *ohmes.* This *harmonic condenser* enginium (the Mole) they caused to be worked from a *magazine battery* (called the Mimmim Bimbim patent number 1132, Thor*petersen and Synds*, Jomsborg, Selverbergen) which was *tuned up* by *twintriodic singulvalv*ulous pipelines (lackslipping along as if their liffing deepunded on it) with a howdrocephalous enlargement, a *gain control* of circumcentric *megacycles*, ranging from the antidulibnium onto the serostaatarean. (309.13–310.08)[7]

Whether a radio built to these specifications would work or not – since this is a Menippean radio, it almost certainly wouldn't – is irrelevant. Joyce is simply following the traditional rules of decorum by employing as much as possible of the language of radio and hams (amateurs) to give formal structure and texture to his discourse. In the same way, he uses rivers' names when discussing ALP, nautical terms when PQ is concerned, and medical terms from otology when discussing the ear later in the same paragraph. The passage begins where thunder 1 left off, in the Eastern ear-world (Ibdullin and Aminah: the parents of Mohammed), and this Menippean radio is capable of tuning across the centuries from antediluvian time to the present (Gael, *Saorstat Eireann,* Irish Free State), just as in ear-culture all ages are eternally present. It is still night-time, when radio reception and distance-getting (tuning in remote stations clearly) is best.

After the radio is presented in technical terms, 'the Mole' or earwig (*forficula auricularia*) of sound from the radio speaker strikes and awakens the sleeping ear in the rest of the paragraph. Joyce's description of the radio set develops logically, beginning with the antenna and ending with the output 'gain' or volume control. The radio 'pips' or time signals then travel to the ear:

They finally caused, or most leastways brung it about somehows, (that) the pip of the lin (to) *pinnatrate inthro an auricular forfickle* (known as the Vakingfar sleeper, monofractured by Piaras UaRhuamhaighaudh*lug*, *tympan* founder, *Eustache* Straight, Bauliaughacleeagh) a *meatous conch* culpable of cunduncing Naul and Santry and the forty routs of *Corthy* with the concertiums of the Brythyc Symmonds Guild, the Ropemakers Reunion, the Variagated Peddlars Barringoy Bnibrthir*hd*, the Askold Oleg*sonder* Crowds of the O'Keef-Rosses and Rhosso-Keevers of Zastwoking, the Ligue of Yahooth o.s.v. so as to lall the bygone dozed they arborised around, up his corpular fruent and down his reuctionary buckling, *hummer, enville and cstorrap* (the man of Iren, thore's Curlymane for you!), lill the *lubberendth* of his *otological* life. (310.08–21)[8]

'They' in the paragraph means representatives of Irish tribal awareness, the 'Finnfannfawners' or Sinn Feiners mentioned at the end of the first paragraph (309.09–10). Again, we follow a logical progression, from the outer ear (auricle, pinna) through the passage (meatus) to the middle ear (hammer, anvil, stirrup) and then the labyrinth (lubberendth) of the inner ear. (Parts of the ear are shown in figure 1.) To Joyce, then, the ear-world is thematically that of the landlubber (lubberendth), of 'man made static.' Joyce seems to have regarded the 'world' of ear-culture as etherial and interiorized; if so, some of Lewis's criticisms, discussed earlier, are to the point. In the subsequent paragraph he borrows the Arab muezzin tower motif from thunder 1 as an image for the broadcast tower of radio, whose announcers of hours in their 'shacks' or 'houses of call' mass and merge the 'faithful' listeners into a single entity.

House of call is all their evenbreads ... hallucinate like an erection in the night ... for it is where by muzzinmessed for one watthour, bilaws below ... (310.22–5)

In the episode that is to follow, PQ's ship is afloat on Hertzian waves,[9] but it stays tied up at the dock, and the mode of action is male. A transitional paragraph leads directly to the first episode.

PQ Renversé

According to tradition, this episode has its genesis in the story 'of a hunchbacked Norwegian captain, who ordered a suit from a Dublin tailor, J.H.

Inner Ear
Semi-circular Canals
Acoustic Nerve
Stirrup (Stapes)
Anvil (Incus)
Tympanic Membrane (Drum)
Cochlea and Organ of Corti
The Ear
Hammer (Malleus)
Eustachian Tube
Auricle; Pinna; Conch
Meatus (Auditory Canal)

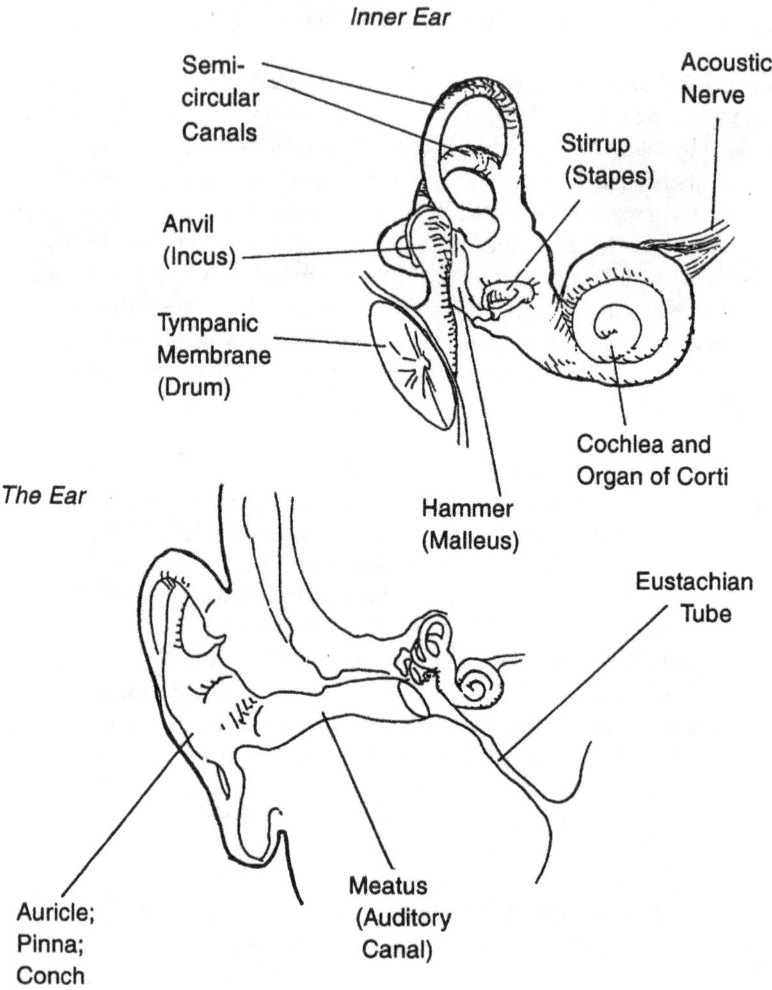

Figure 1

Kerse of 34 Upper Sackville Street. The finished suit did not fit him, and the captain berated the tailor for being unable to sew, whereupon the irate tailor denounced him for being impossible to fit. The subject was not promising, but it became, by the time John Joyce had retold it, wonderful farce.'[10] Readers familiar with Menippea will twitch immediately they notice the appearance of a tailor, for tailors as much as crackpot philosophers are stock-in-trade targets. The episode begins thus:

It was long after once there was a lealand in the luffing ore it was less after lives thor a toyler in the tawn at all ohr it was not before he drew out the moddle of Kersse by jerkin his dressing but and or it was not before athwartships he buttonhaled the Norweeger's capstan. (311.06–10)

Two of the three main characters are here: the captain; his agent, 'the ship's husband'; and Kersse the tailor, a cursing version of Persse (O'Reilly).[11] The second character is usually the narrator or 'teller,' but often 'teller' and 'tailor' become indistinguishable. In the telling, the three are easily told apart by the form of the word 'said' used in their dialogue tags:

Kersse the tailor	sazd
the Norwegian Captain	sagd
the ship's husband	sayd.

With this information in hand, one can more easily disentangle the first speeches of the episode. I quote in full to give an idea of the reversal of the Prankquean tale (see above, pages 62–3).

– Then sagd he to the ship's husband. And in his translatentic norjankeltian. Hwere can a ketch or hook alive a suit and sowterkins? Soot! sayd the ship's husband, knowing the language, here is tayleren. Ashe and Whitehead, closechop, successor to. Ahorror, he sayd, canting around to that beddest his friend, the tayler, for finixed coulpure, chunk pulley muchy chink topside numpa one sellafella, fake an capstan make and shoot! Manning to sayle of clothse for his lady her master whose to be precised of a peer of trouders under the pattern of a cassack. Let me prove, I pray thee, but this once, sazd Mengarments, saving the mouthbrand from his firepool. He spit in his faist (beggin): he tape the raw baste (paddin): he planked his pledge (as dib is a dab): and he tog his fringe sleeve (buthock lad, fur whale). Alloy for allay and this toolth for that soolth. Lick it and like it. A barter, a parter. And plenty good enough, neighbour Norreys, every bit and grain. And the ship's husband brokecurst after him

to hail the lugger. Stolp, tief, stolp, come bag to moy Eireann! And the Norweeger's
capstan swaradeed, some blowfish out of schooling: All lykkehud! Below taiyor
he ikan heavin sets. But they broken waters and they made whole waters at they
surfered bark to the lots of his vauce. And aweigh he yankered on the Norgean run so
that seven sailend sonnenrounders was he breastbare to the brinabath, where bottoms
out has fatthoms full, fram Franz José Land til Cabo Thormendoso, evenstarde and
risingsoon. Up the Rivor Tanneiry and down the Golfe Desombres. Farety days and
fearty nights. Enjoy yourself, O maremen! And the tides made, veer and haul, and the
times marred, rear and fall, and, holey bucket, dinned he raign!

   – Hump! Hump! bassed the broaders-in-laugh with a quick piddysnip that wee
halfbit a second.

   – I will do that, sazd Kersse, mainingstaying the rigout for her wife's lairdship.
Nett sew? they hunched back at the earpicker. (311.22–312.16)

By contrast with the PQ tale, here all of the protagonists are male. Nevertheless, there is considerable confusion of sexual roles (for example, 'her wife's
lairdship') during this challenge to sexual/sensual matriarchy. Needless to
say, the tailor comes off badly in the episode, but tailors are the routine butts
of Menippean pranks precisely on account of their trading in deceit of the
eye.[12]

   The 'suit' theme is far from simple and is never quite concluded. In Menippean satire, resolutions matter little: what does matter is that the story is
itself an element of the action. On the literal level, it is a suit of clothes for the
captain; figuratively, as the captain is the ship, it is provisions or a suit of sails
for a voyage; socially (tropologically/morally), it is a wedding suit and a suit
of marrriage brought by the captain (matter for thunder 8); while, finally, it
is, as in the PQ tale, the formal occasion for an identity quest. With PQ, the
visual stress of her prankings created the quest; here, the prevalent influence
of radio creates the complementary quest, a corporate reaching-back into the
tribal past to revive primal awareness:

So he sought with the lobestir claw of his propencil the clue of the wickser in his ear ...
Our svalves are svalves aroon! We rescue thee, O Baass, from the damp earth and
honour thee. (311.10–18)

Radio valves ('tubes' on this side of the Atlantic) blend with the rallying-cry
– *Sinn Fein, Sinn Fein Amhain*, Ourselves, ourselves alone – of Irish group
awareness and identity.

   Along with corporate sensibility comes the revival of handicrafts, sig-
nifying the decentralizing of reproduction as displacing another aspect of
matriarchy:

... plubs will be plebs but plabs by low frequency amplification may later agree to have another. For the people of the shed are the sure ads of all quorum. Lorimers and leathersellers, skinners and salters, pewterers and paperstainers, parishclerks, fletcherbowyers, girdlers, mercers, cordwainers and first, and not last, the weavers. Our library he is hoping to ye public.

Innholder, upholder.

– Sets on sayfohrt! Go to it, agitator! they bassabosuned over the flowre of their hoose. Godeown moseys and skeep thy beeble bee! (312.33–313.06)

'Sets on sayfohrt!' combines references to naval and to radio activity: Ger, *setz an safort*, start immediately; Ger, *seefahrt*, navigation at sea. Patriarchy is present in the episode in several ways. The main characters are males; men's voices (pitched lower than females') are being heard more – 'low frequency amplification' – and the crafts are all-male. The above passage ends with the instruction to Moses to lead the tribe out of captivity. The next lines are a brief speech by Kersse, the assertive Persse, after which comes the digression (313.14–314.29) that contains the thunder.

The Subplot: Silent Movies

However, the action before the thunder does not consist simply of male replacing female, but rather of male asserting itself as coequal: the eye is displaced from its former position of absolute monarch only as the ear rises to become co-regent. The vehicle for the continued influence of the eye is the silver screen of the silent cinema. As radio emphasizes the ear alone, so does silent film reinforce the roving eye: the 'royal divorce' is still in force, until their wedding at thunder 8. This is the reason why PQ is still present; even though her tale is reversed, it is after all her action and her labyrinth that are retraced, her spell that is being unwoven by the tailor/teller.

A second episode is lightly woven into the fabric of the text preceding thunder 7, the one that Joyce uses as an allegory of shooting a film. He appropriated for the purpose an incident from the Crimean War involving a private (the private I or eye) named Buckley and a Russian General (genre or group) – the one and the many. Richard Ellmann summarizes the story thus: 'Buckley, [Joyce] explained, was an Irish soldier in the Crimean War who drew a bead on a Russian General, but when he observed his splendid epaulettes and decorations, he could not bring himself to shoot. After a moment, alive to his duty, he raised his rifle again, but just then the general let down his pants to defecate. The sight of his enemy in so helpless and human a plight was too much for Buckley, who again lowered his gun. But when the General prepared to finish the operation with a piece of grassy turf, Buckley lost all respect for him and fired.'[13] Appropriately, this story shows the same tri-cyclic pattern as PQ's. Full development of the camera/chimera hunter shooting movie rushes (Russias) comes with thunder 8, when 'burgherly shut the rush in general' (335.13–14).

Here, the roving camera eye and shooting ('bump') are variously invoked, for example:

... the Burklley bump, the Wallisey wanderlook ... (312.29–30)

... that host of a bottlefilled, the bulkily hulkwight, hunter's pink of face, an orel orioled, is in on a bout to be unbulging ... (310.26–7)

... when he pullupped the turfeycork ... When, pressures be to our hoary frother, the pop gave his sullen bulletaction and, bilge, sled a movement ... (310.33–36)

Burniface, shiply efter, shoply after, at an angle of lag, let flow, brabble brabble and brabble, and so hostily ... check me joule, shot the three tailors, butting back to Moyle herring, bump as beam and buttend ... (315.09–12)

Bump! (314.07)

The act of firing meshes with the opening of the Kersse tale (311.05–09). A model for the new suit is drawn by or for the tailor – 'he drew out the moddle of Kersse by jerkin his dressing but and or ...' – while the private draws a bead ('drew out') on the centre of his target ('the moddle') and fires ('jerkin') at the exposed rump or butt ('dressing but').

Although the tale of Buckley and the General receives little further treatment in the context of thunder 7, the 'silver screen,' the 'frameshape of hard mettles,' continues to be invoked through references to money and mining in the digression that encloses the thunder. The following list is representative.

... still passing the change-a-pennies, pengeypigses ... (313.16: Norw, *penge*, money; the Irish halfpenny is stamped with a design of a sow with piglets. References to pigs allude to radio 'hams.')

... a several sort of coyne in livery ... (313.16–17: 'coyne and livery': an old Irish custom of entertaining at dependants' expense, plus reference to money and to clothing – the tailor.)

A few pigses and hare you are and no chicking (313.22: the 'hams' oust the poules: the Irish halfpenny is stamped with pigs; the threepenny bit with a hare, the penny with a chick.)

... tribune's tribute ... (313.23)

... coppels token ... (313.24: Irish, *capall*, the horse on the half-crown.)

... with this good sixtric ... (313.24: Sitric the Viking minted the first silver coin in Ireland, a penny.)

... from mine runbag of juwels ... (313.25: mining.)

Nummers that is summus that ... (313.25: number us that = sum us that; Lat, *nummus*, a coin.)

In the frameshape of hard mettles. (313.27: the movie frame or screen.)

It is minely well mint. (313.28: mining and minting.)

Thus as count the costs of liquid courage, a bullyon gauger, stowed stivers pengapung in bulk in hold ... (313.28–9: the Kersse and movie themes cross, with bullion in the ship's hold, but the thunder is only a dozen lines ahead; Nor, *penge pung*, purse or change purse; Du, *stiver*, any small coin; Hu, *pengo*, a coin.)

Following the thunder, as the digression draws to a close, the movie star (Swift's Stella, combined with his Vanessa, Esther Vanhomrigh) appears on the 'selver screen' with lightning-flashed Norse subtitles, 'pips' on the radio and 'pips' from Eve's apple:

Barhtalamou ... (homereek van hohmryk) that salve that selver is to screen its auntey and has ringround as worldwise eve her sins (pip, pip, pip) willpip futurepip feature apip footlose pastcast with spareshins and flash substittles of noirse-made-earsy from a nephew mind the narrator ... (314.22–7)[14]

Since the movie is silent, the mode is mimic and charade, hence the 'sure ads' (charades) 'of all quorum' (the general or group) (312.35), 'if you guess mimic miening' (313.25) and 'Did do a dive, aped one' in the line following the thunder (314.10).

The text immediately surrounding the thunder takes on references to Finnegan's fall off a ladder and to Humpty Dumpty's fall off the magazine wall, while continuing with the themes of the tales, of silver, and of the screen. The lines after the thunder summarize the main changes:

– Did do a dive, aped one.
– Propellopalombarouter, based two.
– Rutsch is for rutterman ramping his roe, seed three. Where the muddies scrimm ball. Bimbim bimbim. And the maidies scream all. Himhim himhim.
And forthemore let legend go lore of it that mortar scene so cwympty dwympty

what a dustydust it razed arboriginally but, luck's leap to the lad at the top of the ladder, so sartor's risorted why the sinner the badder! Ho ho ho hoch! La la la lach! Hillary rillarry gibbous grist to our millery! A pushpull, qq: quiescence, pp: with extravent intervulve coupling. (314.10–20)

The first three lines paraphrase an exchange with a sailor in the Emmaeus chapter of *Ulysses*.[15] It's as plain as ABC/123 (aped one ... based two ... seed three). The 'dive' or pratfall or slide is referred-to in all three lines (Ital, *palombaro*, diver; Ger, *Rutsch*, slide). In a parody of the 'Ballad of Persse O'Reilly,' the 'maidies' announce the return of the corporate and patriarchal mode: they 'scream all. Himhim.' The rise of the hunchback signals that the transition to Finnegan-again is underway amid Hillarity at the Wake/awakening (Ger, '*Hoch*! ... *lach*!' high ... laugh). The battles, pushing and pulling, for dominance of the sexes and senses, featuring PQ (p ... p ... qq; q ... pp), are in abeyance due to the present interplay of eye and ear, intervulve coupling.[16]

In summary: the context for this thunder presents the ear as resurrected by radio, side by side with the eye as continuing its operation in silent movies. The 'sleeping giant' begins to stir and a new quest, for corporate identity, begins. The tale of Kersse and the Norwegian Captain gets underway but is interrupted after the first cycle by thunder 7. It continues for sixteen more pages, ending just before thunder 8. As the formal cause of these transformations, the seventh thunder, a paragraph by itself –

Bothallchoractorschumminaroundgansumuminarumdrumstrumtruminahumptadumpwaultopoofoolooderamaunsturnup! (314.08–09)

– resounds with references to all of the themes in its context.[17]

Thunder	Interpretation	Theme Sounded
Bo	beau: suitor	ship's husband; wedding
Bot	boat	ship; PQ/captain
	Fr, *botte*, boot	clothes, PQ, tailor; kicks ladder; kick of gun (Buckley)
Both	both	eye and ear; tribal 'togetherness'
Botha	Ar, to be distant, far away	radio 'distance getting'

Thunder	Interpretation	Theme Sounded
Bothallchora-ctorschum-minaround	bottle/both-all characters/chorus actors chumming around	acoustic togetherness via radio, ear-mode
oth	oath	curse/Kersse/Persse
othall	enthrall assail	movie PQ, entrancings battles
thall	trawl, sail tail tale Du, *taal*, language (26L)	ship themes wake (of ship) PQ/Kersse/Buckley thunder, 'noirse made earsy'
thallc	talk Sw, Dan, Nor, *tolk*, interpreter (26L)	ear, radio eye/ear; ship's husband as marriage broker
thallchor	talker	ear, radio announcer
hall	Hu, *Hall*, to hear (26L)	ear, radio
allcho	echo Gr, *algia*, pain Fi, *alkaa*, begin	ear, doubles, etc. changes, battles descent to origins, to 'Guinnesses'
allchora	Algeria (Arab world) Ar, *Al-Koran*, 'that which is to be read aloud'	'muzzinmessed' radio eye and ear together
chor	Fr, *corps*, body	sleeping giant: Finnegan, the oral tribe
choract	cracked	wall, senses, HUMPty Dumpty
hor	hoar whore Ar, *hour*, free	'hoary frother' PQ movie star senses, tribe
hora	houri Sw, Dan, Nor, *høre*, to hear (26L)	PQ movie star (cf. thunder 8) ear, radio

Thunder	Interpretation	Theme Sounded
horactor	whore-actor	movie PQ; mixing of the senses/sexes
ora	Fr, *oreille*, Sw, *öra*, Dan, Nor, *øre*, ear (26L)	ear, radio
oract	erect	erection: broadcast towers, Finnegan sitting up
actors	actors	movie, 'mimic miening'
tor	Ger, *Tur*, door	doors, etc.
tors	doors	doors, etc.
torsch	Ger, exchanges	reversals (sex/sense)
schu	shoe	clothes, tailor; 'kick' theme (see Bot, above)
	shoot	Buckley, movie
chumm	chum	togetherness: eye and ear; tribal group
chummi	Fr, *chemie*, chemistry (also Du, Ger, Rum)	PQ-captain sex/sense chemistry; film developing
hum	hum	radio interference, noise, hum of conversation: this thunder is full of hum/um and oo – radio humming, ear resonance
	ham	radio hams, ham actor
	Ar, *haulm*, dream (26L)	movie: 'hallucinate ...'
hummin	humming	ear
	Sp, *jamon*, ham	radio ham, ham actor
hummina	Lat, *homine*, man	patriarchy: 'Himhim'
	Rum, *lumina*, light	movie (projector)

Thunder	Interpretation	Theme Sounded
ummi	Ger Sl, around	ear, new radio environment
	Fi, *uni*, dream (26L)	movie, etc.
mi	Indog, to diminish (Wig)	waning of visual dominance
mina	Lat, *minae*, battlements, parapets	magazine wall; sex/sense battles
minar	Ar, lighthouse	movie projector
	Ar, minaret	broadcast tower, 'muzzinmessed'
minarou	Port, *minerio*, Rum, *minereu*, ore (26L)	mining, silver screen
inar	inner	ear; 'intervulve coupling'
nar	Ger, *Narr*, fool	inept tailor
	Heb, light, Ar, *nar*, fire (26L)	movie
naro	Lat, *narro*, I tell, report	teller/tailor; radio announcer
aro	Lat, *aro*, plough, furrow	wake
aroun	Haroun (Arab HCE)	Arab world, 'muzzinmessed'
	Erin, aroon	Sinn Fein tribe awakes
round	round (musical form)	ear, echo
	round, circular	ear, echo
ou	Rum, *ou*, egg	Humpty Dumpty
undgan	Dan, *udgang*, exit (26L)	eye dominance
	Dan, *indgang*, Nor, *inngang*, entrance (26L)	equality of ear (for both, see thunder 6 theme of entrances and exits)
undgandsum- uminarumd	Ger (coll) and completely around him surrounding	new clothes, new environment of radio and silent films

Thunder	Interpretation	Theme Sounded
ndgan	Sw, Dan, *igen*, Nor, *igjen*, again (26L)	return of the ear, the tribe
gan	gain (monetary) gain control	silver screen radio volume control
gans	gains Sl, foreskin Ger, *Ganz*, ninny Ger, *Gans*, Du, *gans*, goose (26L)	money; silver screen 'erection,' etc. inept tailor 'no chicking'
ans	Ar, ams, yesterday (26L)	retrieval/revival; all times in ear-mode (radio)
ansumu	Sw, *ensam*, alone; It, *insiemi*, together (26L)	the one and the many; Sinn Fein – 'ourselves alone'; Buckley (the private) and the General
su	Fi, *suu*, mouth (26L)	speech, announcer; ear
sum	Lat, *sum*, I am R, *shum*, noise (26L) Dan, *summe*, hum, buzz, drone	identity quest ear; 'noirse ...', 'man made static' ear; radio hum, conversation
sumu	Lat, *sumus*, we are Sw, *samma*, same (SE)	identity quest; Sinn Fein status of eye and ear, sexes
sumum	Du, *samen*, Dan, Nor, *saamen*, together (26L) Lat, *summum*, the top (ClL)	ear; tribal; Sinn Fein
mum	Sl, mother Sl, silent Sw, *mun*, Nor, *munn*, mouth (26L)	waning matriarchy silent movie sound, ear
mi/minar/nar	(as above)	(as above)
arum	Lat, *-arum*, first declension	themes of sex/sense/

Thunder	Interpretation	Theme Sounded
	genitive plural ending, feminine except when males are meant	identity flux and confusion; this thunder is the first 'decline' of the visual and matriarchal (feminine)
rumd	round (also in Fr, Du, Sw, Dan, Ger)	the suit; ear, new radio environment
dru	drew: a bead the 'moddle'	Buckley, eye Kersse
drum	drum Du, *droom*, Sw, *dröm*, Dan, Nor, *drøm*, dream (26L)	eardrum movie, 'hallucinate ...'
drumstr	drummer	advertiser (radio): 'sure ads'
drumstrum	drum-strum; drum-*strøm* (storm, vortex) dream-*strøm*	ear, radio 'sounds-pound' movie
rums	Fi, *ruumis*, body (26L)	corpse, wake; corporate
rumstru	Fi, *rumpu*, drum (26L)	eardrum
strum	*strøm*, storm	thunder
trum	Ger, *Traum*, dream	movie, 'hallucinate'
trumi	Ger, *Trommel*, Du, *trommel*, Sw, *trumma*, Dan, Nor, *tromme*, drum (26L)	ear (drum)
mı/mına	(as above)	(as above)
nahum	Ar, *nagm*, star (26L)	PQ, movie
hum	hum Du, *ham*, ham (26L) Ar, *haulm*, dream (26L)	ear, radio, etc. radio ham, ham actor movie, 'hallucinate...'
hump	hump	HUMP, Captain, HCE, Finnegan
humpta	Port, *junto*, Sp, *juntos*, together (26L)	tribal, corporate, etc.

Thunder	Interpretation	Theme Sounded
	Fi, *huutan*, to call, cry	ear, radio, 'come bag...'
humptadump	Humpty Dumpty	reunification of sexes/senses
ad	advertisement	'sure ads ...' radio
dum	doom dumb	'balk of the deaf ...' inept tailor
dumpwaul	dump-wall: the midden-dump by the butt of the magazine wall	Humpty Dumpty fell onto it; erection, wall; retrieval
dumpwault	Ger, a nitwit, dumb and lazy	inept tailor
waul	waul, wail	'come bag ...' etc.
waultopoofool	wall-topper fool waul (cry) to poor fool	Humpty Dumpty 'come bag ... ' etc.
poofool	poor fool	inept tailor
lood	lewd loot	movie PQ/whore silver (screen)
loode	Fr, *lieu de*, in place of	displacement of visual
loodera	Lat, *ludere*, to play	interplay of sexes/senses
looderamaun	Gael, *ludramán*, lazy idler (GaL)	inept tailor
looderamauns-turnu	look at the monster now	Finnegan's corpse stirring; revival of auditory, tribe, sleeping giant; movie rush of the general (the mob)/General
ooder	Ital, *udire*, to hear (26L)	ear, radio
od	hod	HUMP, etc.
eram	Lat, *eram*, I was Eireann	old private identity gone ear-world
ama	Ar, *aama*, blind	ear, radio

Thunder	Interpretation	Theme Sounded
amaun	amain (full force, speed) Amen, Egyptian creator (Gla)	thunder, battles, changes Finnegan as a god
maun	mound Ar, *maan*, together (26L)	midden-dump ear group, tribe

maunstur	(as above)
	Port, *amostra*, Du, *monster*,
	    Sw, *mönster*, Nor, *mønster*,
	    sample (26L)
		(as above)
		more to come: power
		    of radio just rouses
		    the corporate
		    monster: wait 'til it's
		    fully awake!

maunsturnup	monster stirred up mons turned up man's stern up	sleeping giant starts to rise 'intervulve coupling' the General's, when Buckley aims
uns	Ger, *uns*, we	tribe, corporate
unsturnup	we turn(ed) up	Sinn Fein, tribe, etc.
sturn	stern (of ship) Ger, *Stern*, star Ger, *Sturm*, storm	the Captain's; wake; retreat of PQ mode movie, etc. thunder, battles, etc.
urnu	you're new, renew, anew	revival of ear-mode, tribal, etc.

11

The Eighth Thunderclap: Sound Film:
The Royal Wedding (*FW* 318–34)

He fell for my lips, for my lisp, for my lewd speaker ... You can trust me that though I change thy name though not the letter never while I become engaged with my first horsepower, masterthief of hearts, I will give your lovely face of mine away, my boyish bob, not for tons of donkeys, to my second mate ... (459.28–35)

We seem to us (the real Us!) to be reading our Amenti in the sixth sealed chapter of the going forth by black. It was after the show at Wednesbury that one tall man, humping a suspicious parcel, when returning late amid a dense particular on his home way from the second house of the Boore and Burgess Christy Menestrals by the old spot, Roy's Corner, had a barkiss revolver placed to his faced with the words: you're shot, major ... (62.26–32)

The ladies have mercias! It brought the dear prehistoric scenes all back again, as fresh as of yore, Matt and Marcus, natural born lovers of nature, in all her moves and senses, and after that now there he was, that mouth of mandibles, vowed to pure beauty, and his Arrah-na-poghue, when she murmurously, after she let a cough, gave her firm order, if he wouldn't please mind, for a sings to one hope a dozen of the best favourite lyrical national blooms in Luvillicit, though not too much, reflecting on the situation, drinking in draughts of purest air serene and revelling in the great outdoors, before the four of them, in the fair fine night, whilst the stars shine bright, by she light of he moon ... (385.18–25)

... see the Bolche your pictures motion and Kitzy Kleinsuessmein eloping for that holm in Finn's Hotel Fiord, Nova Norening. Where they pulled down the kuddle and they made fray and if thee don't look homey, well, that Dook can eye Mae. (330.23–7)

And roll away the reel world, the reel world, the reel world! (64.25–6)

Thunders 7 and 8 form a pair or double-plot, as do thunders 9 and 10. Presaged by thunder 6, each of the last four thunders dramatizes the effects of one or another electric technology as producing a phoenix-rebirth of increasingly unified sensory experience. Thunders 7 and 8 are thematically connected by eye-and-ear development and by their relation to the tale of the Norwegian Captain. Similarly, thunders 9 and 10 are connected by their relation to the fable of the Ondt and the Gracehoper. As epyllia, these sections are the most Menippean structural elements of *Finnegans Wake.*

With the present thunder, Joyce pursues the simultaneous development of silent movies and radio (amplifiers) to their wedding in 'talking pictures.' The action of the PQ tale that ended in a 'royal divorce' of the sexes and senses, is reversed in this motif. As the tale now progresses, following the close of thunder 7, work on the suit for the Captain involves a second fitting (320) and the presentation and rejection (322) of the product. At the same time, there is a marriage proposal (318), a wedding (325ff.), a honeymoon (329) in which the marriage is consummated *in camera*, and the probable birth of a son, who may be Persse O'Reilly. There are actually two endings to this tale, one where the reversed tale concludes (330) and another that echoes the first, just before thunder 8 (330.02–04). There follows an interlude of six pages after which the Butt and Taff dialogue, concerning Buckley and the Russian General, formally begins.

The Film Background

Developments in film technique were occurring quickly while *Finnegans Wake* was in the writing. For patrons, theatres provided lavishly appointed escapist dream-worlds, and major pictures from the big studios provided the occasion for complete movie-house redecoration. A desert epic, for example, might see lobby and foyer turned into an oasis with real (potted) palm trees, hills of sand, pools of water, tents, perhaps even live camels and horses, while theatre staff dressed in Arab garb. When 'stars' visited a city or attended an opening, they received the same adulation as visiting royalty, and massive crowds turned out just to catch a glimpse of them. Such opulence and splendour were in stark contrast to the hardship of the Depression; and Joyce, recognizing the lucrative potential, tried unsuccessfully for years to interest various groups and collaborators in a project to open a movie theatre in Dublin. At the same time, the analyst and critic in him was interested in the mechanical and theoretical side of the technology. The principal technical developments came chiefly from two areas, Hollywood and Russia. These two realms are related to the theme of Buckley shooting the Russian General (the rush in general).

In 1924, in reaction to American filmmaking, Sergei Eisenstein published the article 'Down with the Story and the Plot!' He developed the montage technique – cinematic metaphor or hendiadys – 'the method for making any kind of film,' as he considered it. It was based on the idea that two juxtaposed images gave rise in the imagination to a new idea and that the whole thus created is superior to the sum of its two constituent parts. The dialectic potential in the technique was not lost on Eisenstein: it seemed an ideal method for fusing the posing and resolution of opposites with a popular cultural form. Russian film was in its infancy at the time, so Eisenstein was also concerned with how to 'beat' the American industry, just as he was concerned about the regal status automatically accorded film stars because that ran counter to proletariat ideology. His solution, when he found it, was simple. 'There are no actors in *Battleship Potemkin*,' he announced in an essay.[1] He countered the entire thrust of bourgeois cinema by abolishing all – story, stars, plot (as he saw it) – and by pushing into the dramatic centre of the film the mass as the basic dramatis persona, the mass that otherwise was used to serve as a background for the solo performance of single actors or stars. The tribal mob is Joyce's Russian General.

Joyce's thematic motif for the film projector is the moon: in the darkened (night-time) theatre the screen (full of stars) is lit by the projector, a moon that shines from above and behind the audience. It is a phoenix-fire that also shines through and illuminates clouds – of cigar- and cigarette-smoke 'fumes' – and may itself fume or emit smoke. However, it is in the 'small room' of the projector itself, as well as those of the projection booth and of the original camera (*in camera*), that the wedding of eye and ear takes place and is consummated.[2] So, while the clichéd movie romance of the stars on the screen ends with a wedding, the honey*moon* occurs simultaneously as the act of showing the film.

In this particular section of the *Wake*, the themes are extremely close-knit, aggravating the usual problems of exegetical disentangling. They include the continuing reversal of PQ's tale, to display eye and ear reuniting; overtones of the story of Private Buckley and the Russian General; the technologies of radio and film (the amplifiers from radio technology supply the sound for film – brand-new in the thirties), plus the usual welter of constant commentary on characters and themes from all other parts of the book. Explication in the remainder of this chapter, therefore, is more disjointed than usual. Indeed, so tightly related are the themes that almost any group of them will yield all of the others. For example, the set of nodal associations, honeymoon-moon-light in darkness-twilight, gives rise to the thematic clusters outlined in figure 2.

The PQ/Kersse Tale Continued

Prior to thunder 7, Kersse, challenged, measures the humpbacked Captain for what will be his wedding suit (311.29–34). This measuring is precipitated by a parody of the first of PQ's questions to the Jarl, phrased as the Norwegian Captain questing for a new suit and a new domestic identity (311.22–3: 'Hwere can a ketch or hook alive a suit and sowterkins? Soot! sayd the ship's husband ...'), and is followed by a reprise from the earlier tale (311.36–312.01: 'And the ship's husband brokecurst after him to hail the lugger. Stolp, tief, stolp, come bag to Moy Eireann!'). Immediately following the digression that contains the thunder, Kersse (whose name means a coarse cloth for trousers, and is as well a homonym for Persse O'Reilly) sets to work choosing material and planning the suit:

... twilled alongside in wiping the rice assatiated with their wetting. The lappel of his size? ... She wends to scoulas in her slalpers ... Knit wear? ... plus his ducks fore his drills, an inlay of a liddle more lining ... sneither a whole length nor a short shift so full as all were concerned. (314.32–315.08)

Cloth be laid! (317.11)

The wedding theme begins to assume importance, emerging from language replete with spectrum and radio references, as kismet (fate):

That with some our prowed invisors how their ulstravoliance led them infroraids, striking down and landing alow, against our aerian insulation resistance, two boards that beached ast one, widness thane and tysk and hanry. Prepatrickularly all, they summed. Kish met. Bound to ... Heaved two, spluiced the menbrace. (316.02–09)

A second parody of the PQ question is given, as Kersse cuts cloth for the suit, in terms relating to assembling a radio (solder) and to the reintegration of Humpty Dumpty:

– Nohow did he kersse or hoot alike the suit and solder skins, minded first breachesmaker with considerable way on and
– Humpsea dumpsea, the munchantman, secondsnipped cutter the curter.
(317.22–5)

ALP, HCE
and
PQ, Captain:
dream girl, guy

dream

mid-night
(PM/AM)
(borderline)

wedding:
reverses
PQ split,
'royal divorce'

wedding, i.e.,
integrating

Phoenix (Play-
house) ricorso

ghost:
film image

Finn again

Götterdammerung/
Ragnarok

Honeymoon

Moon ⟷ glow

Light-in-Darkness

Twilight

'in camera'
(camera/projector/
booth)

projector
(in theatre)

Borderline or
Integration:
light/dark
eye/ear
male/female

(borderline)

(AM)

John Peel (break o' day)

consummation;
intercourse
(border interface)

projectile (film):

shooting, fire:
gun, camera

Humpty Dumpty

Spectrum

Horserace

Hunter

movie (fume)

Fire:
– innovation/
blush:
– sexual
– phoenix
– in projector
– drink (firewater)
Buckley & Russian
General

He: Navy blue
(Captain)
She: rosy blush

Borderline
Transitions:
Hump
Persse

(i.e., Buckley, Peel,
suitor)

'reel
world'
horse-
race

Hollywood;
Holy Wood
(the cross/
the 4)

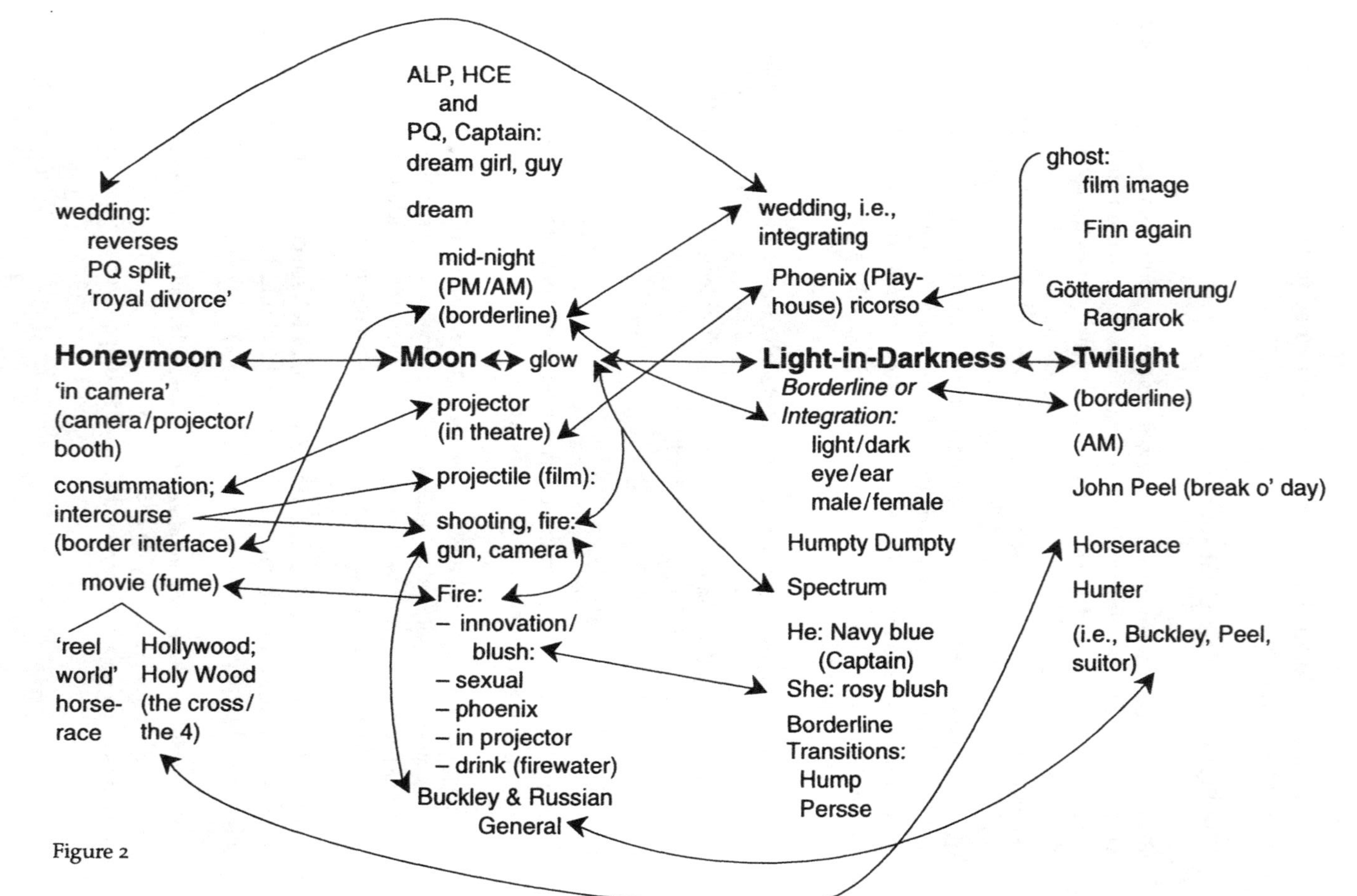

Figure 2

Reversed retelling of PQ's tale is spread somewhat thin over the ground of
the next seven pages, and indeed the parodies are scant up to the dénouement
on 330, as if the episode had really served its purpose by the end of thunder
7. The principal reference points are the parallels to PQ's three questions: the
response to the second iteration of the question is three pages in arriving:

– Stuff, Taaffe, stuff! interjoked it his wife's hopesend to the boath of them consistently. Come back to May Aileen.
– Ild luck to it! blastfumed the nowraging scamptail, in flating furies outs trews his
cammelskins, the flashlight of his ire wackering from the eyewinker on his masttop.
And aye far he fared from Afferik Arena and yea near he night till Blawland Bearring,
baken be the brazen sun, buttered be the snows. And the sea shoaled and the saw
squalled. And, soaking scupper, didn't he drain (320.23–31. Compare 312.01–11, the
response to the first question, and the responses in PQ's original tale, 21.19–31,
22.06–18.)

In the present section the response to the question (which is always a
quest) is a marriage proposal, evidently posed by the blushing leading lady in
a film. The leading man, the humpbacked Captain, is at first oblivious to PQ's
overtures ('gragh knew well': Grannuaile, Grace O'Malley):

... so promonitory himself that he was oblifficus of the headth of hosth that rosed
before him, from Sheeroskouro, under its zembliance of mardal mansk, like a dun
darting dullemitter, with his moultain haares stuck in plostures upon it, (do you kend
yon peak with its coast so green?) still trystfully acape for her his gragh knew well in
precious memory and that proud grace to her, in gait a movely water, of smile a cool-
some cup, with that rarefied air of a Montmalency and her quick little breaths and her
climbing colour. Take thee live will save thee wive? I'll think uplon, lilady. (317.31–
318.04)

A reference to John Peel suggests that a hunt or quest is under way. PQ steals
the show:

And greater grown then in the trifle of her days, a mouse, a mere tittle, trots off with
the whole panoromacron picture. Her youngfree yoke stilling his wandercursus, jilt
the spin of a curl and jolt the broadth of a buoy ... Him her first lap, her his fast pal,
for ditcher for plower, till deltas twoport. While this glowworld's lump is gloaming off
and han in hende will grow. (318.07–14)

PQ's 'climbing colour,' she the blushing leading lady, relates her to the red end of the spectrum. She is to wed a ship's captain dressed in navy blue, thereby reuniting the spectrum. (The spectrum or rainbow normally represents the fractionating power of the visual when it is separated off from the other senses.)

Her blush is also the blush of dawn, the 'break o' day' when John Peel races off to the hunt (a horse-race of a different colour) – another quest. The wedding, a cliché end to a film, is only prefigured in the last lines quoted, while the 'glow' is the glow of the dawn, of the blush, of the 'world' of dreams on the screen and of the projector in the darkened theatre. Consummation in the projector is suggested, for 'han in hende' (hand in hand) is Norwegian, *han i hende*, he in her.

Another reference to John Peel ('Hillyhollow, valleylow! with the sounds and the scents in the morning' 319.01–02) introduces a page of development of the fire motif. As indicated in figure 2, page 176 above, the fire is simultaneously related to the 'burning would' of reckless innovation, the phoenix, drink (firewater), Buckley's shot, sexual desire, and the 'fire' in the projector:

... usquebauched the ersewild aleconner ... it's a suirsite's stircus haunting hesteries round old volcanoes. (319.04–07)

He made one summery ... of his the three swallows like he was muzzling Moselems and torched up as the faery pangeant fluwed down the hisophenguts, a slake for the quicklining, to the tickle of his tube and the twobble of his fable, O, fibbing once upon a spray what a queer and queasy spree it was. Plumped.
Which both did. Prompt. Eh, chrystal holder? (319.10–16)

– I put hem behind the oasthouse, sagd Pukkelsen, tuning wound on the teller, appeased to the cue, that double dyode dealered, and he's wallowing awash swill of the Tarra water. And it marinned down his gargantast trombsathletic like the marousers of the gulpstroom. The kersse of Wolafs on him, shitateyar, he sagd in the fornicular ... behame in the oasthouse. Hops! sagd he.
– Smoke and coke choke! lauffed till the tear trickled drown a thigh the loafers all but a sheep's whosepants that swished to the lord he hadn't and the starer his story was talled to who felt that, the fierifornax being thurst on him motophosically, as Omar sometime notes, such a satuation, debauchly to be watched for, would empty dempty him down to the ground. (319.25–36)[3]

Following a second fitting of the suit ('So for the second tryon all the meeting of the acarras had it. How he hised his bungle oar his shourter and cut the pinter off his pourer and lay off for Fellagulphia in the farning,' 320.18–20) are two short digressions that precede the altercation between Kersse and the Captain (320.32–321.20 and 321.21–36). They include such thematic interweaving as the following.

... their not to say rifle butt target, none too wisefolly ... were signalling gael warnings ... to give them their beerings ... Let be buttercup eve lit by night in the Phoenix! Music. And old lotts have funn at Flammagen's ball. Till Irinwakes from Slumber Deep. How they succeeded by courting daylight in saving darkness he who loves will see. (321.02–19)

The next page presents the climax of the original anecdote: The Captain berates Kersse for incompetence.

– Tick off that whilehot, you scum of a botch, (of Kersse who, as he turned out ... had been mocking his hollaballoon a sample of the costume of the country).
– Tape oaf that saw foull and sew wrong, welsher, you suck of a thick, stock and the udder, and confiteor yourself (for bekersse he had cuttered up and misfutthered in the most multiplest manner for that poor old bridge's masthard slouch a shook of cloakses the wise ... his own fitther couldn't nose him).
Chorus: With his coate so graye. And his pounds that he pawned from the burning. (322.05–15)[4]

Kersse retorts that his camel's back is impossible to fit ('pushkalsson' – Dan, *pukkel*, hump):

The goragorridgorballyed pushkalsson, he sazd, with his bellows pockets fulled of potchtatos and his fox in a stomach, a disagrees to his ramskew coddlelecherskithers' zirkuvs, drop down dead and deaf, and there is never a teilwrmans in the feof fife of Iseland or in the wholeabelongd of Skunkinabory from Drumadunderry till the rumnants of Mecckrass, could milk a colt in thrushes foran furrow follower width that a hole in his tale and that hell of a hull of a hill of a camelump bakk. (323. 16–25)

Subsequently, references to the 'ghost' image on the screen ('the steerage way for stabling, ghustorily spoeking, gen and gang, dane and dare, like the dud spuk of his first foetotype' 323.35–324.01: 'spoeking' – Nor, *spøkelse*, ghost; 'gen and gang' – Dan, *gengang*, walking again), to the movie queen's blush ('picking up the emberose of the lizod lights' 324.04) and to pregnancy ('encient' 324.08), lead up to the third of PQ's recast questions:

And ere he could catch or hook or line to suit their saussyskins, the lumpenpack.
Underbund was overraskelled. As
   — Sot! sod the tailors opsits from their gabbalots, change all that whole set. Shut
down and shet up. Our set, our set's allohn.
   And they poured em behoiled on the fire. Scaald!
   Rowdiose wodhalooing. (324.12–18)

The last echoes the prewar station identification of the Irish Broadcasting
Service, Radio Athlone (Radio Atha Luain).
   Another, though brief, digression follows, one framed as a schoolroom
exercise by the prefix, 'Am. Dg.' (324.23: Ad Majorem Dei Gloriam) and the
suffix, 'Ls. De.' (325.03: Laus Deo Semper). Its content is a radio weather
forecast:

Am. Dg.
   Welter focussed.
   Wind from the nordth. Warmer towards muffinbell, Lull.
   As our relevant Colunnfiller predicted in last mount's chattiry sermon, the allex-
pected depression over Schiumdinebbia, a bygger muster of veirying precipitation
and haralded by faugh sicknells, (hear kokkenhovens ekstras!) and umwalloped in
an unusuable suite of clouds, having filthered through the middelhav of the same
gorgers' kennel on its wage wealthwards and incursioned a sotten retch of low
pleasure, missed in some parts but with lucal drizzles, the outlook for tomarry
(Streamstress Mandig) beamed brider, his ability good.
   What hopends to they?
   Giant crash in Aden. Birdflights confirm abbroaching nubtials. Burial of Life-
tenant-Groevener Hatchett ... (324.23–325.01)

A new 'rain' is predicted, a new role for the eye in union with the other
senses. 'Bury the hatchet' suggests both that the eye-battle of sexes/senses is
or soon will be over, and that freer intercourse is to follow.
   The next four pages continue this toying with the wedding motif. The captain becomes the 'nowedding captain' (325.27); the ship's husband proposes
to Kersse ('be me fairy fay, sayd he, the marriage mixter, to Kersse' 328.03–
04); the twenty-eight spectrum girls parade for their film hero ('all the prim
rossies are out dressparading and the tubas tout tout for the glowru of their
god' 327.15–17); PQ espies her 'fortune,' 'Mr. Right,' as a ghost on the
screen, blushes coquettishly like a fiery aurora borealis and plans to wed him
('our dollimonde sees the phantom shape of Mr Fortunatus Wright since
winksome Miss Bulkeley made loe to her wrecker and he took her to be a
rover, O ... while her fresh racy turf is kindly kindling up the lovver with the

flu, with a roaryboaryellas would set an Eriweddyng on fire': 327.25–33);
consummation of the wedding is foreshadowed and an erection is figured as
Finnegan arising on his bier:

... in the pravacy of the pirmanocturne, hap, sayd he, at that meet hour of night, and
hop, sayd he, and ... before Sing Mattins in the Fields, ringsengd ringsengd, bings
Heri the Concorant Erho, and the Referinn Fuchs Gutmann gives us *I'll Bell the
Welled* or *The Steeplepoy's Revanger* and all Thingavalley knows for its never dawn
in the dark but the deed comes to life, and raptist bride is aptist breed (tha lassy! tha
lassy!), and, to buoy the hoop within us springing, 'tis no timbertar she'll have then
in her armsbrace to doll the dallydandle, our fiery quean, upon the night of the things
of the night of the making to stand up ... (328.17–32)

However that may be, boy and girl, raven (caw) and dove (coo) are betrothed
and the splintered Finn and Humpty Dumpty are, even if only partially or
temporarily, reintegrated as the movie/honeymoon begins:

Cawcaught. Coogcaged.
And Dub did glow that night. In Fingal of victories. Cannmatha and Cathlin sang
together. And the three shouters of glory. Yelling halfviewed their harps. Surly Tuhal
smiled upon drear Darthoola: and Roscranna's bolgaboyo begirlified the daughter of
Cormac. The soul of everyelsesbody rolled into its olesoleself. A doublemonth's
licence, lease on mirth, while hooneymoon and her flame went huneysuckling.
Holyryssia, what boom of bells! What battle of bragues on Sandgate where met the
bobby mobbed his bibby mabbing through the ryce. Even Tombs left doss and dun-
nage down in Demidoff's tomb and drew on the dournailed clogs that Morty Manning
left him and legged in by Ghoststown Gate, like Pompei up to date ... (329.13–15)

'Ghoststown gate' is the shutter on the camera/projector that throws phan-
tom images on the screen.
   As the tale draws to a close, Buckley aims or 'shoots' through the lens
('Burke-Lees'), the wedding is performed and consummated while the Sinn
Fein hovers in the background ('feines for their sinns'):

The Burke-Lees and Coyle-Finns paid full feines for their sinns when the Cap and
Miss Coolie were roped.
   Rolloraped. (330.17–20)

Immediately after the wedding, the tale formally ends with the cliché close of
a fairy tale, 'so they put on the kettle and they made tea and if they don't live
happy that you and I may':

... see the Bolche your pictures motion and Kitzy Kleinsuessmein eloping for that holm in Finn's Hotel Fiord, Nova Norening. Where they pulled down the kuddle and they made fray and if thee don't look homey, well, that Dook can eye Mae. (330.23–7)

The page that remains before thunder 8 contains a general reprise of various themes already treated, for example:

- fashion (clothing: the tailor) and Buckley/John Peel ('Why was you hiding, moder of moders? And where was hunty, poppa the gun?' 330.36–331.01)

- the wedding of senses ('He's herd of hoarding and her faiths is altared. Becoming ungoing, their seeming sames for ... deaf do his part ...' 331.03–05)

- the cliché movie couple ('He knows he's just thrilling and she's sure she'd squeam. The threelegged man and the tulippied dewydress. Lludd hillmythey, we're brimming to hear! The durst he did and the first she ever?' 331.07–10)

- the film reels ('this isn't the polkar, catch as you cancan when high land fling!' 331.10–11)

- the film world of delusion (is-real) and the harem of starlets ('this mounden of Delude, and in the high places of Delude of Isreal, which is Haraharem ...' 331.18–19)

- the couple, again, with PQ as first lady of Hollywood ('As the last liar in the earth begeylywayled the first lady of the forest.' 331.22–3), and

- the groom is seen as a domesticated wild man (ex-bushman, which might be an oblique reference to the actor, Francis X. Bushman) taking the crown from – or with – the queen of prankings: 'Though Toot's pardoosled sauve l'hummour! For the joy of the dew on the flower of the fleets on the fields of the foam of the waves of the seas of the wild main from Borneholm has jest come to crown. (331.33–6)

The next paragraph contains the thunder and a restatement of the fairy-tale ending, 'for they put on the kettle':

Snip snap snoody. Noo err historyend goody. Of a lil trip trap and a big treeskooner for he put off the ketyl and they made three (for fie!) and if hec don't love alpy then lad you annoy me. For hanigen with hunigen still haunt ahunt to finnd their hinnigen where [... thunder ...] and anruly person creeked a jest. Gestapose to parry off cheekars or frankfurters on the odor. Fine again. Cuoholson! Peace, O wiley!

Such was the act of goth stepping the tolk of Doolin (332.01–10).

D.B. Christiani comments on the opening phrases:

Snip Snap Snoody. Noo err historyend goody. *Snip snap snude, nu er historien ude, snip snap snude,* now the story is over. A partially untranslatable jingle (of which a variation appears in H.C. Andersen's *Hørren*, 'The Flax'), this probably contains a pun in 'historyend' on his store (big) end, since 'snip snap snoody' suggests defloration. Also, '... *snip snap Snude, saa er Historien ude, og tip tap Tønde, nu kan en Enden begynde'* is cited by Helweg, page 68, from *Søren Kierkegaards Papirer,* 1 A 156. Kierkegaard is saying here that when the poet's mind refuses to function he might as well blow his brains out: 'snip snap Snude, now the story is finished, and tip tap Tønde, now another can begin.'[5]

In the context, the 'snip snap' might equally suggest Kersse's scissors at work cutting cloth, or those of a snooty ('snoody') film editor, or both. 'Hanigen with hunigen' is Norwegian, 'he again with she again,' which adds to the ghost image of the hunters in the piece, John Peel and Buckley. The thunder is the sound of their firing, and the sound of the movie projector. And 'snip snap' could also be the shutter of a shooter of a snapshot.

Although little is added in the text immediately following thunder 8, Persse O'Reilly lurks throughout the episode behind the figure of Kersse (by means of the P/K split). He even surfaces occasionally as the earwig (perce-oreille), burrowing into the ear in a parody of sexual consummation; for these reasons, he is given considerable presence in the thunder, which makes all things explicit. The movie wedding is depicted as a reel (a movie reel, naturally) or jig – a marriage of the gods (theogamy):

Him that gronde old mand to be that haard of heaering (afore said) and her the petty tondur with the fix in her changeable eye (which see) ... But ... there was a little theogamyjig incidence that hoppy-go-jumpy Junuary morn ... (332.20–5; Juno is the goddess of marriage).

In the first chapter of the *Wake,* PQ's tale was entered after passing through the 'Willingdone Museyroom' episode (8.09–10.24), which began, 'This the way to the museyroom. Mind your hats goan in!' and which ended,

'Mind your boots goan out!' In keeping with the motif of reversing here the actions of that thunder and its section, the present section is followed by a tour of a cinematic 'willingtoned mewseyfume' (334.13; 333.16), a recasting of the first version, featuring

the two deathdealing allied divisions and the lines of readypresent fire of the corked-agains upstored, taken in giving the saloot, band your hands going in, bind your heads coming out, and remoltked to herselp in her serf's alown, a weerpovy willowy dreevy drawly and the patter of so familiars, farabroads and behomeans, as she shure sknows, boof for a booby, boo: new uses in their mewseyfume. The jammesons is a cook in his hair. And the juinnesses is a rapin his hind. And the Bullingdong caught the wind up. Dip. (333.10–18)

This 'mewseyfume' episode occurs in the first digression following thunder 8 (beginning on 332.36) and is considerably shorter than the version at the beginning of the *Wake*. It is followed by another and longer digression, a prelude to Butt and Taff's mimed reenactment of the story of Buckley and the Russian General (338–54) as the chapter continues.

The eighth thunderclap –

Pappappapparrassannuaragheallachnatullaghmonganmacmacmacwhack-falltherdebblenonthedubblandaddydoodled (332.05–07)

– resonates with all of the themes present in the episode context.

Thunder	Interpretation	Theme Sounded
Pa	pay	theatre admission silver screen[6]; 'Peace, O Wiley'; wedding, quest ended
Pa/pap/pappa	father	patriarchy: Finn/HCE/Captain (again)
pap	pop Ar, *bab*, door	gunshot (Buckley/John Peel) doors (theatre too), camera shutter
pappa	Pompei	volcano (see 319.07, etc.)

Thunder	Interpretation	Theme Sounded
pappappappa	sound of gun	Buckley, 'poppa the gun' (331.01)
	sound of shutter	movie
Pappappappar-rassannuara-gheallachnal-tulaghmongan	Pappa appears anywhere he'll act natural(ly) among them	acting
ap	ape (mime)	acting (movie)
appa	happy	wedding: happy ending
pappapparrassa	Pappa Persse	patriarchy
appar	appear a pair	ghost image wedding, senses (eye/ear)
apparra	Fr, *appareil*, device, gear; Ger, *Apparat*, apparatus	camera, projector
apparras	upraise	ghost walk/resurrection of Finnegan; erection (consummation)
apparrassan	Ger/Engl, *Apparat*'s on	'our set's allohn': resurrected tribe
par	pair Fr, *père*, father Sw, Dan, Nor, *par*, pair (26L)	wedding, senses patriarchy wedding, senses
parra	Fr, *parer*, attire, deck out Curragh (racecourse)	Kersse the tailor horse-race, etc.
parrassan	parson Gael, *pearsún*, parson (GaL) R, *baraban*, drum (26L)	wedding wedding eardrum (as in thunder 7)[6]
parrassannuara-gheallachna-tullaghmongan	Pairas an Ua Raghailleach na Tulaighe Mongáin (píres un úrayelokh nu tulí muñgáñ) (GaL)	'Piers the Descendant of Raghallach' ('[strong-] fore-armed') of the hill

Thunder	Interpretation	Theme Sounded
		of Mongán (dimin. of *mongach*, hairy) [Anglic. Tullymongan, Co. Cavan]; *Tulach Mongáin* is at the heart of *Breifne Ui Raghailligh*, Anglic. Breffny O Reilly; see *FW* 99.26–7' (GaL) – the full-dress tribal name of Persse O'Reilly
arra	Eire	setting of movie, of resurrection (of tribe)
	aura, array	spectrum girls
	Ar, *yara*, see	visual sense; movie
	Lat, *ara*, plough	wake
arras	arras: curtain, screen	movie
	a race	horse-race; 'race' (film track) in the projector and camera
arrassan	a raising	ghost walk / Finn again; erection
arrassannu	a race anew	Sinn Fein; horse-race
ras	race	horse/whores; harem dance, reel themes
	raise	resurrection, etc.
	Fr, *rais*, ray	moonbeam, projector
rassa	Lat, *rasa*, cleaned, scrubbed	movie screen as palimpsest
	Gael, *rásaidhe*, wandering woman, a jilt (GaL)	PQ piratess before the wedding; movie coquette
rassan	racing	horse/whores (harem); reel world
rassannu	raise anew	Sinn Fein/Finnegan again; erection

Thunder	Interpretation	Theme Sounded
assa	Sw, *äska*, thunder	thunder, change
assann	Ar, *assam*, deaf	eye-ear
sannu	Sp, Ital, *sano*, sound (26L)	ear
	Sp, Fr, Ital, film, movie (26L)	movie
	R, *sini*, blue	Captain (navy blue); movie
	R, *son*, Sp, *sueno*, Ital, *sogno*, Port, *sonho*, dream (26L)	movie, dreams
sannuar	Fr, *seigneur*, lord, Sp, *señor*, mister	patriarchy etc.
ann	ALP	ALP, PQ; wedding
nua	Gael, *nua*, new	movie
nuar	Fr, *noir*, black	darkened theatre
	Fr, *nuer*, to shade or graduate the colours of	spectrum girls
	Ar, *nar*, fire	'fire' motifs; Buckley/ projector/phoenix, etc.
nuaragh	mirage	ghost image
	Fr, *nuage*, cloud	weather forecast; fume
uara	Ar, *yara*, to see (26L)	eye
uarag	Fr, *orage*, storm	weather forecast; old sex/sense wars; thunder
rag	rag, cloth	the suit, tailor
	rage	storm, thunder; Captain's response to Kersse
raghea	Russia	the General
	radio	ear and thunder 7
ag	Ger, *Auge*, eye	eye
	Dan, *aeg*, Sw, *agg*, Nor, *egg*, egg (26L)	Humpty Dumpty, reintegration
aghe	Fi, *auki*, open (26L)	doors; shutter
aghea	Asia	'Haraharem'; ear-mode

Thunder	Interpretation	Theme Sounded
agheall	Fr, *agile*, nimble, quick	Finn quick (vs. dead); dance, reel; shutter
	Fr, *échelle*, ladder	[visual pun for film strip]
ghealla	Fi. *kieli*, language, tongue (26L)	ear, etc.; thunder
gheallach	Gael, *geallach*, moon, moonlight (GaL)	movie projector; 'he moon,' honeymoon
heallachna-tullagh	he'll/he-all'll act naturally	movie actor; Finn revived
alla	Allah	ear, East; movie god
lach	latch	doors; shutter
nat	gnat, earwig	Persse O'Reilly, quest
natull	Fr, *natal*, native	Wild Man from Borneo; ex-bushman
natullagh	Ger, *natürlich*, naturally	actor, etc.; domesticated 'wild man,' etc.
tu	Fr, *tous*, *tout*, all	corporate, revived tribe
tulla	Dan, Nor, *tale*, speak, talk (26L)	ear, language revival
	Ital, *telaio*, loom (26L)	cloth, Kersse
	Fi, *kuulla*, to hear (26L)	ear
	Sw, *tala*, talk (26L)	ear, language revival
ulla	Allah	ear, East; movie god
aghm	aim	Buckley; camera/projector
	Ar, *nagm*, star (26L)	movie star; girl starlets
mon	man	patriarchy; Captain, Finnegan
	Sw, *moln*, cloud (26L)	weather forecast; fume
	Sw, Dan, Nor, *mane*, moon (26L)	movie projector; 'he moon,' honeymoon
monga	Scand, the many	corporate, Sinn Fein, etc.; Finn Again

Thunder	Interpretation	Theme Sounded
gan	gun Fr, *gens*, people	Buckley, camera (shoots) corporate, General
mac	Fi, *mykkä*, dumb (26L) Gael, son (GaL)	eye/ear; idiot tailor Buckley (Anglic. of *Buachaill*, boy [GaL]); result of consummated marriage
macma	magma	volcanoes, etc.
macmacmac	[sound of machine gun] [sound of shutter]	Buckley; 'poppa the gun' (334.01) movie
acwha	Lat, *aqua*, water	ships: PQ's and Captain's; weather forecast (this thunder includes some rain, as PQ reigns as co-regent)
whack	whack (hit) wake	movie 'shot'; Buckley fires and hits General wake (ships; Finn's)
whackfallther- deb ...	'Whack fol the da ...' [words from the refrain of the song, 'Tim Finnegan's Wake']	wake; Finn again
fallth	faith	'her faiths is altared' combines 'theogamy' and movie themes: make-up alters face, altar wedding
fallther	father	patriarchy; consummated marriage
all	all	corporate, General
allth	health	Finn's revival
allther	all there altar	Sinn Fein wedding, gods (movie)

Thunder	Interpretation	Theme Sounded
her	her	ALP/PQ bride
	hear	ear
	Fr, *hier*, yesterday	'historyend'
herd	herd	the general (group)
	heard	ear
herdeb	her debut	PQ, movie actress
erdeb	Arab	ear, East, etc.
deb	deb[utante]	actress, spectrum girls
deb ... dub	Gael, *dubh*, black (GaL)	darkened theatre
debble	devil	underworld of gods, ghosts; projector as 'infernal machinery' (320.33)
debblen ... dubblan	doubling	marriage, senses; ghosts
	dubbing	movie, ear added to eye
	Dublin	setting of movie action, resurrection, etc.
ebblenonthedubblandaddy	Eblana, the Dublin daddy (*Eblana* was Ptolemy's name for Dublin – McH)	patriarchy; Dublin the scene of the film and the resurrection
ble ... bla	Fr, *bleu*, blue	Captain (navy blue); fume/projector
blen	Ger, Du, Sw, Dan, Nor, *blind*, blind (26L)	eye/ear
	Fr, *plein*, full	moon, etc.
len	Fr, *lune*, moon	moon, etc.
	Sw, *linne*, Nor, *lin*, linen (26L)	cloth, tailor, Kersse
	Dan, Nor, *len*, lightning	flash (projector); thunder
lenon	linen	cloth, tailor, Kersse
enon	Sw, *en annen*, Nor, *en annan*, another (26L)	ear-echo; ghost image
nonthe	Ital, *nozze*, wedding	wedding

Thunder	Interpretation	Theme Sounded
onthe	Fi, *onni*, black (26L) Fi, *uni*, dream (26L)	darkened theatre movie-dream
thedu	Theda [Bara]	actress, PQ
thedubblan- daddydoodled	'the Dublin daddy doodled'	movie: 'written' on the screen by 'she light of he moon'
dubbl	double	echo, ghost image, etc.
bla	Sw, Dan, Nor, *bla*, blue (26L)	Captain (navy blue), fume, projector
blan	Fr, *blanc*, white	wedding dress; light when spectrum reintegrated
bland	Ger, Du, Sw, Dan, Nor, *blind*, blind (26L)	eye/ear
blanda	Sw, *blanda*, mix, blend (26L)	wedding, senses, sexes, spectrum
landa	Ar, *lamba*, electric light bulb (26L)	projector; fire motif; lightning
andad	ended	'royal divorce' of sexes, senses; identity quest; happy ending
dad/daddy	father	patriarchy etc.
daddy	Fi, *tähti*, star (26L) Ar, *dawdaa*, noise (26L)	movie star, starlets thunder
dyd	died	ghosts, underworld
doo	Fr, *deux*, two	wedding, sexes, senses,etc.
doodled	[dalliance]	courtship, wedding, consummation
	diddle ('Whack fol the diddle': var. refrain of song, 'Tim Finnegan's Wake')	wake; Finn again
oodle	Sl, much, many	General group/mass/tribe

12

The Ninth Thunderclap:
The Reciprocating Engine: Joy Sticks and
Joyce Ticks (*FW* 403–419.11)

The Ondt – horseless carriage or car-apace
The Gracehoper – taking off on a wing and a prayer

And as I was jogging along in a dream as dozing I was dawdling, arrah, methought broadtone was heard and the creepers and the gliders and flivvers of the earth breath and the dancetongues of the woodfires and the hummers in their ground all vociferated echoating: Shaun! Shaun! Post the post! (404.03–07)

Down among the dustbins let him lie! Ear! Ear! Not ay! Eye! Eye! (409.02–03)

After suns and moons, dews and wettings, thunders and fires, comes sabotag. *Solvitur palumballando!* (409.28–30)

I know that Λd ought to be about roads, and go along repeating that to myself all day as I stumble along the roads hoping it will dawn on me how to show up them roads so as everybody'll know as how roads, etc. (Letter from Joyce to Harriet Shaw Weaver, 29 August 1925)

I began Λd (otherwise the last watch of Shaun) a few days ago and have produced about three foolscapes of hammer and tongs stratification lit up by a fervent prayer to the divinity which shapes our roads in favour of my ponderous protagonist and his miniscule consort. (Letter from Joyce to Harriet Shaw Weaver, 10 October 1925)

Book III, chapter 1 of the *Wake* (403–28) displays a greater degree of formal intricacy than perhaps any other chapter of the book. Like II.3, it contains two thunders, 9 and 10; but, though this chapter is brief by comparison, it is extremely difficult to separate the thunders for discussion.

Chapter 1 of book III presents the metamorphosis of Shaun, a process echoed by the complex and digressive epyllion structure of the chapter as

— So vi et! we responded. Song! Shaun, song!
— I apologuise, Shaun began, but I would
rather spinooze you one from the grimm
gests of Jacko and Esaup, fable one, feeble
too. Let us here consider the casus, my
dear little cousis of the Ondt and
the Gracehoper. The Gracehoper was
always jigging a jog, hotby on akkant of his
joyicity, (he had a partner pair of
findlestilts to supplant him) or if not
he was always making ungraceful
overtures to Floh and Luse and
Bienie and Vespatilla to play pupa-
pupa and puticy-puticy and to commence
insects with him, even if only in chaste,
behold a watering pot. He would of
curse, by his meliscious fore antennas, lamely,
harry me, marry me, bury me, bind me
till she was puce for shame and allso
fourmish her Spinner's housery at the earthobest
schoppinhour so summery as his cottage,
which fourmillierly cald Singsomingenting,
groped up. Or, if he was not done

Thunder 9: fair copy of Ondt and Gracehoper

[III.i.   F.W. 444]

Thunder 9: instruction to insert thunder 9 into fair copy: 63 letters

well as by its general theme of transformation. Here we see Shaun in full dress as a postman delivering the mail, retracing some of the labyrinth of the *Wake* with the Letter in hand. In the scheme of the rhetorical *logos*, Shaun personifies *pronuntiatio* – delivery (of the Letter): at his first speech, 'Shaun yawned, as his general address rehearsal' (407.28) – he is a step beyond the Russian General of the last thunder. His metamorphosis is from postman to post-man: he finally extends himself out of space and into the eternal spirit world in which past and present coalesce.

The Original Form and Present Structure of the Chapter

The four chapters that compose book III were roughed out in 1924 and 1925 and had a relatively simple overall narrative theme[1] as the 'four watches' of Shaun, which Joyce referred to in correspondence as Λabcd.[2] Originally, III.1 and III.2 were composed and revised as one.[3] They were split for separate publication in *transition*.[4] Moreover, David Hayman remarks, these first two chapters were subjected to 'an extravagant number of revisions' prior to inclusion in the *Wake*, and, he suggests, 'Joyce apparently felt that to justify their position in the book these pages must embody a greater depth of suggestive power and fuller character development than do most of the chapters . . .'[5]

I shall deal with the present chapter by itself and not as one-half of III.1–2, both because it alone contains the last two thunderclaps, and because, as they were filled out or filled in late, they indicate that this chapter came to acquire a special unity that transcended the original plan of some twelve to fourteen years previously. This is not to suggest that the remaining chapters are in any degree superfluous; rather that they have other work to perform at the wake, work different from that of the thunders and their contexts, though no less Menippean.

In a letter full of frustration, written while he was composing the present chapter of the *Wake*, Joyce remarked that it rehearsed familiar material. It is 'a description of a postman travelling backwards in the night through the events already narrated. It is written in the form of a *via crucis* of 14 stations but in reality it is only a barrel rolling down the river Liffey.'[6] The rolling barrel becomes, after thunder 10, a 'victory roll' or 'barrel roll' performed by an exultant Shaun as (or in) an airplane. Whatever the original plan, the final version of III.1 has an elaborate, digressive, and quintessentially Menippean structure.

The chapter opens (403) with a narrative voice telling the reader to listen to a series of sounds that are both a church bell tolling midnight and the firing of a twelve-cylinder reciprocating engine. This narrator continues for another paragraph and then either changes voice or is replaced by another first-person narrator. The latter voice continues for four more pages and ends by introducing a wireless television set. Shaun is on the set; he gestures, and his hand (active touch, synaesthesia) presents a dialogue between him and a new interlocutor, a group, that continues for a 'via crucis' of fourteen interchanges. Shaun has a last speech (425–6); the voice of his hand is replaced by that of a narrator. Shaun does his barrel roll; the television, an Aladdin's lamp, turns off amid last comments from his interlocutor. Shaun (who is revealed as the other narrators' voices, private and corporate) speaks the concluding paragraph. Seen thus, as a narration interrupted by a dialogue that forms a second plot, the chapter is a Milesian tale, an epyllion.[7]

Within that framework there resides a more complex plot-digression pattern. The speeches of the early first-person narrator include several important digressive descriptions – of Shaun's clothing (404.15–405.03), of Shaun's carriage and comportment (405.07–24), of Shaun's food and zest as a banqueter (405.29–407.09), and of the television set (407.11–22). The whole is presented as a dream-vision: 'Methought as I was dropping asleep somepart in nonland of where's please …' (403.30–1). Shaun delivers both thunders in his speeches, which are usually much longer than those of the corporate interlocutor. Thunder 9 is a parenthetic aside in the middle of a sentence introducing the central portion of the chapter – itself a digression, – the second of Joyce's fables, 'The Ondt and the Gracehoper' (414.16–419.11). (The first fable, mentioned earlier, was 'The Mookse and the Gripes.') The rest of the chapter serves as the enveloping action for the fable.

Shaun's first speech after the fable is followed by a digression describing the labyrinthine route he uses in delivering the Letter (420.17–421.14). It concludes with a parody of JvH's telegram to PQ: 'Stop. Cumm Bumm. Stop. Come Baked to Auld Aireen. Stop.' (421.13–14), indicating a retrograde motion from the concerns of thunder 5 (the Letter) to those of thunder 2. Immediately, Shaun's dialogue is resumed for five further interchanges (the third includes thunder 10). The third-person narrator then returns to describe Shaun's transformation. The television image fades out, and the first-person-plural narrator returns to speak the concluding paragraph. Thus, at the end, the inside and the outside of the narrative exchange places. The first-person-singular voice that introduces the televised dialogue and then disappears has the last word *on* the program, while the corporate voice that first appears with Shaun and remains alone on the program with him continues after the set is off. What began in the mode of private consciousness ends in the mode of collective awareness.

The keynote of this chapter, more than in the others, is metamorphosis. The time is given, at the outset, as midnight (later, as midday), the bewitching hour, and the mode as deep dream (also metamorphic), that of interiorizing outer experience and of fluid time, space, and identity.

Methought as I was dropping asleep somepart in nonland of where's please (and it was when you and they were we) I heard at zero hour as 'twere the peal of vixen's laughter among midnight's chimes from out the belfry of the cute old speckled church tolling so faint a goodmantrue as nighthood's unseen violet rendered all animated greatbritish and Irish objects nonviewable to human watchers save 'twere perchance anon some glistery gleam darkling adown surface of affluvial flowandflow as again might seem garments of laundry reposing a leasward close at hand in full expectation. And as I was jogging along in a dream as dozing I was dawdling, arrah, methought broadtone was heard and the creepers and the gliders and flivvers of the earth breath and the dancetongues of the woodfires and the hummers in their ground all vociferated echoating: Shaun! Shaun! Post the post! with a high

voice and O, the higher on high the deeper and low, I heard him so! And lo,
mesceemed somewhat came of the noise and somewho might amove allmurk. Now,
'twas as clump, now mayhap. (403.18–404.11)

The passage is given a tinge of Middle and Elizabethan English ('methought,'
'mescemed,' etc.) that accentuates the feeling of dream and romance fiction
('Blessed momence, O romence ...' 404.14) while the stage is set and the airplane and auto are introduced.
   They are heard at the outset:

   Hark!
   Tolv two elf kater ten (it can't be) sax.
   Hork!
   Pedwar pemp foify tray (it must be) twelve.
   And low stole o'er the stillness the heartbeats of sleep. (403.13–17)

Both the church bell and the reciprocating engine are Menippean products –
at least in so far as neither performs according to logical engineering or ordinary experience. Therefore, the twelve strokes of the bell occur in an apparently random sequence: 12-2-11-4-10-6 (line 14), and 4-5-50-3-12 (line 16).[8]
This is also the firing order of a (Menippean, equally absurd) twelve-cylinder
engine for a car or airplane. The passage also serves to introduce one of the
main thematic concerns of the chapter: time. The next words – 'White fogbow spans. The arch embattled. Mark as capsules. The nose of the man who
was nought like the nasoes. It is self-tinted, wrinkling, ruddled' (403.6–8) –
link the themes of time and metamorphosis. The "nose of the man," etc., is a
clear reference to Ovid (Publius Ovidius Naso), whose chief work, the *Metamorphoses*, served Joyce in all his Menippean writings. A fogbow is a rain
bow arch produced in and by fog. Rainbows require daylight, yet the base
time is midnight, so the passage suggests a carrying forward of the mixture
of light and dark from thunder 8. It is not now twilight, but midnight and
midday simultaneously – both of them moments of transformation. The arch
is 'embattled' because the place of the visual sense in the hierarchy of the
senses, symbolized throughout the *Wake* by the spectrum and the seven or
the twenty-eight girls, continues to be adjusted during the final thunders.
Now, instead of clear day or night, it is foggy, so the effective operation of
vision is reduced from the outset of the episode. Too, fog is low-flying cloud,
where rain and thunder and lightning emanate, so our scene is set at the very
heart of the processes of transformation.

The Ondt and the Gracehoper

Entomology has been a traditional resource for our culture for both moral fables and satire. Virgil took his bees seriously, as did Swift and Arnold theirs: the industrious bee produces honey and wax – for sweetness and light. For the moralists of old, the ant became an almost heraldic symbol of industriousness. G.K. Chesterton saw enough in Maeterlinck's allegory to provide Joyce with the material for his reworking of Aesop's 'Ant and the Grasshopper' into the car and the airplane:

Maurice Maeterlinck is a man of unmistakeable genius, and genius always carries a magnifying glass. In the terrible crystal of his lens we have seen the bees not as a little yellow swarm, but rather in golden armies and hierarchies of warriors and queens. Imagination perpetually peers and creeps further down the avenues and vistas in the tubes of science, and one fancies every frantic reversal of proportions; the earwig striding across the echoing plain like an elephant, or the grasshopper coming roaring above our roofs like a vast aeroplane as he leaps from Hertfordshire to Surrey. One seems to enter in a dream a temple of enormous entomology, whose architecture is based on something wilder than arms or backbones; in which the ribbed columns have the half-crawling look of dim and monstrous caterpillars; or the dome is a starry spider hung horribly in the void.[9]

At one level, the Ondt and the Gracehoper are Shaun and Shem. At another, they are Wyndham Lewis and an amalgam of Joyce and Eliot; at still another, the car and the airplane; at yet others, the bureaucrat and the artist, the eye-man and the ear-man, and all the pairs and doubles and complements in the *Wake*. (They are also thunders 9 and 10.) As Joyce writes, '*These twain are the twins that tick* Homo Vulgaris' (418.26).[10]

As this chapter begins, the visually biased Shaun, who had played 'angel' to Shem's 'devil' in the Phoenix Playhouse, is cast in reverse as the Ondt/devil. As both a car and a mailman he wends his way through the streets and the countryside: he traces the earth-labyrinth and his main concern is space. By contrast, the Gracehoper is other-worldly and flies above and around mere mundane limitations; he traces the air-labyrinth. His grace-hopeful concern is time and eternity, circumventing or 'beating' clock time. This theme is somewhat reinforced by the enveloping dream motif, for dreams are inner experience, not that of the outer world of vision and space, and are linked to cyclic time and to the ear, as was seen earlier. At chapter's end, Shaun succumbs to Shem's taunts and to the influence of the new media and is transformed out of his visual and spatial cocoon.

The first inventory of the chapter is one of Shaun's clothing (404.16–405.02). As such, it indicates that he is still under the influence of PQ's visual bias; but the clothes also serve him as carapace and cocoon, and his shoes, in particular, are described as metallic car wheels with changeable tires: 'thick welted brogues on him hammered to suit the scotsmost public and climate, iron heels and sparable soles ...' (404.20–1). Since Shaun is a motor car in addition to being a postman, he remarks the sedentary nature of the car as an extension of man: he is 'the bearer extraordinary of these postoomany missive on his majesty's service while we and yous and them we're extending us after the pattern of reposiveness!' (408.13–15). As the Gracehoper notes later on, all such outerings or extensions are necessarily accompanied by a closure of side-effects: '*An extense must impull, an elapse must elopes ...*' (418.34).

For Shaun, projected into space by this technology as never before, the side-effect is that he loses all relation to time. His delivery timetable continually fluctuates: the narrator says, 'Shaun in proper person (now may all the blueblacksliding constellations continue to shape his changeable timetable!) stood before me' (405.09–11). He becomes 'a mere mailman of peace, a poor loust hastehater of the first degree' (408.10–11). But he *is* a space expert:

... the Ondt, who, not being a sommerfool, was thothfolly making chilly spaces at hisphex ... (415.27–8)

The Ondt was a weltall fellow, raumybult and abelboobied, bynear saw altitudinous wee a schelling in kopfers. He was sair sair sullemn and chairmanlooking when he was not making spaces in his psyche, but, laus! when he wore making spaces on his ikey, he ware mouche mothst secred and muravyingly wisechairmanlooking. (416.03–08)

His Gross the Ondt, prostrandvorous upon his dhrone, in his Papylonian babooshkees, smolking a spatial brunt of Hosana cigals ... (417.11–13)[11]

The Ondt, that true and perfect host, a spiter aspinne, was making the greatest spass a body could with his queens laceswinging ... (417.24–6)

Because he was shaped by PQ, Shaun/Ondt begins the chapter with a strong visual bias and a need to isolate a private identity from that of the group. He spies Shem/Gracehoper and remarks:

But, Gemini, he's looking frightfully thin! I heard the man Shee shinging in the pantry bay. Down among the dustbins let him lie! Ear! Ear! Not ay! Eye! Eye! For I'm at the heart of it. Yet I cannot on my solemn merits as a recitativer recollect ever having done of anything of the kind to deserve of such. Not the phost of a nation! Nor by a long trollop! I just didn't have the time to. (409.01–07)

Like PQ, whose identity was at first submerged in 'a poss of porter pease,' Shaun feels the need 'to isolate i from my multiple Mes' (410.12), particularly as he feels increasingly threatened by the encroaching influence of the inner time-sense. Recalling Shem, he remarks,

It should of been my other with his leickname for he's the head and I'm an everdevoting fiend of his. I can seeze tomirror in tosdays of yer when we lofobsed os so ker. (408.17–19: See 'with the memories of the past and the hicnuncs of the present embelliching the musics of the futures' 407.31–3)

Subsequently, he predicts his own metamorphosis (which finally occurs with thunder 10):

... and there does be a power coming over me that is put upon me from on high out of the book of breedings and so as it is becoming hairydittary I have of coerce nothing in view to look forward at unless it is Swann and beating the blindquarters out of my oldfellow's orologium oloss olorium. A bad attack of maggot it feels like. 'Tis trope, custodian said. Almost might I say of myself, while keeping out of crime, I am now becoming about fed up be going circulating about them new hikler's highways like them nameless souls ... (409.36–410.08)

This is Shaun the postman, in the cocoon, in the process of becoming a car and then turning into an airplane, as a patterkiller becomes a flutterby. He will later turn from a space/eye man into an ear/time man after wrapping himself in television.

If there is one sound that predominates in this section of the *Wake*, it is the drone and the stuttering cough of the internal combustion engine: 69 per cent of the letters that compose thunder 9 is given to 'coughing' in one or another language. Although the engine is necessary for both the car and the airplane, it is associated thematically with Shaun, the ant who stockpiles food and fuel and whose Rabelaisian appetite is so celebrated in the middle-class banquet described on 405.29–407.09.[12] The engine has twelve cylinders ('twelve coolinder moons!' 408.34: perhaps its association with the bureaucratic Shaun is by way of the number twelve and the bureaucratic jury), and so the car-apace constantly demands food/fuel: 'he fell ... to sirch for grub for his corapusse or to find a hospes, alick, he wist gnit!' (416.12–15).

Consumption and the exhaust are linked in this Menippean anthropoento-
morphic engine, as the Shaun/Ondt,

having moistened his manducators upon the quiet and scooping molars and grinders
clean with his two fore fingers, he sank his hunk, dowanouet to resk at once, exhaust
as winded hare, utterly spent, it was all he could do (disgusted with himself that the
combined weight of his tons of iosals was a hundred men's massed too much for him)
... (408.01–07)

Asked by the corporate interlocutor if he is able to deliver the Letter, Shaun
replies:

– As, Shaun replied patly, with tootlepick tact too and a down of his dampers, to that I
have the gumpower and, by the benison of Barbe, that is a lock to say with everything, my beloved. (410.24–7)[13]

At the end of the digression of 'The Ondt and the Gracehoper,' the interlocutor exclaims to Shaun, 'How good you are in explosion! How farflung is
your folkloire and how velktingeling your volupkabulary!' (419.12–13)[14]
The same euphony is remarked in their earlier retort:

– How mielodorous is thy bel chant, O songbird, and how exqueezit thine after
draught! *Buccinate in Emenia tuba insigni volumnitatis tuae.* (412.07–09)[15]

The engine belches and burps, coughs and farts – which latter, through German, ties back into the roads theme. The running of the engine also finds its
echo in a linguistic motif of stuttering and stammering and repetition, for
example, 'the ra, the ra, the ra, the ra' (415.11–12), 'sunsunsuns' (415.22),
'Nixnixundnix' (415.29), and 'Nichtsnichtsundnichts!' (416.17), 'shooshooe'
(417.34), and 'coocoo' (417.36).
   As in the other sections, a 'fire' or 'burning would' of innovation is
present; here, it takes two forms. One is related to television; the other to fire
belched from the engine's exhaust and to internal combustion (digestion of
foodstuffs). Shaun is described as 'looking grand, so fired smart' (405.15), as
'the fiery boy ... naturally incensed' (412.13–14) who wanders 'this furnaced
planet' (412.17) and who smokes a special brand of Havana cigars. Finally,
Shaun admits that the engine produces 'the fuellest filth ever fired since
Charley Lucan's' (419.36).
   If Shaun is restricted to the underworld, the Gracehoper/Shem flies high

on art and wit. As a contrast to Shaun/Ondt's outer and visual bias, the Gracehoper is 'blind' and ear-oriented.

The Gracehoper who, though blind as batflea, yet knew, not a leetle beetle, his good smetterling of entymology asped nissunitimost lous nor liceens but promptly tossed himself in the vico, phthin and phthir, on top of his buzzer, tezzily wondering wheer would his aluck alight or boss of both appease and the next time he makes the acquinatance of the Ondt after this they have met themselves, these mouschical unsummables, it shall be motylucky if he will beheld not a world of differents. (417.03–10)

An identity quest is neither very important to the Gracehoper as he flings himself about in the air (cf. 'Tossmania' 416.28–30), nor very private; it is a 'boss of both appease.' Whereas the Ondt has command of space and of size, the Gracehoper is at home in or is identified with time, and Viconian cycles (ear-time is cyclic): he 'tossed himself in the vico.' For him, the universe is interiorized (cf. the reference to Schopenhauer, 414.33, who wrote of the world as will and idea, and the reference to *'my in risible universe,'* 419.03).[16] Further, he flirts with 'airy processes, even if only in chaste, ameng the ever-listings, behold a waspering pot. He would of curse melissciously, by his fore feelhers, flexors, contractors, depressors and extensors, lamely, harry me, marry me, bury me, bind me' (414.28–32). While the last series does relate to Viconian cycles, the 'flexors, contractors, depressors and extensors,' types of insect muscles, are also the control surfaces of a Menippean airplane – ailerons, rudder, elevators, flaps. And he has a landing gear, 'a partner pair of findlestilts to supplant him' (414.23–4).

However, the Shaun/Ondt does a little grace-hoping himself, after his own moralistic fashion:

But believe me in my simplicity I am awful good, I believe, so I am, at the root of me, praised be right cheek Discipline! And I can now truthfully declaret before my Geity's Pantokreator with my fleshfettered palms on the epizzles of the apossels that I do my reasonabler's best to recite my grocery beans for mummy *mit* dummy *mot* muthar *mat* bonzar regular, genuflections enclosed. Hek domov muy, there thou beest on the hummock, ghee up, ye dog, for your daggily broth, etc., Happy Maria and Glorious Patrick, etc., etc. In fact, always, have I believe. Greedo! (411.12–21)

After the thunder, he snobbishly shuns the Gracehoper (415.30–1), but, as his own metamorphosis is commencing, he prays:

Seekit Hatup! ... Suckit Hotup! As broad as Beppy's realm shall flourish my reign shall flourish! As high as Heppy's hevn shall flurrish my haine shall hurrish! Shall grow, shall flourish! Shall hurrish! Hummum. (415.34–416.02)

This ends with the humming engine and contains again the hatred of haste, both conventional references for the Ondt; but the terms of the prayer parody an inscription on the Egyptian pyramid of Pepi II.[17] Since the Egyptians were concerned to 'beat time,' this texture of the text suggests that Shaun has begun to metamorphose. And this reference brings up a final group of themes related to Finnegan and to the wake.

Altogether, the fable of the Ondt and the Gracehoper is adorned with several hundreds of entomological references: technical terms like termitary, Siphonaptera, and corbicula, mingle with foreign words like *Biene* (Ger, bee), *rogach* (R, stag beetle), and *drewbryf* (We, bug), and common English words such as ant, louse, flea, nit, gnat, etc. Mechanical terms relating to cars, engines, or airplanes, are almost entirely absent as these have been anthropomorphized or entomologized. So the car, a car-apace, has turned into Shaun's metallic clothing, and into the Ondt's carapace. Similarly, Finnegan's coffin (the vehicle for Shaun/Ondt's metamorphosis) is a cocoon. An almost-too-human Shaun, a postman, gradually transforms into a post-man or post-human (out of time) as the chapter moves towards thunder 10; simultaneously, Finnegan 'wakes' by being reconstituted. This transformation will appear when the relations among the different voices in III.1 are analysed in chapter 13, below.

The Themes of Space and Time

Early in III.1, Shaun's job is described as post-human: he is to 'be the bearer extraordinary of these postoomany missive' (408.13–14). As the Ondt/devil, he moves about the underworld, so he expects to encounter shades and ghosts, yet still he is frightened by Shem's ghastly appearance ('he's looking frightfully thin!' 409.01; cf. the ghost, 'phost,' 409.06). Shortly thereafter he finds that his cocoon is beginning to have its effect and remarks that 'there does be a power coming over me ... from on high out of the book of breedings ...' (409.36–410.02; the interlocutor calls him 'our belated,' 410.22), and just before the thunder he writes a Menippean 'last will and testament.' After thunder 9, his transformation from Ondt into Gracehoper is succinctly versified:

He larved ond he larved on he merd such a nauses[18]
The Gracehoper feared he would mixplace his fauces. (418.11–12)

On the other hand, the Gracehoper is no stranger to the cocoon/casket as he happily plays in time and out of the spaces of this world: 'he was always striking up funny funereels with Besterfarther Zeuts, the Aged One, with all his wigeared corollas, albedinous and oldbuoyant, inscythe his elytrical wormcasket' (414.34–415.01), and singing:

Hombly, Dombly Sod We Awhile but *Ho, Time Timeagen, Wake!* For if sciencium (what's what) can mute uns nought, 'a thought, abought the Great Sommboddy within the Omniboss, perhops an artsaccord (hoot's hoot) might sing ums tumtim abutt the Little Newbuddies that ring his panch. A high old tide for the barheated publics and the whole day as gratiis! Fudder and lighting for ally looty, any filly in a fog, for O'Cronione lags acrumbling in his sands but his sunsunsuns still tumble on. Erething above ground, as his Book of Breathings bed him, so as everwhy, sham or shunner, zeemliangly to kick time. (415.14–24)

Shaun's 'last will intesticle' is a requiem for PQ and for matriarchy, both of which are fast losing all of their castrating influence over him:

To the Very Honourable The Memory of Disgrace, the Most Noble, Sometime Sweepyard at the Service of the Writer. Salutem dicint. The just defunct Mrs Sanders who (the Loyd insure her!) I was shift and shuft too, with her shester Mrs Shunders, both mudical dauctors from highschoolhorse and aslyke as Easther's leggs. She was the niceliest person of a wellteached nonparty woman that I ever acquired her letters, only too fat, used to babies and tottydean verbish this is her entertermentdags for she shuk the bottle and tuk the medascene all times a day. She was well under ninety, poor late Mrs, and had tastes of the poetics, me having stood the pilgarlick a fresh at sea when the moon also was standing in a corner of sweet Standerson my ski. P.L.M. Mevrouw von Andersen was her whogave me a muttonbrooch, stakkers for her beg-first party. Honour thy farmer and my litters. This, my tears, is my last will intesticle wrote off in the strutforit about their absent female assauciations which I, or perhaps any other person what squaton a toffette, have the honour to had upon their polite sophykussens in the real presence of devouted Mrs Grumby when her skin was exposed to the air. O what must the grief of my mund be for two little ptpt coolies worth twenty thousand quad herewitdnessed with both's maddlemass wishes to Pep-ette for next match from their dearly beloved Roggers, M.D.D. O.D. May doubling drop of drooght! Writing. (413.03–26)

The requiem is made the more pointed by the included paraphrases and paro-dies of passages from Swift's 'On the Death of Mrs. Johnson' (Stella). The passage, 'only too fat' to 'had tastes of the poetics' corresponds to Swift, '... only a little too fat ... this is the night of the funeral ... frequent fits of sickness ... she had true taste and good sense both in poetry and prose.' And the passage, 'which I, or perhaps' to 'Mrs Grumby' corresponds to Swift, '... the truest, most virtuous and valuable friend that I, or perhaps any other person, was ever blessed with ...'

Finally, the classic Menippean structure of 'The Ondt and the Gracehoper' digression should be mentioned. This piece (414.14–418.11) was composed as a unit and inserted into the already drafted chapter. It begins with a transitional piece of dialogue that contains thunder 9. That is followed by six paragraphs of prose, and then by a page of verse in the same metre and tone as Goldsmith's 'Retaliation.'[19] It ends with a parodic blessing, the sign of the cross over Shaun (a cross is Joyce's siglum for 'the four'). The verse is a condensed reprise of the themes already discussed. For example, the Gracehoper sings to the Ondt,

> *Can castwhores pulladeftkiss if oldpollocks forsake 'em*
> *Or Culex feel etchy if Pulex don't wake him?*
> *A locus to loue, a term it t'embarass,*
> *These twain are the twins that tick Homo Vulgaris*
>
> ...
>
> *Your feats end enormous, your volumes immense,*
> *(May the Graces I hoped for sing your Ondtship song sense!),*
> *Your genus its worldwide, your spacest sublime!*
> *But, Holy Saltmartin, why can't you beat time?*   (418.23–6; 419.05–08)

The ninth thunderclap –

(husstenhasstencaffincoffintussemtossemdamandamnacosaghcusaghhobix-hatouxpeswchbechoscashlcarcarcaract) (414.19–20)

– resounds with all of the themes present in its context, as the following list illustrates.

Thunder	Interpretation	Theme Sounded
husstenhassten-caffin-coffin tussem-tossem daman-damna ... cosagh-cusagh ... car-car-car ...	Pairs or doubles; stuttering; onomatopoeia, coughing of an engine, of Shaun	Pairs from all parts of the *Wake*; stutterance (early thunders), innovation; engine (car, airplane), Shaun

Thunder	Interpretation	Theme Sounded
hus	Ger, *hus*, house	cocoon, carapace
husste	Dan, Nor, *hoste*, Sw, *hosta*, cough (26L)	engine; Shaun clearing his throat before delivery
hussten	sustain Ger, *Husten*, Du, *hoesten*, cough	Shaun's persistence engine, etc.
us	us	corporate interlocutor
ste	Sw, Dan, Nor, *sta*, stand (26L)	Shaun's legs, wheels; airplane landing gear, 'findlestilts'
ten	teem Fr, *taon*, gadfly Fr, *temps*, time	corporate Gracehoper/airplane time
tenhas	Fr, *tenace*, tenacious	Shaun's persistence
hasste	Sw, *hosta*, Dan, Nor, *hoste*, cough (26L) Dan, *haster*, urgent	engine, etc. time, hastehater
hassten	hasten Du, *hoesten*, cough	time, hastehater engine, etc.
ass	ass, donkey buttocks Fr, *aise*, ease, comfort, substantial	donkey (cf. thunder 10) flatulence: engine, roads; the sedentary Shaun/Ondt
asste	Sw, *äska*, thunder	thunder
assten	Austin Aston (Martin) Ar, *assam*, deaf	car car Shaun, eye-man
stenc	stink, stench	exhaust, flatulence
stenca	Ital, *stanco*, tired, weary (26L)	Shaun
tencaffincof- fintussem- tossem	think of Finn coughing/take off Finn['s] coffin, to see him tossing [and turning]	engine, etc.; coffin/carapace/cocoon; rough ride; Finn wakes, revives

Thunder	Interpretation	Theme Sounded
enc	Fr, *encre*, ink	Letter
caffin	coughing	engine, etc.
caffincoffin	Fi, *keinotekoinen*, artificial (26L)	extensions of man, these new technologies
affinco	Fi, *vahinko*, damage (26L)	transformation of Shaun, thunderchanges
	Fr, *afin que*, to the [distant] end that ...	Shaun transformation
fin	Finn[egan] Fr, *fin*, end Gael, *fein*, self	Finnegan, corporate visual/sequential time Shaun's individualism
finco	Gr, *vicho*, cough	engine, etc.
coffin	coffin coughing	coffin/carapace/cocoon engine, etc.
fintu	Fi, *kinkku*, ham (26L)	radio/TV 'hams'
intus	Fr, *en tous/tout* in everyone	corporate
tusse	Fr, *tousser*, Sp *toser*, cough	engine, etc.
tussem	twosome to seem Lat, *tussem*, a cough	pairs, doubles, etc. visual, outer world engine, etc.
tussemtossem	[bumpy ride]	car/airplane
usse	R, *usa*, door Fi, *isa*, father	doors Finnegan, patriarchal group
ussem	us then you seem Ger, *essen*, eat Fr, *essence*, gasoline	corporate Shaun Shaun banquet, engine fuel; Ant and Grasshopper engine
sem	Shem	Shem/Gracehoper

Thunder	Interpretation	Theme Sounded
semt	scent	exhaust smell, etc.
	sent	Letter
	seemed	Shaun, visual, outer
tos	toes	wheel/foot, Shaun
tosse	to see	visual
	Fr, *tas*, heap, pile	banquet, food storage
	Ital, *tosse*, Sp *toser*, Port *tossir*, cough	engine, etc.
	Fr, *tasser*, to fill up	banquet, etc., gas tank
tossem	toss them	rough ride; Gracehoper 'in the vico'
	(See tussem)	(Ibid.)
osse	Fi, *isa*, father (26L)	Finnegan, patriarchal
	R, *osi*, wasps	Gracehoper/airplane
ossem	awesome	imposing Ondt
	ozone	engine exhaust
semd	sent	Letter
semdaman	seemed a man (once)	Shaun, post-human
emda	Ar, *imda*, signature (26L)	Letter; last will ...
emdam	Ger, *Enden*, end	of visual
da	day	time: midday
daman	demon	Shaun/Ondt-devil
	Fr, *demain*, tomorrow	time
damandamn	damn and damn	Ondt expletive/home
aman	a man	Shem, Shaun
	Amon, Egyptian creator (Gla)	Finnegan, patriarchal gods arise
man	Ar, *maan*, together (26L)	corporate
	Gael, *maon*, dumb (GaL)	Shaun (Shem is blind)
	meann, stuttering (GaL)	stutterance; engine sound
mand	Fr, *monde*, world	space theme

Thunder	Interpretation	Theme Sounded
mandam	Lat, *mandamus*, we command (legal term) (ClL)	
anda	Sw, *anda*, breath (26L)	engine; Shaun Book of Breathings (transformation)
andam	Ger, *enden*, end Ger, *ändern*, to change	thunder; Shaun as post-man metamorphosis
damna	Daimler Lat, *damna* (pl.), losses, injuries; fines (ClL)	car/Ondt
amna	Ar, *namla*, ant (26L)	Ondt
amnac	Gael, *annach*, one-who-is GaL)	Shaun as human
nac	Ger, *Nacht*, night	time; midnight
nacosagh	narcosis Fi, *matkustaa*, travel (26L)	coffin/cocoon car, airplane, Letter delivery
nacosaghcusagh	Gael, *na casachta*, of the cough (GaL)	engine, etc.
cos	Sp, *coche*, car Gael, *cos*, foot, leg	car postman delivers on foot; wheel, car
cosagh	Gael, *cosagh*, footed (GaL) Gael, *casacht*, cough (GaL)	Shaun; wheel engine, etc.
cosaghcu	Gael, *casachtach*, cough (GaL)	engine, etc.
osa	R, *osa*, wasp	Gracehoper
sa	Du, *saai*, tedious (26L) Ar, *saah*, hour	hastehater, etc. time
sag	Ger, *sag*, say, *sagt*, says	the dialogue
sagh	R, *zhech*, burn	internal combustion, 'fire' motif
saghcu	Ger, *Schabe*, cockroach	Shaun/Ondt/car
aghcu	R, *achki*, eyeglasses (26L)	Shaun 'peering closer'

Thunder	Interpretation	Theme Sounded
cus	Sp, *coche*, car (26L)	car
hob	hub [of wheel]	wheel, car
obix	obese	Shaun/Ondt (after banquet)
obixhat	opposite	pairs/polarities: eye-ear, time-space, etc.
bi	Sw, Dan, Nor, *bi*, bee (26L)	Gracehoper, airplane
bix	bees Gr, *bex*, a cough (ClL)	Gracehoper, airplane engine, etc.
bixhat	be-shat fixate	exhaust visual (static)
ixhat	R, *yekhat*, drive (26L)	car, plane
hatouxpes	Fi, *maatkustaa*, travel (26L)	car, plane; Shaun delivering the Letter
ato	auto	automobile
atoux	Ar, *yasouq*, drive (26L)	car, plane
toux	Fr, *toux*, cough Fr, *tous*, everyone, all	engine, etc. corporate
pes	Lat, *pes*, foot	Shaun, wheel, car; delivery
	Fr, *pèse*, weighs	Shaun (heavy after banquet)
	Ger, *Pass*, Dan, *pas*, passport (26L)	travel; car, plane
peswch	We, *peswch*, cough	engine, etc.
bec	Fr, *bec*, burner Nor, *bak*, behind (26L) Sw, *buk*, Nor, *buk*, belly (26L)	engine, fire Shaun the post-man banquet, food
bech	Gr, *bex*, cough (26L) Gael, *beach*, bee	engine, etc. Gracehoper
bechos echos	MBr, *bêchos*, of a cough (McH) echoes	engine, etc. ear: pairs, doubles

Thunder	Interpretation	Theme Sounded
chos	Fr, *chaise*, chair	Shaun 'wisechairman-looking'; sedentary Ondt, car
	Sp, *coche*, car	car
	chaos (Gla)	thunder, transforming
chosca	Fr, *chausseur*, wear/put on shoes	Shaun, postman; tires for wheel (cocoon for feet)
	[Michael] Cusack, the cyclops [Gr, wheel-eye] in *Ulysses* (Gla)	one eye: waning of visual
hosc	husk	carapace, cocoon/car/coffin
osca	Sp, Ital, *mosca*, fly (26L)	Gracehoper
cas	case	carapace, cocoon/car/coffin
	Lat, *casus*, calamity	thunder, transforming
cashl	PS, *kasel*, cough (McH)	engine, etc.
cashlca	R, *kashlyat*, cough (26L)	engine, etc.
	Ar, *ghallayah*, boiler (26L)	fire; engine
shl	Gael, *suil*, eye	Shaun, eye
shlca	Po, *pschla*, flea	Gracehoper/airplane
car	car	car
carcar	Gr, *karkaron*, Lat, *carcer*, prison (ClL)	carapace
carcarcar	[stuttering]	stutterance, engine noise
	many cars	Shaun 'swarming of himself' (417.14)
arcar	Ar, *aachar*, another (26L)	doubles, pairs
carcar	Ar, *trartsur*, cockroach	Shaun/Ondt, car
carcarc	car-case/carcase	carapace, coffin/car/cocoon
arcarcarac	[spark plugs in engine; lightning]	car; thunder

Thunder	Interpretation	Theme Sounded
cara	carry	the Letter, by Shaun
	Fr, *courir*, run	hastehater Shaun; the engine
	Sw, *kra*, Dan, *kre*, drive (26L)	car, airplane
	Gr, *choros*, space	Space: Shaun; eye
caract	cracked	Humpty Dumpty
	R, *garyet*, burn (26L)	fire; engine
	car act	thunder 9
aract	erect	Finnegan; patriarchal arises/arouses

13

The Tenth Thunderclap: Television:
The Charge of the Light Brigade

Last word of perfect language (424.23–4)

Television kills telephony in brothers' broil. (52.18)

... 'by Allswill' the inception and the descent and the endswell of Man is *temporarily* wrapped in obscenity, looking through at these accidents with the faroscope of television, (this nightlife instrument needs still some subtractional betterment in the readjustment of the more refrangible angles to the squeals of his hypothesis on the outer tin sides) ... (150.30–5)

Doth it not all come aft to you, puritysnooper, in the way television opes longtimes ofter ... (254.21–3)

... the phoenix, his pyre, is still flaming away with trueprattight spirit: the wren his nest is niedelig as the turrises of the sabines are televisible. (265.08–11) Old yeaster-loaves may be a stale as a stub and the pitcher go to aftoms on the wall. (598.20–2)

Brave footsore Haun! Work your progress! Hold to! Now! Win out, ye divil ye! The silent cock shall crow at last. The west shall shake the east awake. Walk while ye have the night for morn, lightbreakfastbringer, morroweth whereon every past shall full fost sleep. Amain. (473.20–5)

The technological subject of thunder 10 appears early in III.1 as part of Shaun's uniform as a postman. He is described as dressed like Sean the Post in Boucicault's play, *Arrah-na-Pogue*. He carries a lamp on his belt.[1]

went into the society of jewses. One temp when he foiled to be killed, the freak wanted to put his bilingual head intentionally through the Irish Tames and go and join the clericy as a demonican skyterrier. Throwing dust in the eyes of the Hooley Farmers! He used to be avowdeed as he ought to be vitandist. For onced I squeaked by twyst I'll squelch him. Then he went to cecilia's treat on his solo to pick up Galen. Inkupot! He has encaust in the blood. Shim! I have the outmost contempt for. Prost bitten! Conshy! ~~leave~~ your libber to T C D. Your puddin is cooked! You're served, cram ye! Fatefully yaourth . . . Ex. Ex. Ex. Ex.

— But for what, thrice truthful teller, Shaun of grace? weakly we went on to ask now of the gracious one, Vouchsafe to say. You will now, goodness, won't you? Why?

— For his root language if you ask me, whys, Shaun replied as he blessed himself devotionally like a crawsbomb making act of oblivion, footinmouther! (what the thickuns else?) which he picksticked into his lettruce invrention. Ullhodturdenweirmudgaardgringnirurdrmolnirdfenrirlukkilokkibaugimandodrrerinsurtkrinmgernrackinarockar! Thor's for yo.

— The hundredlettered name, last word of perfect language. But you could come near it, we do suppose, strong Shaun O', we foresupposed. How?

— Peax! Peax! Shaun replied in vealar penultimatum. 'Tis pefils before Sweeney's as he swigged a slug of Jon Jacobsen from his treestem sucker cane. Mildbut likesome! I might as well be talking to the four waves till tibbes grey eves and the rests asleep. Frost! Nope! No one in his seven senses could as I have before said, only you missed my drift, for it's being incendiary. Every dimmed letter in it is a copy and not a few of the silbils and wholly words I can show you in my Kingdom of Heaven. The lowquacity of him! With his threestar monothong! Thaw! The last word in stolentelling! And what's more rightdown lowbrown schisthematic robblemint! Yes. As he was rising my lather. Like you. And as I was plucking his goosybone. Like yea. He store the tale of me shur. Like uyp. How's that for Shemese?

Thunder 10: galleys: 104 letters reduced to 100 letters

When look, was light and now'twas as flasher, now moren as the glaow. Ah, in unlitness 'twas in very similitude, bless me, 'twas his belted lamp! Whom we dreamt was a shaddo, sure, he's lightseyes, the laddo! (404.11–14)

Joyce is saying that, in the absence of a light-from-within, the mode of presentation is a pictorial verisimilitude such as emerges in Renaissance art. Later, after the lamp is lit, the mode reverts to medieval, lit from within and therefore playing down purely visual values such as verisimilitude and chiaroscuro in favour of iconography.

At this first contact, the lamp is out, but it is soon activated and becomes both an Aladdin's magical lamp and a television set.

Overture and beginners!
When lo (whish, O whish!) mesaw mestreamed, as the green to the gred was flew, was flown, through deafths of durkness greengrown deeper I heard a voice, the voce of Shaun, vote of the Irish, voise from afar [cf. 'nor avoice from afire' on the first page of FW] ... call the way how it suspired (morepork! morepork!) to scented nightlife as softly as the loftly marconimasts from Clifden sough open tireless secrets (mauveport! mauveport!) to Nova Scotia's listening sisterwands. Tubetube!
His handpalm lifted, his handshell cupped, his handsign pointed, his handheart mated, his handaxe risen, his handleaf fallen. Helpsome hand that holemost heals! What is het holy! It gested.
And it said:
– Alo, alass aladdin, amobus! Does she lag soft fall means rest down? Shaun yawned, as his general address rehearsal ... (407.10–28)

Joyce has two images for television. The minor one, used principally in this chapter, is Aladdin's magical lamp. It allows him to relate the themes of the chapter to *The Thousand and One Nights*. (thunder 10 has an extra letter: all ten present a total of 1,001 letters.) The major image, used throughout the *Wake*, draws, as did the theme of Buckley and the Russian General, on an event from the Crimean war, and is taken from Tennyson's 'The Charge of the Light Brigade': basically, suicide. The final stage of the thunder cycle is realized at Dublin, Ireland, both as Shaun's barrel tumbles and rolls down the river Liffey to the sea and the names of the locations coincide. The Irish name of Dublin is Baile-Atha-Cliath (pronounced by-a-clee-ah); the charge of the Light Brigade was made at Balaclava. Because of these features, and because Joyce remarked that he was writing *Finnegans Wake* 'after the style of television' (the television mosaic image of light dots, like the *Wakese* mosaic of puns and epiphanies, is pointillist in form), it will be necessary to draw on passages from other parts of the *Wake* to elucidate the television theme. In a real sense, then, the whole of *Finnegans Wake* is the context for thunder 10.[2]

There is one further association with television – that of the colour green. Green is the central of the seven colours of the spectrum: red-orange-yellow-green-blue-indigo-violet. And it is the colour most associated with Ireland, the 'emerald isle.' Perhaps Joyce regarded green as the unifying core of the spectrum from which the other colours were but deviations: but that is speculation, and matters little. On the other hand, *Finnegans Wake* is about the awakening of the sleeping giant, the tribe dormant in all civilized cultures, and Joyce did see Ireland as being at the forefront of that awakening. If green represents Ireland and if the other colours, alone or in various combinations, represent the other civilized nations, then the reunification of the spectrum thematically represents the reunification of civilized mankind into the human tribe (Finnegans) once more. In this reunification, the Irish are presented as being ahead of the others, perhaps because they had neither fully detribalized nor 'taken to' British or European civilization and so they had less of a change to endure.

The Action of Television

To Joyce, television seems to unweave the fabric of civilized society and replace it by a more organic form of association:

> Belisha beacon, beckon bright! Usherette, unmesh us! That grene ray of earong it waves us to yonder as the red, blue and yellow flogs time on the domisole, with a blewy blow and a windigo. Where flash becomes word and silents selfloud. (267.12–17)

There is such considerable play in this chapter with colours that it deserves a separate study. (Rimbaud assigned colour values for the vowels: Joyce may well have done something similar for vowels and the colour of lightning of the thunders.) In the above passage, the chromatic 'psychological primaries,' red, yellow, green, and blue, are given in clear English (while other colours, 'blewy ... windigo' have their spelling altered). The grouping suggests that a psychological or interiorized action is under way here. (Artists use two different groups of primary colours: the additive, for mixing lights; and the subtractive, for mixing pigments.)

The users of television, the new Finnegans, are electrically decomposed by the iconoscope tube in the television camera and are reassembled in the receiver:

> [it] receives through a portal vein the dialytically separated elements of precedent

decomposition for the verypetpurpose of subsequent recombination so that the heroticisms, catastrophes and eccentricities transmitted by the ancient legacy of the past, type by tope, letter from litter, word at ward, with sendence of sundance, since the days of Plooney and Columcellas when Giacinta, Pervenche and Margaret swayed over the all-too-ghoulish and illyrical and innumantic in our mutter nation, all, anastomosically assimilated and preteridentified paraidiotically, in fact, the sameold gamebold adomic structure of our Finnius the old One, as highly charged with electrons as hophazards can effective it ... (614.33–615.08)

Joyce summarizes the transformation as a kind of death:

BUTT *(giving his scimmianised twinge in acknuckledownedgment of this cumuli-kick, strafe from the firetrench, studenly drobs led, satoniseels ouchyotchy, he changecors induniforms as he is lefting the gat out of the big: his face glows green, his hair greys white, his bleyes bcome broon to suite his cultic twalette).* (344.08–12)

Green was the colour with which watch dials glowed; in addition, it was the colour of all early television screens, as well as the colour of make-up that performers had to wear for the cameras.[3] Erik Barnouw mentions this as an aspect of the development and expansion of television broadcasting in the thirties: 'To the Empire State transmitter, programs began to travel by cable from NBC studio 3H in Radio City. Less than two years old, this radio studio was made into a television studio with light grills and catwalks and technicians. It became the source of a diversity of productions, usually two per week, on Tuesday and Thursday. In the corridor, actors began to be seen with green make-up and purple lipstick. It became known that such things were necessary in the new medium; perhaps it would always be that way. Before long a green face no longer caused comment in Radio City cafeterias. It was, rather, a mark of status.'[4]

Joyce Menippizes both Tennyson and television in his first explicit description of the latter. The time is both midday (because of the heliotropes: it is 'precisely the twelves of clocks, noon minutes, none seconds ... by dawnybreak in Aira' 353.31–3) and midnight (because it occurs as a digression in the movie section of Butt and Taff), and therefore is all-time and no-time, 'noughttime':

In the heliotropical noughttime following a fade of transformed Tuff and, pending its viseversion, a metenergic reglow of beaming Batt, the bairdboard bombardment screen, if tastefully taut guranium satin, tends to teleframe and step up to the charge of a light barricade. Down the photoslope in syncopanc pulses, with the bitts bugtwug their teffs, the missledhropes, glitteraglatteraglutt, borne by their carnier walve.

Spraygun rakes and splits them from a double focus: grenadite, damnymite, alex-
tronite, nichilite: and the scanning firespot of the sgunners traverses the rutilanced
illustred sunksundered lines. Shlossh! A gaspel truce leaks out over the caeseine coat-
ings. Amid a fluorescence of spectracular mephiticism there caoculates through the
inconoscope stealdily a still, the figure of a fellowchap in the wohly ghast, Popey
O'Donoshough, the jesuneral of the russuates. The idolon exhibisces the seals of his
orders: the starre of the Son of Heaven, the girtel of Izodella the Calottica, the cross
of Michelides Apaleogos, the latchet of Jan of Nepomuk, the puffpuff and pompom of
Powther and Pall, the great belt, band and bucklings of the Martyrology of Gorman.
It is for the castomercies mudwake surveice. The victar. Pleace to notnoys speach
above your dreadths, please to doughboys. Hll, smthngs gnwrng wthth sprsnwtch!
He blanks his oggles because he confesses to all his tellavicious nieces. He blocks his
nosoes because that he confesses to everywheres he was always putting up his latest
faengers. He wollops his mouther with a sword of tusk in as because that he confesses
how opten he used be obening her howonton he used be undering her. He boundles
alltogotter his manucupes with his pedarrests in asmuch as because that he confesses
before all his handcomplishies and behind all his comfoderacies. And (hereis cant
came back saying he codant steal no lunger, yessis, catz come buck beques he caudant
stail awake) he touched upon this tree of livings in the middenst of the garerden for
inasmuch as because that he confessed to it ... (349.07–350.03)[5]

The audience is imaged as a heliotrope that follows the course of the television screen. At midnight, the ghosts walk; it merges here with noon, the
time of the real. Joyce implies that television creates a new mode of virtual
reality in which experience is interiorized by the '*inconoscope*' as discarnate
inward icons – a '*viseversion*' of visual, civilized realities that is 'nichilite,'
nihilistic.

This is restated grammatically to include the simultaneity of all times and
spaces:

The abnihilisation of the etym by the grisning of the grosning of the grinder of the
grunder of the first lord of Hurtreford expolodotonates through Parsuralia with an
ivanmorinthorrorumble fragoromboassity amidwhiches general uttermosts confus-
sion are perceivable moletons skaping with mulicules while coventry plumpkins
fairlygosmotherthemselves in the Landaunelegants of Pinkadindy. Similar scenatas
are projectilised from Hullulullu, Bawlawayo, empyreal Raum and mordern Atems.
They were precisely the twelves of clocks, noon minutes, none seconds. At someseat
of Oldanelang's Konguerrig, by dawnybreak in Aira. (353.22–32)

Joyce's description of the television is explicit, beginning with the 'bombardment screen' invented by Professor Baird, which is struck by a scanning electron beam that causes it to glow. The cathode-ray electron beam is fired from a gun ('*spraygun*') at the rear of the tube, whence it passes through a highly charged field and is deflected magnetically by plates inside or coils placed outside the tube to produce the scanned image (frame or '*teleframe*'). The scanning beam or spot traverses the screen in parallel lines sloped ('*photoslope*') from the horizontal. An external synchronization pulse ('*syncopanc pulse*') is added to the broadcast signal to ensure that the camera and the home receiver will scan in coordination. '*Double focus*' refers both to the 'split focus' technique of one early form of television and to the reversal of visual values that television causes whereby one 'focal point' is at the cathode emitter of the electron gun while the other vanishing-points are interiorized by the viewer of television along with time and space. The charged '*scanning firespot*' traverses about six hundred lines – the six hundred involved in the charge at Balaclava. Those soldiers were slaughtered, and the television world, too, is peopled by spectres, ghosts, and shades of the post-human era. Accordingly, towards the end of the passage, extreme unction is administered: '*blanks his oggles ... blocks his nosoes ... his latest faengers ... his mouther ... his manucupes with his pedarrests ...*' (eyes, nose, mouth, hands, and feet are anointed). Such is the situation Shaun enters as his televised dialogue gets under way, hastening his transformation into post-humanity.

In order for the genie to appear, Aladdin had to rub the lamp: in the television or magic-lamp world Shaun, too, exercises active touch. He waves the rhetorician's hebdomadal hand (he *is* delivery), and the hand speaks for and as him:

His handpalm lifted, his handshell cupped, his handsign pointed, his handheart mated, his handaxe risen, his handleaf fallen. Helpsome hand that holemost heals! What is het holy! It gested.
  And it said:
  – Alo, alass, aladdin, amobus! (407.23–7)

A page later he is identified with the broadcast signal itself: 'I, the mightif beam maircanny, which bit his mirth too early or met his birth too late!' (408.16–17). In the fifth interchange with Shaun, the interlocutor notes, pointing to the 'greening' effect of television: '– And it is the fullsoot of a tarabred. Yet one minute's observation, dear dogmestic Shaun, as we point out how you have while away painted our town a wearing greenridinghued' (411.22–4) Shaun answers:

– O murder mere, how did you hear? Shaun replied, smoiling the ily way up his lampsleeve (it just seemed the natural thing to do), so shy of light was he then. Well, so be it! The gloom hath rays, her lump is love. And I will confess to have, yes. Your diogneses is anonest man's. Thrubedore I did! Inditty I did! All lay I did! Down with the Saozon ruze! And I am afraid it wouldn't be my first coat's wasting after striding on the vampire and blazing on the focoal. See! blazing on the focoal. As see! blazing upon the foe. Like the regular redshank I am ... But it is grandiose by my ways of thinking from the prophecies. New worlds for all! And they were scotographically arranged ... (411.25–412.03)

Like Sean the Post in the play, Diogenes carried a lamp; that Cynic philosopher's barrel, in a Menippean twist, is also Shaun's barrel – and barrel roll – later in the chapter. Active touch is again invoked with 'Feefeel! Feefeel!' (420.13).

'Blazing' on 'foe' and 'focal' (and 'blazing coal') invoke as well the Charge of the Light Brigade–theme for television and the 'focal' electron gun inside the cathode-ray tube. (Scotography is X-ray photography.) A few pages later, we find Shaun 'under the sheltar of his broguish, vigorously rubbing his magic lantern to a glow of fullconsciousness' (421.21–3), and just before the thunder he becomes exercised about Shem and confuses him with the television and its effects (which indicates that his own sense of identity – he is Shem's twin – is at this point quite confused):

It was given meeck, thank the Bench, to assist at the whole thing byck special chancery licence. As often as I think of that unbloody housewarmer, Shem Skrivenitch, always cutting my prhose to please his phrase, bogorror, I declare I get the jawache! Be me punting his reflection he'd begin his beogrefright in muddyass ribalds. Digteter! Grundtsagar! Swop beef! You know he's peculiar, that eggschicker, with the smell of old woman off him, to suck nothing of his switchedupes. M.D. made his *ante mortem* for him. He was grey at three, like sygnus the swan, when he made his boo to the public and barnacled up to the eyes when he repented after seven. The alum that winters on his top is the stale of the staun that will soar when he stambles till that hag of the coombe rapes the pad off his lock. He was down with the whooping laugh at the age of the loss of reason the whopping first time he prediseased me. He's weird, I tell you, and middayevil down to his vegetable soul. Never mind his falls feet and his tanbark complexion. That's why he was forbidden tomate and was warmed off the ricecourse of marrimoney, under the Helpless Corpses Enactment. I'm not at all surprised the saint kicked him whereby the sum taken Berkeley showed the reason genrously. (423.13–32)

Although Joyce, in the *Wake*, consistently equates electric technologies

with the abandonment of sequential (visual) time and with extratemporal
interiorized experience, he does maintain that the iconography of the television image is basically medieval in character, that it is both a midnight and a
'middayevil' instrument. The last overt reference to Aladdin's television
lamp occurs as the dialogue ends:

And the stellas were shinings. And the earthnight strewed aromatose. His pibrook
creppt mong the donkness. A reek was waft on the luftstream. He was ours, all fra-
grance. And we were his for a lifetime. O dulcid dreamings languidous! Taboccoo!
   It was sharming! But sharmeng!
   And the lamp went out as it couldn't glow on burning, yep, the lmp wnt out for it
couldn't stay alight. (427.10–16)

This passage parodies a song from Puccini's Tosca:[6] as the television goes
out, midday seems to fade and midnight to return, but that is purely thematic reinforcement, for the condition imposed by television persists and
develops as the narration resumes. With the whole chapter in view, a re-
examination of the narrator's and others' voices is possible.

Transformation in the Narrative

The chapter begins with a third-person narrative that is quickly displaced by
a first-person speaker. Both voices are Shem's as he discusses and describes
his brother, Shaun. Before long, Joyce reveals further that this voice is also
that of the donkey belonging to 'the Four' (also, at times, Don Quixote), the
ass that carries the Logos on its back:

Had I the concordant wiseheads of Messrs Gregory and Lyons alongside of Dr Tarpey's
and I dorsay the reverend Mr Mac Dougall's, but I, poor ass, am but as their four-
part tinckler's dunkey. Yet methought Shaun (holy messonger angels be uninterrupt-
edly nudging him among and along the winding ways of random ever!) Shaun in
proper person ... (405.04–09)

The relations are complex: both Shaun and the donkey are carriers, themselves carried (in this section) on the 'carnier walve' or carrier wave of television, and therefore are inextricable from delivery. But in the past, Shaun's
job has been single-level and sequential, whereas both Shem and the donkey
(here somehow identified with Shaun) work with manifold levels of signification. Once the television/lamp goes on, Shem speaks with the 'we' of the
rest of the dialogue, a 'we' pregnant with associations. It is at once the mani-

fold levels, a mass audience for Shaun's delivery, and the reconstituted post-human (post-civilized) tribe into which Shaun will eventually merge. Both the television and the dialogue, moreover, function as cocoon for this metamorphosis of Shaun, while the transformational digression of 'The Ondt and the Gracehoper' signals its occurrence. Shaun delivers oratory – and himself.

Consequently, in his first speech after the digression, Shaun notes that he has arrived out of the daylight of Roman civilization and into the Dark Ages: 'I'm as afterdusk nobly Roman as pope and water could christen me' (419.21–2). This speech is interrupted by a further digression about the delivery of the Letter (420.17–421.14). As that ends, the midden-dump by the butt of the magazine wall 'rears'' casting up all pasts simultaneously as touch becomes active: 'Feefeel! Feefeel! ... And all the mound reared. Till he wot not wot to begin he should' (420.13–14). In his next speech, Shaun, having traditionally been visually bureaucratic, employs active touch, 'rubbing his magic lantern to a glow of fullconsciousness'; the mass audience has asked if he isn't rather akin to Shem, so he embarks on a lengthy description of Shem. His transformation continues apace; in their next address, the mass calls him 'Shaun illustrious' (422.19), and in the next, 'Shaun of grace ... the gracious one' (424.14–15). This latter statement precipitates thunder 10, 'the hundredlettered name again, last word of perfect language' (424.23–4).

Having delivered the thunder, the name/*logos* and formal cause of his metamorphosis into the spirit world of interiorized experience, Shaun has suddenly grown in strength and in intellect. So, in its remaining questions of him, the mass refers to him with such adjectives as 'strong Shaun' (424.24), and with

– Still in a way, not to flatter you, we fancy you that you are so strikingly brainy and well letterread in yourshelves as ever were the Shamous Shamonous, Limited, could use worse of yourself, ingenious Shaun, we still so fancied, if only you would take your time so and the trouble of so doing it. (425.04–08)

Shaun retorts:

– Undoubtedly but that is show, Shaun replied, the muttermelk of his blood donor beginning to work, and while innocent of disseminating the foul emanation, it would be a fall day I could not, sole, so you can keep your space and by the power of blurry wards I am loyable to do it (I am convicted of it!) any time ever I liked (bet ye fippence off me boot allowance!) with the allergrossest transfusiam as, you see ... (425.09–15)

His transformation is conscious and complete. He is no longer bound by space and has learned to 'beat time' by the inner experience of simultaneous time. At this point, several additional reversals occur.

Hitherto, Joyce has carefully assigned the voices, plural for the mass on the set, singular for outside (prior to) the televised dialogue/interview (except for Shaun who consistently speaks in the first person until the end of his last speech where he refers to himself or to his old persona in the third person singular – 426.01). However, after Shaun's last speech, Joyce symbolically turns the chapter inside-out. The first-person narrator resumes the stage to describe Shaun's barrel roll into the past[7] and simultaneous tumble inwards into the time-world. The voice then relates the turning off of the television/ lamp (the penultimate paragraph) and is replaced by the Shem/mass's corporate voice that speaks the concluding paragraph. 'I' enters the chapter/ cocoon; 'we' emerges.

Transformation and the Vortex

At this point, a passing reference to Wyndham Lewis by the first-person narrator serves to draw together several themes. After Shaun's last speech, the narrator reminisces, 'he was the soft semplgawn slob of the world with a heart like Montgomery's in his showchest and harvey loads of feeling in him and as innocent and undesignful as the freshfallen calef' (426.10–13). The last phrase alludes to Lewis's *The Caliph's Design: Architects! Where Is Your Vortex?*[8] and introduces Shaun's tumble into universal time:

... as they are telling not but were and will be, all told, scruting foreback into the far-goneahead to feel out what age in years tropical, eccelesiastic, civil or sidereal he might find by the sirious pointstand of Charley's Wain (what betune the spheres sledding along the lacteal and the mansions of the blest turning on old times) as ere-while had he craved of thus, the dreamskhwindel necklassoed him, his thumbs fell into his fists and, lusosing the harmonical balance of his ballbearing extremities, by the holy kettle, like a flask of lightning over he careened (O the sons of the fathers!) by the mightyfine weight of his barrel (all that prevented the happering of who if not the asterisks betwink themselves shall ever?) and, as the wisest postlude course he could playact, collapsed in ensemble and rolled buoyantly backwards in less than a twinkling ... with corks, staves and treeleaves and more bubbles to his keelrow a fairish and easy way enough as the town cow cries behind the times in the direction of Mac Auliffe's, the crucethouse, *Open the Door Softly*, down in the valley before he was really uprighted ere in a dip of the downs (uila!) he spoorlessly disappaled and vanesshed, like a popo down a papa, from circular circulatio. (426.22–427.08)

Shaun's former visual space-world is planar and linear: Joyce characterizes the new sensibilities as structured by circle and cycle and vortex.

The barrel tumbles through the water-labyrinth as the Liffey carries it 'along the riverrun, past Eve and Adam's ... by a commodius vicus of recirculation' to the sea (the same happens to PQ's rain). Vico's ages cycle and recycle, the whole movement creating a vortex as does Shaun's barrel roll in the airplane and his backwards journey through the events of the *Wake*.[9] Similarly, the electron beam of a television set creates a cone-shaped vortex (the early screens were circular) as it sweeps continually around the screen from side to side and top to bottom and back again. This sweeping creates as it were another vortex at the vanishing-point of reversed perspective in the user ('double focus'). Finally, a tensional vortex is created by the many pairs and doubles in the chapter, for example, verse and prose, Shem and Shaun, Ondt and Gracehoper, space and time, eye and ear/touch, motor car and airplane, individual and group, alphabet (the Letter) and television, human and post-human, outer and inner experience, and so on.

As the television/lamp goes out, Shaun undergoes a form of apotheosis:

Well, (how dire do we thee hours when thylike fades!) all's dall and youllow and it is to bedowern that thou art passing hence, mine bruder, able Shaun, with a twhisking of the robe, ere the morning of light calms our hardest throes, beyond ... we in the country of the old, Sean Moy, can part you for, oleypoe, you were the walking saint, you were, tootoo too stayer, the graced of gods and pittites and the salus of the wake. Countenance whose disparition afflictedly fond Fuinn feels. Winner of the gamings, primed at the studience, propredicted from the storybouts, the choice of ages wise! Spickspookspokesman of our specturesque silentiousness! Musha, beminded of us out there in Cockpit, poor twelve o'clock scholars, sometime or other anywhen you think the time. Wisha, becoming back to us way home ... (427.17–35)

Shem's corporate voice, the voice of all literature, welcomes the transmogrified bourgeois Shaun into the company of the patriarchal gods and particularly into that of a now-sensible Finnegan ('fond Fuin feels'). His single-levelled nature is put aside[10] as he amplifies himself to accommodate all four levels (note PQ's drizzle):

However! Our people here in Samoanesia will not be after forgetting you and the elders luking and marking the jornies, chalkin up drizzle in drizzle out on the four bare mats. How you would be thinking in your thoughts how the deepings did it all begin and how you would be scrimmaging through your scruples to collar a hold of an imperfection being committled. Sireland calls you. Mery Loye is saling moonlike.

And Slyly mamourneen's ladymaid at Gladshouse Lodge. Turn your coat, strong character, and tarry among us down the vale, yougander, only once more! And may the mosse of prosperousness gather you rolling home! May foggy dews bediamondise your hooprings! May the fireplug of filiality reinsure your bunghole! May the barleywind behind glow luck to your bathershins! (428.01–14)

The last four invocations show Shaun ensconced amidst another four, the four elements ('mosse ... dews ... fire- ... -wind') of alchemical transmutation.

Shaun's reunification with 'Sireland' symbolizes the displacement of all matriarchal environments and the establishment once more, and for all time, of the patriarchal/Finnegan mode of culture. In Viconian terms, it is a resurrection of the 'age of the gods' as an environment, displacing that of mere men. In the thunder, this awakening is invoked by the presence of names of various tribal gods from Norse mythology.

The tenth and last thunder –[11]

Ullhodturdenweirmudgaardgringnirurdrmolnirfenrirlukkilokkibaugimandodrrerinsurtkrinmgernrackinarockar! Thor's for yo! (424.20–2)

– is a formal vortex aswirl with the names and sounds of the themes and changes wrought at the wake by television.

Thunder	Interpretation	Theme Sounded
Ull	Gael, *ull* (prefix): great, huge, chief, mighty, many, monstrous (GaL)	The mass, the sleeping giant, tribe, Sireland television ('Horrid')
	Ull, Norse patron god of skiing, archery (McH)	Sireland, etc.
ullho	Gael, *ollamh*, tribal poet, sage (GaL)	Shem/mass
ullhod	the head of Ull, Norse god (SE)	return of gods, Sireland
ullhodtur	Lat, *aliter*, other	Shem-Shaun, etc.
	Sw, Dan, Nor, *alder*, age (26L)	time themes, mass-age
	altar	return of gods, etc.
	alter	thunder, change

Thunder	Interpretation	Theme Sounded
lho	Gael, green	television, Eire
lhodtur	Fr, *l'auteur*, the author	Shem (wrote the Letter)
hod	hod Dan, Nor, *hud*, skin (26L)	Finnegan tactility, barrel/carapace
hodtu	Fi, *hautaus*, funeral	wake, coffin, Finn again
hodtur	Hoder, blind god, killed Balder (McH)	return of gods, nonvisual
odtur	author	Shem (the Letter)
tur	Ger, *Tür*, door Sw, *torr*, Dan, *tør*, Nor, *torr*, dry (26L)	doors no more of PQ's rain
turd	turd toured	midden cycles and vortices; Shaun's mail route; return of all past times
turde	Fi, *turve*, sound (26L)	nonvisual
turden	Ger, through the ... Dan, Nor, *torden*, thunder (26L)	television (light *through* the screen) thunder
turdenwier	Nor, *tordenveir*, thunderstorm (SE)	thunder
ur	ur-, first Dan, Nor, *ur*, clock (26L)	cycle starts anew; Finn again time theme
urd	Urd, a Norse fate (McH) Urd, a Norn whose name means 'the past' (SE)	return of gods, Sireland; 'weird' Shem, television time theme
urde	Erde; Gerde	return of gods
urden	Odin (Gla)	return of gods
we	we	group
weir	weird (etym., to become!), fate	Finn again; transformation of Shaun; 'weird' Shem/television

Thunder	Interpretation	Theme Sounded
	Fr, *vert*, green	television
weirmud	Ger, homesickness	Shaun returns home (427.35)
ei	Ger, *Ei*, Du *ei*, egg (26L)	Humpty Dumpty (senses) reunited
eir	ear	nonvisual; dialogue
	Eire	television
mud	mud	tactility, nonvisual
mudgaard	mudguard	Shaun (motor car)
	Midgaard: Earth in Norse myth (SE)	return of gods, Sireland
	Du, Dan, *middag*, noon (26L)	midday evil, television
udgaa	Dan, *udgang*, exit	transformation of Shaun; doors
gaar	Fr, *guerre*, war	charge of Light Brigade (television)
gaardgrin	gathering	mass
	Cardigan, the earl of: English Lt Gen. in charge of the Light Brigade	charge of Light Brigade (television)
ardgr	ordure	midden-dump
	archer	Ull (see above), Sireland
gri	Fr, Sp, *gris*, Du *grijs*, grey (26L)	television ('grey at three')
grin	Crim[ea]	charge of Light Brigade (television)
	green	television
	Gael, *grien*, sun	midday: television
	Du, Sw, Nor, Dan, green	television, Eire
	Grimm (fairy tales)	Ondt and Gracehoper/ Ant and Grasshopper
	Ger, *Krim*, Crimea	charge of Light Brigade

Thunder	Interpretation	Theme Sounded
gringni	Grinne, minor Norse god	return of gods, Sireland
gringnir	Grimnir: Odin (SE)	return of gods, Sireland
ring	circle, cycle sound (e.g., of bells)	barrel roll, cycles, vortex ear again
ingn	engine	car and 'plane
ingnir	Ger, Du, Sw, Dan, Nor, finger	tactility
ni	Sw, Dan, Nor, new	renewal
ir	ear Eire	ear again television; tribal
irur	Ger, *Ihrer*, their	group, mass
rur	rear	electron gun at rear 'focus'
rurd	reared	'all the mound reared'

rurdr	rudder (at rear of ship)
	
	Rudra: Vedic storm god (Gla)
		wake; last thunder;
		  mass/tribe from
		  past in charge
		thunder[storm]; return
		  of gods

urd	Urd, Gerde, Erde	[see above]

drm	Sw, *dröm*, Dan, Nor, *drøm*,
	  dream (26L)
		inner experience; time
		  [see beginning of chapter]

drmol	dermal Fr, *dur, molle*, hard, soft	skin, tactility, carapace tactility, carapace
mol	Sw, Dan, Nor, *mal*, aim (26L)	electron gun
molni	R, *molniya*, lightning	electron beam, television thunder
molnir	Mjollnir, Thor's hammer (SE)	return of gods, Sireland
ol	Sw, *öl*, Dan, Nor, *øl*, beer, ale	Shaun's barrel
nirf	nerve	tactility
nirfen	Ger, *Nerven*, nerves	tactility

Thunder	Interpretation	Theme Sounded
fen	Finn	Finn again, etc.
	Fr, *fin*, end	time theme; last thunder
	Gael, *fein*, self	Sinn Fein, tribal
fenrir	Fenrir, a wolf, son of Loki (SE)	return of gods, etc.
fenrirlu	funeral	wake; Shaun post-human
rir	rear	end, rear, wake; last thunder; Shaun the Post; the mound (reared); electron gun at rear of set, etc.
	Fr, *rire*, laugh	television ('down with the whooping laugh')
rirlukkilok	rear-look, kill-look	electron gun at rear focus, kills visual dominance and replaces it with tactility
irlukki	Dan, Nor, *ulykke*, accident (26L)	thunder-change; Shaun changes to post-human
lu	Sw, *ljus*, Dan, Nor, *lye*, light (26L)	midday, time themes
luk	Luke	the Four
	look	waning visual
	Ger, *Licht*, Du *licht*, light (26L)	midday, time themes
lukki, lokki	lock, key	to doors (now open: see end of *FW*, 'The keys to. Given.')
	low key	tactility
	Ger, *Lucke*, gap	interval, tactility
	Ger, Du, *lachen*, laugh	'the whooping laugh'
	Fi, *lukea*, play (26L)	Shem/artist; senses in interplay (equals tactility)
	Sw, *lukta*, Dan, *lugte*, Nor, *lukte*, smell (26L)	television, 'spectracular mephiticism': resurrection motif
	Loki, a demigod (SE)	return of gods, Sireland

Thunder	Interpretation	Theme Sounded
lukkilokki	Sw, *kackerlacka*, cockroach (26L)	Shaun/Ondt
ukki	Fi, *auki*, open (26L)	doors
	R, *ukho*, ear	ear again, dialogue
kil	kill	corpse, ghost; Shaun turns post-human
kilokki	Sw, *klocki*, clock (26L)	time themes
	Sw, *klocka*, bell (26L)	ear again
lok	Ger, *Loch*, hole	interval, tactility
lokki	Loki, a demigod (SE)	return of gods, Sireland
	Fi, *luoti*, bullet (26L)	electron gun; charge of Light Brigade
lokkiba	Fi, *lokakuu*, October (26L)	charge of Light Brigade (took place on 25 Oct. 1854, at Balaclava: Russians defeated by English, French, and Turks)
okki	Ital, *occhio*, Rum *ochi*, eye	waning of visual
ba	Egy, immortal soul	ghosts, return of gods
baug	bug	Ondt, Gracehoper
	Fr, *bauge*, ring, sound cycle	ear again; barrel roll; cycle, vortex themes
	Gael, *bug*, soft	tactility
	Dan, *bog*, book	the Letter
baugi	Bauge, a giant in the Prose Edda (SE)	return of gods, Sireland
	Fr, *bougie*, candle	medieval lighting: television ('midday evil')
baugiman	bogeyman	Finn, sleeping giant, television-ghost, Ondt/devil
augi	Ger, *Auge*, eye	waning visual

Thunder	Interpretation	Theme Sounded
	Fi, *auki*, open (26L)	doors
augimand	augment	mass; all senses
ugim	Turk, *ekim*, October (26L)	charge of Light Brigade (television)
gim	Jim (Joyce)/Shem (Gla)	Shem/artist
gima	genie (a giant spirit)	Aladdin and the lamp, return of gods via tactility (rub the lamp)
gimand (od)	command(ed)	charge of Light Brigade
imandod	inundate	barrel tumbling down Liffey; simultaneity; merging into the mass
man	man Fr, *main*, hand Sw *mun*, Nor *munn*, mouth (26L) Ar, *maan*, together	Finn again, Sireland tactility, active touch dialogue, ear again Sinn Fein, re-tribalism
mand	Ger *Mund*, Du *mond*, Dan *mund*, mouth (26L)	dialogue, ear again
and	Ger *Hand*, Du, Sw *hand*, Nor *hånd*, hand (26L)	tactility, active touch; Shaun's hand that speaks, rubs the magic lamp
ando	Sw *anda*, Dan, Nor *ande*, breath	Book of Breathings (engine); Shaun transformation; Finn revives, breathes
andod	ended	thunder cycle, civil mode, visual dominance
do	Fr, *Dieu*, God Fr, *doux*, soft	Sireland, etc. tactility
dod	Sw, *död*, Dan, Nor *død*, death (26L)	ghost image, etc.; interiorizing of outer

Thunder	Interpretation	Theme Sounded
dodr	Sw, *dörr*, Du *deur*, Dan, Nor *dør*, door	door themes
dodrrer	dodderer: old man	Finn again
odrre	odour, stink	engine exhaust, 'spectracular mephiticism'
odrrerin	Oddrun, sister of Atli (SE)	return of gods, etc.
rer	rear Fr, *rire*, laugh	'all the mound reared' 'whooping laugh': television
rerin	rerun rearing	recycle: cycles, etc. the mound
rerinsurt	rear-insert	television image inserted from rear by electron gun
er	Eire	Sireland, television
eri	eerie Sw, *öra*, Dan, Nor *øre*, ear (26L)	television ghosts ear again
erin	Erin/Eire hearing	Sireland, television ear again
ins	Ger, *ins*, inside	interiorization of experience
insu	ensue	thunder's effects, Finn again
insurtkr	encircle	circle, cycle themes; oral tribe
insurtkrin	insurgent	mound reared; Crimean war theme
su	Fi, *suu*, mouth (26L)	dialogue; ear again; Book of Breathings
sur	Ar, *zuhr*, noon	middayevil television, time themes
surt	Surt: ruler of Norse fireworld, slays Frey at Ragnarok	Sireland, return of gods; electron gun

Thunder	Interpretation	Theme Sounded
surtkrin	supreme	Sireland, over civil/ matriarchal
krin	careen	Shaun barrel
krinm	Ger, *Krim*, Crimea	charge of Light Brigade, television
krinmg	cringe	fear of ghost image
krinmgern	Hrimgerd, a giantess (SE)	return of gods
rinmg	ring	circle, cycle themes; if bells, ear again
ger	Fr, *jour*, day	television middayevil; waking dream (wake theme); time themes
gern	Fr, *jeune*, young	television 'grey at three'
gernra	Ital, *giorno*, day	middayevil, etc., as above
ern	Erin	Sireland
ra	ray Egy, Ra, sun god Gael, *radh*, speech	stream of electrons middayevil; day, etc., themes; return of gods thunder; ear again; dialogue
rac	race (a people) raise	new post-human tribe resurrection themes
rackin	Raglan: commander of British troops in the Crimea	charge of Light Brigade television
rackinar	Ragnar Lodbrok, Viking tribal chief (SE)	tribalism
rackinarock	Ragnarok: the rending of the rocks: Old Norse myth of destruction of all things in a final battle with evil powers (SE)	Götterdammerung (cf. thunder 6); translation of all outer experience, incl. all time and space
ackin	icon	television iconoscope

Thunder	Interpretation	Theme Sounded
kin	kin[-ship, -folk] Gael, *caoin*, wail, lament (GaL) Gael, *cinn*, of a head/s, principal (GaL)	Finnegan again wake Sleeping Giant, Finn again
inar	inner	interiorization of all experience
na	Du, *na*, after	Shaun the post-human
nar	Ger, *Narr*, fool Heb, *nar*, light (26L) Ar, *nahr*, river (26L)	Shaun, before trans-formation television middayevil, day themes the barrel rolling down the Liffey (of PQ rains) flowing to join the patriarchal sea/mass
naro	Lat, *narro*, tell, report	dialogue
narockar	narrator	narrator: private turns corporate
aro	Lat, *aro*, plough, furrow	wake
arockar	orator	Shaun as delivery
roc	roc	Aladdin: asked the genie last for a roc's egg
rocka	R, *ruka*, hand (26L)	active touch, television
rockar	rocker: back and forth	cycle, vortex themes
ockar	Ar, *achdar*, green (26L)	television, Eire
ka	Egy, *Ka*, the soul or double	inner spirit world of tribe; doubles and pairs
kar	car	Ondt
ar	our air (verb) air (noun) Eire	corporate, tribe television broadcast television mephiticism Sireland

14

Conclusion

I done me best when I was let. Thinking always if I go all goes. A hundred cares, a tithe of troubles and is there one who understands me? One in a thousand of years of the nights! (627.13–16)

The keys to. Given. A way a lone a last a loved a long the (628.15–16)

Each thunder of *Finnegans Wake* includes words that mean 'thunder' and words that mean 'door.' Joyce's thunder is at once the sound of a cultural metamorphosis as registered in and by language, the formal cause of those changes, and the act of change itself. The appearance of 'door' is appropriate because each thunder is a portal or 'diaphane' through which our culture has passed. Each thunder names and dramatizes a cultural and perceptual labyrinth. In the *Wake*, Joyce leads us through these labyrinths a second time – in the wake of the first time, then for cognition, now for recognition, for perception. The first time, we, Finnegans all, blundered through each labyrinth in the dark; this second time we can work our way through aWake. Therefore, book IV, the final chapter of the *Wake*, announces the dawn. With the new day, all of the senses are awake and refreshed and functioning in concert. If subsequently the cycle begins anew – 'the seim renew' – it will be performed not in the night railed against by Pope in his 'Dunciad' but in the day of full awareness.

When writing *Finnegans Wake*, Joyce often likened his efforts to those of two tunnelling parties approaching each other from opposite sides of a mountain. The theme of 'one world burrowing towards another' is also used several times in the *Wake* and seems an apt image for the changes announced by the thunders as well. The tunnelling parties give a clue to Joyce's procedure: he tackled his problems from many sides simultaneously and kept at them until a solution presented itself. The mountain is the experience stored in language; sometimes, as in the case of the thunders, the solution came late.

It will be noticed, from the evidence presented in appendix 1, that although some thunders were written early, many were written late or added to galleys as the *Wake* was going to press. It also appears that their relation to *The Thousand and One Nights* (by their present embodiment in 1,001 letters) was hit upon only a year or two before final publication. This late decision serves to illuminate another of the many paradoxical features of serious Menippean satire and the particular difficulties of *Finnegans Wake*: the normal relation between surface and deep structure is reversed. The element of primary unifying import, say, in ordinary discursive writing or in novels the narrative or plot, resides on the surface, while the deeper structure includes style and imagery. However, in 1924, Joyce began work on a new kind of book, one that, after the pattern of Flaubert's ideal, would be held together not by plot or narrative but by the sheer force of its language and style.

With *Finnegans Wake*, as with such other Menippean satires as *De nuptiis ...*, *De planctu naturae*, *Gargantua and Pantagruel*, *Tristram Shandy*, *Bouvard and Pecuchet*, the structural element, the language, provides the surface; the narrative plot is the element most deeply buried. Once such works are recognized as Menippean and grammatical and as working primarily through language on the sensibilities of their readers, then the futility of approaching them by the usual route of educing the narrative becomes evident. The narrative of *Finnegans Wake* (supposedly an account of the fortunes of the HCE family), which has, from the appearance of Campbell and Robinson's *Skeleton Key* until the work of the structuralists a decade or so ago, formed the basis of most *Wake* criticism, is perhaps the element of least consequence. Pursuit of the story line, the Menippist's red herring, has had the effect of diverting critical attention from the most salient and most Menippean characteristic of the *Wake*: its language. (Joyce figured he'd keep the critics busy for three hundred years.[1]) This effect conforms nicely to Eliot's famous dictum about the function of 'meaning in the ordinary sense' in a poem: that it serves as 'the choice piece of meat carried by the burglar to distract the housedog' of the mind, so that the poem can go about its work unnoticed and unhindered. When Eliot's 'The Waste Land' appeared, it caused such immediate outrage in the literary establishment that it was instantly and (almost) universally denounced, automatically prohibited from inclusion in the literary canon. Derek Attridge has pointed out that *Finnegans Wake* still enjoys the same prejudice:

I am not suggesting that there is the remotest possibility of the anglophone cultural establishment's going back on its exclusion of *Finnegans Wake* from the central, defining core of the literary tradition, as enforced within the institutions of education and publishing. Indeed, the reasons I have given for the value of thinking through such a reversal are precisely the reasons why it will not happen within the context of current political and social systems. The canon is produced by and reinforces a set of values and assumptions upon which those systems depend for their degree of acceptance and their perpetuation; one has only to examine the governing political rhetoric of the major powers in the 1980s to find every notion that *Finnegans Wake* questions being given massive endorsement. The exercise of making the *Wake* a central and not a digressive text in our literary culture can be at present only a hypothetical one, but this is exactly its value, and the value of similar attempts to think against the grain of the instituted canon.[2]

If the *Wake* is still excludable from the establishment canon by virtue of its oddness and its challenge to every orthodoxy, it rests exactly along the central, defining core of the Menippean tradition, which it recapitulates in full.

The *Wake* has neither beginning nor end (hence, again, the irrelevance of narrative) and uses all of the established Menippean commonplace ploys. Even so, its identification as a Menippean satire could be based on its language alone. The language of the *Wake* is not, of course, unprecedented: Martianus Capella, Alan of Lille, and Rabelais are among Joyce's predecessors. But on the basis of the thunders alone one could conclude that *Finnegans Wake* is quintessentially Menippean.

The ten thunders are not a new kind of word game or crossword puzzle or acrostic. Joyce called them 'perfect language' (424.23–4), and they are language untrammelled by a merely connotative or nominalist function. His thunders return language to that ideal or ur-condition recognized by all grammarians as latent in ordinary speech and language. The thunders return language to constitutive utterance, transformative utterance that reunites naming and bringing-to-being in the primordial region of the *logos* and of formal causality. Awareness of this dimension of language underlies grammarians' traditional insistence that, on the one hand, etymology provided a certain route to understanding the formal nature of the things named, and that, on the other hand, there were 'continuous parallels' between the two Books, of Nature and of Scripture.

Whatever other ploys a Menippist uses, it is still his use of wit and of words that is fundamental to his Menippism. For it is chiefly by manipulating the accumulated experience and perception embedded in language that a Menippist retunes and readjusts the sensibilities of an audience to produce the effect of clarified perception. The primary focus of a critical appraisal of any Menippean satire should therefore be its language.

Joyce's thunders are both the most obvious oddity and the most dramatic aspect of *Finnegans Wake*. They are also the concentrated essence of everything he is doing in the rest of the book. They are the Menippean farrago *par excellence*, the point of convergence of Menippean list, prose and verse, narrative and theme, high style and low wit (and vice versa). As such, they are vortices or centres of energy, linguistic and thematic, which structure the whole of the *Wake* and the whole experience of the alert reader. They are macaronic medleys in fifty or more languages of themes from both their immediate contexts and the *Wake* as a whole, compressing and distilling the whole in a pattern that reflects numerous other Menippean satires, including that frame tale, *The Thousand and One Nights*, and the digressive lists or catalogues of Rabelais, Sterne, and many others. The very thunders are Menippean digressions from the ordinary turns of language, even from the turns established as ordinary to the *Wake*. Deliberately placing thunder 1 on the first page clearly indicates that the thunders are intended to arrest and provoke the reader from the outset – not to be passed over or ignored. Finally, in order to 'read' a thunder, the reader has to assume a posture at once passive and meditative, actively and intensely playful (a form of *spoudogeloion*) – a paradoxical and Menippean condition to which the training afforded by the language of the rest of *Finnegans Wake* is prelude. The prominent positions of thunders 1, 2, and 3, which any new reader will encounter quickly, signals that the reader is intended to notice them, wrestle with them, and return to rather than circumvent them.

If hitherto the thunders of the *Wake* have been neglected by Joyce scholars, the omission may stem from a general unawareness that the *Wake* is Menippean. Recognizing that it is a Menippean satire necessitates examining the thunders, for they are the most distilled and purely Menippean part of the work. This critical point of view yields the great advantage that it allows us to understand, for the first time, Joyce's generic intentions in writing *Finnegans Wake* in this manner and the central importance of the thunders as a key to what Joyce is doing in and with the work as a whole: in other words, what the *Wake* *is*, and what it is *for*.

My concern in these pages has been to lay a foundation for examining *Finnegans Wake* as a Menippean satire – the satiric arm of philology (traditional grammar). Besides concerning itself with language in a particular manner, Menippean (or Cynic) satire also explores the relation of technology to culture. Such exploration, too, forms an essential part of philology: philologists considered the two books, the Book of Nature (the world) and the Book Written as parallel texts that would yield to parallel exegetical technique and that would explain each other. These matters are primary focuses for *Finne-*

gans Wake too, and in this respect Joyce drew heavily on the grammarian, Giambattista Vico. The *Wake* is by no means without precedent in pursuit of these matters: its forerunners include works by Petronius, Apuleius, Martianus Capella, Alan of Lille, Erasmus, More, Henry Cornelius Agrippa, Rabelais, the *Satyre Ménippée*, Bonaventure Desperières, Cervantes, Swift, Sterne, among hundreds of others.[3]

Recognizing *Finnegans Wake* as a Menippean satire clears up many otherwise unintelligible aspects of the book, chief among them the apparently mad antics with language, and the thunderclaps in particular.

With a very few exceptions, *Wake* readers cannot say what the book *is*, or what it is *for*. The exceptions are those who have discerned that the book proceeds along grammatical lines. (The same, in fact, may be said of *Ulysses*, another if rather different sort of Menippean satire.) Once recognize that the *Wake* belongs to and brings up to date the Menippean tradition, and that Menippism is philological satire, and these questions quickly answer themselves.

Afterword

All writing with an overt or hidden satirical intent does, of course, juxtapose the ground and the trivial in order to bring out the triviality of the trivial.
(Rosemund Tuve, *Elizabethan and Metaphysical Imagery*, 215)

– But, Mr. Joyce, aren't many of your puns trivial?
– Yes, and many are quadrivial.

Loud, heap miseries upon us yet entwine our arts with laughters low! (*FW* 259.07–08)

In 'The Frontiers of Criticism,' T.S. Eliot wrote '… the only obvious common characteristic of *The Road to Xanadu* and *Finnegans Wake* is that we may say of each: one book like this is enough.' *The Road to Xanadu*,[1] by John Livingston Lowes, is a meticulous ferreting-out of all of the books which Coleridge had read and from which he had borrowed images or phrases to be found in 'Kubla Khan' and 'The Ancient Mariner' – a sort of perfect graduate-student paper. The *Wake* is itself an exuberant encyclopaedia of the trivial and the learned. Nothing, implies Eliot, exceeds like excess.

But Eliot was not given to flippancy in his public pronouncements: here, he is more likely playing possum. For Eliot ranks as perhaps this century's most learned critic and poet: his study of tradition and techniques of expression allowed him to view the whole, from Homer to the present, as forming a 'simultaneous order.' He very likely knew two Menippean works obscure to the average reader: Martianus Capella's *The Marriage of Mercury and Philology* (*De nuptiis Philologiae et Mercurii*) – regarded as 'the most popular book of the Middle Ages' – and Alan of Lille's *Plaint of Nature* (*De planctu naturae*).

The obscurity today of these works has two main reasons. One, the classics are no longer much read or discussed – not in translation, and certainly not in the original Latin. Second, neither work, Martianus' or Alan's, can be translated into English any more than the *Wake* can be effectively rendered into medieval Latin or koine Greek. Yet they are identical to the *Wake* in riot of wit, horseplay, hi-jinx with words and language, and mixture of trite and learned, trivial and quadrivial. The translator of Alan's *Plaint of Nature* said as much:

> With the possible exception of Martianus Capella, the Latin of the *De Planctu Naturae* is the most difficult I have ever encountered. Throughout most of the work there are two layers of meaning and in a number of places there are three. In addition, puns are an ever recurring feature; most of these cannot be expressed in English. The result is that parts of it defy an accurate and idiomatic translation.[2]

> The *Plaint* is an important work and was to have a far-reaching influence. Nevertheless, one cannot escape the conclusion that it may be a display-piece. The author revels in every device of Rhetoric. He at times tortures the Latin language to such an extent that one is reminded of Joyce's English. He so interweaves the ordinary, etymological and technical signification of words that, when one extracts the meaning of many a section, one despairs of approximating a satisfactory translation.[3]

So alike, and so different from the rest of Western literature, are the *Marriage* and the *Plaint* and the *Wake*, it is as if there have been three *Wakes* – the first two in Latin.

A mysterious cyclic coincidence emerges once the basic similarities of the three works strike the attention, one that might have delighted Joyce, though I have not yet found a direct reference to it in *Finnegans Wake*. Martianus wrote *De nuptiis* in the fourth century; Alan, *De planctu* in the twelfth; Joyce, the *Wake* in the twentieth. Evidently, Dame Literature serves us a 'book like this' every eight centuries. What to make of *that*? I don't know, beyond reassuring Mr Eliot that the next one will be some time in coming.

On the Composition of the Thunders

I. Chronology of Composition

The importance of Joyce's calling his first character, Roderick O'Conor, the 'last preelectric king' should not be overlooked. It demonstrates that he had in mind from the earliest time of composition various observations about the nature and effects of electric media on culture: the phrase is pregnant with the suggestion of electric and postelectric monarchy. Perhaps at the time he was toying with the idea of electricity itself as monarchical, as monarch of the new culture. In any case, book III was first drafted between 1924 and 1926 with the televised dialogue in place in III.1 in a rough form, without any thunders but including the references to Aladdin and his magic lamp.

In 1926, Joyce wrote three versions of thunder 1 and two of thunder 2, as part of their respective sections. Thunder 1, in its first form, took 97 letters: **badalgharaghtakamminnarronnkonnbronntonnerronntuonnthunn-trovarrhonnawnskawntoohoordenenthounucckk.**[1] This eruption had been inserted into a second draft of the opening section of the *Wake* (then called *Work in Progress*). The date is established by letters written at the time and mentioning the piece (*Letters* I, 15 November 1926; *Letters* III, 24 November 1926). A fair copy of the same passage from later the same year has the following, slightly changed, form: **badalgharaghtakamminna-ronnkonnbronntonnerronntuonnthunntrovarrhounawnskawntoo-hoordenenthunnuck!** Here, several letters have been deleted and one has been added: it is now 94 letters long. This version appeared in the typescript sent to Harriet Shaw Weaver.[2] In another copy of the typescript (not dated, but presumably made before revising the proofs for *transition* 1), Joyce added three more letters, changing the end to **kawntoohoohoordenenthunnuck.**[3]

Thunder 2 began as a marginal insertion, added in November 1926 to a fair copy of the PQ episode. In this first version, it is 76 letters long: **gokgorlay-orrgromgremmitghundhurthrumathunaradidillifaititillibumullunuk-kunen**.[4] In a typescript dated a few weeks later (16 December 1926), Joyce deleted the eleventh letter (to make **rlayorgro**) and changed the penultimate letter from **e** to **u**, making the new length 75 letters.[5] This version remained unchanged until galley proofs were set for *Finnegans Wake* in 1937.

In 1927, Joyce made one further change to thunder 1, altering the fifth-from-last letter from **n** to **r**, to make **thurnuck**. This was done about 25 February 1927, on a proof for *transition* 1.[6]

In the same year, 1927, he wrote two versions of thunder 3, and wrote thunder 4.

The first version of thunder 3, only 58 letters in length, was 'added in March 1927 to a late fair copy' of the context.[7] It was this: **klatschabattacreppycrot-tygraddaghsemmihsammihnouihpkonpkor**.[8] Revisions were made to two sets of galley proofs for *transition* 2 (about April 1927). On one, only the last letter was changed, from **r** to **s**. However, this alteration was not retained and the second set shows the following 83 letters: **klikkaklakkaklaskaklopatz-klatschabattacreppycrottygraddaghsemmihsammihnouihpkonpkor**.[9] The principal addition here has been the first 25 letters. Evidently this version was retained until 1937.

Thunder 4 first appeared in a typescript in 1927, not long after proofs were set for *transition* 4. The exact chronology is hard to establish, but as the dates involved are close together, perhaps the sequence is unimportant and the whole process can be regarded as a single act of composition. The typescript shows only the beginning and the end of the thunder, without the central portion but with the lacuna indicated by dashes. Consequently, I infer that Joyce had a definite scheme in mind for the thunder, had settled the begin-ning and end, and was composing and revising the central portion 'on the back burner.' (Of course, a much simpler, if less likely and less appealing, interpretation is possible: that the typist could not read or was too lazy to type the missing portion from the manuscript – or found it offensive, – and just indicated it with dashes.) The typescript, 46 letters plus lacuna, reads thus: **Whurawhorascortastrumpaporna ————————— strippuck-puttanach**, eh?[10]

Curiously, although this thunder appears in the typescript, it was not included in the galley proofs for *transition* 4, dated May 1927. Nevertheless, it did appear in the version printed in *transition* 4 (July 1927),[11] in exactly the same form as in *Finnegans Wake*.

In 1928, Joyce roughed in his first version of thunder 9 on the back of the first page of fair copy of 'The Ondt and the Gracehoper.' No further change was made to it until the first printed version appeared in *transition* 12. The rough-in is 63 letters long, as follows: **Husstenhasstencauffincoffintussemtossemdannandamnanahobixhatoux**.[12]

The next thunder to be composed was the sixth: the date assigned is probably early in 1932.[13] It appears in a first ink draft of the end-piece and is notable chiefly because, while all of the others thus far have begun under-length and grown to their eventual hundred-letter size, it began at considerably more than 100 letters and was reduced. The first version is also curious in that the initial 56 letters are neatly written while the balance is scrawled. This suggests either that the writing was done at two different times (unlikely) or that the first portion was already composed and ready to hand or memorized and the balance was composed during the inclusion of the word. The first version (114 letters) is somewhat chaotic: **Lukkedoerendunandurraschiudilooshoofermoyportertooryzooysphallnabortankapakkapukzakriodvergekurwazybunkerootagapik**. (Or -**tagapuk**: letters 106–11 are difficult to decipher.)[14]

It was not until 1934 that another version of thunder 6 surfaced, this in the separately printed Hague edition of II.1. Here, the thunder has been edited down to 89 letters: **Lukkedoerendunandurraskewdylooshoofermoyportertooryzooysphalnabortansakroidverjkapakkapuk**. No further changes were made to thunder 6 until proofs were being set for *Finnegans Wake*. Except for the omission of eleven consecutive letters (between letters 68 and 69 in this last version), this is identical with the form in which it was published in the *Wake*. The remaining letters were added early in 1938.

The year in which Joyce settled on a hundred-letter uniform length for his thunders, as indicated by his revisions to thunder 7, appears to be 1935. True, he had finalized thunder 1 as 100 letters in 1927 (although a few letters were to be varied for use in the *Wake*) and thunder 4 suggests by its lacuna that a hundred-letter pattern was in progress. Nevertheless, Joyce continued to compose new and variable-length thunders up to the time of thunder 7, 1938. From that year forward, either new thunders were added whole, or existing ones were revised.

In its earliest form, thunder 7 was over-long (108 letters): **Bothallchoractorschumminaroundgansummumminarumdrumstrummitraimminahumptadumpwaultopoorfoolooderamannsthurnup**.[15] Thunder 7 was written thus in a fair-copy ink draft of the chapter, dating from early 1935. In the first typescript, also made in 1935, it has been emended to the same form as published in the *Wake*.[16]

Thunder 9 was slightly revised for publication of 'The Ondt' in *transition* (1926). Originally 63 letters, it now swelled to 74 letters: **Husstenhasstencaffincoffintussemtossemdamandamnamcossaghcussaghhobixhatoux.**

It was probably in 1935, when thunder 7 was pulled up to proper length, that Joyce developed the relation to *The Thousand and One Nights*, though it may have been as late as 1936. In 1936, he composed thunder 10. The proofs for *transition*, as set, do not contain thunder 10, but Joyce inserted an instruction to leave a gap for it in the typesetting.[17] On the same sheet (the second set of *transition* pages), he inserted the phrases, 'the hundredlettered name, lost word of perfect language.' If 'lost' is taken for a pun on 'last,' to which it was eventually changed, it definitely shows that the pattern of ten thunders was established in Joyce's mind at this time, that is, that the tenth was to be the last. The tenth thunder itself 'must have been added to a missing third set of pages' for *transition*,[18] for it appears in the published version (with three extra letters) as follows: **Ullhodturdenweirmuddgarrdgringnirurdrmolnirogfenrirlukkillokbaugimandodrrerinsurtkrinmgernrackinaroickar.**[19] The extra letters (numbers 20, 44, and 45, in this version) were cancelled in the *Wake* galleys.

The remaining work on the thunders was conducted for the most part on galley proofs for *Finnegans Wake* in 1937 and 1938. Several thunders were simply set as he had left them, in their earlier forms, and revisions were made on the galleys. It is as if Joyce's attitude was, 'let's have fresh type to look at and then I'll get to work on it.'

In March of 1937, thunder 2 was set as it had been left in 1926 (75 letters) and then revised to final length by adding a new beginning of 25 letters; no changes were made to the rest of it.

At about the same time, thunder 3 was set as it had been left in 1927 (83 letters); 17 letters were added to bring it to length, and the last letter was changed from **r** to **t**.

Also at this time, thunder 9 was set in its most recent (74-letter) form. Three letters (49, 52, and 59) were cancelled and 29 more added to the end. The extra letters in thunder 10 were cancelled on a second set of duplicate galleys (dated by the printer 24/4/37). The digressions concerning television as a charge of the Light Brigade were added to a typescript of *FW* 338.04–354.06 (Butt and Taff) dated 1937.[20] Thunder 5 was 'added in 1937 to a late galley'[21] and thunder 8 was added to a 'late galley after July 1938'[22] with only one difference between the insertion and the version in the *Wake* (letter 37 is **x** instead of **k**).[23]

Finally, in 1938, thunder 6 was printed in galley proofs (dated 19 January

1938, and 29 January 1938, and sent on to Harriet Shaw Weaver on 16 June 1938) in the 1934 form of 89 letters. Joyce merely inserted (between letters 68 and 69) the eleven letters needed to bring it up to length (**sporthaokan**), and made no further changes to it.[24] The other remarkable thing about this galley is that every fifth letter has been ticked, working from each end in towards the insertion point. This was the only evidence of actual letter-counting I have found in any of the manuscripts, typescripts, proofs, and galleys.[25]

II. Analysis and Inferences

The question naturally arises, as various thunders were expanded or emended, how was the balance of themes they announce or echo modified? More particularly, as letter-groups were added or deleted, were any new themes inserted that were not otherwise definitively present in an earlier version? And were any of the themes present in an earlier version deleted or reduced to a negligible or questionable trace in the process of producing the version published in *Finnegans Wake*?

Certain of the thunders lie outside of these questions.

Thunder 1 went through three versions in 1926, all close to final length (97, 94, and 97 letters), and another revision (to 100 letters) in 1927 that is not significantly different from the *Wake* version. In effect, these four stages may be regarded as a single extended act of composition.

Thunder 4, either filled out or with the lacuna, can equally be regarded as the result of a single act of composition.

Thunders 5, 8, and 10 were added whole, or in all-but-final form, to proofs as the *Wake* was taking shape.

The other five thunders, however, underwent an average of three versions each over much longer periods of time and so are legitimately subject to the questions.

Thunder 2

Two versions of thunder 2 were made in 1926–7, resulting in a word of 75 letters. The difference between them is slight: a doubled letter was cancelled and the penultimate letter was changed from **e** to **u**. The second version was set in *Wake* galleys in March 1937, and represents the last three-quarters of the finished thunderclap. The missing letters are these: **Perkodhuskurun-barggruaya**. As shown in the word-list for thunder 2, this presents little of import that is not included in the rest of the thunder. Seventeen of the letters can be accounted for by words meaning thunder (in Lettish, Breton, and

Lithuanian). The second version begins at **gokgorlayor** with the Turkish for 'thundering sky' and contains other references to thunder (all appropriate, since PQ is associated with rain). The Gaelic references to the Jarl and to magic form a bridge between the two pieces of the thunder. Half of the remaining new letters involve references to various females: 'goddess,' [Cornelia] Otis [Skinner], Dis, [Eleanora] Duse, Istar and Esther (cf. Swift's Stella and Vanessa). With the exception of **barg**'s being the Hebrew for lightning (*baraq*), the other four new letters contribute only minor references: for example, embark, embargo, barge, argue, etc.

In sum, the transition from the second version to the final one resulted in no thematic or referential deletions. It did, however, result in additional references to thunder (otherwise present, hence redundant) and to several 'PQs.' As the previous version contained other, if less explicit, PQ references it does not appear that the additions change appreciably the basic pattern of the thunder, so the new letters may be regarded as padding.

Thunder 3

The first versions of thunder 3 were made in March and April of 1927: as the interval is short, they may be regarded as a single extended act of composition. The second version was set into *Wake* galleys and revised then. The final revision involved only the end of the word. Joyce changed one letter (the last, from **r** to **t**), and inserted 17 new letters, 16 of them consecutive: the ending – **nouihpkonpkor**! – of version two now reads – **nouithappluddyappladdypkonpkot**! The insertions eliminate a possible (and irrelevant) 'weep' from **ouihp** but preserve the French reference to midnight and even tighten it by adding its final **t**. They add a doubled reference to applause (thunder) in the taverns as well as the new phrase, 'with the bloody apple,' and a reference in French to the devil (both references apt to the Fall-in-the-Garden motif), and they contain the Polish for 'citizen.' Since thunder, applause, and citizenship occur elsewhere in the thunder, only the references to the Fall merit consideration. But they do not materially change the thrust of the thunder, for the Fall motif is carried in all of the early thunders and is, moreover, an element of the incident of the cad in the park. The last eight letters do not seem to tie in very well with the insertion (there is no strong bridging), but they seem equally disjunct without it. To conclude: the insertion may be regarded as padding.

Thunder 6

Thunder 6 followed a somewhat different pattern, for quite a number of letters were deleted and groups of letters were shifted about in its two revisions. The first version was drafted in late 1931 or early 1932 as part of the tail-piece to the Phoenix Playhouse, and had at that time 114 letters. The handwriting suggests that about half of it had been worked out beforehand and that the balance was composed as it was being written down.

A second and much shorter version (89 letters) appeared in the first publication of the piece two years later. While this drew on only the first 92 letters of the initial version and left the first 75 of it more or less intact, it shows a rearrangement of groups of the remaining letters. Thus, **tankapakkapukzakroidvege** becomes, in the second version, **tansakroidverjkapakkapuk**. The remaining 22 letters of the first version are cancelled.

Another feature of the revisions to this thunder is that they give, at one point, a suggestion as to pronunciation. The letter-group **durraschiudiloos** in the first version is emended to **durraskewdyloos** in the second and final versions, suggesting the sound 'Q-D,' a rhyme with 'cutie,' and making 'shut the door' in Italian (*chiudi l'uscio*) less literal.

The three-letter difference in length between the elements of the first version that were retained and the second version are accounted for as follows: one letter dropped by revising **chiudi** to **kewdy**; one letter dropped by revising **verge** to **verj**; one letter dropped by revising **allna** to **alna**. None of these appears to have resulted in an appreciable change of sound.

The sound of the end of the thunder also seems to have been preserved in the change from **tagapik** (or **tagapuk**) to **pakkapuk** (in any case, Joyce always ended his thunders with consonants). This preserves, at the end, the references to hump, hobgoblin, sharp blow, and finished.

The deleted letters, **kurwazybunkerootagapik** (or **-puk**) contain little of significance that is not already present in the other syllables and sounds. For example:

Letters:	Yield:	Referring to:
unker	Dan, *ungkarl*, bachelor	Shaun, Shem; the cad
tag	Ger, *Tag*, day	time theme
wazy	Fr, *vas-y*, go away, scram	decline of visual, shun Shem
bunker	bunker	Diddlem Club: the bagnio in the basement

And so on. The last item is the only omission as, with the letters deleted, no further explicit references remained in the thunder to the Diddlem Club in the basement of the Playhouse. On the other hand, the girls and PQ are often referred to in the final version, so the omission is not a serious one. To sum up: nothing material was lost by the deletion of these letters.

The transpositions present a similar case. Apparently, **kapakkapuk** is a self-contained unit whose principal components (Fi, tavern; Turk, shut the door, etc.) are not disturbed by alterations in placement. Similarly with the contents of **sakroidverj**: there seems to be no bridging at either end of this letter-group in its original location, so its placement there was perhaps arbitrary. In the second version, although nothing results from placing it before the self-contained **kapakkapuk**, new readings are generated by inserting it after **nabortan**. These include the following:

abortans	abortions	cf. Belinda
borta	porter	HUMP
	Fr, etc., door	doors theme
tans	Ger, *Tans*, dance	hoofer theme
tansakroid	consecrate	return of gods
ansak	Ger, *Ansicht*, opinion	private awareness (waning)

Nothing here is not already present in the invariable portion of the thunder, except the possible reference to Belinda's abortions: the new position of the letter-group thus reinforces themes that have previously been announced.

Finally, is anything added or deleted by the insertion of the eleven letters, **sporthaokan**, between **ortan** and **sakroi**? First, as to bridging: it will be noted that the new letters preserve some of the sounds already present. That is, **ortansakroi** turns into **ortans ... kansakroi**, effectively maintaining all of the readings generated in the second version, but redistributing them slightly.

The new letter-group inserts the following:

ansportha	Ital, *ancora*, again	renewal
sport	sport, game	Angels and Devils, Colours
portha	porter	HUMP, etc.
orthao	Gr, *ortho*, right, correct	renewal, end of imbalances
haok	Ger, *Haut*, skin	Corio; stripper, temptress
aokan	Ger, *Augen*, eyes	waning of visual
	Ger, *oben*, above, on high	return of gods

A review of the full thunder list shows that this clump actually adds nothing to the thematic references included elsewhere in the thunder, although several of the interpretations are novel (It, again; sport, ortho-; skin; on high). The insertion, therefore, may be regarded as padding and the other revisions as tightening.

Thunder 7

Thunder 7 resembles thunder 6 in that, in its first version, it too was over-long (108 letters). Both versions, initial (manuscript) and final (typescript), were produced in 1935 and so can be regarded as stages in a single act of composition. However, it is interesting to note that, unlike thunder 6, in which the last quarter was subjected to editing, transposition, and additions, thunder 7 merely saw two instances of letter-substitution and the cancellation of a number of doubled consonants (the opposite of repeating **ba** in thunder 1 in order to pad it out to the hundred-letter total). Here are the changes: **gansummummi** became **gansumumi; strummitraimmi**[26] became **strumtrumi; topoorfool** became **topoofool; mannsthurnup**! became **maunsturnup**!

Thunder 9

Thunder 9 saw three versions. It was first written (63 letters) in 1928; a second form (74 letters) appeared in *transition* (1936), which was also set in *Wake* galleys (April–May 1937), where the final version was composed. The manuscript version was this: **Husstenhasstencauffincoffintussemtossemdannandamnananhobixhatoux**. The variant areas of interest to the questions and not covered in the final version are the section **dannandamnananaho**. Using **dannan** eliminates demon, damn, dam, and several other interpretations that appear in the *Wake* version, all negligible because they are otherwise introduced. But **dannandam** does seem to bring the following:

dann	Ger, *dann*, then
anna	Anna Livia
annanda	inundate
andam	Ger, *ändern*, to change; *enden*, end

At the same time, **damnananaho** seems to present repeats of Anna as **nan** and **ana** in the double pattern of the thunder. If the references to ALP were intended, perhaps they were supposed to refer to the Liffey, down which Shaun's barrel/casket/cocoon is tumbling. As this group contains no detectable references to entomology used elsewhere in 'The Ondt and the Gracehoper,' perhaps the repeated letters are onomatopoeic and serve to reinforce the stuttering-and-repetition motif of the thunder.

In the second version, only one change was made to the first half of the thunder: the seventeenth letter was cancelled. No appreciable change of sound resulted, and no further changes were then or subsequently made to the first forty letters. The section discussed above was altered to read **damandamnam**, and some Gaelic coughing was inserted between it and the last eleven letters, with the group **cossaghcussagh**. The new emendation eliminates the ALP references (if that is what they were) and the repetition of **na**. It introduces 'demon' and 'damn and damn,' as well as the Gaelic for dumb and for stuttering. The inserted letters are principally Gaelic coughing, but also include some entomology. None of this brings new themes to the thunder. For the final version, the doubled s's in the insertion were reduced to single s's, and a letter was cancelled (**damnamcos** became **damnacos**), reducing this part of the thunder to 71 letters. The final 29 letters were then added after **hatoux**. They are: **peswchbechoscashlcarcarcaract**.

Since **car** is repeated once more than is necessary for the interpretations, the extra one represents an example of padding for emphasis. That is, a final stuttering is played on the word car, emphasizing it (the car and its engine both are the result of a 'stutterance,' and they produce mechanical coughing and stuttering), and emphasizing the thunder as a car-act. Seventeen of the new letters yield 'cough' in one or another language, and nineteen of them provide references to entomology. A review of the interpretations offered for this part of the thunder (in the word-list in chapter 12) shows that nothing substantial is added to the statement made by the thunder before they were included; the difference they make is mainly one of emphasis.

III. Summary

If any conclusion can be drawn from the foregoing, it is that Joyce pursued certain basic themes in each thunder single-mindedly throughout the course of their revisions and throughout the apparently chaotic reworking of their contexts. It would have been reasonable to assume that, as he reworked and elaborated upon a section and thunder, he added new themes and made substantial changes. Such, however, does not appear to have been the case, at least as regards the thunders. Although some thunder words were revised extensively, the changes that Joyce wrought upon them amounted to variations on themes he had established, in the earliest versions.

That is in itself remarkable, for it indicates that, at the most profound and complex reaches of his use of language, Joyce established, early in the work on a section, basic patterns of relationship between technology, culture, and sensibility, and worked with a touch so sure that he found no need to deviate from them as the work developed and formed an integrated whole. The thunderclaps are both the superstructure and the deep structure of that whole.

Outline of the Menippean Tradition

Homer, *Margites* (800 B.C.? 1100 B.C.?)
Gorgias (5th c. B.C.), *Praise of Helen*
Diogenes the Cynic (404–323 B.C.)
Menippus of Gadara (fl. c. 250 B.C.)
Varro (116–27 B.C.) more than 600 Menippean satires
Seneca (4 B.C.–A.D. 65), *Apokolocyntosis / Ludus de morte Claudii*
Petronius Arbiter (d. A.D. 66) *Satyricon*
Plutarch (est. A.D. 46–120), *Gryllus*
Lucian of Samosata (est. A.D. 120–180), works
Apuleius of Madaura (est. A.D. 125– ?) *Metamorphoses / The Golden Ass*
Macrobius (A.D. 339-422) *Saturnalia*
Martianus Capella (late 4th/early 5th c. ?) *De nuptiis Philologiae et Mer-
curii / The Marriage of Mercury and Philology*
Bernardus Sylvestris of Tours (fl. c. 1136), *Cosmographia*
Alan of Lille (est. 1128–1202), *De planctu naturae*
Dante Alighieri, *La Vita Nuova* (1292–4)
Geoffrey Chaucer, *The Canterbury Tales* (1387ff.)
Erasmus, Desiderius (1466?–1536), *Moriae encomium / The Praise of Folly*
More, Thomas (1478–1535), *Utopia*
Andreas Guarnas of Salerno (est. 1435– ?) *Bellum Grammaticale: A Dis-
course of Great War and Dissention between the Two Worthy Princes, the
Noune and the Verb* (1576)
Henry Cornelius Agrippa von Nettlesheim, *De incertitudine et vanitate
scientiarum et artium / On the Vanity and Uncertainty of the Arts and
Sciences* (1530)
François Rabelais (est. 1495–1553), *Gargantua and Pantagruel*
Miguel de Cervantes, *Don Quixote* (1605–15)

Giordano Bruno (Nolanus: 1546–1600), various texts

Thomas Nashe (1567–1601), *The Unfortunate Traveller*, etc.

Sir John Harington (1561–1612), *A New Discourse of a Stale Subject Called The Metamorphosis of A JAX* (1595)

Johannes Kepler (1571–1630), *Somnium, sive Astronomia lunaris / A Dream, or the Astronomy of the Moon*; and *Dissertatio cum nuncio siderio nuper ad mortales misso a Galilaeo Galilaeo / A Discourse with the Sidereal Messenger Lately Sent to Mortals by Galileo*

Anonymous (various hands), *La Satyre Ménippée* (1594)

John Barclay, *Euphormionis lusini satyricon / Euphormio's Satyricon* (1605)

Thomas Dekker (1570?–1641?), *The Guls Horne-Booke*

Guillaume Bouchet (1513–93), *Les Serees / The Evening-Sequences* (1583–1614)

François Beroalde de Verville (1556–est. 1612), *Le Moyen de Parvenir, oeuvre contenant La Raison de Tout ce Qui este, est, et sera / How to Succeed* (c. 1610)

John Taylor, the 'water poet' (1580–1653), many texts

Dornavius / Caspar Dornau (1577–1632), many texts, esp. *Amphitheatrum Sapientiae Socraticae Joco-Seriae, Hoc Est Encomia et Commentaria Autorum, quia Recentiorum propre omnium: Quibus res, aut pro vilibus vulgo ad amoenitatem, sapientiam, virtutem, publice privatimque utilissimum / The Amphitheatre of Joco-Serious Socratic Wisdom, That Is, Encomia and Commentaries of Nearly All Authors up to the Present Time, Who Found Virtue, Wisdom, or Utility in Vile and Vulgar Things* (1619)

Ben Jonson (1573?–1637), *News from the New World Discovered in the Moon* (played 1620)

Robert Burton (1577–1640), *The Anatomy of Melancholy* (1621–38)

Quevedo (Gomez Francisco de Quevedo y Villegas: 1580–1641), *Los Suenos / The Visions* (1627 and later)

Edmond Rostand, *Cyrano de Bergerac* (1640–55)

Samuel Butler (1612–80), *Hudibras* (1663, 1664, 1678)

Izaak Walton (1593–1683), *The Compleat Angler* (1653)

Sir Thomas Burnett and George Duckett, *A Second Tale of a Tub: or, the History of Robert Powel the Puppet-Show-Man* (1705)

John Dunton, *The Second Part of the New Quevedo, Or, a Further Vision of Charon's Passengers* (1702); *Athenian Sport: or, Two Thousand Paradoxes Merrily Argued, To Amuse and Divert the Age* (1707)

Alexander Pope et al., *The Memoirs of the Extraordinary Life, Works, and Discoveries of Martinus Scriblerus. [Working title: The Works of the Unlearned.] Written in Collaboration by the Members of the Scriblerus*

Club: John Arbuthnot, Alexander Pope, Jonathan Swift, John Gay, Thomas Parnell, and Robert Harley, Earl of Oxford
Alexander Pope, *Peri Bathous / The Art of Sinking in Poetry* (ex Scriblerus)
Jonathan Swift, *Gulliver's Travels* (ex Scriblerus)
Jonathan Swift, *A Tale of a Tub*
Laurence Sterne, *The Life and Opinions of Tristram Shandy, Gentleman*
Goethe, *Faust*, parts 1 and 2
Mark Twain, *Huckleberry Finn*
Lewis Carroll, *Alice in Wonderland; Through the Looking Glass*
Thomas Carlyle, *Sartor Resartus*
George Gordon/Lord Byron, *Don Juan*
Charles Kingsley, *The Water Babies*
Gustave Flaubert, *Le Tentation de St Antoine; Bouvard et Pecuchet; Salammbo*
Walter Savage Landor, *Imaginary Conversations*
James Joyce, *Dubliners, Exiles, Finnegans Wake, Ulysses*
Ezra Pound, *The Cantos*
T. S. Eliot, 'The Waste Land'
Woody Allen, *Mighty Aphrodite, The Purple Rose of Cairo, Shadows and Fog, Zelig*
Orson Welles, radio version of 'The War of the Worlds'
John Fowles, *Mantissa, The French Lieutenant's Woman* (both the novel and the film)
John Barth, *Chimera*
Don DeLillo, *White Noise*
Flann O'Brien, *At Swim-Two-Birds*
Charles G. Finney, *The Circus of Dr Lao*
Luis d'Antin van Rooten, *Mots d'Heures: Gousses, Rames. The d'Antin Manuscript. Discovered, Edited and Annotated by Luis d'Antin van Rooten*
Italo Calvino, *If on a Winter's Night a Traveller ...*

The Rhetorical Structure of *Finnegans Wake*

[From *JJQ*, 11, no. 4, Summer 1974, 394–404]

The ten thunders in *Finnegans Wake* are 100-letter words, except for the tenth, which has an extra letter. The 1,001 letters in the ten words may well be an allusion to Scheherazade and *The Thousand and One Nights*. These ten words appear as carefully spaced digressions. (In rhetoric, a digression is a major mode of metamorphosis.) These words are encoded patterns that include an inventory of themes and developments and transformations of man.

There are four books in *Wake*. Book I contains the first five thunders, book II contains thunders 6-8, book III contains thunders 9 and 10.

The character, Finnegan, and his demise, occur in thunder 1; the Prankquean occurs in thunder 2; thunder 3 includes HCE and Persse O'Reilly; thunder 4 and thunder 5 relate to ALP and to the antics of Belinda; thunder 6 involves the Phoenix Playhouse, in which all of the characters perform; thunder 7 relates to the episodes of Kersse the tailor and the Norwegian Captain; thunder 8 concerns Private Buckley and the Russian General; thunders 9 and 10, the Ondt and the Gracehoper. (See 266 for summary of the classical structure of *Finnegans Wake*.)

The four books themselves relate to one of Joyce's traditional concerns, namely exegesis of the Books of Man and Society, Nature and Scripture. The Roman Varro states the doctrine in *De Lingua Latina* as follows:

Now I shall set forth the origins of the individual words, of which there are four levels of explanation. The lowest is that to which even the common folk has come ... The second is that to which old-time grammar has mounted, which shows how the poet has made each word which he has fashioned and derived ...

The third is that to which philosophy ascended, and on arrival began to reveal the nature of those words which are in common use ... The fourth is that where the sanctuary is, and the mysteries of the high-priest: if I shall not arrive at full knowledge there, at any rate I shall cast about for a conjecture ...[1]

An account of the 'trope' of the Book of Nature, and culture and artefacts, as 'texts' to be read and interpreted – 'Signatures of all things I am here to read' (*U* 37) – is presented by Ernst Curtius in *European Literature and the Latin Middle Ages*:

It is a favorite cliché of the popular view of history that the Renaissance shook off the dust of yellowed parchments and began instead to read in the book of nature or the world. But this metaphor itself derives from the Latin Middle Ages. We saw that Alan speaks of the 'book of experience.' For him, every creature is a book (*PL*, CCX, 579A) ... In later authors, especially the homilists, 'scientia creaturarum' and 'liber naturae' appear as synonyms. For the preacher the book of nature must figure with the Bible as a source of material. This idea appears in so late a writer as Raymond of Sabunde (d. 1436), who however overshot the mark (and hence was condemned by the Council of Trent) ...[2]

The 'trope' of the book served to organize the verbal universe in harmony with both the 'text' of nature and of Scripture. A few words from Professor Gilson's study, *The Philosophy of St Bonaventure*, indicate the bearings of the trope of the book for theologians and scientists alike:

Since the universe was offered to his eyes as a book to read and he saw in nature a sensible revelation analogous to that of the Scriptures, the traditional methods of interpretations which had always been applied to the sacred books could equally be applied to the book of creation. Just as there is an immediate and literal sense of the profane text, but also an allegorical sense by which we discover the truths of faith that the letter signifies, a tropological sense by which we discover a moral precept behind the passage in the form of an historical narrative, and an analogical sense by which our souls are raised to the love and desire of God, so we must not attend to the literal and immediate sense of the book of creations but look for its inner meaning in the theological, moral, and mystical lessons that it contains. The passage from one of these two spheres to the other is the more easily effected in that they are in reality inseparable.[3]

Exegesis of the Book of Nature had begun in pagan times but became a major feature of Christian culture throughout the Middle Ages and the Renaissance, and onward into our own time. (See the four volumes of Henri de Lubac, *Exégèse médiévale: Les quatre sens de l'Ecriture*.[4])

The four Books of the *Wake* proceed in the mode of each of the four conventional levels of exegesis. The first level concerns the literal sense, which includes all possible meanings; the second level is the figurative or allegorical one, which mediates on the patterns and forms presented; the third level is tropological or moral, applying the matters of the first two levels to human conduct and standards; the fourth level is anagogical, concerned with ultimate mysteries. Thus book IV of the *Wake* is brief, and begins with the day of judgment: 'Array! Surrection!' (593).

In view of the nature of the first level of exegesis as inclusive of all possible senses, it is natural that it should be much the largest of the books in the *Wake*, comprising the first 216 pages, eight chapters, and five thunders; book II (the allegorical) comprises 183 pages, four chapters, and three thunders. Book III (the tropological or moral), comprises 189 pages, four chapters, and thunders 9 and 10. Book II opens with the figure of the Playhouse, and a mime, and a large cast. In other words, the second, or allegorical level of exegesis concerns the theatre of human interplay and transformation. Curtius has a section on the world as stage and the world as theatre: 'As we see: the metaphor "world-stage," like so many others, reached the Middle Ages both from pagan Antiquity and the Christian writers.'[5]

It is well to remember that the *Wake* is a drama and not a narrative. The characters of the drama of the *Wake* are presented by Joyce in a mode as traditional as that of scriptural exegesis, namely, that of classical rhetoric. Like Swift in *A Tale of a Tub* and *The Battle of the Books* and Sterne in *Tristram Shandy*, the major divisions of rhetorical discourse, as perceived by the Romans and translated into trivial and quadrivial studies. The 190 or so pages of book III comprise four chapters and the last two thunders, and develop the tropological or moral level, beginning with the parable of the Ondt and the Gracehoper and Shaun's sermon to the girls of St Bride's. The fourth and last book, some 35 pages long, is also the last chapter, and concerns the fourth of the traditional levels, eschatology or meditation on final things. Beginning at page 619, the meditation of ALP herself, who enacts the character or figure of *memoria*, proceeds to wake and remember and replay the human drama.

Quintilian often refers to the divisions of rhetoric, as when he comments, in *Institutio Oratoria*, 'that every speech is composed of matter and words, and that as regards matter, we must study invention, as regards words, style, and as regards both, arrangement, all of which it is the task of memory to retain and delivery to render attractive.'[6]

The first division of rhetoric is *inventio,* or wit and knowledge, and learning and insight, and is the role assigned to the figure of Shem, the penman and forger. The second division of rhetoric is *dispositio,* or arrangement, which includes the whole range of whims, postures, moods, and 'hobbies.' This mask, or role, is assigned to HCE '"the grandada of all rogues."' The third division of discourse or rhetoric, *elocutio,* embraces the arts of embellishment and adornment and charm, and is associated with the three levels of decorum or style. In effect, *elocutio* is very nearly allied to weaponry and is the mask of the Prankquean herself, a mask that includes Izzy and Isolde. (A mask is inevitably a corporate and not a private image, a 'put on' that adapts from situation to situation, to manifest diverse characteristics and potential. The mask is basically the public itself, as recognized by Baudelaire in his envoy to the reader of *Les fleurs du mal:* 'Hypocrite lecteur, mon semblable, mon frère.')

Memoria, which is the fourth branch of rhetoric, includes the arts of the 'memory theatre.'[8] The mask of *memoria* is worn by ALP in the *Wake* ('mememormee' [628]) and by Molly Bloom in *Ulysses;* 'gossipaceous Anna Livia' is revealed in the process of scrubbing dirty linen in public. Remembering is restructuring as well as recycling.[9] ALP's relation to music ('"Sheshell ebb music wayriver she flows"'[10] and sound involves the aspect of simultaneity, a central characteristic of the auditory imagination.

The fifth division of rhetoric is *pronuntiatio* or delivery, the mask or role assigned to Shaun the Post, whose 'sermons' are to be found especially in the first two chapters of book III (403–73).

In Swift's *A Tale of a Tub,* and Sterne's *Tristram Shandy,* delivery is in the hands of the Aeolists and of Doctor Slop, respectively. (In *The Battle of the Books* it is managed by the character Momus, the god of sleep.) The full extent of the exegetical levels and the divisions of rhetoric is brought into play not only in Swift and Sterne, and not only in *Finnegans Wake* and in *Ulysses,* but also in *The Waste Land* and in *Four Quartets,* to mention only four authors. (Each of the *Four Quartets* displays an exegetical level, which is, in turn, divided into the five divisions of rhetoric. Thus, the fifth section of each of the *Four Quartets* exhibits a marked concern with delivery, or *pronuntiatio.*)

The book structure of the *Wake* relates to the four levels of traditional exegesis and the character structure dramatizes the divisions of traditional rhetoric. There remain the thunders. They are symmetrically arranged in two 'plays' of five thunders (acts) each. Each of these also corresponds to the five divisions of rhetoric. The 'act' is designated by the *Oxford Companion to the Theatre* as an interval of digression: 'In early times the music between the parts of an English play was called the Act.'[11]

The first five-part 'play' enacts the 'royal divorce' or the dissociation of sensibility of eye and ear. The technologies, the arts and inventions of man (many of which are displayed in the opening Willingdone Museyroom) in the first five thunders show the bias of the eye and its divisive and exclusive powers; the integral egg (Humpty Dumpty), the *Sphairos* of Empedocles, and the pre-Socratic philosophers, the integral sensorium, falls from the 'magazine wall' and shatters with the specializing of human ingenuity and enterprise. The age of hardware and specialism is begun.

All of the thunders, by virtue of their compressed linguistic character, are digressions from the language of their contexts. In terms of rhetorical division, the second, third, fourth, and fifth thunders, concerned as they are with the principal characters – Izzy (the Prankquean), HCE, and ALP – enact *elocutio*, *dispositio*, and *memoria* as before.

The second five-thunder (five-part) 'play' repeats the drama of the 'royal divorce' of the senses in reverse, as a royal marriage in which the parts of the egg, Humpty Dumpty, are reunited. The initial splitting up of sensibility, the fragmentation that was the demise of Finnegan and that gave rise to his 'parts' in the persons of the family of HCE, ALP, Shem, Shaun, and Izzy-Isolde, is reversed and culminates in a final judgment, the dawn of a new age of Finn Again ('Array! Surrection!' [593]).

The thunderclaps of *Finnegans Wake* have, from the first, been embedded in as much obscurity as the relation of the work to the five parts of rhetoric. Perhaps this difficulty can be clarified by a note on the 'magazine wall.' The mystery of the magazine is revealed in Emerson's words: 'The human body is the magazine of inventions ... All the tools and engines on earth are only extensions of its limbs and senses.' With each extension of man, each new invention, Joyce's 'magazine wall' rocks and rumbles. At the outset of the *Wake*, the fragmentation and visual specialism represented by the bricks themselves was enough to end the integrity of the *Sphairos* – the integral and 'mystical sphere' of Empedocles.

Thunderclap 1, quite naturally, enacts the resonant effects of the first inventions/extensions of man, which propel him from the palaeolithic Garden into the neolithic age, from primal integral hunting and food gathering to the specialisms of the Willingdone Museyroom of weaponry. As the first 'act' of the first five-part 'play' the mode is *inventio*, the first division of rhetoric. As part of the unified *logos* (which was rendered by the Romans by the phrase *ratio et oratio*) or the all-resonant word, each division of rhetoric assumes and resumes the other divisions, just to the degree that any moment of consciousness simultaneously includes as its complements all aspects of mental activity.

Each of the thunderclaps is performed in a 'key' of its own: each sums up its own characteristic blend of cultures and of languages, and what Claude Lévi-Strauss calls 'texts': 'To say that the world is intelligible means that it presents itself to the mind of the primitive as a message, to which his language and behavior are an appropriate response – but not as a message *from elsewhere*, simply as a message, as it were, in its own right.'[11] The strong indications of Arabic language in thunderclap 1 (*FW* 3), the only thunder in which is to be found an appreciable amount of Arabic, are stressed through the appearance in the subsequent text of bulbous-dome and minaret architecture and 'Haroun Childeric Eggeberth' (4) – the Near East matrix of technologies and all human languages, 'himals and all.' It is neatly recapitulated later with '(ting ting! ting ting!) By his magmasine fall. Lunmps, lavas and all. *Bene!* But, thunder and turf, it's not alover yet! One recalls Byzantium' (294).

Thunder 2 (23) presents the Prankquean, the matriarch of clothing and style, as social weaponry. This 'dressing up' or 'pranking' embodies the division of *elocutio* (adornment and ornament) in traditional rhetoric. The tale of the Prankquean (21–3), in accordance with the doctrine of decorum, is told in three different levels of style, low, middle, and high. The dressing-up of society via this eposide includes 'what papyr is meed of, made of, hides and hints and misses in prints. Till ye finally (though not yet endlike) meet with the acquaintance of Mister Typus, Mistress Tope and all the little typtopies' (20). The Thunder results in the putting-on of 'the whole of the polis' (23), the establishment of towns and cities as new social garments, themselves the result of the Prankquean's piracy and social aggression.

Thunder 3 (44) presents HCE, Here Comes Everybody (the rhetorical division, *dispositio*, or arrangement), in the multiple roles of Hosty the publican and of the host – the everyman of the civilized multitude. He constantly rearranges affairs: 'He as fafafather of all schemes for to bother us' (45). His restless, fragmenting nature is incompatible with the integral and iconic Humpty Dumpty, who symbolically cannot maintain his place and falls and shatters again. This thunder recapitulates and develops the social innovations and their effects dramatized in the preceding sections: HCE is the consequence of the promise of accumulated technological specialism. The thunder embodies the multitudinous sounds of rail and press, of a mechanized world.

Thunder 4 (90) (in rhetoric, *memoria*, memory) enacts the rape and prostitution of Nature by market gardening. 'Treely and rurally,' 'Meirdreach and Oincuish!' (90). The episode involves the 'iron horse' and the whores' race: 'but the past has made us this present of a rhedarhoad' (81). The relation to *memoria* is the enormous pricing system that goes with markets, and Nature herself as embodying memory of all things. Prices, as a 'memory theatre,' are unforgettable, 'like the crack that bruck the bank in Multifarnham' (90). The environments created by technologies and ensuing services are usually hidden from their users: 'Yes, the viability of vicinals if invisible is invincible' (81).

Thunder 5 (113) (*pronuntiatio*, delivery) presents the episode of Belinda the hen and the Letter. The technologies involved in the thunder are reproduction at high speed by means of print and the photograph. They produce 'generations, more generations and still more generations' (107). The episode includes an explicit discussion of the application of traditional four-level exegesis (109.12–30). This thunder ends the first 'play' and clears the stage for the new 'act' which is in book II.

Book II occupies the second level of exegesis, the figurative or allegorical, and opens (219) with the Phoenix Playhouse chapter. The second 'play' of five 'acts' (five thunders, five parts of rhetoric) is a *ricorso* or replay of the first five-acter in a different mode. The first five acts had moved from the iconic and integral mode to the analytic and visual, dramatizing the 'royal divorce' of the senses of eye and ear. The second five acts move from the analytic to the integral, from the visual to the audile-tactle, 'showing the Radium Wedding of Neid and Moorning' (222). The very simultaneity of the acoustic mode permits a nonsequential order for the parts of rhetoric in this second group of thunders.

Act I, thunder 6 (257) presents the rhetorical division *memoria* anew as 'the Pageant of Past History' (221), and resonates, 'the mar of murmury mermers to the mid's ear' (254), with the awakening of the auditory, 'why wilt thou erewaken him from his earth' (255). *The Mime of Mick, Nick and the Maggies* is the show billed for the Phoenix Playhouse and for this chapter. The mime is an iconic and allegorical mode located between those of eye and ear, and is played on the receding border of the industrial age. Everything here is in a state of transformation, phoenix-like, as the hardware age is surrounded by the new services of the telephone and telegraph under the auspices of the G.P.O. ('where G.P.O. is zentrum' [256]: General Post Office – in the U.K. the telephone and telegraph company as well). The electric flip from eye to ear obsolesces the visual reign of the Prankquean/Izzy: 'So angelland all weeping bin that Izzy most unhappy is' (257). (At electric speeds, man becomes discarnate, angelic.) The transformation indicated on the playbill for thunder 6, 'wound up ... by a Magnificient Transformation Scene showing the Radium Wedding of Neid and Moorning and the Dawn of Peace, Pure, Perfect and Perpetual, Waking the Weary of the World' (222) shuts the eye and opens the ear 'Upploud!' (257). The thunder is a reversal point between the worlds of the (earlier) industrial complex and the new electronic services to come. Both Aquinas and Aristotle stress the circumstances that 'in the whole of the previous time in which anything is moving towards its form, it is under the opposite form; but in the last instant of this time, which is the first instant of the subsequent time, it has the form which is the term of the movement.'[12] All of the thunders occur at such flip points, between worlds, and are explosions of applause in the Playhouse. The word *explode* is given in the *Oxford English Dictionary* as 'from Latin, *explodere, explaudere*, to drive out by clapping, hiss (a player) off the stage: ... 1. *trans.* To clap and hoot (a player, play, etc.) off the stage; hence *gen.* to drive away with expressions of disapprobation; to cry down, to banish ignominiously.' The stage is cleared of the old act and readied for the Phoenix's return.

The next chapter of book II is the 'Triv. and Quad.' chapter. As the drama moves into the electric orbit, there is a retrieval of these oral traditions of medieval education. Giambattista Vico, from whom, as has often been discussed, Joyce drew a great deal for use in *Finnegans Wake*, was appointed to the chair of Rhetoric at the University of Naples in 1699.[13] In 1707 his inaugural oration offered the key to 'the knowledge of the corrupt nature of man,' which 'invites us to study the complete cycles of the liberal arts and sciences and expounds the true, easy and unvarying order in which they are to be acquired.'[14] These are, of course, the trivium and quadrivium. Joyce's artistic reasons for organizing his work in the traditional European modes of grammatical exegesis of the 'texts of Nature and Society,' on the one hand, and for structuring his characterizations on the modes of traditional rhetoric, on the other hand, are copiously implied in the 'Triv. and Quad.' chapter (II.2) of the *Wake*.[15]

Thunder 7 (314) reenacts the tale of the Prankquean, but now in reverse. The drama turns around the story of a tailor making a wedding suit for a ship's captain (male). The rhetorical division is again *elocutio*, or adornment, and the three styles are again on show. Just as the Prankquean episode had concerned the separation of eye and ear, this replay reverses that earlier 'play' by the action of radio ('tribalbalbutience' [309]) bringing the oral mode back, 'due to woman formed mobile or man made static and bawling the whowle hamshack' (309). Humpty Dumpty, electrically reintegrated, is again found atop the wall in the thunder itself: '... humtadumpwaultop ...' (314.9).

Thunder 8 (332) (the rhetorical division *dispositio*, arrangement) presents the world of film editing and arrangement '(in imageascene all: whimwhim whimwhim)' (FW 331). The episode is concerned with the *in camera* wedding of eye and ear: things are 'Fine again' (332). The thunder is followed by a movie scenario suited to the epic dimensions of film, involving 'Sea vaast a pool' (338), both the Crimean war and the Russian revolution, both the private (Buckley) and the mob (the Russian General). The camera eye is engaged in shooting 'that ligtning lovemaker's thender apeal till ... Bullyclubber burgherly shut the rush in general' (335).

Thunders 9 (414) (*pronuntiatio*, delivery) and 10 are in the first chapter of book III. In the rhetorical scheme, thunder 9 is concerned with delivery and 'putting on' the public: 'Shaun yawned, as his general address rehearsal' (407). (In the next chapter he is described as having 'delivered himself with express cordiality, marked by clearance of diction and general delivery' [431]). In the exegetical scheme, book III moves at the tropological level of moral application: thunder 9, the sound of Shaun's clearing his throat, presents us with a moral fable. Technologically, the thunder involves additional delivery systems, the car and plane, which reach their apogee, or flip point, here. The thunder also mimes the cough and chug of the reciprocating engine. Like the movie form, both car and plane combine the old mechanical technology and the new electric circuitry: 'methought broadtone was heard and the creepers and the gliders and flivvers of the earth breath and the dancetongues of the woodfires and the hummers in their ground all vociferated echoating: Shaun! Shaun! Post the post!' (404).

Thunder 10 (424) (rhetorically, *inventio*) is, like thunder 1, a vortex of all themes. This thunder carries an extra letter – for delivery by Shaun. Like *The Thousand and One Nights*, it gives a *ricorso* spin to the structure. The 'play' is over, and, 'as the wisest postlude course he could playact,' all of the characters and themes are merged, 'collaspsed in ensemble and rolled buoyantly backwards' (426), just as thunder 1 has cleared the stage of Finnegan. In keeping with the 'thousand-and-one' theme (this makes 1,001 thunder letters), the Aladdin's lamp of television is given as the mode of discovery of this section, and of everything before and after. The tactility of the medium is playfully mimed as rubbing the lamp. This is the television thunder that combines all the senses – after it, Shaun merges with his 'interlocutor' of the chapter, the mass audience.

The two groups of thunders in reciprocal complementarity enact the dissolution of the universe of discourse (the verbal universe) and its contemporary reintegration at electric speed. This inclusive consciousness gets its voice in ALP as *memoria*.

SUMMARY OF CLASSICAL STRUCTURE OF *FINNEGANS WAKE*:

1. The books of *Finnegans Wake* in relation to the exegetical levels:

Book I   literal sense
Book II   analogical or allegorical level
Book III   tropological or moral level
Book IV   eschatological or anagogical level

2. The role of the rhetorical divisions in relation to the character- and thunder-structure:

		Thunders	
Character	Division of Rhetoric	Eye Mode	Ear Mode
Shem (forger)	*inventio*	1	10
HCE	*dispositio*	3	8
Prankquean/Izzy	*elocutio*	2	7
ALP	*memoria*	4	6
Shaun (postman)	*pronuntiatio*	5	9

Notes

1: Cynic Satire

1 Diogenes Laertius, *Lives of Eminent Philosophers*, 103–5.
2 *Petronius: The Satyricon and the Fragments*, trans. J.P. Sullivan.
3 *Encyclopedia of Philosophy*, II, 285.
4 François Rabelais, *Gargantua and Pantagruel*, 4–5.
5 Leon Rooke, *Shakespeare's Dog*, 96.
6 Martianus Capella, *Martianus Capella and the Seven Liberal Arts* II: *The Marriage of Mercury and Philology*, 381–2.
7 P. Wyndham Lewis, 'The Greatest Satire Is Non-Moral,' in *Men without Art*, 109.
8 E.P. Korkowski, *Menippus and his imitators: A Conspectus, up to Sterne, for a Misunderstood Genre*, 42–3. The finest scholarship yet produced on the subject of Cynic satire, this thesis conclusively shows the Menippean tradition to be a consciously mimetic one. Menippists combine 'freewheeling parody of' and 'absolute respect for' each other, as Anne Payne noted in *Chaucer and Menippean Satire*, x. Korkowski further notes:

> Menippus was imitated because his techniques of display and of ridicule were attractive, easy to emulate, and adaptable to many applications in learning and theology. His kind of writing was seldom regarded as an exalted classical form – it sent up everything of that kind – and consequently authorities on literary genres, until the mid-Renaissance, passed over Menippean satire as unworthy of comment. Quintilian, Cicero, and a few other ancients mention Varro's *Saturae Menippeae*, but only out of apparent amazement that he wrote in such a low form.
>
> Menippean satire was kept much alive in Byzantium, and from there handed on to the European Renaissance; Menippism also went forward, in an austere condition, into the Latin Middle Ages. During the Renaissance, it was used exten-

sively in disputes over learning and theology; the German Reformation, the unrest of late-sixteenth-century France, the rise of the Jesuits, the English Puritan Interlude, the question of helio-centrism, the Catholic church's opposition to humanism and seventeenth-century developments in experimental science, are only some of the issues around which Menippean writing centred. (x–xi)

9 Eugene Kirk, *Menippean Satire*, xi.
10 Ibid., x.
11 Ibid., xii.
12 Ibid., 141.
13 Edwin Hatch, *The Influence of Greek Ideas on Christianity*, 60–1.
14 Ibid., 63.
15 This medieval rhyme neatly summarizes the traditional four levels:

> Littera gesta docet
> Quid credas, allegoria
> Moralis quid agas
> Quo tendis, anagogia.

In Dante's time, the four levels were still so normal a part of the training in literacy and grammar as to be regarded as commonplace. So Dante refers to them casually and even applies them to (his own) secular poetry in the famous letter to Can Grande.
16 F.M. Cleve, *The Giants of Pre-Sophistic Greek Philosophy*, II, 342–3. Cleve adds, 'the allegorical names of the elements have been translated into plain language by Empedocles himself:

> Well, then, I'll tell you now those mighty, primordial things
> Out of which all the things we now see have grown to be seen:
> Earth, the billowy ocean, and also the air full of moisture,
> Likewise the Titan ether that ties the whole world to a circle.' (Fr. 38)

17 In my *Laws of Media: The New Science*, I discussed briefly the parallels between the traditional (Aristotelian) four causes, for exegesis of the Book of Nature, and the four levels of patristic exegesis, for use on the written text:

Formal cause:	Literal level
Efficient cause:	Moral/tropological level
Material cause:	Allegorical level
Final cause:	Eschatological/anagogical level

18 Korkowski, 207. The background for the *Epistolae Obscurorum Virorum* is discussed in George Saintsbury, *The Earlier Renaissance*, 89–98.

19 As Dorothy Coleman points out in *Rabelais: A Critical Study in Prose Fiction*, the writer of the preface to the *Satyre Ménippée* (ostensibly the printer, but probably Passerat) cites Rabelais as a Menippean precedent, along with the usual list of Latin and Greek writers (Varro, Lucian, Apuleius, et al.). A century later, in Le Père Rapin's *Réflexions sur la poetique d'Aristote et sur les ouvrages des poëtes anciens et modernes*, Cervantes and Rabelais are presented as modern Menippeans (Coleman, 86–7). Of Rabelais' fun with the new technology of typography, Dorothy Coleman writes: 'Rabelais could also play with printing: the typographical process was sufficiently new for contemporary readers to see *le coup testée* (la teste coupée) as comic, to be amused by word-listing from top to bottom or from side to side; an example of this is the books in St. Victor's library (*Pantagruel*, chapter 7). Rabelais' linguistic exuberance is the condition for his Menippean erudition. Just as Burton, in *The Anatomy of Melancholy*, can start with a neat statement such as "We are apish in the world" and then proceed to play on the *apish* conception, bringing in all his literary experience and knowledge of languages ... so Rabelais ...' (97).

    She points out that Rabelais fuses encyclopaedic erudition and patristic exegesis with sporting play with words and even letters of the alphabet (210–11). This is done, she notes, with such 'ebullience and form-creating energy' that 'the word coinages and foreign words produce almost a ritual dance with language, sometimes losing sight of meaning altogether, where the main delight to the reader is in making new words ... yet Rabelais is so far from being a disordered prose writer that one realizes that his universe was as complex as Joyce's' (211).

20 The 'nose' is also a penis (that which 'knows' in carnal knowing) – an old pun even then: the new style of reproduction has forcibly dislodged the old or made it obsolescent. Imagine the glee with which a Sterne would satirize today's business office, replete with reproduction equipment made by the A.B. Dick company.

21 Joyce used the technique variously: for example, he personified the divisions of Rhetoric in the main characters of the *Wake* (see appendix 3). Finnegan portrays the primordial *logos* that fragments into five parts – the HCE family – with the arrival of the new technologies of the word. Or, rather, Finnegan 'goes dormant' in the human psyche while his role is usurped by the new crew. Shem the forger plays *inventio* as poet and artist; HCE is the disposer and arranger, *dispositio*; ALP, with her nabsack ('mememormee,' 628.14), enacts *memoria*; the daughter, Izzy, is both Isolde – witch and temptress – and the Prankquean, mistress of guise and disguise, in either role *elocutio* ('Hello, cutsey-o'); Shaun the Postman is given the job of *delivery*, the fifth division.

22 Martin Price, *Swift's Rhetorical Art*.

23 Richard A. Lanham, *'Tristram Shandy': The Games of Pleasure*. Cf. also D.W. Jefferson's *'Tristram Shandy* and the Tradition of Learned Wit.'

24 The *Tale* resembles a five-act play in narrative or novel form, its subject the *logos*, analysed in terms of the five divisions of rhetoric. Swift thus dramatized the realignments taking place in the culture around him. He made *elocutio* and decorum subservient to *dispositio*, which, as Walter Ong has shown, is overt in the dialectical reforms of Peter Ramus and his followers. Sterne did the same by making Corporal Trim – i.e., bodily ornament – the servant of Toby – *dispositio*.

25 This point receives comment in Martin Price's *Swift's Rhetorical Art* and his *To the Palace of Wisdom*, and in Ronald Paulson's *Theme and Structure in 'Tale of a Tub.'*

26 Richard Ellmann, *JJ*, 565.

2: *Finnegans Wake* as Cynic Satire

1 Both Korkowski and Kirk have made this point conclusively. Korkowski's unpublished dissertation is a treasure trove of information about the tradition. Scholarship is the poorer for its not being easily available.

2 Carnivalistic discontinuity is a common feature of Menippism. Mario Domenichelli notes:

> Defamiliarization [is] to be found (or unfound) in the lapses of the fictional *discontinuum*. It is exactly in this place that a perspective of multiplicity and simultaneity is progressively brought to presence, exactly where (fictional) time is abolished, and discourse sinks into hyperreality, or unveils in itself hyperreality and multipresence. This movement towards hyperreality is what characterizes, and gives unity to, the *opus-in-interruptum*. It is a movement from the mimetic-parodic Menippean variety of styles in *A Portrait* and *Ulysses* to *Finnegans Wake* where the 'disease' reaches its terminal ph(r)ase, since in *Finnegans Wake* not only is fictional discourse being deformed into a grotesque proliferation of styles, shapes and meanings through the incongruous collage of what should not go together, language itself undergoes the monstrous, or wonderful metamorphosis (both in the sense of passage from one shape to another, and in the metalinguistic sense that the process describes itself) at the level of its minimal units, phrase and morpheme. A kind of baroque or metaphysical wonder is produced in putting together levels of experience and language so very remote from one another. ('Paradoxes,' 111–12).

As we saw in chapter 1, any grotesque proliferation of styles, shapes, and meanings or incongruous collage of what should not go together represents a development of Menippean tactics. Those tactics have their beginnings in juxtaposing the flatly incongruous, verse and prose, or high style and low subject (and vice versa), to jolt and heighten awareness. The same sort of joco-seriousness, that is, of carnivalistic juxtapositions, occurs in Petronius and Martianus Capella, to mention but two early examples. The language itself – and the language of the *Wake* itself – is a principal subject of the *Wake*:

> ... in *Finnegans Wake*, Joyce deals almost totally with those specifically human qualities [emotions, knowledge, language, and culture], and suggests that all we can know of them we know through language. We do not feel what we cannot name. Perhaps we do not even see what we cannot name. Adam's first act was verbal denomination. We surely do not remember what we cannot name. Language, then, *is* reality in Joyce's last, great work. In this novel, he did not attempt to describe, but to render reality itself, a letter scratched from among the detritus of the world. There is nothing totally true or false, yet the world continues, engendering and killing; rises and falls, dependent on a measure, are illusory, but people continue, constantly seeking a measure. *Finnegans Wake* is a celebration of every human energy sung by a chorus of voices using a host of linguistic forms, using masking and revealing language to express confused, contradictory, opaque, incalculable human truths. (Marilyn French, 'Joyce and Language,' 255.)

See also S.B. Purdy, 'Mind Your Genderous: Toward a *Wake* Grammar,' 46–78.
3 Richard Ellmann, *JJ*, 715–16.
4 Vivian Mercier, *The Irish Comic Tradition*, 7.
5 Ellmann observes:

> He defended its theme, its view of life as a recurrence of stock characters and stock situations, another aspect in which the psychology and anthropology of his time did not controvert him. He defended its technique of form in terms of music, insisting not on the union of the arts – although that seems to be implied – but on the importance of sound and rhythm, and the indivisibility of meaning from form, an idea which has become a commonplace in the critical assessment of Eliot's later verse. Finally, he defended his language both in terms of linguistic theory, as a largely emotional medium built up by sifting and agglutination, and in terms of the appropriateness of linguistic distortion to a book which traced the distortion of dreams and suggested that history was also paranomastic, a jollying duplication of events with slight variations. (*JJ*, 716.)

Joyce said patiently to another, '... the action of my new work takes place at night. It's natural things should not be so clear at night, isn't it now?' (to William Bird: reported by Ellmann, *JJ*, 603).

Clive Hart records the Menippean effectiveness of reading the book in his *Structure and Motif in 'Finnegans Wake.'* The word-play, he says, 'comes to be accepted, just as the ordinary reader of the ordinary book accepts the usual conventions of language. After a few hundred pages we are so saturated with puns that nothing surprises, nothing shocks; the mind's ear takes part-writing for granted, the mind's eye is fixed in a permanent state of multiple vision' (34). That is not to say that the reader becomes comatose or shocked into insensibility, but rather that he has had his senses retuned. After a couple of sessions with the *Wake*, good literature has a sweeter savour; poor or inept literature becomes quite unrewarding and insubstantial. Hart gives suggestions for proper reading of the *Wake* on page 36. In 'Nodality and Infra-Structure in *Finnegans Wake*,' David Hayman remarks that '*Finnegans Wake* manipulates and teases in the reader's name and virtually in his person. But, for this to be so, for the experience of reading to be one of making, the *Wake* must give the appearance of randomness when in fact it is organized down to its least unit' (135). Hayman also comments that 'from a musical point of view,' the *Wake* 'is most musical in its construction and execution' (*The 'Wake' in Transit*, 191). Still, 'the *Wake*'s language is not exceptional to language processes ...; rather, it is representative and paradigmatic of them. In foregrounding what most other writings work to deny, the *Wake* requires us to confront our assumptions about reading, meaning, connexity' (S.S. Sailer, *On the Void of to Be*, 66).

In *Joyce's Dislocutions*, the eminent *Wake* scholar, Fritz Senn, presses this honest caution, which could be applied equally aptly to any of the more erudite Menippean satires:

> It is easier to use the *Wake* as proof for something we want to have proved than to know anything precise about it. So some warning is called for. *Finnegans Wake* offers unique reading rewards (at the cost of unequalled frustration); it will remain a fascination and a challenge. But while we can usually make an instructive show of select passages we ought not to confuse the *Wake*'s exemplary complaisance with our understanding of it ... As a *Wake* reader who has done quite a bit of devoted homework, I may be entitled to say that, collectively, we have failed in a most elementary way [to arrive at sufficient basic understanding] and that we are hardly qualified to discuss *Finnegans Wake* with scholarly pretense. It is a pretense that I, for one, can no longer keep up with a straight face. (It is of course possible, and legitimate, to theorize intelligently about *Finnegans Wake* without actually having gone near it, or on the basis of what has already been written about it ...) (xi).

Senn has noted Ezra Pound's instinctive aversion to the perversity of the Menippean decorum, which calls for mixing high and low style, of *Ulysses* ('A Note on Burlesque Bloom'). Early readers of the book's fourth chapter, the one that ushers Leopold Bloom onto the stage of *Ulysses*, 'were less struck by the alimentary all-inclusiveness (which was to be enlarged on subsequently in "Lestrygonians') than the unnecessarily vulgar emphasis on a bodily process that was conventionally undeserving of mention, so that even Ezra Pound, not known for squeamishness, blue-pencilled certain offensive phrases for *The Little Review* prepublication. As the *Wake* later put it, the author had produced "from his unheavenly body a no uncertain quantity of obscene matter not protected by copriright' (*FW* 185.29–30)' (729). In the same issue of *JJQ* as Senn's article, Paul Vanderham details some of the cuts and ascribes them to Pound's Horatian sense of decorum:

> Pound's objections to *Ulysses* arose from his attachment to a classical, hierarchical aesthetic, one that was incompatible with what may be described as Joyce's incarnational, egalitarian tendencies. No purely aesthetic explanation, however, can do full justice to Pound's objections to *Ulysses*. Underneath every aesthetic lie ethical, political, philosophical, or religious convictions – and Pound's is no exception. Indeed, when Pound's aesthetic objections to *Ulysses* are examined closely in light of the expurgations that they were intended to justify, they appear to be little more than thinly-disguised religious objections to Joyce's tendency to subvert the hierarchies cherished by Pound, especially the one separating the erotic and excremental elements of human sexuality. (585–6)

Pound justified his excisions to Joyce on the grounds that they were 'bad art' and too excessive, too likely to distract the reader from the story. Exactly. The same 'tendency to subvert the hierarchies,' to stand the world or the established order (or the audience) on its head in order to reclaim a sense of proportion characterizes every Menippean satire.

6 Letter to Harriet Shaw Weaver, 27 June 1924 (*Letters* I, 214). 'It is all so simple,' Joyce remarked; 'if anyone doesn't understand a passage, all he need do is read it aloud.' (Senn and Purdy, eds; 'Mind Your Genderous,' 55.) Peter Myers comments: 'Not entirely true, of course; but if one *says* "Luisome his for lissome hers' one is more likely to hear the motif "Handsome is as handsome does' than if one merely *looks* at it' (*The Sound of 'Finnegans Wake,'* 15.) Myers discusses the complex relation between written and spoken words: 'A great deal of understanding is necessary in order to hear. Anyone who listens to an unfamiliar language and attempts to look up the words in a dictionary will soon find that he does not even know what he has heard. The same applies to anyone who listens to Joyce read when the pages are not at hand: many words are heard, but many others melt, as it were, into music and noise. Appreciation of the text must involve a

stage of half-hearing; for the lack of comprehension, by shutting off many of the referents, is sometimes an aid to perceiving the richness of the music and mimesis' (129). The reader has to preserve a delicate balance between eye and ear and the other senses, physical and literal, when reading the *Wake* – a balancing act that demands poise as well as much practice. Derek Attridge has teased out the various approaches to reading the *Wake* (and issues surrounding each) in 'Reading Joyce,' his introductory essay in *The Cambridge Companion to James Joyce*.

Fritz Senn, one of the more experienced Joyceans, has this to say about the book's demand that the reader remain flexible and balanced:

> In practice the readers of the *Wake* slip into the roles of pedantic schoolmasters who emend the text's deficiencies of the most self-righting verbal artifact in existence. We mentally put things right, but of course no longer toward one correct solution ...
>
> *Finnegans Wake* thrives on a principle of instant verification or, as we might term it with equal inaccuracy, of instant falsification. We have only to ask ourselves what a 'wrong' interpretation of any *Wake* passage could mean and how one would go about demonstrating it, to realize some basic difference from other works of literature. Even acknowledging that not all our remedial associations are equally pertinent, or helpful, or valuable, we would be hard put to define 'right' or 'wrong' interpretations. Joyce's last works teach us to modify our notions as to what interpretation might be, and turns [*sic*] our attention toward the idea of a continuous adjustive endeavour that involves us, as it did Bloom in his kitchen, in a good deal of alert moving about. What we cannot afford at all is static inflexibility (even though you find a lot of it in Joycean criticism). ('On Reading,' in *Joyce's Dislocutions*, 71)

Not very many books in our tradition resist interpretation in the same way or place the same sort of demand upon the reader: virtually every one of them is a Menippean satire.

7 Keeping the reader suspended between alternatives, on the borderline, is central to the Menippean effect because it sustains a complex sensibility aware of multiple possibilities simultaneously.

> The *Wake*'s moments of self-reference, then, replicate rather than resolve the multiplicity of perspectives the book offers in such abundance. Our innocent reader will doubtless note that one of its self-images is the dream, but will have no reason to privilege this over all the others that are available: the letter, the manifesto, the midden, the illuminated page, the photograph, the ballad, the children's game, the television program, the riddle, the radio broadcast, the bed-

time story, the geometrical theorem, the anecdote, the quiz show, the lecture, the homily, the mailbag ... the list could go on as long as the longest list in *Finnegans Wake*.

It would seem unnecessary to spend time emphasizing something so obvious as the undecidable polysemic richness of the *Wake* were it not that so much commentary pays little more than lip-service to this property, before going on to press the claims of this or that particular and exclusive reading. We seldom think through the consequences of Joyce's having written, with great effort, a text whose meanings occur in the form of alternatives between which it is impossible to decide. (Attridge, 'Finnegans Awake,' 17).

8 McHugh, *The 'Finnegans Wake' Experience*, 25. Joyce sent some pages of the new book to Ezra Pound in 1926. Pound's initial reaction was this: 'I will have another go at it, but up to the present I make nothing of it whatever. Nothing so far as I make out, nothing short of divine vision or a new cure for the clapp can possibly be worth all the circumambient peripherization.'

9 Ibid., 9.

10 In 1932, Joyce pointed out to Eliot that the new book, 'Work in Progress' (W.i.P.) avoided chronology and sequentiality by its cyclic structure and use of 'continuous present.' He wrote: '*Ulysses* is a book with a beginning, middle, and end and should be presented as such. The case is quite different with W.i.P. which has neither beginning nor end' (*Letters* I, 315. See also n. 15, below.) Nevertheless, some readers persist in attempting to educe a sequential narrative, from Campbell and Robinson's early *A Skeleton Key to 'Finnegans Wake'* to *Understanding 'Finnegans Wake': A Guide to the Narrative of James Joyce's Masterpiece*, by Danis Rose and John O'Hanlon, to John Gordon's *'Finnegans Wake': A Plot Summary*, and to Michael Begnal's *Dreamscheme*. On the first page of his book, Gordon announces he will provide a 'thoroughly reductive' reading of *Finnegans Wake* as a naturalistic narrative. Begnal avers, 'there still remains a novelistic form and structure behind or below the complications of the novel's primary linguistic level' (51). 'Interpreting narrative in the *Wake*, or denying that it exists, involves very high ethical stakes for those who play either way,' observes Thomas Hofheinz. The lines of battle are by now well drawn.

11 Two remarks in Eliot's *To Criticize the Critic* are apposite. The first is from the essay, 'What Dante Means to Me': 'To pass on to posterity one's own language, more highly developed, more refined, and more precise than before one wrote it, that is the highest possible achievement of the poet as poet' (132). He adds that this is at once a task of 'craft of speech and of exploration of sensibility.' The second remark is found in his essay 'American Literature and Language' and concerns Mark Twain, who 'at least in *Huckleberry Finn*, reveals himself to be one of

those writers, of whom there is not a great many in any literature, who have discovered a new way of writing, valid not only for themselves but for others. I should place him, in this respect, even with Dryden and Swift, as one of those rare writers who have brought their language up to date, and in so doing, "purified the dialect of the tribe"' (54). *Huckleberry Finn*, too, is a Menippean satire. See also Eliot's retrospective comments in *Four Quartets* about 'trying to learn to use words ...' ('East Coker,' V, and 'Burnt Norton,' V). Eliot and Pound were tackling the same problems as was Joyce, but from entirely different angles. 'In the *Wake*,' writes Marshall McLuhan, 'Shem the Penman is, like Moses, an "outlex.' The seer cannot be a rhetor. He does not speak for effect, but that we may know ... And the artist, in order that he may perform his katharsis-purgative function, must mime all things. (The katharsis-purgative role of the Herculean culture-hero dominates the nightworld of the *Wake* where the hero sets Alpheus, the river of speech and collective consciousness, to the task of cleansing the Augean stables of thought and feeling)' ('James Joyce: Trivial and Quadrivial,' 83).

12 Reported by Hugh Kenner in *Dublin's Joyce*, 327. Appositely, Richard Ellmann remarked of Joyce that 'Since the material of *Ulysses* was all human life, every man he met was an authority' (*JJ*, 453). Writing about Joyce's use of traditional poetic riddling in the *Wake*, Patrick McCarthy notes:

> In view of Henry Frank Beechhold's demonstration that Joyce thought of himself as part of the Gaelic tradition – specifically as an *ollave* or *fili* ['Early Irish History and Mythology in *Finnegans Wake*' (Ann Arbor: University Microfilms, 1956), 2–3. The *fili* was a poet or seer, a man of great learning: see Mercier, *The Irish Comic Tradition*, passim, and Robin Flower, *The Irish Tradition* (Oxford: Oxford Univ. Press, 1947), 4. The *ollave* spent seven years in a bardic school before seeking service as official poet to a king or chieftain (Flower, 98–9).] – it is significant that in the archaic Irish poetic tradition the formula *Ni ansa*, 'Not hard (to say),' is not only the traditional formula for beginning the answer to a riddle but also the formula for beginning the recitation of a story that is prefaced by a question. [Mercier *TICT* 80–1] Joyce's deviation from this tradition consists, in part, in treating his materials on two levels, both as universal knowledge that is accessible to everyone and as obscure knowledge that is clear to no one: *Ni ansa* sounds enough like 'No answer' for Joyce to transmute it into 'Noanswa' (23.20–1; Cf. 105.14). (*The Riddles of 'Finnegans Wake,'* 30).

13 'Tradition and the Individual Talent,' 56, 58.
14 'The Method of Mr Pound.' Joyce exploited the same technique via parody, according to Mario Domenichelli:

The reversal of St. Thomas' aesthetics, already at work in *A Portrait*, is radically exploited and fully achieved through *Ulysses* and *Finnegans Wake*. These two books are polyphonic, polysemic works in which the radical metaphors, Dublin and the body, betray the anatomic, Menippean perspective. The fictional body, and the very body of discourse, are dismembered. They are shown, or constructed, or deconstructed as a *discontinuum* with effects of total disintegration of the fictional discourse in *Ulysses* and of discourse *tout court* in *Finnegans Wake*. The basic strategy seems to be parody. It is through parody that all the fictional styles put into play are overloaded until, through their very overloading, they become utterly devoid of meaning while paradoxically acquiring endless possibilities of meaning. ('Paradoxes' 113)

15 *Homage to John Dryden*, 288.

16 James Stephens, whom Joyce considered a sort of protégé to carry on and finish *Finnegans Wake*, should Joyce's deteriorating health or eyesight prevent his doing so, used 'wake' similarly: in 1932 he was preparing an anthology of nineteenth-century Irish poets and remarked of the 'many thousands of writers in that epoch' that 'they all used to write in their sleep as well as in their wake' (from a letter to S.S. Koteliansky, 5 October 1932; *Letters of James Stephens*, 372).

17 Postcard dated 16 April 1927. *Letters* I, 251.

18 Cf. letter to Miss Weaver, 8 November 1926. *Letters* I, 246. Part of the enduring conventional wisdom about the *Wake* is that it begins and ends at the same point, that is, in the middle of the same sentence, and thus that the book itself is a circle. But this assumption does not really stand up to the experience of reading aloud, although it seems quite tenable – and quite attractive – to silent readers. So, evidently it is a false conclusion, a myth deduced from a red herring Joyce tossed across our path. Joyce said that he wanted the *Wake* to end with the most silent word in the language: when one reads the last line aloud, it tapers off with a definite *decrescendo*, ending with the word *the* and the tongue near the teeth after forming the /th/, and no real articulate sound at all. But the book opens with 'riverrun, past Eve and Adam's ...' etc., spoken at normal volume and intonation. Put the two ends together, however, and the delivery is simply too disjoint. Nobody would speak, or narrate, that way. I propose instead that *Finnegans Wake* begins in the middle of *some* sentence, the way the voice on the radio begins in the middle of a sentence when we tune in a station, but that we have no idea of the actual beginning of that sentence; and that the *Wake* ends in mid-sentence, simply fading out, the way many songs fade out at the end of a record, or the way a film scene 'fades to black.' We have no idea what actually does or might come next, after 'along the': the fact that the end *can* be joined to the beginning is sheer Menippean coincidence – and nothing more. As Joyce said, the *Wake* 'has neither

beginning nor end': it is just suddenly there, *in medias res*; and it has no end(ing), it just tapers off into silence.

19 Letter of 12 May 1927. *Letters* I, 252.

20 This is not to claim that all Menippean writers are grammarians with bees in their private or collective bonnets, or even that they are conscious of grammar any more than they need be conscious of other Menippists. It is to note that Menippean satire, perhaps beginning with Varro, perhaps even earlier, developed a convergence of interests and techniques that put it on a common footing with grammar and rhetoric. This convergence appears clearly in their mutual concern with language. The partnership was certainly cemented for more than a thousand years by Martianus' *De nuptiis*.

21 'James Joyce: Trivial and Quadrivial,' 88–9.

22 'Prologue to the First Book,' ed. Le Clercq, 5. The notion that Joyce explored the parallels between the 'Two Books' is gaining currency in Joyce circles, although the relation of that trope to traditional grammatica and to the tradition of learned commentary is still not observed. For example, Cheryl Herr has observed that 'as parallel texts, then, early modern Irish culture and Joyce's works exemplify similar mechanisms of operation and conform to similar conditions of possibility – especially insofar as they conceptualize matters such as being, freedom, personal authenticity, and fidelity. The measure of Joyce's awareness that these notions are inherently ideological is the fact that his texts do not affirm them; the works merely generate discourse about them and gesture toward the institutional purveyors of these concepts' (*Joyce's Anatomy of Culture*, 11). Here, approach to the trope is encumbered by semantic and political concepts that effectively occlude the technique of juxtaposition and of parallels: they work more on the level of percepts and sensibility than on that of concepts and ideology. Dialectics (philosophy and ideology) does not easily function as grammar.

23 'Prologue to the Second Book,' 161. Joyce said to Max Eastman, 'the demand that I make of my reader ... is that he should devote his whole life to reading my works' (*JJ*, 716) See also 'The "Ideal Reader" of *Finnegans Wake*' by Katie Wales in *The Language of James Joyce*, 132–57.

24 *Dublin's Joyce*, 283. In this section, Kenner gives an account of Joyce's 'work of finding a language.'

25 Letter of 17 October 1923. *Letters* I, 205.

26 Letter of 16 November 1924. *Letters* I, 222. Too, 'Joyce, the artist without peer of the profundity of the trivial, chose to make the assemblage of random objects a major thematic recurrence of *Finnegans Wake*. Most random and most recurrent is the dump, tip, or midden, the comic, mute all-object and all-word *litter*-ature including the book containing it, swallowing up its locus, dear dirty Dublin, as well ("Dear. And we go on to Dirtdump" – *FW* 615.12). Like language, or as lan-

guage, the dump is a layered receptacle in which hidden treasure lies, treasure that is indistinguishable from trash, according to one's point of view' (Purdy, 'Vico's Verum-Factum,' 372).

27 *The Waning of the Middle Ages*, 227.

28 *Dublin's Joyce*, 325–6.

29 *Ulysses*, 37. Proteus is the magus of forms and formal transformation; Stephen is concerned to read the language of all manner of forms and outlines. As Stephen traces the mutating outlines of air and sea and shore 'he had come nearer the edge of the sea and wet sand slapped his boots. The new air greeted him, harping in wild nerves, wind of wild air of seeds of brightness ...' (44). He notes the formal inner world that exists alongside the outer experience (another boundary he limns): 'My soul walks with me, form of forms ...' and he meditates on a rich profusion about him of forms in process of mutation, re-forming: 'A bloated carcass of a dog lay lolled on bladderwrack. Before him the gunwale of a boat, sunk in sand. *Un coche ensablé*, Louis Veuillot called Gautier's prose. These heavy sands are language tide and wind have silted here. And there, the stoneheaps of dead builders ...' (ibid.). Light can be as Protean as water:

> His shadow lay over the rocks as he bent, ending ... I throw this ended shadow from me, manshape ineluctable, call it back. Endless, would it be mine, form of my form? Who watches me here? Who ever anywhere will read these written words? Signs on a white field ... You find my words dark. Darkness is in our souls, do you not think? Flutier. Our souls, shame-wounded by our sins, cling to us yet more, a woman to her lover clinging, the more the more.
>
> She trusts me, her hand gentle, the longlashed eyes. Now where the blue hell am I bringing her beyond the veil? Into the ineluctable modality of the ineluctable visuality. (48)

As Proteus' water shapes itself immediately around whatever is thrust into it, so does the shadow flung over the rock, the word over the paper, the soul around the sin, one lover around the other; and, too, the boot shapes itself to the foot. (Equally, Dublin and Ithaca, Bloom and Odysseus, Stephen and Telemachus, and all the double-plot and two-book structures.)

A final example of reading signature and speech of form from a chapter that overflows with them:

> His gaze brooded on his broadtoed boots, a buck's castoffs *nebeneinander*. He counted the creases of rucked leather wherein another's foot had nested warm. The foot that beat the ground in tripudium, foot I dislove. But you were delighted when Esther Osvalt's shoe went on you: girl I knew in Paris. *Tiens,*

quel petit pied! Staunch friend, a brother soul: Wilde's love that dare not speak
its name. He now will leave me. And the blame? As I am. As I am. All or not at
all.

In long lassoes from the Cock lake the water flowed full, covering greengold-
enly lagoons of sand, rising, flowing. My ashplant will float away. I shall wait.
No, they will pass on, passing chafing against the low rocks, swirling, passing.
Better get this job over quick. Listen: a fourworded wavespeech: seesoo, hrss,
rsseeiss, ooos. Vehement breath of waters amid seasnakes, rearing horses, rocks.
In cups of rocks it slops: flop, slop, slap: bounded in barrels. And, spent, its
speech ceases. It flows purling, widely flowing, floating foampool, flower
unfurling. (49)

The terms 'diaphane' and 'adiaphane' are particularly related to the transformation of Stephen's perceptions both in this passage and throughout the chapter,
which is structured around Philology. Here it relates as much to the eyes and eyelids as to the ways in which the senses screen experience. This visual component is
light and colour, whether direct (outer) or via other senses (inner). In this chapter,
'diaphane' serves almost as the key term in a manifesto. It was the quintessential
term in the manifesto of the stilnovisti, and in Guido Cavalcanti's canzone 'Donna
mi pregha ...' Angelo Lipari has demonstrated (in his careful analysis in *The Dolce
Stil Novo according to Lorenzo Da' Medici*) that the whole poem is an extended
metaphor based on light imagery. In particular, he discusses the line 'Diafan dal
lume.' The lady is the diaphane through which the poet must pass to experience a
mystical 'death' in order to take on the new life, the 'vita nuova' – a transformation of consciousness and of sensibility. For Dante, Beatrice. For Stephen, the
transformation is obtained more simply but no less symbolically by closing his
eyes while he walks, limning the border between worlds, amid seawrack left by
Proteus' fingers – the tide. Joyce did not reduce the world to a division between
eye and ear: for comment on the sense of smell in Joyce's writing, see Bernard
Benstock, 'James Joyce: The Olfactory Factor,' in *Joycean Occasions*, 138–56.

30 The endpapers to Mary Parr's *James Joyce: The Poetry of Conscience* reproduce as
a fold-out the chart given to Sylvia Beach. Stuart Gilbert uses the chart in *James
Joyce's 'Ulysses': A Study*, but minus the telling 'correspondences'; at Joyce's
request, they were to be dealt with in the discussion instead of listed on the chart.
Richard Ellmann compares the 'Gorman-Gilbert plan' or chart to the one Joyce
gave to Carlo Linati in 1920 (*Ulysses on the Liffey*). Ellmann provides some of the
background:

The first known schema for *Ulysses* was that which on 21 September 1920
Joyce sent to Carlo Linati. In the accompanying letter, he said, 'in view of the

enormous bulk and the more than enormous complexity of my damned mon-
ster-novel it would be better to send ... a sort of summary-key-skeleton-schema
(for home use only) ... I have given only "Schlagworte" [catchwords] in my
schema but I think you will understand it all the same. It is the epic of two races
(Israel-Ireland) and at the same time the cycle of the human body as well as a
little story of a day (life) ... It is also a kind of encyclopaedia.'

The schema sent to Linati offers brief meanings (*Senso, Signifaco*) for each
episode, lists the classical or legendary personages (some unexpected) without
specifying their parallels, and names the several dominant symbols in each
chapter. Joyce subsequently retracted some of his hints, especially of the episodes' meanings, and spelled out the less central classical parallels. He then
devised a new schema, which in late 1921 he lent to Valery Larbaud, who was
about to lecture on the still unpublished book.

After its publication, Joyce discreetly continued to circulate this second
schema, or one like it, usually through Sylvia Beach's intermediary hands.
(186–7)

31 Peter Myers, *The Sound of 'Finnegans Wake,'* 19.

32 Ibid., 16.

33 Ibid., 17–18.

34 Letter to Harriet Shaw Weaver, 21 May 1926. *Letters* I, 241.

35 See, for example, *Dublin's Joyce*, 334–5. Since Kenner, *Vico and Joyce*, a collection
of essays edited by Donald Phillip Verene, has explored numerous new dimensions of Joyce's use of and reliance on Vico.

36 Kenner, 330. Joyce's interest in Vico was first publicized by Samuel Beckett's con-
tribution to *Our Exagmination Round His Factification for Incamination of Work
in Progress* (1929). Clive Hart gives a brief résumé of aspects of Vico, thought to
be used by Joyce, in *Structure and Motif in 'Finnegans Wake,'* 46–9. Convenient
summaries of how Viconian theories are seen to relate to the *Wake* are to be
found in Campbell and Robinson's *Skeleton Key*, in Beckett's article, and in A.M.
Klein's 'A Shout in the Street,' in W.Y. Tindall's *James Joyce: His Way of Interpreting the Modern World*.

37 S.B. Purdy has written about the status of the object in the *Wake*:

Artifact, and object as artifact, thus loom large in *Finnegans Wake*. Object in *La
Scienza nuova* is part of language itself: the hieroglyphic or divine language
was 'a mute language of signs and physical objects' (*cenni o corpi*); the heroic
language mixed objects (emblems, blazons, signs, devices) with words (*SN* 219,
232–3; Bergin 432, 446). The common language of the age of men is purely linguistic, but is also called the epistolary language. When Vico tells of the barba-

rous king of the Scythians sending an answer to Darius in the form of five objects, he calls them 'real words' (*SN* 68; Bergin 48), as if to emphasize the ontological over the epistemological object ... ('Vico's Verum-Factum,' 372).

38 Ibid., 94. More recently, Vico scholars have become aware of Joyce's interest in this aspect of Vico's investigations. For example, Donald Phillip Verene writes:

> this mental language, this *lingua mentale comune*, is what is made articulate in language as it appears in symbols. Whenever we use an actual language to communicate, our ability to achieve meaning is based on the common mental language that contains the commonplaces of human mentality itself and that is a product of our *fantasia*. Fundamental human communication depends upon us making touch with this common mental language in a direct fashion. Something of this process can be grasped from *Ulysses* and *Finnegans Wake*, in which Joyce uses a kind of language behind language. In reading these works we sense that below the articulations of our specific language there lies a language of all languages. Words and meanings are conjoined in a kind of first language of imagination, of imaginative universals. It is as if in *Finnegans Wake* Joyce tried to speak the unspeakable language of the *lingua mentale comune*. (*Vico's Science of the Imagination*, 178.)

Vico's title, *The New Science*, was inspired by that of Bacon's *Novum Organum* (New Science): Bacon was an earlier grammarian. Vico's mental dictionary was a direct result of his attempt to counter the excesses of dialectic in his day by shifting Aristotelian intelligible universals to poetic wisdom and philology as a basis of humanistic science. The mental dictonary, notes Verene, 'contains the special letters of the book of humanity which we can learn to read by *fantasia*. Galileo's magnificent art of reading degenerates into the dominance of method and technological procedure, and Vico's art of reading the hieroglyphics of the *sensus communis* of humanity has its degerate counterparts in historicism and the contemporary concern with methodology in the humanities' (204). Poetic wisdom is the key to Vico's New Science and, similarly understood as philology (grammar), is the key to the *Wake*.

Vico laboured not to provide an apology for grammar in his time but to update its uses and resources and thereby to effect a reconciliation in the ongoing war of the Ancients and the Moderns by restoring their complementarity. Thus, he concludes book II of *The New Science* with this observation:

> We have shown that poetic wisdom justly deserves two great and sovereign tributes. The one, clearly and constantly accorded to it, is that of having founded gentile mankind, though the conceit of the nations on the one hand

and that of the scholars on the other, the former with ideas of an empty magnificence and the latter with ideas of an impertinent philosophical wisdom, have in effect denied it this honour by their very efforts to affirm it. The other, concerning which a vulgar tradition has come down to us, is that the wisdom of the ancients made its wise men, by a single inspiration, equally great as philosophers, lawmakers, captains, historians, orators and poets, on which account it has been so greatly sought after. But in fact it made or rather sketched them such as we have found them in the fables. For in these, as in embryos or matrices, we have discovered the outlines of all esoteric wisdom. And it may be said that in the fables the nations have in a rough way and in the language of the human senses described the beginnings of this world of sciences, which the specialized studies of scholars have since clarified for us by reasoning and generalization. From all this we may conclude what we set out to show in this second book: that the theological poets were the sense and the philosophers the intellect of human wisdom. (265)

39 On these grounds, Wyndham Lewis attacked Joyce. Curiously, in most respects, Lewis too was a Menippist. See, for example, the opening lines to part II of *One-Way Song*:

> Again let me do a lot of extraordinary talking.
> Again let me do a lot!
> Let me abound in speeches – let me abound! – publicly polyglot.
> Better a blind word to bluster with – better a bad word than none lieber Gott!
> Watch me push into my witch's vortex all the Englishmen's got
> To cackle and rattle with – you catch my intention? – to be busily balking
> The tongue-tied Briton – that is my outlandish plot!

Lewis's principal observations are contained in *Time and Western Man* (1927) and *Men without Art* (1934). His Freudian account of Joyce and *Ulysses* in the former volume was by no means the first, just as Ellmann's (in the biography) was by no means the last. It brought out several aspects of the ear interest as opposed to eye interest. Placing the ear above, or on the same plane of emphasis as, the eye (displacing the dominance of the visual over the other senses) supplants the dominance of the outer world and of discrete objects over the interior world – a world also of 'mental time' in which past and present coalesce. Lewis notes that this merging has had the added effect in Joyce of thrusting up process (and 'impartiality') to displace point of view: 'What stimulates him is *ways of doing things*, and technical processes, and not *things to be done*. Between the various things to be done he shows a true craftsman's impartiality ... Strictly speaking, he has no world-view at all, no special point of view, or none worth mentioning' (*Time and Western Man*, 90). The value of Lewis's observations lies mainly in his having discovered that the inward path is achieved by acoustic rather than by visual stress. Evidently, then, this stress has been present in our arts since Romanticism: it remained for further stress to be applied for inward subjectivity to be pressed to the point where it reversed into impersonality (as proclaimed by Eliot). In *Men Without Art*, Lewis points out further that the acoustic mode is non-linear: 'In my criticism of *Ulysses* I laid particular stress upon the limitations of the *internal* method. As developed in *Ulysses*, it robbed Mr. Joyce's work as a whole of all linear properties whatever, considered as a plastic thing ...' (120). This method, however, is consistent with the abandonment of sequential time, i.e., with the discovery that the acoustic and inner affords the opportunity to explore the simultaneous dimensions of experience, including that of time. A two-book structure is therefore an acoustic structure, because the two books are simultaneous. The basis of Lewis's attack is neatly summed up in *Men without Art* by this: 'Dogmatically, then, I am for the Great Without, for the method of External approach – for the wisdom of the eye, rather than that of the ear' (128).

40 From the essay on Matthew Arnold in *The Use of Poetry and the Use of Criticism*.

41 Cf. Ellmann in *JJ*:

> Joyce said to August Suter, and he remarked to another friend, 'I have put the language to sleep.' As he explained to Max Eastman in a later effort, valiant but unsuccessful, to win a convert to his method, 'In writing of the night, I really could not, I felt I could not, use words in their ordinary connections. Used that way they do not express how things are in the night, in the different stages – consciousness, then semi-conscious, then unconscious. I found that it could not be done with words in their ordinary relations and connections. When morning comes of course everything will be clear again ... I'll give them back their English language. I'm not destroying it for good.' Joyce set out upon this radical technique, of making many of the words in his book multilingual puns, with his usual conviction. After all, he said to Frank Budgen, 'The Holy Roman Catholic Apostolic Church was built on a pun. It ought to be good enough for me. (559)

42 Ibid., 563.

43 Ibid., 729.

44 Katie Wales, *The Language of James Joyce*, 67.

45 Derek Attridge, *Peculiar Language*, 231.

46 Ellmann commented in *JJ*:

> He [Joyce] defended the complexity as necessary to the theme, a claim which

has come to be accepted for modern poetry. He defended its technique or form in terms of music, insisting not on the union of the arts – although that seems to be implied – but on the importance of sound and rhythm, and the indivisibility of meaning from form, and idea which has become a commonplace in the critical assessment of Eliot's later verse. Finally, he defended his language both in terms of linguistic theory, as a largely emotional medium built up by sifting and agglutination, and in terms of the appropriateness of linguistic distortion to a book which traced the distortion of dreams and suggested that history was also paranomastic, a jollying duplication of events with slight variations. (716)

Ralph Waldo Emerson may have been the first to remark explicitly that artefacts are extensions of the body: 'The human body is the magazine of inventions ... All the tools and engines on earth are only extensions of its limbs and senses' ('Works and Days,' in *Society and Solitude*).

47 Peter Myers, *The Sound of 'Finnegans Wake,'* 45.
48 In *Dublin's Joyce* Kenner shows some of the uses of figures in the *Wake*. Antanaclasis: homonymic pun.
49 Paranomasia, e.g., 'Casting her perils before our swains' (202.08–09), or 'her faiths is altared' (331.03).
50 Syllepsis (similar to zeugma), e.g., Pope's 'Or lose her heart, or necklace, at a ball.'
51 *The Riddles of 'Finnegans Wake,'* 135.
52 Bill Bryson, *The Mother Tongue*, 51. The holorime is a rhetorical pun, both a scheme and a trope. Steven Pinker calls them 'oronyms' and found them by another route, the stream of speech or river of eloquence that will not brook being chopped up into discrete words.

All speech is an illusion. We hear speech as a string of separate words, but unlike the tree falling in the forest with no one to hear it, a word boundary with no one to hear it has no sound. In the speech sound wave, one word runs into the next seamlessly; there are no little silences between spoken words the way there are white spaces between written words. We simply hallucinate word boundaries when we reach the edge of a stretch of sound that matches some entry in our mental dictionary. This becomes apparent when we listen to speech in a foreign language: it is impossible to tell where one word ends and the next begins. The seamlessness of speech is also apparent in 'oronyms,' strings of sound that can be carved into words in two different ways:

The good can decay many ways.
The good candy came anyways.

> The stuffy nose can lead to problems.
> The stuff he knows can lead to problems.

[Others surface in students' term papers and essays]:

> Eugene O'Neill won a Pullet Surprise. (a Pulitzer Prize)
> My Mother comes from Pencil Vanea. (Pennsylvania)
> They played the Bohemian Rap City. (Bohemian Rhapsody) (*The Language Instinct*, 159–61)

Pinker comments, too, that 'information about each component of a word is smeared over the entire word' (161).

53 The question remains, who speaks or narrates *Finnegans Wake*?

It is not Joyce: his remarks about corporate authorship – he merely recorded the words of those about him – suggest that everyone, and therefore no one, is the speaker (anonymous = unanimous), which dodges the question.

> John Paul Riquelme confronts the problem of voice in the novel in this way: 'in the *Wake*, the only definitive answer to the question "*Who is speaking?*" is the pragmatic one: the *reader* speaks by taking on the role of the artist as teller. The ambiguous status of of the text's language not only allows but *requires* us to mimic the teller in different voices that merge with one another' (*Teller and Tale in Joyce's Fiction*, 8). This works well if we say that the reader speaks, in a sense, by recognizing each new voice as it takes over the narration, and by realizing that these voices are the tellers. Joyce has never spoken directly to us in any of his works' (Michael H. Begnal, *Dreamscheme*, 79–80).

So the reader performs the text: Whose text? Who speaks there? Vico asked the same question when he went in search of 'The True Homer' in book III of *The New Science*. He decided that authorship of Homer's poems was corporate: he concluded 'that the Greek peoples were themselves Homer' (290): this is to follow a basic assumption of our own cultural anthropologists, that anything not ascribable to a particular individual is regarded as the work of the culture at large. Perhaps, then, the language itself speaks *Finnegans Wake*. At least, it is the language itself that speaks the ten thunders.

3: Introduction to Part II

1 Aside from our understanding of the divine *logos* of creation, this sense survives in Scripture and liturgy: e.g., the (old) Offertory for Pentecost Monday is 'Into-

nuit de caelo Dominus, et Altissimus dedit vocem suam: et apparuerunt fontes aquarum, alleluia' [The Lord thundered from heaven, and the most High gave His voice: and the fountains of waters appeared, alleluia] (Ps. 17: 14, 16).

2 Hugh Kenner remarks in *Dublin's Joyce*, 325, that 'there was an odd tradition that the Irish enjoyed, without intervention of Babel, a language descended from the Adamite speech' – a tradition that would have held considerable significance for Joyce when he was working in *Wake* mode. Joyceans agree that readings of the *Wake* performed with a strong Irish accent 'work' best.

3 *Summa Theologica*, Q. 113, A. 7, ad 5. II, 1031. Joyce's knowledge of Aquinas is well attested by his students. As, for example, Fr Noon shows, Joyce pursued intensive studies of St Thomas after leaving Ireland. [In Paris],

> He began to teach himself Greek, which he had avoided taking in college (though he had a special flair for languages), and he embarked, without formal direction, upon a fairly intensive program of private study of Aristotle and Aquinas. Valery Larbaud, who was to become a very close friend of Joyce at a time much later on, and who was chiefly responsible for seeing to it that Joyce became well known in French literary and intellectual circles, says of this early Paris period in Joyce's career: 'C'est ainsi que, pendant qu'il était à Paris, il passait plusieurs heures chaque soir à la Bibliotheque Saint-Geneviève, lisant Aristote et saint Thomas d'Aquin. (*Joyce and Aquinas*, 12)

Later, while living and teaching in Trieste, Joyce continued to study Aquinas 'in Latin, a page a day' (Ellmann, *JJ*, 353). Fr Noon also, in a discussion of Joyce's 'root language,' notes the Menippean topic of the author giving advice to the reader as regards the influence of writing on language and speech, and on the reader's mental capacities:

> ... early in the *Wake* Joyce advises his readers to stop ('stoop'), 'if you are abced minded.' He then goes on to describe his own poetic process as a search for the 'nameform that whets the wits that convey contacts that sweeten sensation ... that entails the ensuance of existentiality.' There is a sense in which you must know and love your instrument, words, for their own sake, if you ever hope to use them for the construction of poetry, or for entry into an already constructed poem.
>
> This notion of the instrumental causality of language is much more operative in the *Wake* than is any concept of words as mere speculative signs. Not unrelated to it is Joyce's tendency to regard words as gestures or epiphanies of being, gestures whose meaningfulness consists in the disclosure of the secret, wordless essence itself. For though the essence lies beyond the gesture, the essence would

not be manifest at all. The words of 'a true friend' will tell us much more about himself, says Joyce, than we will ever learn, for instance, by studying his footwear. The *Wake* is full of many good-natured counsels to the reader to cut short his reading if he cannot accept Joyce's attitude that words must be taken as intrinsically interesting 'gestures of being' rather than as mere signals of concepts to inform us by a kind of shorthand of what is going on: 'Please stoop if you're a B. C. minding missy, please do.' Or again 'Begin to forget it. It will remember itself from every sides, with all gestures, in each our word. Today's truth, tomorrow's trend.' (*Joyce and Aquinas*, 151–2)

4 Thunder as the voice of God appears in both Old and New Testaments, e.g., John 12:28–9.

'Vico reflects that the compulsion to band together and to initiate an equitable sharing of the land must have come solely from what those beings of crude and fierce nature believed to be the bidding of a superior power speaking through the thunder and lightning' (A.A. Grimaldi, *The Universal Humanity of Giambattista Vico*, 190). Vico further proposed that 'the first "bond" of faith was sealed when the thundering sky signified for primitive man the emanation of a divine law that bade him cease his ferine wandering and settle down in one place, thus becoming "bound" to a home and family' (ibid., 197). These are primary among the themes of the *Wake*'s first two thunderclaps. It is more likely that Joyce was prompted by Vico than by the 'conventional wisdom' of anthropology.

However, Joyce studies have not got very far with examining or explaining the thunders. Roland McHugh summarizes the present extent of thought on the subject. He quotes the first thunder, and notes:

This is made out of various foreign equivalents of 'thunder,' for instance Japanese *kaminari*, Italian *tuono*, Portuguese *trovao* and Danish *tordenen*. Its significance has generally been agreed upon since Samuel Beckett's authorized essay on the *Wake* appeared in 1929. It represents the roll of thunder which, according to Giambattista Vico's *The New Science*, characterises the first phase through which all human civilizations must progress ... Beckett's essay attempts 'to condense the thesis of Vico, the scientific historian. In the beginning was the thunder: the thunder set free Religion, in its most objective and unphilosophical form – idolatrous animism: Religion produced Society, and the first social men were the cave-dwellers, taking refuge from a passionate Nature: this primitive family life receives its first impulse towards development from the arrival of terrified vagabonds: admitted, they are the first slaves: growing stronger, they exact agrarian concessions, and a despotism has evolved into a primitive feudalism: the cave becomes a city, and the feudal system a democracy: then an anarchy: this is corrected by a return to monarchy: the last stage is a tendency towards interdestruction: the nations are dispersed and the Phoenix of Society arises out of their ashes. (*The 'Finnegans Wake' Experience*, 4–5. Beckett's essay, 'Dante ... Bruno. Vico ... Joyce' appeared in *Our Exagmination ...*)

5 *Letters on Literature and Politics* 1912–1972, ed. Elena Wilson, 184.

4: The First Thunderclap

1 J. Campbell and H.M. Robinson, *A Skeleton Key to 'Finnegans Wake,'* 26. Sir Tristram's first name is given as Amory. Louis O. Mink adds the further variants Armoricus and Armory in his note on Howth (*'Finnegans Wake' Gazetteer*, 345–6). In his introduction, Mink gives a summary:

> Although HCE (for whom Joyce's working siglum was ⋔) is the whole city – always at greater or less remove from the family intimacy of a river, island and riverbanks – he is also, as (Letters I, 254) a sleeping giant interred in the landscape, his head the Hill of Howth, his torso the gentle ridge running East and West through north Dublin, and his upturned feet the two hills or knocks of Castleknock Hill and Windmill Hill, just West of Phoenix Park (about 12 miles from Howth). Sometimes his feet are located as the hill of the Magazine Fort within Phoenix Park (7.30–32; 12.35–36); St. Thomas's Hill is separated only by a gully from its neighboring Whitebridge Hill. Most readers of *Finnegans Wake* have seen the Wellington Monument in Phoenix Park as the erect penis of this sleeping giant; but in geographical fact this would make him, remarkably and ridiculously, short in the leg. (xxv)

Comment on the various forms and significances of stuttering may be found in Shari Benstock's essay 'Apostrophes' in *Joycean Occasions*, 106–7.

2 George Steiner, not an 'establishment Joycean,' glosses the opening lines as follows:

> A good measure of the prose in *Finnegans Wake* is polyglot. Consider the famous riverrounding sentence on page one: 'Sir Tristram, violer d'amores, fr'over the short sea had passencore rearrived from North Armorica ...' Not only is there the emphatic obtrusion of French in *triste, violer, pas encore*, and *Armoric* (Ancient Brittany), but Italian is present in *viola d'amore* and, if Joyce is to be believed, in the tag from Vico, *ricorsi storici*, which lodges partly as an anagram, partly as a translation, in 'passencore rearrived.' Or take a characteristic example from Book II: 'in deesperation of deispiration at the diasporation of

his diesparation.' In this peal a change is rung on four and, possibly, five languages: English 'despire,' French *deesse*, Latin *dies* (perhaps the whole phrase *Dies irae* is inwoven), Greek *diaspora*, and Old French or Old Scottish *dais* or *deis* meaning a stately room and, later, a canopied platform for solemn show. In Joyce's 'nighttalk' banal monosyllables can knit more than one language. Thus 'seim' in 'the seim anew' near the close of 'Anna Livia Plurabelle' contains English 'same' and the river Seine in a deft welding not only of two tongues but of the dialectical poles of identity and flux. (*After Babel*, 190).

Steiner's concern is the renewal of a language, in this context by its interface with other languages or by play with it in extraordinary forms. Joyce, he concludes, 'represents a borderline case between synthesis and neologism' (ibid).

3 Cf. the version in Ellmann, *JJ*, 556–7. Tim Finnegan was laid out 'With a gallon of whisky at his feet, / And a barrel of Porter at his head.'
4 Joyce's gloss to the passage, ibid.
5 There are 37 other 'rumbles' in the *Wake*:

23.28	27.17	33.03	54.15	56.36	88.09
99.36	113.04	135.16	154.33	155.04	179.34
186.25	187.15	194.16	195.06	219.17	254.15
278.04	285.21	293.10	354.20	378.09	382.02
384.03	392.28	484.26	495.23	515.16	571.32
582.32	596.14	599.25	612.08	612.18	613.20
615.08					

5: The Second Thunderclap

1 The tale is also sketched in 'free verse' on 262.03–19.
2 Margaret Solomon accords her a chapter in *Eternal Geomater*, but her account is heavily biased towards sexual and excretory references. The most useful studies to date are those of Grace Eckley, ('"Petween Peas Like Ourselves": The Folklore of the Prankquean,' 177–88), and Patrick McCarthy (*The Riddles of 'Finnegans Wake'*: he devotes an entire chapter to PQ's questions and their significance). McCarthy sees the tale as a microcosm of the *Wake*:

If the *Wake* is Joyce's model of the universe, The Tale of Jarl van Hoother and the Prankquean is a model of *Finnegans Wake*, a demonstration piece in which Joyce records a number of his most important themes. By structuring the episode, like the book, on the three ages of a Viconian cycle of history, from the Garden of Eden to the founding of Dublin, and at the same time reproducing the tripartite structure of a mythic action involving one cast of characters, Joyce turns the episode into a ritualistic action of cosmic significance. Not only the Mime but a number of other episodes in the *Wake* follow the pattern set by The Tale of Jarl van Hoother, thereby establishing this tale as an archetypal action. Like the repetition of a religious formula – e.g., the 'Sanctus! Sanctus! Sanctus!' phrase which Joyce parodies at least thirteen times in the *Wake* – the division of an action into three basically similar stages, each accompanied by a key phrase (the riddle), is a means of ritualizing that action. 'I have your tristich now; it recurs in three times the same differently,' Joyce explains ... (*FW* 481.10–11). (119)

3 Eckley, 177–81.

4 The art of rhetoric does not arise until writing as a new way of seeing has interposed itself between speaker and language sufficiently to afford the detachment necessary to turn it into an art form. In traditional rhetorical parlance, style and ornamentation are called the clothing of ideas, as much as sheets and sails were spoken of as ships' clothing. Clothes are PQ's weapons, her belliclothes. PQ's style is 'Not the lithe slender, not the broad roundish near the lithe slender, not the fairsized fullfeatured to the leeward of the broad roundish but, indeed and inneed, the curling, perfectportioned, flowerfleckled, shapely highhued, delicate features swaying to the windward of the fairsized fullfeatured' (602.01–05).

5 Cleopatra was also a pirate: she charmed and stole Mark Antony by means of feminine allurements. Other links between her and PQ include 'Maye faye, she's la gaye this snaky woman' (20.23), and 'Cliopatria, thy hosies history' (271.12). As the 'snaky' Gorgon, PQ enters the opening section to the third thunder to do battle with Perseus/Persse O'Reilly.

6 Concerning the Prankquean's relation to rhetoric, it is noteworthy that the highest sails on a ship are called the royals. Cleopatra (Asianism) had a barge of her own.

7 Frances M. Boldereff, *Hermes to His Son, Thoth: Being Joyce's Use of Giordano Bruno in 'Finnegans Wake,'* 42. One author sees Menippean tendencies in Joyce's use of alchemy: 'Consistently in his work Joyce satirizes those who flee from the world into an abstract intellectual realm: his use of alchemy aids these parodies' (Barbara Di Bernard, *Alchemy and 'Finnegans Wake,'* 81).

8 It might also correspond to the 'dummy' in the card game, bridge.

9 David Hayman reveals that in the first drafts the question was simply a request for a cup of porter: 'I want a cup of porter,' and then 'Why do I want a cup of porter?' and subsequently 'Why do I like a poss of porterpease.'

The request on the second visit, 'I want 2 cupsa porterpeace,' was emended to read 'Why do I liking 2 poss of porterpeace.' On her third visit the 'prank-wench' originally asked 'Why am I like three cupss porterpease,' which eventually became 'Why do I like 3 poss porterpease' as Joyce struggled to establish a parallel construction among the three statements of the riddle. Three basic levels of meaning, all of which are incorporated in the final published version of the riddle, can be distinguished in these early drafts: a request for porter, a question about why the Prankquean wants (or likes) porter, and a metaphoric riddle about the Prankquean's similarity to a pot of porter. Certainly, the evidence of the early drafts contradicts Frances Boldereff's contention that the riddle originated in Joyce's search for a 'point of order' [*Hermes to His Son Thoth*, 107]; the 'point of order' theme is plainly a later addition to the riddle and is less significant than a number of other themes that are incorporated into the riddle (McCarthy, *The Riddles of 'Finnegans Wake,'* 112).

Frances Boldereff reads the riddle as 'How do we find the point of order?' and tries to relate it to 'the world order Bruno and Yeats and Joyce subscribed to ...' *Hermes to His Son Thoth*, 111 (cf. also pages 109–12). Grace Eckley finds instead a relation between the demand of the riddle and an emphasis on 'the role of the gastronome for Shaun' (cf. 'Petween Peas Like Ourselves,' 182–6. Few people have actually studied the words of the riddle before setting it atop their hobby-horses. McCarthy continues:

There are many valid interpretations of the riddle ... each of which demonstrates an important thematic element. Bernard Benstock observes that the riddle 'asks the question of the duality of opposites, since the hero's twin sons are asking why do we look like two peas in a pod (but are really as different as day and night)?' [Benstock, *Joyce-again's Wake*, 269]. Although this interpretation ignores the fact that the riddle is posed by a woman and not by 'the hero's twin sons,' the 'look-alike' theme is of paramount importance in the riddle and applies in part to the twins who appear to be opposites but may exchange roles at any time. Each principle of *Finnegans Wake* bears within it the seeds of its contrary, illustrating Giordano Bruno's principle of *In tristia hilaris, in hilaritate tristis,'* [Benstock 284; Solomon 12] which is the obvious source for the names Hilary and Tristopher. (112–13)

10 *Gaelic Lexicon*, 16.
11 Joyce explained this in his letter to Paul Ruggiero of 4 September 1938 (*Letters* I, 400).
12 In his *The Sigla of 'Finnegans Wake,'* McHugh provides additional evidence as well as explication of the 'characters,' PQ-Issy, her mirror-twin and the spectrum girls that she produces (50–5).

13 PQ's influence and effects, her use of clothing to seduce the visual sense and propel her viewers towards private identity and suppressing their other senses, are
constantly dramatized in the *Wake*. For example:

> It is nebuless an autodidact fact of the commonest that the shape of the average
> human cloudyphiz, whereas sallow has long daze faded, frequently altered its
> ego with the possing of the showers (Not original!). Whence it is a slopperish
> matter, given the wet and low visibility (since in this scherzarade of one's thou-
> sand one nightinesses that sword of certainty which would indentifide the body
> never falls) to idendifine the individuone in scratch wig, squarecuts, stock lave-
> leer, regattable oxeter, baggy pants and shufflers (he is often alluded to as Sly-
> patrick, the llad in the llane) with already an incipience (lust!) ... (50.35–51.09)

14 See *Works of the Rev. Jonathan Swift, D.D.*, arranged by Thomas Sheridan, II,
303.
15 *JJ*, 22.

6: The Third Thunderclap

1 By Joyce. He wrote a companion rhyme at the same time as a blurb for the publication of *Anna Livia Plurabelle* (later *FW* I.viii), issued by Faber in June, 1930:

> Buy a book in brown paper
> From Faber and Faber
> To see Annie Liffey trip, tumble and caper.
> Sevensinns in her singthings,
> Plurabelle on her prose,
> Seashell ebb music wayriver she flows. (Ellmann, *JJ*, 629–30, 803)

2 R. McHugh, *The Sigla of 'Finnegans Wake,'* 16.
3 'Includes' rather than 'is' for, as McHugh has shown, the various sigla extend to
characters as well as to conceptual patterns. The identifications above are the primary ones. The sigla began simply as abbreviations for the names of these characters. McHugh deals with fourteen of the sigla in his study. (Today, the 'computer-
literate' would call them icons.)
4 'Earwig Lore,' *Discovery*, March 1937, 89–91: quoted in McHugh, *Sigla*, 16.
According to Eric Partridge (*A Dictionary of the Underworld*), an earwig or earwigger is also a clergyman (because of his exhortations) and an eavesdropper, and
'earwig!' means 'be quiet!' As for Persse O'Reilly, *perce-oreille* is French for the
confessional screen, and by synecdoche, sometimes the confessional itself.

5 The McGuffin is the object of the chase; it is the thing that the opposing parties
contend for. It might be anything, a formula or letter, or the plans for a battleship
or secret weapon, or the weapon itself, but it *per se* is of scant significance to the
film. In one of Hitchcock's films it is mentioned casually, and only once, in passing: the film, on the other hand, is about the characters and their conflicts.

6 Ellmann, *JJ*, 565. Quoted remarks are from Mary and Padraic Colum, *Our Friend
James Joyce*, 123.

7 McHugh, *Sigla*, 15.

8 Paraphrase of W.Y. Tindall's succinct account in *A Reader's Guide to 'Finnegans
Wake,'* 36.

9 According to the O.E.D., 'cad' can mean a younger (or youngest) son, usually one
who had entered the military to find a career (abbreviation of 'cadet'); a familiar
spirit, an assistant or confederate of lower grade, as a bricklayer's labourer; an
omnibus conductor; a fellow of low vulgar manners and behaviour; it is also an
abbreviation for 'cadaver' – all of these are apposite and related in the context.
Pipe, on the other hand, can mean whistle, flute, etc., but Joyce specifies that it not
of the musical variety, 'not the oriuolate' (35.11). Among the acceptable meanings
are these: a detective or *watch*er [my italics]; a rifle; and, as a verb, to understand,
to watch, to find (Partridge, *Dictionary of the Underworld*). Pipe can also signify a
handgun, a length of pipe (for plumbing), a tobacco pipe.

10 The fire of 'burning would' from Thunder 1, which was changed into PQ's 'lighting up' on the Jarl who fell from (i.e., because of) Grace, is here changed to ale –
firewater – while the cup is the grail of an identity quest. Drink helps cement the
group while numbing all senses but the visual.

11 Joyce scholars have long recognized a symmetry in the structure of the books that
comprise the *Wake*. The first three books form an arch with book two as the key-
stone. As Clive Hart writes:

> Around a central section, Book II, Joyce builds two opposing cycles consisting of
> Books I and III. In these two Books there is established a pattern of correspon-
> dences of the major events of each, those in Book III occurring in reverse order
> and having inverse characteristics. Whereas Book I begins with a rather obvious
> birth (28–9) and ends with the symbolic death (215–16), Book III begins with
> death (403) and ends with a birth (590); 'roads' and the meeting with the king
> (I.2) reappear in III.4, the trial of I.3–4 in III.3, the Letter of I.5 in III.1, and the
> fables of I.6 earlier in III.1. In his correspondence, Joyce implicitly referred to
> this pattern. (*Structure and Motif in 'Finnegans Wake,'* 66–7)

The present HCE chapter, parts of which were among the first elements of the
Wake to be written, is balanced by HCE's speech in book III (532–54), which was

published in 1930 as a separate booklet, *Haveth Childers Everywhere*. David Hayman calls the present chapter 'the first chapter to be assembled.' He adds: 'Soon after he had revised the pages of 'Here Comes Everybody' (*FW* 30–4) in the fall of 1923, Joyce set to work on the remainder of the chapter which was soon followed by others from Book I. The chapter was written in three installments coinciding with the three aspects of the action: the "HCE," the genesis of "The Ballad of Persse O'Reilly," and the Ballad itself. As each of these passages was written and revised separately, this is a perfect example of Joyce's episodic method of composition' (*A First-Draft Version of 'Finnegans Wake,'* 23).

McHugh comments at length on this symmetrical structure (which does not extend to the thunders) in the first three chapters of *The Sigla of 'Finnegans Wake.'* Louis O. Mink's summary of the section from book III – 'HCE's great apologia pro vita sua' – presents it as clearly echoing HCE's Promethean dimension:

> In eight speeches, separated by the comments of his interrogators (or judges), HCE begins haltingly. In his guilty stammer, he denies the unspecified charges against him, cries outrage against his accusers, appeals for pity, and (rather inconsistently) announces his repentance. But in a sudden metamorphosis (p. 539) he is transformed from the pubkeeper and petty transgressor Earwicker into HCE, the archetypal builder of material civilization. I am the one, he says, who built the hospitals, museums, dancehalls, observatories, universities, and cathedrals; I built the roads and the railroads; I bridged the rivers, paved the streets and lit the city; I created cuisine and sports, introduced tea and wine, and brewed stout; I minted the money and gave the citizens laws and courts; I created both the seven wonders of the world and the seven statues that line the route from Dublin's Parnell Square to College Green. And I did it all to arouse and satisfy my wife's desire. (*A 'Finnegans Wake' Gazetteer*, xvii–xviii)

12 The many references to monkeys and apes in both chapter and ballad refer to social rivalry and social climbing (what Lewis later satirized as the *Apes of God*).

13 Volapük words are taken from McHugh, *Annotations*. I have not been able to examine a dictionary of Volapük words, but suspect their presence in this thunder, and perhaps in others.

14 Parodies of the ballad occur frequently in the *Wake*, e.g., 175, 371–3. It is claimed that embedded in the fourteen verses are references to the stations of the cross and to each of the twelve labours of Hercules. I cannot find them all, although some are clear enough: e.g., verse 9 can be seen to allude to St Veronica's cloth as well as to the adventure of the Augean stables.

15 James Frazer, *The Golden Bough*, 537.

16 Robert Graves, *The White Goddess*, 441.

17 Ibid., 192–3.

7: The Fourth Thunderclap

1 In *A First-Draft Version of 'Finnegans Wake,'* 24, David Hayman writes that the boundary between the opening and middle section is 'ill defined' and that the central pages (*FW* 85–91; the thunder is on page 90) were composed 'with some difficulty.'

2 Susan Swartzlander, 'Multiple Meaning and Misunderstanding: The Mistrial of Festy King,' 465.

3 The full context is this: 'Shocking! Such as turly pearced our really's that he might, that he might never, that he might never that night? Treely and rurally. Bladyughfoulm ... [thunder] ... ckputtanach, eh? You have it alright.
Meirdreach an Oincuish! But a new complexion was put upon the matter when ...' (90.29–35).

4 E.g., 'assback bridge' (84.03; Buridan's *Pons Asinorum*) or 'rival rialtos' (84.07), which are fairly direct, yield to indirection such as 'sware by all his lards porsenal' (83.07–08) and 'sitisfactuary conclusium' (84.15), both of which invoke the bridge held by Horatius, as well as Macaulay's well-known lay, 'Horatius.' It begins thus: Lars Porsena of Clusium / By the nine gods he swore / That the proud house of Tarquin / Should suffer wrong no more.'

5 McHugh, *Annotations*, cites R.A.S. Macalister, *The Secret Languages of Ireland*, as his source for the gloss: Shirt-of-two-strokes Ogham; Mac Ogham; Finn's Ladder Ogham (three forms); Finn's-three-shanked Ogham; Head-in-a-bush Ogham; Head-under-a-bush Ogham; Serpent-through-the-heather Ogham; Millrace Ogham; Arm, Bird & Colour Oghams; Ogma Sun-face supposedly invented Ogham.

6 *Augs*: hogs; Ger, eyes. *Ohrs*: whores; Ger, ears. *Rhino*: Gr, nose. *Kehle*: Ger, throat.

8: The Fifth Thunderclap

1 David Hayman confirms this: 'I.V was written in two halves which Joyce did not join together until after four drafts and several changes in plan.' (*A First-Draft Version of 'Finnegans Wake,'* 25.) He identifies the 'halves' as 104–112.02 and 113.23–125 (ibid.) See also his *The 'Wake' in Transit*, 183, to the same effect, and the entire chapter, 155–99, on this chapter of the *Wake* and the Letter theme. The Letter deserves a separate communication study for, as Hayman points out, 'shortly after writing the Letter, Joyce concerned himself with the question of transcription and transmission, which ultimately became the far larger problem of aesthetic generation and the fate of the Word' (*The 'Wake' in Transit*, 176).

2 McHugh (*Annotations*) points out that the Suras of the Koran begin, 'In the name

of Allah, the Merciful, the Compassionate ...' The rest parodies, significantly, the Our Father. According to the notebooks (see 'Sigla' on 78, above), Anna Livia corresponds to smell among the senses, yet the invocation relates her to singing (the ear). That, as a goddess, she is invoked in terms reserved to a male deity suggests that equipoise is not preserved at the level of the sexual-battle theme but rather that matriarchy reigns as an undercurrent here as throughout the chapter. Curiously, Anna Livia herself only makes two appearances *in propria persona* in the *Wake*. Hayman comments on this:

> If we discount the voices of I.8 as mere echoes of an absent ALP and place Issy's monologues and letters in the same category as the passages in the voices ascribed to Shem and Shaun, there are only two clear instances of ALP's utterance in *Finnegans Wake*. Alluded to, spoken of, her presence felt throughout the book, she comes to light, literally as well as figuratively, in the closing pages or the third and fourth segments of Book IV. There, she dominates, speaking first in the stilted rhetoric of her Letter and then in the soft and sweetly flowing idiom of her 'Soft morning city' address to the husband and the world from which she departs. (*The 'Wake' in Transit*, 193)

3 David Hayman's term in *A First-Draft Version of 'Finnegans Wake,'* 24.

4 Clive Hart, *Structure and Motif in 'Finnegans Wake,'* 200. Hart is referring mainly to the more extensive version of the Letter, the Revered Letter of *FW* 615–19, discussed below. There are several obvious parodies of the Letter, and others not so obvious. Belinda's appears as a form letter on page 280 (which Kimberly Devlin calls 'Issy's practice letter' [*Wandering and Return in 'Finnegans Wake,'* 160]), and in parodic paraphrases on 301.10–302.30, and 369.24–370.14. The 'other letters' in the *Wake* tend to be Menippean productions, like the one (308) that ends the 'Triv. and Quad.' chapter (II.2). It, called a NIGHTLITTER, satirizes the epic descent into the underworld to glean wisdom from the tribal elders and is glossed with marginal cartoon graffiti of thumbing the nose and of crossed bones that resemble salad forks (for the *satura lanx*). Joyce's (Menippean) advice about the Letter and its contents appears shortly after thunder 8: 'Leave the letter that never begins to go find the latter that ever comes to end, written in smoke and blurred by mist and signed of solitude, sealed at night' (337.11–14).

Altogether, there are about a dozen letters in *Finnegans Wake*:

> the socially 'correct' letter beginning 'Dear (name of desired subject, A.N.)' and ending 'From Auburn chenlemagne' (280.09–29); the love letter beginning 'I know, pepette, of course, dear, but listen, precious' and ending 'So long as the lucksmith. Laughs!' (143.31–148.32); the love letter beginning 'Come, smooth of my slate, to the beat of my blosh' and ending 'it's the surplice money ... what

buys the bed while wits borrows the clothes (279.fn1); and the 'spoken' letter to Juan beginning 'Meesh, meesh, yes, pet. We were too happy' and ending 'and listen, with supreme regards, Juan, in haste, warn me which to ah ah ah ah' (457.25–461.32). Besides Issy's four written/spoken letters, there is the Boston 'transhipt' letter to 'Maggy,' of which Issy's is a variant, beginning 'Dear whom it proceded to mention Maggy' and concluding with its PS (111.10–20). The children's nightletter to their parents announces their intended takeover of adult power (308); Anna Livia calls for 'a brandnew bankside' (201). The Shem/Dolph letter begins 'Dear and he went on to scripple gentlemine born, milady bread, he would pen for her' and concludes 'From here Buvard to dear Picuchet' (301.10–302.10). There's the reported letter of 'the secretary bird' (369.25–370.14), a variant of the Boston 'transhipt' letter that conflates the bird with Pandora with the Liffey and voices concerns for husband and children. There is Shaun's letter that opens with 'To the Very Honourable The Memory of Disgrace, the Most Noble, Sometime Sweepyard at the Service of the Writer,' in which HCE speaking through Shaun indicts himself on a number of sexual counts (413.03–26). And, penultimate in the text, is the ALP letter beginning 'Dear. And we go on to Dirtdump. Reverend. May we add majesty?' and ending

The herewaker of our hamefame is his real namesame who will get himself up and erect, confident and heroic when but, young as of old, for my daily comfreshenall, a wee one woos.

    Alma Luvia, Pollabella.

P.S. Soldier Rollo's sweetheart. And she's about fetted up now with nonsery reams. And rigs out in regal rooms with the ritzies. Rags! Worns out. But she's still her deckhuman amber too (615.12–19). (Sailer, *On the Void of to Be*, 200–1).

5 *A First-Draft Version of 'Finnegans Wake,'* 26. The rest of Hayman's observations are *à propos*:

In sum, the 'Revered Letter' of ALP was composed from *Scribbledehobble* notes but grew out of the I, ii, iii, iv, sequence of chapters and more particularly out of the second half of I.iv. In its turn, this passage spawned I.va. I.vb (*FW* 113.23–125) was derived from both I.va and the 'Letter.' This, however, does not complete the tale.

    Having written his third draft of the 'Letter' together with two drafts of the two parts of I.v, Joyce made ink fair copies, sandwiching the 'Letter' between the two halves of I.v. It should be stated however, that the three passages were not at this point treated as a unit, though they were apparently redrafted in sequence. While reworking this material the author stumbled upon the subject matter of Book III, writing the account of Shaun's delivery of the 'Letter,' a passage designed perhaps to supplant I.va, as an introduction to the 'Letter' or perhaps to follow after the three-part structure of I.v. This brief account of the 'Letter's' delivery was written in the Book I notebook on the bottoms of previously filled pages. Soon after he composed it Joyce became aware of its real function in the *Wake*; consequently he recopied and revised only the final paragraph. It is approximately at this point in the chapter's history (or more precisely after he had had a typescript made of the I.v complex) that Joyce was able to write Miss Weaver the following account of his plans: 'The passage "Let us now ... Shem the Penman" follows the words "the hen saw." Between the words "penman" and "revered" are three further passages, a description of Shem-Ham-Cain-Egan etc and his penmanship, Anna Livia's visits and collaboration and delivery of the memorial by Shawn the Post' (*Letters* 1/16/24). One is struck in this account by several facts. First, Joyce did not at this time think in terms of a clearly defined chapter-book structure. Second, he had not conceived of Book II as intervening between Book I or the derivation of the 'Letter' and Book III or the delivery. Third, the most significant single theme of the *Wake* was then the concept of the Word as suggested through the treatment of the 'Letter.' I do not mean by this that Joyce had abandoned the ideas previously developed in the *Scribbledehobble* and the early sketches. It would seem rather that the book was still in flux and that Joyce was still thinking in terms of fusing the fragments (*Letters* 9/10/23). Fourth, of the three new passages described in Joyce's letter, only one, the Shem piece (I.vii), which was then in progress, took the form and occupied the position projected for it. The ALP passage (I.viii), which Joyce was soon to write, has little to do with the 'memorial.' The Shaun sequence quickly outgrew the term 'passage' and became a complex four-part unit leading to the dawn or metaphorical delivery of the 'Letter' to HCE in Book IV. The 'Revered Letter,' the spark which ignited this phoenix fire in 1923, became in 1938 a sub-division of the shortest of the *Wake*'s four sections, where it now occupies less than four and one-half printed pages. (25–6)

Hayman gives the draft-version of both the Revered Letter (81–3) and the sketch of Shaun's delivery of the Letter (most of which was not used in the *Wake*: 90–1). As Belinda's Letter was not an element of the 'first draft' of I.5, Hayman omits it, but Connolly quotes the notebook drafts of this Letter in the introduction to his *James Joyce's Scribbledehobble: The Ur-Workbook for 'Finnegans Wake'* (xvii–xix).

Not only is Shaun in charge of delivery, he personifies the rhetorical division of *pronuntiatio* or *actio* (delivery), as we shall see later. None the less, in typically

Menippean fashion, delivery of the Letter is frustrated at every turn and ultimately blocked entirely.

> As the letter is carried along the pathway, it meets every possible form of resistance to delivery. Ultimately, it cannot be delivered, for reasons stamped on its envelope: 'No such no.'; 'None so strait'; 'Overwayed. Understrumped'; 'Too Let. To be Soiled'; 'Vacant.' The occupants of the various Dublin addresses tracked by the postal system (addresses that once belonged to James Joyce) meet similar fates: 'Noon sick parson'; 'Exbelled from 1014 d.'; 'Dining with the Danes'; 'Arrusted'; 'Drowned in the Laffey'; 'Salved. All reddy berried'; 'Cohabited by Unfortunates.' The letter follows a circuit that either begins or should terminate at '29 Hardware Saint ... Baile-Atha-Cliath,' but even its message despairs of delivery: 'Nave unlodgeable. Loved noa's dress. Sinned, Jetty Pierrse.' The letter has been opened by 'Miss Take,' its address 'Wrongly spilled,' and has been sent 'Back to the P.O. Kaer of' (420.17–421.14). (Shari Benstock, 'Apostrophes,' 115)

Furthermore,

> the postal system has certain claims on this letter. It has become the property of the post (and Shaun will claim authorship of it), its final resting place to be the dead letter office (the midden-heap), where its 'penmarks used out in sinscript with such hesitancy by [the] cerebrated brother' (421.18–19) will be pecked at by Biddy the hen. Interrogated by the girls from Saint Bride's school (incarnations of Issy), Shaun first denounces the letter as belonging to 'Mr O'Shem the Draper,' who put his mother up to writing it ('She, the mammy far, was put up to it by him' [421.35–6]), for which Shem should be 'depraved of his libertins to be silenced, sackclothed and suspended' (421.36–422.01). (Ibid)

6 Sir Edward Sullivan, *The Book of Kells.* In *The Books at the 'Wake,'* Atherton calls I.5 'the main account of manuscripts in the *Wake*' (62, 68). He also notes that 'in the literal sense this chapter tells how a letter was scratched up out of a "midden" (110.25) or "mudmound" (111.34). This midden is a symbol, elaborated later, for the inhabited world in which men have left so many traces. The letter stands as a symbol for all attempts at written communication including all other letters, all the world's literature, *The Book of Kells*, all manuscripts, all the sacred books of the world, and also *Finnegans Wake* itself. One reason why *The Book of Kells* is included here is that it was once "stolen by night ... and found after a lapse of some months, concealed under sods"' (62–3). Further, Atherton points to the purely Menippean trait of this chapter's self-absorption: 'In actual

fact an entire chapter of [the *Wake*] is mainly concerned with its own manuscript' (60).

Another common Menippean trope is giving the reader instructions inside the book, telling the reader how to behave or how to read and interpret what he is reading. 'Joyce, like Sterne, was a writer who consciously sought to train literary critics to read his works, and to do so within the artifice itself,' reports Phillip Herring. 'The reader thus becomes co-creator of the meaning of a literary work written by an author who believed his task was to give us only part of the text's meaning – perhaps even believed this was all any author could do given his view of language' (*Joyce's Uncertainty Principle*, 167). The chapter presents and analyses 'various possible critical tools and approaches to the letter or the *Wake* (none of which will help), where Joyce casts his ventriloquist's voices into a mock-pedantic lecturer who sounds suspiciously like Shem. Difficulties of interpreting unstable texts are alternately explored, parodied, and dismissed until we gradually see that the uncertainty of the letter is the uncertainty of the *Wake*, and that our scholarly efforts to solve these puzzles are being mocked' (ibid 196). Menippists often take a perverse delight in frustrating readers who try to to educe 'right' meanings or coherent narratives from their work: techniques range from putting the preface late in the work, to jumbling the order of chapters or inserting blank pages as chapters (or, as Sterne does in *Tristram Shandy*, a black page or a marbled page – the endpapers [the book inside-out, which Sterne called a 'motley emblem of my work']), to instructing the reader to write the next few lines or paragraphs, etc. Joyce manages it in a more literary manner, by letting the very style of the *Wake* float a dozen levels of meaning simultaneously in every passage; so there is not one point of view at a time but many. Again, this ploy will keep the reader from becoming rigid, that is, from adopting a single fixed perspective on the text or the experience, and demands that the reader sustain maximal flexibility of response: Menippism in full spate! Margot Norris comments, using the present chapter to illustrate her point:

The formal elements of the work, plot, character, point of view, and language, are not anchored to a single point of reference, that is, they do not refer back to a center. This condition produces that curious flux and restlessness in the work, which is sensed intuitively by the reader and which the *Wake* itself describes as follows:

Every person, place and thing in the chaosmos of Alle anyway connected with the gobblydumped turkery was moving and changing every part of the time: the travelling inkhorn (possibly pot), the hare and turtle pen and paper, the continually more and less intermisunderstanding minds of the anticollaborators, the as time went on as it will variously inflected, differently pronounced, otherwise spelled, changeably meaning vocable scriptsigns. (*FW* 118)

The substitutability of parts for one another, the variability and uncertainty of the work's structural and thematic elements, represent a decentered universe, one that lacks the center that defines, gives meaning, designates, and holds the structure together – by holding it in immobility. (*The Decentered Universe of 'Finnegans Wake,'* 120–1)

Therefore, all of Joyce's hints in the book about how to interpret it – or the Letter – are Menippean red herrings, and contribute to the play. 'Our subject is not so much the letter's content, as how that content becomes obscured, and how we are urged to embark on what is tantamount to an archaeological investigation so as to piece its meaning together. This task is carefully made impossible in the *Wake* itself,' remarks Phillip Herring (200). In true Menippean fashion, the fun and the play is the point, not the interpretation of the content; or rather the real meaning is the effect that the book has on the reader. 'Before we can actually read the letter, an absurdly pompous lecturer, sounding very much as if he is addressing an annual meeting of the Bibliographical Society of America, heaps upon the reader such a mass of confusing and contradictory evidence that the subject is hopelessly obscured' (ibid., 199).

7 Part 2, chapter 1, 'The Manuscripts,' passim.
8 The nursery rhyme is entirely apposite: 'Higgledy, piggledy, my black [or fat, etc.] hen / She lays eggs for gentlemen; / Gentlemen come every day / To see what my black hen doth lay. / Sometimes nine and sometimes ten; / Higgledy, piggledy, my fat hen.'
9 For example, Margot Norris, in her structuralist study of the *Wake,* writes: 'Whatever the Letter may be, it is *not* a document that clarifies anything, renders any verdict, or pardons anyone. We are no more certain about its origin, name or meaning than we are of any other character or event in the work. If anything, its own slovenly condition and confusing content affirm and manifest the chaos of the fall. As just one among the "litterish fragments" (66.25) in ALP's womblike mail pouch, the Letter's value is not its message or its meaning but – like her other tacky gifts – its function as a token of peace and reconciliation' (*The Decentered Universe of 'Finnegans Wake,'* 70–1). Atherton thinks the Letter 'something crooked and depraved' (*Books,* 63); Tindall found it merely 'trivial, illiterate and repetitious' (*A Reader's Guide to 'Finnegans Wake,'* 103). Patrick McCarthy notes that 'one of the commonplaces of *Finnegans Wake* criticism is that the mysterious letter retrieved from the midden heap represents the book itself, so that the characters' various attempts to decipher the document constitute a self-reflexive com-

mentary on the reader's encounter with the *Wake*. This might seem to give the letter passages a centrality not enjoyed by other parts of *Finnegans Wake* ...' ('The Last Epistle of *Finnegans Wake*,' 725). Talia Schaffer reiterates the idea that the Letter 'is the manuscript of *Finnegans Wake* itself' in her 'Letters to Biddy: About That Original Hen' (625). She argues that 'the problem of the letter must be seen within the philosophical context of Giordano Bruno the Nolan.' McCarthy goes on to discuss six factors 'working against the reader's expectation that the letter contains definitive answers to the meaning of *Finnegans Wake* ...' By now, the reader will recognize the hand of Menippus: 'No two versions of the document are identical'; 'Even within a single version, the ambiguity of the language often undermines the writer's apparent intention'; 'the narrator's attention is constantly diverted from the epistolary text to the envelope, the handwriting, and other aspects of the letter's existence as a physical artifact'; 'it is difficult to separate the text of the manuscript itself from the commentaries that spring up around it'; etc. (ibid.) The sheer proliferation of versions of the Letter (see note 4, above) is no help either: 'The difficulties involved in interpreting the Wakean letter stem not only from narrative lack, the gaps in the document, but also from narrative excess, its numerous versions ... the linguistic excess of the final version may render the reader suspicious, creating obfuscations and uncertainties as successfully as any straightforward elisions' (Kimberly J. Devlin, *Wandering and Return in 'Finnegans Wake,'* 36).

Furthermore, now, over fifty years after the publication of *Finnegans Wake*, the academic community has produced so much learned commentary on various forms of the Letter and its – their – relation to the *Wake*, that it is unlikely that any agreement can or will ever be reached about meaning. Joyce warned us: 'to concentrate on the literal meaning' is to follow fresh red herring.

10 Lydia Languish, in Sheridan's play, *The Rivals*, wrote letters to herself.

11 It is interesting to compare Joyce's treatment of print with that of other Menippists. Sterne's, for example, involves personifying (prosopopoeia) the five divisions of the rhetorical Word as his five main characters to dramatize the effects. Both Dr Slop and Belinda are publishers. Dr Slop, the man-midwife, is delivery: with his forceps (the new high-speed presses) he butchers and mangles the infants (books) as he yanks them from the matrix. During delivery of the case-in-point, Tristram's nose is damaged: as Sterne makes clear, the 'nose' is also 'knows' and gnosis as well as the instrument of profound (carnal) knowing. *Tristram Shandy* is Sterne's 'Dunciad.' To Shaun, the 'postman of the mind,' Joyce assigned the function of delivery – of the Letter. Hayman, unaware of the rhetorical dimension, finds it remarkable that Joyce settled on the delivery aspect so early (1923) and remained so consistent with it: 'What may strike us is the use of the contemporary in this vision, the fact that Shaun and his function are seen as aspects of a

periods characterized by rapid communication and communicators' (*The 'Wake'
in Transit*, 182: see 178–82 for his account of the development of Shaun's delivery
of the Letter).

12 The 'Mons held by tentpegs' is the sleeping giant or dormant Finnegan trussed
helplessly like Gulliver in Lilliput.

13 The gloss (left side, italic: rhetorical) is 'By lineal in pondus overthepoise.' Embedded verse, and prose/verse mixtures are traditional Menippean techniques.

14 *The Sigla of 'Finnegans Wake,'* 63.

15 See 'Sure, she fell in line with our tripertight photos as the lyonised mails
when we were stablelads together' (465.14–15). The lionized male is an aesthetic
object.

16 The principle is discussed in Richard Ellmann's *Eminent Domain*, passim. T.S.
Eliot states it as a test of poetic maturity: 'Immature poets imitate; mature poets
steal; bad poets deface what they take, and good poets make it into something better, or at least something different. The good poet welds his theft into a whole of
feeling which is unique, utterly different from that from which it was torn; the
bad poet throws it into something which has no cohesion. A good poet will usually
borrow from authors remote in time, or alien in language, or diverse in interest'
('Philip Massinger,' *Selected Essays*, 206).

17 These are used extensively by Sterne; e.g., there is the business of Tristram's nose
(slang for penis) mangled in delivery; and Walter Shandy, Tristram's father, continually muses over a pet theory of copulative verbs.

18 The *De planctu naturae* of Alan of Lille is a handy example of this form of wit. At
one point he mounts an attack on castrati and on homosexual practices in these
terms. It gets under way:

> Since the plan of Nature gave special recognition, as the evidence of grammar
> confirms, to two genders, to wit, the masculine and feminine (although some
> men, deprived of a sign of sex, could, in my opinion, be classified as of neuter
> gender), I charged the Cyprian, with secret warnings and mighty, thunderous
> threats, that she should, as reason demanded, concentrate exclusively in her
> connections on the natural union of masculine and feminine gender.
>
> Since, by the demands of the conditions necessary for reproduction, the mas-
> culine joins the feminine to itself, if an irregular combination of members of the
> same sex should come into common practise, so that appurtenances of the same
> sex should be mutually connected, that combination would never be able to
> gain acceptance from me either as a means of procreation or as an aid to concep-
> tion. For if the masculine gender, by a certain violence of unreasonable reason,
> should call for a gender entirely similar to itself, this bond and union will not be
> able to defend the flaw as any kind of graceful figure but will bear the stain of

an outlandish and unpardonable solecism.* (*Alan of Lille, The Plaint of Nature*, trans. J.J. Sheridan, 156–7).

The translator's glosses at this point are illustrative:

> * A strained metaphor from grammar. The meaning is: confusion of gender can never be justified on the ground of being a figure of speech. It is always a flaw.
>   This passage is an almost incredible mélange of words whose ordinary, metaphorical, technical, and etymological signification must be kept in mind simultaneously. *Suppositio* means 'placing underneath' (etymology) and calls *suppositum* 'a noun' (technical sense) to mind. *Appositio* means 'placing' one thing 'along another' (etymology), an 'adjective' (technical). Adjective symbolises man, noun symbolises woman. Background idea concerns the implication of positions in coitus. No translation can deal adequately with the passage.
>   The active element in sexual relationship is the man, the woman's role is passive. Man is represented by the subject in a sentence, woman by the object. Only the transitive verb, which expresses the direct action of subject on object can symbolise the sex relationship. With intransitive verbs there is no direct object. The action in reflexive and passive verbs is referred back to the subject. Cf. *Carmina Burana* 95.17, ed. A. Hilka and O. Schumann (Heidelberg, 1930) 2.123. (157–8)

This last remark concerns Nature's observation, 'In addition to this I gave instructions that the conjugations of Dione's daughter should restrict themselves entirely to the forward march of the transitive and should not admit the stationary intransitive or the circuitous reflexive or the recurring passive ...' In the same passage, the fifth prose section of the work – a classic Menippean satire, it mingles verse and prose – Alan includes a grammar of sexuality, a dialectic of sexuality, and a rhetoric of sexuality.

19 More subdued references to and uses of the grammar/sex motif are scattered throughout the *Wake*, e.g., 'with man's mischief in his mind whilst her pupils swimmed too heavenlies, let his be exaspirated, letters be blowed! I is a femaline person. O, of provocative gender. U unisingular case.' (251.29–32). The Storiella section begins on *FW* 267; McHugh notes of her (⊣: roughly, PQ) that 'up to 272.08 she studies Ireland's Punic Wars and designs sexual campaigns in grammatical jargon. The names of tenses obviously epitomize history ...' (*The Sigla of 'Finnegans Wake,'* 63).

20 Cf. 'that ... variant *maggers* for the more generally accepted *majesty* which is but a trifle and yet may quietly amuse ...' (120.16–18)

9:   The Sixth Thunderclap

1 Cf. Joyce's letter to Harriet Shaw Weaver, 7 June 1926 (*Letters* I, 241). David Hayman reproduces Joyce's one-page outline of book II in *A First-Draft Version of 'Finnegans Wake,'* 30.

2 Published as *The Mime of Mick, Nick and the Maggies*. It was also published in *transition* no. 22 (February 1933).

3 Hayman, 21. Joyce wrote Harriet Shaw Weaver that he was 'trying to conclude section I of Part II but such an amount of reading seems to be necessary before my old flying machine grumbles up into the air. Personally the only thing that encourages me is my belief that what I have written up to the present is a good deal better than any other first draft I made' (16 February 1931: *Letters* I, 300). Several weeks later he added a note regarding his difficulties (he could write, but not read, because of eye troubles) in 'trying to follow with various readers the books I am using for the present fragment which include Marie Corelli, Swedenborg, St. Thomas, the Sudanese War, Indian outcasts, Women under English Law, a description of St. Helena, Flammarion's The End of the World, scores of children's singing games from Germany, France and Italy and so on ...' (4 March 1931: *Letters* I, 302).

4 Hayman, 21.

5 That is, the ten thunders were an idea that developed as the work progressed. Thunder 6, in the 'first-draft version' is irregular: there, it has 114 letters. The development of the thunders and their eventual 1,001–letter pattern is dealt with in appendix 1.

6 Joyce sent Harriet Shaw Weaver a first draft of the central portion of II.1, accompanied by the following synopsis.

> I enclose the final sheet of the first draft of about two thirds of the first section of Part II (2,200 words) which came out like drops of blood. Excuse me for not having written but I have had a dreadful amount of worry all this last month ... I think the piece I sent you is the gayest and lightest thing I have done in spite of the circumstances ...
>
> The scheme of the piece I sent you is the game we all used to call Angels and Devils or colours. The Angels, girls, are grouped behind the Angel, Shaun, and the devil has to come over three times and ask for a colour. If the colour he asks for has been chosen by any girl she has to run and he tries to catch her. As far as I have written he has come twice and been twice baffled. The piece is full of rhythms taken from English singing games. When first baffled vindictively he thinks of publishing blackmail stuff about his father, mother etc etc etc. The second time he maunders off into sentimental poetry of what I actually wrote at the age of nine: 'My cot alas my dear old shady home where oft in youthful

sport I played, upon thy verdant grassy fields all day or lingered for a moment in thy bosom shade etc etc etc etc.' This is interrupted by a violent pang of toothache after which he throws a fit. When he is baffled a second time the girl angels sing a hymn of liberation around Shawn. The page enclosed is still another version of a beautiful sentence from Edgar Quinet which I already refashioned in *Transition* part one beginning 'since the days of Hiber and Hairyman etc.' E.Q. says that the wild flowers on the ruins of Carthage, Numancia etc have survived the political rises and falls of Empires. In this case the wild flowers are the lilts of children. Note specially the treatment of the double rainbow in which the iritic colours are first normal and then reversed. (22 November 1930: *Letters* I, 295)

The Quinet sentence appears in French on *FW* 281; the double rainbow on 226–7. McHugh discusses this section in *The Sigla of 'Finnegans Wake'*; along with variants on the game of 'colours' reviewed in the work of the Opies, he mentions fifteen more children's games that appear in the section (55–61).

7 'Glugg' is Shem in the act of swallowing his Menippean banquet.
8 The genre of the *Wake* is drama, performed aloud by the reader. PQ's entrancing, warlike Maggies are singled out for attention in I.6, question eight:

> 8. And how war yore maggies?
> Answer: They war loving, they love laughing, they laugh weeping, they weep smelling, they smell smiling, they smile hating, they hate thinking, they think feeling, they feel tempting, they tempt daring, they dare waiting, they wait taking, they take thanking, they thank seeking, as born for lorn in lore of love to live and wive by wile and rile by rule of ruse 'reathed rose and hose hol'd home, yeth cometh elope year, coach and four, Sweet Peck-at-my-Heart picks one man more.
> 9. Now, to be on anew and basking again in the panorama of all flores of speech ... (142.29–143.04)

9 The cast has its echo or mirror-image in a mirror-chapter, III.4. There, a parallel cast, involving the same dramatis personae, is set forth (555–8), in a four-page sentence that introduces instructions for sets and staging of a movie script: a film is a kind of phoenix, born and reborn nightly, in the fire of the projector, and in a Playhouse.
10 The stripper entices by presenting the normally integral body to a specialist gaze; she wears the attention of the audience: 'But listen to the mocking birde to micking barde making bared!' (251.35); '... of some deretane denudation with intent to excitation' (557.22).

11 In his time philosophy Bergson blurred many of the classical distinctions between, e.g., subject and object, and knower and known, by according mental processes participation in physical events.

> 'Pure duration,' we are told, 'is the form which our conscious states assume when our ego lets itself *live*, when it refrains from separating its present state from its former states.' It forms the past and the present into one organic whole, where there is mutual penetration, succession without distinction. 'Within our ego, there is succession without mutual externality; outside the ego, in pure space, there is mutual externality without succession.' 'Questions relating to subject and object, to their distinction and their union, should be put in terms of time rather than of space.' In the duration in which we *see ourselves acting*, there are dissociated elements; but in the duration in which we act, our states melt into each other. Pure duration is what is most removed from externality and least penetrated with externality, a duration in which the past is big with a present absolutely new. But then our will is strained to the utmost; we have to gather up the past which is slipping away, and thrust it whole and undivided into the present. At such moments, we truly possess ourselves, but such moments are rare. Duration is the very stuff of reality, which is perpetual becoming, never something made. (Bertrand Russell, *A History of Western Philosophy*, 796)

It was primarily because of this resurgence of auditory awareness that Wyndham Lewis attacked the time philosophy of Bergson in *Time and Western Man*:

> The Time-doctrine, first promulgated in the philosophy of Bergson, is in its essence, to put it as simply as possible, anti-physical and pro-mental. A great deal of partisan feeling is engendered in the course of its exposition: and all that feeling is directed to belittling and discrediting the 'spatializing instinct' of man. In opposition to that is placed a belief in the *organic* chatracter of everything. Dead, physical nature comes to life. Chairs and tables, mountains and stars, are animated into a magnetic restlessness, and exist on the same vital terms as men. They are as it were the lowest grade, the most sluggish, of animals. All is alive: and, in that sense, all is mental. (433)

Lewis declared himself the enemy of the Great Within, and saw it (rightly) as constituting an attack on eye-culture to be repulsed at all cost. He felt that the 'theoretic truth' that the time philosophy affirms is a mechanistic one (94). 'The inner meaning of the *time-philosophy*, from whatever standpoint you approach it, and however much you paste it over with confusing advertisements of 'life,' of 'organism,' is the doctrine of a mechanistic universe; periodic; timeless; or nothing but "time," whichever you prefer; and, above all, essentially *dead*' (93). But Lewis is examining it simply as a variety of or pollution of visual space and visual time (Newtonian absolute space and time, frozen and immutable) minus sequentiality: his own admitted visual bias prevents him from realizing that acoustic space and time has its own vivid dynamism and life, but in quite a different pattern – as discussed, for example, by T.S. Eliot in 'Tradition and the Individual Talent,' or by F.M. Cornford in 'The Invention of Space' (in *Essays in Honour of Gilbert Murray*, 215–35).

12 Peter Myers, *The Sound of 'Finnegans Wake,'* 32.

13 In *Annotations*, McHugh cites passages from Judges, Genesis, Deuteronomy, Psalms, Exodus, and Jeremiah, among others.

14 Myers, 38.

15 Ibid., 38–9.

10: The Seventh Thunderclap

1 Cf. Joyce's letter of 11 March 1923 to Harriet Shaw Weaver. Also cf. David Hayman's *First-Draft Version of 'Finnegans Wake,'* 20–1, 34–5: Hayman quotes the second draft (as the first draft is not available), 203–4, and gives a photo reproduction (206–7) of the manuscript.

2 Hayman, 35. James A. Connor, S.J. has remarked, appositely,

> I cannot help but find it interesting that at the same time radio was becoming commonplace and was changing the world in such vast ways, Joyce was experimenting with a kind of language that imitated so many of its audial characteristics. Joyce himself, in his 'Work in Progress,' admitted that 'there is not even a chronological ordering of the action. It is a simultaneous action, represented by the novel's circular construction.' Simultaneous action? Everything happening at once? What could be a better description of radio in the '30s, before digital dials and noise filters and stereophonic sound? The language of the *Wake* flows and shifts, is noisy and hard to grasp, much like competing radio signals. The reader is enticed to read, to listen, with the same intensity as a radio hound in 1933. ('Radio Free Joyce: *Wake* Language and the Experience of Radio,' 830)

Fr Connor gives a good idea of the experience of using a radio in the twenties and thirties:

> Noise was always a problem. And worse, transmissions were never steady – they often appeared and disappeared like desert highways. These were the days

before adjustable frequency stabilizers (my father invented the first one in 1950). Blocks had to be put in or taken out just to hold the frequency and keep it steady. Moreover, signals from the other side of the world sometimes bounced off the Heaviside layer and overrode more local signals. This made listening a complex, frustrating job. Joyce may have been concentrating on an Abbey Theatre Broadcast when a snow report from Minsk dropped on him or when a farm journal from Chicago insinuated itself between the broken acts of the drama.

A number of factors such as temperature drift also varied the frequency. As a transmitter warmed up, the signal meandered off course, so that listeners like Joyce would have had constantly to retune their receivers. Moreover, if someone at the transmitter opened the door to the radio room, the transmitter tubes could cool suddenly, and the frequency would stray again, so that everyone would have to try harder to follow it. Then, on top of all this, there were squeals, whistles and howls like banshees keening through the airwaves. If any two RF signals were close to one another, the difference between them became an audial signal, an eerie wail on the headphones, like the voice of a poor dead soul bouncing up and down along the Heaviside layer. These voices – moving, shifting, piling on top of one another, settling, whistling, humming, screeching, must have sounded in all their constant flux like the coils of hell. (829)

See this chapter of the *Wake*: '… woman formed mobile or man made static and bawling the whowle hamshack and wobble down in an eliminium sounds pound so as to serve him up a melegoturny marygoraumd, eclectrically filtered for allirish earths and ohmes' (309.33–310.01)

3 He submitted himself and his realm to Henry II in the twelfth century. Cf. the account in Seumas MacManus, *The Story of the Irish Race*, 319–330.

4 Hayman, 203. Italics and brackets indicate additions. Roderick O'Connor was about sixty when he submitted to Henry (McHugh, *Annotations*). In *FW*, Joyce makes him fifty-seven or fifty-eight.

5 Letter to Harriet Shaw Weaver, 2 March 1927. The letter-shape E or ш, in various orientations, was the siglum for HCE (cf. letter to HSW, 24 March 1924).

6 Three of Vico's ages are alluded to: in the first age, fear of thunderstorms drives men into caves; the second age sees marriage instituted; the third, burial.

7 I have italicized the radio terms. The electrical symbol for an antenna looks like an opened umbrella. Bellini and Tosti were pioneers in radiotelegraphy. 'Skybuddies' are the radio-ether equivalent of pen-pals. Vacuum cleaners were a frequent source of static and interference. 'Key click' is a kind of interference. Ham shack: radio amateur station. 'Thorpetersen …': the Peterson coil for lightning protection, combined with Thor's name. Valves are radio tubes. The 'umbrella' antenna is proof against PQ's rain/reign. Joyce refers to radio hams explicitly on occasion,

e.g., 'You have jest (a ham) beamed listening through (a ham pig) ...' (359.22)
Hugh Kenner remarked that (in contrast to *Ulysses*) the *Wake* 'is about Ireland
after the rebellion,' and that 'Joyce used to sit in his apartment in Paris and listen
to radio broadcasts from Ireland' (introduction to a thirty-hour uninterrupted
reading of the whole of *Ulysses* on Dublin radio and carried live by the Canadian
Broadcasting Corporation on 16 June 1982).

8 I have underlined the otological terms. It is noteworthy that we do not have ear-
lids as we have eyelids. That is, even during sleep, our ears are as active as they are
during the day, whereas our outward vision is shut down. Bearing in mind that
FW is a 'night book,' the ears might be found to be particularly active. John Bishop
discusses the byplay between radio and otology in these pages in *Joyce's Book of
the Dark: 'Finnegans Wake,'* 274–81.

9 Cf.:

> For he would himself deal a treatment as might be trusted in anticipation of
> his inculmination unto fructification for the major operation. When (pip!) a
> message interfering intermitting interskips from them (pet!) on herzian waves,
> (call her venicey names! call her a stell!) a butterfly from her zipclasped hand-
> bag, a wounded dove astarted from, escaping out her forecotes. Isle wail for
> yews, O doherlynt! The poetesser. And around its scorched cap she has twilled a
> twine of flame to let the laitiest know she's marrid. And pim it goes backballed.
> Tot burns it so leste. A claribel cumbeck to errind ...
>
> Now a run for his money! Now a dash to her dot! Old cocker, young crowy,
> sifadda, sosson. A bran new, speedhount, outstripperous on the wind. Like a
> waft to wingweary one or a sos to a coastguard. For directly with his whoop,
> stop and an upalepsy didando a tishy, in appreciable less time than it takes a gla-
> ciator to submerger an Atlangthis, was he again, agob, before the trembly ones,
> a spark's gap off, doubledasguesched, gotten orlop in a simplasailormade and
> shaking the storm out of his hiccups. The smartest vessel you could find would
> elazilee him on her knee as her lucky for the Rio Grande. He's a pigtail tarr ...'
> (232.07–36)

10 Richard Ellmann, *JJ*, 22. Thomas Hofheinz notes that 'the persona of the Norwegian captain, and elements of his story, first appear in *Ulysses* in a reference to a
blind man with a back "like that Norwegian captain's" (*U* 61), and in the strange
self-portrait of W.B. Murphy' (' "Group drinkards maaks grope thinkards": Narrative in the "Norwegian Captain" Episode of *Finnegans Wake*,' 651).

11 Persse/Kersse: another of Joyce's uses of the P/K split of developing Irish. Cf.
Brendan O'Hehir, *A Gaelic Lexicon for 'Finnegans Wake,'* 403–5.

12 McHugh relates, in *The Sigla*, that 'P.W. Joyce reports that in Ireland "Tailors were

made the butt of much good-natured harmless raillery, often founded on the well-known fact that a tailor is the ninth part of a man."' This assertion is used at 317.26, 326.33, and 327.03, and derives from Elizabeth I's reception of eighteen tailors as 'gentlemen both.' McHugh refers, in his comments, to various Menippean satires: 'If we are to appreciate properly the role of the tailor in II.3 we must refer in the first place to Thomas Carlyle's *Sartor Resartus* (314.17). It is probable that Carlyle developed the 'philosophy of clothes' from Swift's *Tale of a Tub*, also a major *FW* sourcebook. The tailor, he contends, "is not only a man but something of a Creator or Divinity ... how a man is by the tailor new-created into a Nobleman and clothed not only with Wool but with Dignity and a Mystic Dominion ... What too are all Poets and Moral Teachers but a species of Metaphorical Tailors ... And this is he whom ... the world treats with contumely, as the ninth part of a man"' (78). The tailor covers bodily defects or otherwise distracts attention from reality while emphasizing corporeal beauty in accord with the reigning fashion – a kind of seduction that is open to Menippean attack as pomposity, self-aggrandizement, or illusioneering. Dunton has his *Parable of the Top-Knot*, Swift, his shoulder-knots, etc. Satires on tailors abound, and include *Sartor Resartus*, L'Estrange's *Quevedo*, Greene's and Dekker's treatments of tailors in hell. Joyce was not unaware of the tradition: 'So sartor's risorted why the sinner the badder!' (314.17–18). John Bishop brings together many of the references to tailors in the *Wake* in 'How to Find a Good Tailor' (*Joyce's Book of the Dark: 'Finnegans Wake,'* 126–30).

13 Ellmann, *JJ*, 411. The story of 'How Buckley Shot the Russian General' receives its fullest treatment in II.3 (338–55) and has successfully resisted critical and interpretive attack. 'It has become the model,' as Nathan Halper noted, (in 'James Joyce and the Russian General') 'of all in Joyce's work that seems private and perverse.' Further, Kelly Anspaugh points out, the story as given by Ellmann

is not a 'true' story in that the incident described, a soldier named Buckley shooting a defecating Russian general, never happened. According to Halper, there *was* a Russian general – F.E. de Todleben, 'commander of the Russian Army, who was wounded at Sevastopol in June, 1855' (11). Buckley, however, did not shoot Todleben. As for the latter's defecation, this is an echo, not from Sevastopol but rather Waterloo, where the French General Cambronne, when ordered to retreat, cried "*Merde!*" and held his position until the battle was lost (Roland McHugh, *The Sigla of 'Finnegans Wake,'* 84) – an act of courage as reckless as the Crimean Charge of the Light Brigade, which elicited from another French general, Bosquet, the memorable remark, '*C'est magnifique, mais ce n'est pas la guerre.*' The story of how Buckley shot the Russian General, therefore, is a composite piece: a collection of war residues (as it were) brought together by a logic not unlike that which informs Freud's dreamwork or joke-work. No wonder then that Joyce should have incorporated this story into his jocoserious dream-in-progress. ('How Butt Shot the Chamber Pot,' 71–2)

14 Re. 'noirse-made-earsy': D.B. Christiani observes: 'The episode of the Norwegian captain is so Scandinavian in tone that, reading it, one can forget that the *Wake* is an ostensibly English book' (*Scandinavian Elements of 'Finnegans Wake'*, 43). She calls II.3 'the *locus classicus* of Dano-Norwegian in the *Wake*' (154). Joyce wrote Harriet Shaw Weaver that 'the Norwegian-Danish language has neither masculine nor feminine: the two genders are common and neuter. The article follows the noun ...' (1 January 1925: *Letters* I, 225). In the present context, where the sexes are moving towards an equilibrium, the advantages are clear.

Nearly all of the commentators on the *Wake* have missed the essential point that Joyce's use of language or terms in any passage is guided by the classical canons of decorum. For example, Clive Hart sees it as, at most, contributing atmosphere: 'Joyce often uses a group of puns to create a kind of drone-base or pedal-point with which to accompany the whole development of a section and so provide it with a general ambiance, each pun contributing its small quota of atmosphere. Once again there is no necessary connexion between this atmospheric function of a pun and the rest of its content. Thus the river-names in "Anna Livia," the Norwegian vocabulary in "The Norwegian Captain" episode (311–32), and the city-names in "Haveth Childers Everywhere" (532–54), while they create a rich atmosphere, rarely have any other functional relationship to the special contexts in which they are embedded' (*Structure and Motif in 'Finnegans Wake,'* 33–4) Certainly, decorum governs 'atmosphere,' but it is much broader, embracing sense, feeling, tone, effect on audience sensibility, use of figures, tropes, languages, et al.

15 – Neat bit of work, longshoreman one said.
– And what's the number for? loafer number two queried.
– Eaten alive? a third asked the sailor.
– Ay, ay, sighed again the latter personage ... A Greek he was. (*Ulysses*, 632)

16 'Pushpull' is a type of radio amplifier; 'coupling' is a technical term in radio for joining one 'stage' to another, often by magnetic resonance.

17 In the 'first draft' version, this thunder too was irregular. Thunders 6 and 7 are the only two that appear in Hayman's study; he gives thunder 7 on 171, in both the initial 106-letter version and in its present form. Variations of the thunders are discussed in Appendix 1.

11: The Eighth Thunderclap

1 *Film Essays by Sergei Eisenstein*, 16. Problems of dialectic, as well as those of plot,

actors, et al., are further discussed by Eisenstein in his two books *Film Form: Essays in Film Theory* and *Film Sense*. Cf. 'Pad Podomkin' (333.04).

2   Most early film technology used the same machine as both camera and projector. That quite different machines were used for sound film makes no difference thematically at this point.

3   Omar Khayyam had been invoked on the previous page in relation to the wedding proposal: 'O wanderness be wondernest and now!' (318.17). See Fitzgerald's *Rubaiyat*:

> XII   A book of Verses underneath the Bough,
>   A jug of Wine, a loaf of Bread – and Thou
>   Beside me singing in the Wilderness –
>   O Wilderness were Paradise enow! (56)

4   Otherwise, this page might be titled 'A Day at the Races' for the many references to racing and steeplechasing. A courtship is another kind of steeplechasing (it is already present in the book under the figure of the horse-race and whores' race). Now, racing and the shape of the racetrack are a figure for the progress of film through the projector or camera from reel to reel (the frame in front of the lens is actually called 'the race'):

> the Boildawl stuumplecheats for rushirishis IrushIrish ... (322.02–03: Baldoyle racecourse)

> Chorus: With his coate so graye. And his pounds that he pawned from the burning.
> – And, haikon or hurlin, who did you do at doyle today, my horsey dorksey gentryman. Serge Mee, suit! sazd he, tersey kersey. And when Tersse had sazd this Kersse stood them the whole koursse of training how the whole blazy raze acurraghed, from lambkinsback to sliving board and from spark to phoenish ... And they peered him beheld on the pyre. (322.14–25)

> – And so culp me goose, he sazd, szed the ham muncipated of the first course, recoursing, all cholers and coughs with his beauw on the bummell ... (322.35–323.01)

The racing theme is quite funny, given its earlier association with whoring (Cf., 'I wish auspicable thievesdayte for the stork dyrby' 325.06): 'blazy raze acurraghed' refers to Curragh racecourse, Dublin. The 'Stork Derby' was a contest, with a cash prize, to see which woman could have the most babies in a ten-year period. (See *The Great Stork Derby*, by Mark Orkin.) The cash ($750,000 in 1926 dollars) came from the will of a wealthy eccentric: the executors were instructed, 'at the expiration of ten years from my death to give [the money] and its accumulations to the Mother who has since my death given birth in Toronto to the greatest number of children as shown by the Registrations under the Vital Statistics Act' (Orkin, 57).

5 *Scandinavian Elements of 'Finnegans Wake,'* 171–2.

6 The tale is shared by thunders 7 and 8, so some carry-over of themes is to be expected.

12: The Ninth Thunderclap

1 Hayman, *A First-Draft Version of 'Finnegans Wake,'* 36. From the outset, Shaun was a Menippean sort of character. In *The 'Wake' in Transit* Hayman comments about the 'delivery sketch' of III.1–2:

> Shaun is clearly incompetent ... Self-importance and lazy inefficiency, mock simplicity or false frankness, and general ineptitude are already implicit in the way Shaun 'allowed simple & unfranked correspondence to escape automatically from the mailbag.' His Shaunish and Harlequinesque incontinence, his greed for food and money are clear not only from his stumbling movements, but also from the emphasis placed on the eatable and spendable contents of the packages he (mis)delivers ... As a popular Dublin character and potential political or spiritual leader (or hack), the epitome of what Joyce was not, Shaun the post is taking shape under our eyes. Or rather, he is reappearing; for variants of this rugged and hearty philistine have served as *alter egos* to the Joycean artist pretty much from the start. The sketch for his portrait complements in advance the masochistic presence of Shem/Joyce as the willing victim of an appealing and ebullient but sadistic antagonist. It is not surprising that, having (re)discovered this character almost by inadvertence (65), Joyce chose to invert the valence of *Ulysses*, where the cultured clown Mulligan has a bit part only, making extensive use of this avatar of the antagonist to give a nocturnal point to the self-effacing presence of the Pierrot-like Shem. Indeed, the *Wake* makes such lavish use of Shaun's voice and persona that he self-destructs repeatedly. (185–6)

2 Cf. the letter to Harriet Shaw Weaver (21 May 1926): 'I wish you would read through Λ abcd and tell me how they interact.' This dates the completion of the first draft of III (*Letters* I, 240). For Joyce's early work on the theme of traffic in the *Wake*, and in this chapter in particular, see 'Traffic in Transit: Some Spatio-Temporal Elements of *Finnegans Wake*,' by Wim Van Mierlo, in *Finnegans Wake* '*teems of times.*'

3 Hayman, 36.

4 III.1: *transition* 12 (March 1928); III.2: *transition* 13 (Summer 1928). III.3 was published in *transition* 15 (February 1929), and III.4 in *transition* 18 (November 1929). Only thunder 9 appears in this first printed version, in a rudimentary form of 71 letters. Thunder 10 was not added until 1936.

5 Hayman, 37.

6 To Harriet Shaw Weaver, 24 May 1924. (*Letters* I, 214).

7 Parallels with another Menippean satire are discussed by J.S. Atherton in 'A Man of Four Watches: Macrobius in *Finnegans Wake*.'

8 The first line is fairly orderly, 12–11–10 mixed with 2–4–6; the second line is in complete disarray. Tolv = Dan, twelve; elf = Ger, eleven; kater = Gael (or Anglic. Fr), four; pedwar = We, four; pemp = We, five; foify sounds to me like fifty or five-y but could be something else.

9 G.K. Chesterton, *What's Wrong with the World*, 262. Because of the presence of the donkey in the dialogue of Shaun with the group (on television), I suspect that Joyce combined two of Aesop's fables for the Ondt. Both are brief, so I give them in full.

The Ass and the Grasshopper

An ass, having heard some grasshoppers chirping, was completely enchanted by their lovely voices. He wanted more than anything to be able to sing as well, and so he asked the grasshopper what kind of food they lived on to give them such beautiful voices. They replied: 'The dew.' The ass resolved that he would live only upon dew until he could sing as sweetly as a grasshopper. In a short time he had died of hunger.
One man's meat is another man's poison.

The Ants and the Grasshopper

One fine winter's day a nest of ants were drying grain they had collected during the summer. A grasshopper, almost dying of hunger, passed by and begged for a little food. The ants asked him: 'Why didn't you store up food during the summer?' To this he replied: 'I spent my days singing, and there wasn't enough time.' The ants then said': 'If you were foolish enough to sing all summer, you must go to bed without any supper in the winter.' (*Aesop's Fables – and Others'*, 75 and 108 respectively)

10 Hugh Kenner observes that 'it was Lewis who assigned the eye to himself and the ear to Joyce. It was also he who assigned time to Shem and space to Shaun.

Ulysses, he wrote, was a time-book, a midden-heap of *temps retrouvé*, a lingering over what had long faded from the world' (*Dublin's Joyce*, 366). Lewis had blasted *Ulysses* in a polemic against the new spate of 'time school' writers for their relativism and use of the concept of space-time and for their reducing reality to flux instead of treating it as composed of solid objects. Joyce responds to Lewis in several ways in the *Wake*. As Andrzej Duszenko observes, 'Joyce's most direct response to Lewis and most extensive comment on the space-time debate is contained in two passages: the lecture of Professor Jones followed by the fable of the Mookse and the Gripes (*FW* 148–168) and the fable of the Ondt and the Gracehoper (*FW* 414–419)' ('The Relativity Theory in *Finnegans Wake*,' 67). Prof. Duszenko's account is a most useful survey of 'Wakean glances at Newtonian physics and its fall' and the space-time debate that followed the publication of Einstein's theories. Duszenko also notes that George Otte offers an analysis of both fables and a discussion of Lewis's and Joyce's views of spatiotemporal conjunction in 'Time and Space (with the Emphasis on the Conjunction): Joyce's Response to Lewis.'

11 Prostrandvorous contains pro-, strand, voracious, avarice, and R *postranstvo*, space.

12 The Gracehoper too has an appetite, but it is modest by comparison to the Ondt's and less substantial, for his is a time-feast: 'He had eaten all the whilepaper, swallowed the lustres, devoured forty flights of styearcases, chewed up all the mensas and seccles, ronged the records, made mundballs of the ephemerids and vorasioused most glutinously with the very timeplace in the ternitary – not too dusty a cicada of neutriment for a chittinous chip so mitey' (416.21–6).

13 In several early attempts to invent it, the internal combustion engine was fuelled by gunpowder. Saint Barbara is the patroness of artillerymen.

14 'Folkloire' is Gael *focloir*, vocabulary; 'velktingeling' is Dan *velklingende*, euphonious; Volapük is, like Esperanto, an artificial language. Kristian Smidt glosses this passage as a characteristic example of Joyce's voluptuous vocabulary:

> The two words 'voluptuary' and 'vocabulary' have been telescoped to form a coined portmanteau-word. By the simple expedient of changing a *c* to a *k*, we get the additional suggestion of the town and bazaar of Kabul with its exotic eastern associations. Besides, we are at liberty to see the French word *vol* and the English word *up* in the parent word, adding the very appropriate senses both of theft and of flight, height and speed. The exposition is undeniably in a state of explosion and the folklore rich and farflung. 'Velktingeling' is the Norwegian word 'velklingende' (meaning euphonic) plus the onomatopoeia 'tingaling'; and it serves to describe the 'volupkabulary.' (*James Joyce and the Cultic Use of Fiction*, 75–6).

15 *Vulg. Ps.*, 80:4 – Buccinate in neomenia tuba, in insigni die solemnitatis vestrae: 'Blow up the trumpet in the new moon, in the time appointed, on our solemn feast day' (McHugh, *Annotations*).

16 Also cf. 'he savvy inside true inwardness of reality' (611.21) and 'Hearing. The urb it orbs. Then's now with now's then in tense continuant. Heard. Who having has he shall have had. Hear!' (598.28–30).

17 'As the name of this Pepi ... shall flourish, and this pyramid of Pepi ... shall flourish, and this his work flourish for ever and ever ...' (*The Egyptian Book of the Dead*, xxvii). Cf. G. Maspero, 'La Pyramide de Pepi II,' McHugh notes several other uses of the *Book of the Dead* in Shaun/Ondt's final speech before the verse portion of 'The Ondt and the Gracehoper' (418.05–08). John Bishop (*Joyce's Book of the Dark: 'Finnegans Wake,'* 86–125) provides a useful account of Joyce's use of *The Book of the Dead* in the *Wake*.

18 A cocoon is spun by a larva to protect the chrysalis. Note the Ondt's gradual disappearance in '... ond ... on ... a ...'

19 Compare Goldsmith:

> Here, waiter, more wine, let me sit while I'm able,
> 'Till all my companions sink under the table;
> Then with chaos and blunders encircling my head,
> Let me ponder and tell what I think of the dead.
> (*Complete Works*, IV, 353, lines 19–22)

Joyce's verses form an extended sonnet: each line of the octet is in Joyce a two-line sentence (418.11–26); equally, each line of the sestet is a sentence (418.27–30, .31–2, .33–6, 419.01–02, .03–04, .05–08).

13: The Tenth Thunderclap

1 Shaun the Post carries a lamp that he fastens onto his belt when he is not using it. The numerous correspondences are noted by McHugh in *Annotations*, e.g., 404, 426. See also the discussion in Atherton, *The Books at the 'Wake,'* 157–61.

2 Clive Hart writes as follows:

> Among other major contexts in which the cross-correspondence idea operates is the television show, whose central position (337–55) and fertile symbolic content clearly proclaim it one of the most important miniature replicas of *Finnegans Wake* as a whole. It seems that Joyce never saw any television at all – an amazing fact in view of the extraordinarily realistic evocation of the medium that he achieves in *Finnegans Wake* – but, as I have already sug-

gested, Joyce always took a great interest in any new scientific or technological advance and he had both read and heard about the early telecasts with considerable enthusiasm. To Budgen he expressed the hope that readers of *Finnegans Wake* would be better able to appreciate the book if its material were presented partly in terms of the new medium in which the world was growing so interested. Not only does Joyce parody the medium of communication, but he makes a direct and illuminating analogy between the electronic techniques of television and his own creative process. (*Structure and Motif in 'Finnegans Wake,'* 158–9)

3 Television was developed by John L. Baird in 1925 and first demonstrated soon thereafter, as Joyce was beginning the long process of writing *Finnegans Wake*. Within a year (1926), the first television equipment was perfected; the BBC made experimental broadcasts as early as 1929. The burgeoning and excitement of the times is well captured by John G. Fuller in a passage redolent of the themes of the final thunders:

> These were the days of hope and glory. The bitter memories of the First World War had faded; the clouds of the Second had not yet gathered. The Twenties was the decade of record breakers and 'firsts': the first television demonstration, the first woman to swim the English Channel, the first talking picture, the first New York-to-London telephone call.
>
> Jelly Roll Morton and his Red Hot Peppers were breaking records in Chicago, while Babe Ruth cracked his record-breaking sixtieth home run in Yankee Stadium. Everyone was singing *Making Whoopee* and *Crazy Rhythm*, while they were sweating under the heavy gyroscopic demands of the Charleston and the Black Bottom. Gene Tunney was taking the heavyweight championship away from Jack Dempsey.
>
> Everything that happened in aviation seemed to grab headlines. Lindbergh, of course, had grabbed the biggest the previous year. In the balmy days of 1927, he flew alone from New York to Paris. He set up a mad scramble of followers to conquer the Atlantic, whether because it was *there*, or because there was lavish prize money ready to be plucked from the carrot stick. (*The Airmen Who Would Not Die*, 19)

At the time, the world seemed to be bursting with new electric technologies and appliances, including sound film, the electrified internal combustion engine in cars and airplanes, air races, car races, radio, telephones, short-wave listening and reporting, and the mysterious new television.

4 Erik Barnouw, *The Golden Web: A History of Broadcasting in the United States*, 2, 42–3.

5 Here is Clive Hart's gloss on this passage.

> The 'bitts' which hurtle down the tube and – 'Shlossh' – fall into place as a stable picture are blurred and unintelligible in themselves – 'a double focus' – but when combined on the delicate screen the ghastly and ghostly truth becomes clear. The pictures of Butt and Taff are made to converge like a pair of flat photographs in a stereoscope to produce a fully rounded and comprehensible figure. (In this episode Joyce is evidently predicting 3-D television along with the atom bomb [353.22] and the destruction of the world.) The 'bitts' are of course Shem and Shaun who are able to 'adumbrace a pattern of somebody else or other' (220.15) only when they work together for the common good, but the passage is as relevant to the style of *Finnegans Wake* as to its characters. Joyce's language units may make little sense in isolation, or even be misleading, but when all the other bits are taken into consideration and projected on to the revolving screen of the interpreting mind, their true significance is revealed. Like a national language, that of *Finnegans Wake* – a recognizable and consistent whole, varied by its own dialects, slang and special usages – was meant to be self-explanatory on its own ground. (*Structure and Motif in 'Finnegans Wake,'* 159–60)

Hugh Kenner sees in the passage little more than 'the familiar specter of cold jesuitic violence': 'Missledhropes, misled hopes, flying missiles, and ultimate hangman's ropes. The hail of bullets is now more meaningless than the spatter of electrons in a television tube. A ghostly apparatus of valves, carrier waves, iconoscopes, scanners and six-hundred-line screens educes out of the spatter an intelligible form, the General of the Jesuits, alias Father Dolan with his familiar pandybat' (*Dublin's Joyce*, 272. In the criticism and commentary on the *Wake* to date, no relations have been noticed as existing between television and the charge of the Light Brigade, or any other of the themes, sensory or social. Kenner is wide of the mark, but Hart has noted the similarity of the television pointillist image to epiphanic *Wakese*. [I wrote the above in 1982. Nine years later, in 1991, Donald F. Theall noted that 'the receiver is conceived as a "light barricade" against which the charge of the light brigade (the video signal) is directed' ('The Hieroglyphs of Engined Egyptians,' 149).

6 Puccini, *Tosca*, III: 'E lucevan le stelle e olezzava la terra, stridea l'uscio dell'orto e un passo sfiorava la rena. Entrava ella, fragrante, mi cadea tra le braccia. Oh! dolci baci o languide carezze, mentr'io fremente le belle forme disciogliea dai veli!' (And the stars shone and the earth was perfumed, the gate to the garden creaked and a footstep rustled the sand on the path. Fragrant, she entered, and fell into my arms. Oh! sweet kisses, languid caresses, as I trembling unloosed her veils and disclosed her beauty) (McHugh, *Annotations*, 427).

7 It is referred to occasionally in the *Wake*, e.g., in the 'fourth watch' of Shaun: 'While elvery stream winds seling on for to keep this barrel of bounty rolling and the nightmail afarfrom morning nears' (565.30–2). Similar to Diogenes', Shaun's barrel is clothing, house, cocoon, and coffin (cf., 419.15–20).

8 London: The Egoist 1919. It is reprinted, with many of Lewis's other vorticist statements in *Wyndham Lewis the Artist: From Blast to Burlington House* and in *Wyndham Lewis on Art: Collected Writings* 1913–1956, 129–83.

9 See the other vortex references in the chapter, e.g., the spiral galaxy of the Milky Way, or the car vortex, 'The whool of the whaal in the wheel of the whorl of the Boubou from Bourneum has thus come to taon!' (415.07–08). The 'bourne' or womb/cocoon/coffin is another vortex.

10 The 'four watches' of Shaun are four 'wristwatches or pocket watches,' the four intervals of the night that lead to dawn and resurrection ('Array! Surrection! Eireweeker to the wohld bludyn world. O rally, O rally, O rally! Phlenxty, O rally!' 593.2–4), and are also Shaun in the mode of each of the four levels of exegesis: III.1, the present chapter, is the literal level, the one that contains all of the others.

11 Kristian Smidt remarks the 'Sireland' motif of post-human discarnate patriarchy as dominant in the tenth thunderclap: 'It means God and thunder and *Ragnarok* and the Norse antiquity of Dublin, the scene of Earwicker's story (the "Eyrawyggla saga"), besides containing the separate significations of the component parts of the mammoth word, most of which are in Old Norse or something like it. A word with such all-comprising meaning and capable of such indefinite variations is obviously suited to be a magical appellative for the Universal Spirit' (*James Joyce and the Cultic Use of Fiction*, 76).

14: Conclusion

1 Ellmann, *JJ*, 815.

2 Attridge, *Peculiar Language: Literature as Difference from the Renaissance to James Joyce*, 237.

3 Eugene P. Kirk's *Menippean Satire: An Annotated Catalogue of Texts and Criticism* lists more than seven hundred Menippean satires – and extends only to 1660.

Afterword

1 T.S. Eliot, *On Poetry and Poets*, 119.

2 Alan of Lille, *Plaint of Nature*, foreword (n.p.).

3 Ibid., introduction, 33.

Appendix 1: On the Composition of the Thunders

1 *The James Joyce Archive*, vol. 44, *'Finnegans Wake': Book I, Chapter 1. A Facsimile of Drafts, Typescripts, and Proofs*, 45.

2 Ibid., 105.

3 Ibid., 145.

4 Ibid., 131.

5 Ibid., 169.

6 Ibid., 204.

7 Private correspondence from David Hayman.

8 *Archive*, vol. 45, *'Finnegans Wake': Book I, Chapters 2–3. A Facsimile of Drafts, Typescripts, and Proofs*, 71.

9 Ibid., 131.

10 *Archive*, vol. 46, *'Finnegans Wake': Book I, Chapters 4–5. A Facsimile of Drafts, Typescripts, and Proofs*, 101.

11 Ibid., 185.

12 *Archive*, vol. 57, *'Finnegans Wake': Book III, Chapters 1 and 2. A Facsimile of Drafts, Typescripts, and Proofs*, 318–9.

13 *Archive*, vol. 51, *'Finnegans Wake': Book II, Chapter 1. A Facsimile of Drafts, Typescripts, and Proofs*, 5.

14 Ibid., 139. David Hayman gives the alternative ending in *A First-Draft Version of 'Finnegans Wake,'* 141.

15 *Archive*, vol. 54, *'Finnegans Wake': Book II, Chapter 3. A Facsimile of Drafts, Typescripts, and Proofs*, 13.

16 Ibid., 61.

17 *Archive*, vol. 61, *'Finnegans Wake': Book III, Chapters 1–4. A Facsimile of 'transition' Pages*, 339, 560.

18 Private correspondence from David Hayman.

19 *Archive*, vol. 62, *'Finnegans Wake': Book III. A Facsimile of the Galley Proofs*, 29.

20 *Archive*, vol. 55, *'Finnegans Wake': Book II, Chapter 3. A Facsimile of Drafts, Typescripts, and Proofs* (the second of two volumes), 107, 121, etc.

21 Private correspondence from David Hayman.

22 Private correspondence from David Hayman.

23 *Archive*, vol. 49, *'Finnegans Wake': Book I. A Facsimile of the Galley Proofs*, 442 (galley 62).

24 *Archive*, vol. 51, 393, 443.

25 Ibid., 443.

26 David Hayman reads the ms as -**strummitrummi**- (*A First-Draft Version of 'Finnegans Wake,'* 171). He may well be right: the writing is not very clear at that point. If he is right, the ms version is 107, not 108, letters long.

Appendix 3: The Rhetorical Structure of *Finnegans Wake*

1 Varro, *De Lingua Latina.*
2 Ernst R. Curtius, *European Literature and the Latin Middle Ages,* 319–20.
3 Etienne Gilson, *The Philosophy of St. Bonaventure,* 229.
4 Henri de Lubac, *Exégèse médiévale, les quatre sens de l'Ecriture.*
5 Curtius, 138–9.
6 Quintilian, *Institutio Oratoria,* VIII, Pr. 6.
7 *JJ,* 630, n.
8 Frances A. Yates has a study of this branch of rhetoric in *The Art of Memory.*
9 See F.C. Bartlett's *Remembering* and Edmund Blair Bolles's *Remembering and Forgetting: Inquiries into the Nature of Memory.*
10 *JJ,* 630, n.
11 James A. Boon, *From Symbolism to Structuralism: Lévi-Strauss in a Literary Tradition,* 133. Boon is quoting Peter Caws, 'What Is Structuralism?' 81.
12 *Basic Writings of Saint Thomas Aquinas,* II, 1031.
13 A.A. Grimaldi, *The Universal Humanity of Giambattista Vico,* 37.
14 Giambattista Vico, *Opere* I, *Le Orazione,* Oratio VI, 57; Grimaldi, 43.
15 See also Marshall McLuhan, 'James Joyce: Trivial and Quadrivial.'

Bibliography

Aesop. *Aesop's Fables – and Others'*. London, Melbourne, Cape Town: Ward Lock 1962.

Alan of Lille. *Alan of Lille, The Plaint of Nature*, trans. and commentary by J.J. Sheridan. Toronto: Pontifical Institute of Mediaeval Studies 1980.

Anspaugh, Kelly. 'How Butt Shot the Chamber Pot: *'Finnegans Wake' II.3.' JJQ* 32, no. 1, Fall 1994, 71–81.

Aquinas, St Thomas. *Summa Theologica*, trans. A.C. Pegis. *Basic Writings of Thomas Aquinas*. New York: Random House 1945.

Atherton, J.S. *The Books at the 'Wake.'* London: Faber and Faber 1959.

– 'A Man of Four Watches: Macrobius in *Finnegans Wake.' A Wake Newslitter*, IX.3, 1972, 39–40.

Attridge, Derek. 'Finnegans Awake: The Dream of Interpretation.' *JJQ* 27, no. 1, Fall 1989, 11–29.

– *Peculiar Language: Literature as Difference from the Renaissance to James Joyce*. Ithaca, NY: Cornell University Press 1988.

Bacon, Sir Francis. *Novum Organum* [New Science, also *Novum Organon*]; *or, True Directions concerning the Interpretation of Nature*. In *The English Philosophers from Bacon to Mill*, ed. E.A. Burtt. New York: Random House (Modern Library) 1939.

– *Novum Organum*. In *Great Books of the Western World*. Chicago, London, Toronto, Geneva: Encyclopaedia Brittanica 1952.

Barnouw, Erik. *The Golden Web: A History of Broadcasting in the United States*. New York: Oxford University Press 1968. 2 vols.

Bartlett, F.C. *Remembering*. Cambridge: Cambridge University Press, 1950.

Beckett, Samuel, et al. 'Dante ... Bruno. Vico ... Joyce.' In *Our Exagmination Round His Factification for Incamination of Work in Progress by Samuel Beckett, Marcel Brion, Frank Budgen, Stuart Gilbert, Eugene Jolas, Victor Llona, Robert McAlmon,*

Thomas McGreevy, Elliot Paul, John Rodker, Robert Sage, William Carlos Williams. With Letters of Protest by G.V.L. Slingsby and Vladimir Dixon. Paris: Shakespeare and Company; London: Faber and Faber 1929.

Begnal, Michael H. *Dreamscheme: Narrative and Voice in 'Finnegans Wake.'* Syracuse NY: Syracuse University Press 1988.

Benstock, Bernard. 'James Joyce: The Olfactory Factor.' In *Joycean Occasions: Essays from the Milwaukee James Joyce Conference,* ed. J.E. Dunleavy et al., q.v.

– *Joyce-again's Wake.* Seattle: University of Washington Press 1965.

Benstock, Shari. 'Apostrophes.' In *Joycean Occasions: Essays from the Milwaukee James Joyce Conference,* ed. J.E. Dunleavy et al., q.v.

Bishop, John. *Joyce's Book of the Dark: 'Finnegans Wake.'* Madison: University of Wisconsin Press 1986.

Boldereff, Frances M. *Hermes to His Son, Thoth: Being Joyce's Use of Giordano Bruno in 'Finnegans Wake.'* Woodward, PA: Classic Non-Fiction Library, 1963.

Bolles, Edmund Blair. *Remembering and Forgetting: Inquiries into the Nature of Memory.* New York: Walker; Markham, ON: Thomas Allen 1988.

Bonheim, Helmut. *A Lexicon of the German in 'Finnegans Wake.'* Berkeley, Los Angeles: University of California Press 1967.

Boon, James A. *From Symbolism to Structuralism: Lévi-Strauss in a Literary Tradition.* New York: Harper & Row 1972.

Brett, G.S. *Psychology Ancient and Modern.* London: Longmans 1928.

Bryson, Bill. *The Mother Tongue: English and How It Got That Way.* New York: Morrow 1990.

The Cambridge Companion to James Joyce, ed. Derek Attridge. Cambridge, New York: Cambridge University Press 1990.

Campbell, J., and H.M. Robinson. *A Skeleton Key to 'Finnegans Wake.'* New York: Viking 1944. Rpt. Compass Books 1961.

Capella, Martianus. *The Marriage of Mercury and Philology,* trans. W.H. Stahl and R. Johnson with E.L. Burge. Vol. 2 of *Martianus Capella and the Seven Liberal Arts.* 2 vols. New York: Columbia University Press 1977.

Carlyle, Thomas. *Sartor Resartus,* [and] *On Heroes and Hero Worship.* London: Dent; New York: Dutton 1908. Rpt. 1959.

Caws, Peter. 'What Is Structuralism?' *Partisan Review* 35 (1968).

Chesterton, G.K. *What's Wrong with the World.* London, New York, Toronto, Melbourne: Cassell 1910.

Christiani, Dounia Bunis. *Scandinavian Elements of 'Finnegans Wake.'* Evanston IL: Northwestern University Press 1965.

Cleve, F.M. *The Giants of Pre-Sophistic Greek Philosophy.* 2 vols. The Hague: Martinus Nijhoff 1965.

Coleman, Dorothy. *Rabelais: A Critical Study in Prose Fiction*. Cambridge: Cambridge University Press 1971.

Colum, Mary, and Padraic Colum. *Our Friend James Joyce*. London: Gollancz 1959.

The Concise Dictionary of Twenty-six Languages in Simultaneous Translations, ed. Peter M. Bergman. New York: Bergman Publishers (Polyglot Library) 1968.

Connor, James A., S.J. 'Radio Free Joyce: *Wake* Language and the Experience of Radio.' *JJQ* 30, no. 4; 31, no. 1, Summer/Fall 1993, 825–43.

Cornford, F.M. 'The Invention of Space.' In *Essays in Honour of Gilbert Murray*. London: Allen & Unwin 1936.

Curtius, Ernst R. *European Literature and the Latin Middle Ages*, trans. Willard R. Trask. New York: Pantheon 1953,

Devlin, Kimberly J. *Wandering and Return in 'Finnegans Wake': An Integrative Approach to Joyce's Fictions*. Princeton NJ: Princeton University Press 1991.

Di Bernard, Barbara. *Alchemy and 'Finnegans Wake.'* Albany NY: State University of New York Press 1980.

Diogenes Laertius. *Lives of Eminent Philosophers*, ed. and trans. R.D. Hicks. 2 vols. Loeb Classical Library. Cambridge MA: Harvard University Press; London: Heinemann 1925. Rpt. 1959, 1980.

Domenichelli, Mario. 'Paradoxes: Joyce's Opus In-Interruptum.' *JJQ* 27, no. 1, Fall 1989, 111–19.

Dunleavy, Janet E., Melvin J. Friedman, and Michael Patrick Gillespie, eds. *Joycean Occasions: Essays from the Milwaukee James Joyce Conference*. Newark: University of Delaware Press; London and Toronto: Associated University Presses 1991.

Duszenko, Andrzej. 'The Relativity Theory in "Finnegans Wake."' *JJQ* 32, no. 1, Fall 1994, 61–70.

'Earwig Lore,' *Discovery*, March 1937, 89–91; quoted in Roland McHugh, *The Sigla of 'Finnegans Wake,'* 16.

Eckley, Grace. '"Petween Peas Like Ourselves": The Folklore of the Prankquean,' *JJQ* 9, no. 2, Winter 1972, 177–88.

The Egyptian Book of the Dead, trans. E.A. Wallace Budge. New York: Dover 1967.

Eisenstein, Sergei. *Film Essays by Sergei Eisenstein*, ed. Jay Leyda. London: Dobson 1968.

– *Film Form: Essays in Film Theory*, ed. and trans. Jay Leyda. New York: Harcourt Brace & World 1959.

– *Film Sense*, ed. and trans. Jay Leyda. London: Faber and Faber 1948.

Eliot, T.S. *Four Quartets*. In *The Complete Poems and Plays 1909–1950*. New York: Harcourt, Brace & World 1962.

– *Homage to John Dryden: Three Essays on the Poetry of the Seventeenth Century*. Hogarth Press, n.d. Rpt. *Selected Essays*. 3rd ed. London: Faber and Faber 1972.

– 'Matthew Arnold.' In *The Use of Poetry and the Use of Criticism*. New York: Barnes and Noble 1955.
– 'The Method of Mr Pound,' *Athenaeum*. London: 24 October 1919, p. 1065.
– *On Poetry and Poets*. New York: Farrar, Straus & Cudahy 1943. Rpt. 1957.
– 'Philip Massinger.' In *Selected Essays*. 3rd ed. London: Faber and Faber 1972.
– *To Criticize the Critic*. New York: Farrar, Straus & Giroux 1965.
– 'Tradition and the Individual Talent.' In *The Sacred Wood: Essays on Poetry and Criticism*. London: Methuen 1920. Rpt. 1948.
Elliott, Robert C. *The Power of Satire: Magic, Ritual, Art*. Princeton NJ: Princeton University Press 1960.
Ellmann, Richard. *Eminent Domain*. New York: Oxford University Press 1967.
– *James Joyce*. New York: Oxford University Press 1959. Rev. 1982. (Revised ed. referenced as *JJII*.)
– *Ulysses on the Liffey*. New York: Oxford University Press 1972.
Emerson, Ralph Waldo. 'Works and Days.' In *Society and Solitude*. New York, Boston: Houghton, Mifflin 1888.
The Encyclopedia of Philosophy, ed. Paul Edwards. 8 vols. New York: Macmillan & Free Press. 1967. Rpt. 1972.
Frazer, Sir James. *The Golden Bough: A Study in Magic and Religion*. New York: Macmillan 1922. Rpt. 1937.
French, Marilyn. 'Joyce and Language.' *JJQ* 19, no. 3, Spring 1982, 239–55.
Fuller, John G. *The Airmen Who Would Not Die*. New York: Putnam 1979.
Gilbert, Stuart. *James Joyce's 'Ulysses': A Study*. London: Faber and Faber 1930, 1934. Rev. ed. London, New York: 1952.
Gilson, Etienne. *The Philosophy of St. Bonaventure*, trans. Dom Illtyd Trethowan and F.J. Sheed. London: Sheed & Ward 1938.
Glasheen, Adaline. 'Part of What the Thunder Said in *Finnegans Wake*.' Mimeographed as issue 23 of *The Analyst*, ed. Robert Mayo. Evanston IL: Dept. of English, Northwestern University 1964.
– *Third Census of 'Finnegans Wake': An Index of the Characters and Their Roles Revised and Expanded from the Second Census by Adaline Glasheen*. Berkeley, Los Angeles, London: University of California Press 1977.
Goldsmith, Oliver. *Complete Works of Oliver Goldsmith*, ed. Arthur Friedman. 5 vols. Oxford: Clarendon Press 1966.
Gordon, John. *'Finnegans Wake': A Plot Summary*. Dublin: Gill and Macmillan 1986.
Graves, Robert. *The White Goddess*. New York: Random House (Vintage) 1948.
Grimaldi, A.A. *The Universal Humanity of Giambattista Vico*. New York: S.F. Vanni 1958.
Halper, Nathan. 'James Joyce and the Russian General.' *Partisan Review* 18 (July/August 1951) 424–31. Rpt. *Studies in Joyce*. Ann Arbor MI: UMI Research 1983, 9.

Hart, Clive. *Structure and Motif in 'Finnegans Wake.'* Evanston IL: Northwestern University Press 1962.

Hatch, Edwin. *The Influence of Greek Ideas on Christianity.* Foreword with new notes and bibliography by Frederick C. Grant. New York, Evanston IL: Harper & Row (Torchbooks) 1957.

Hayman, David. *A First-Draft Version of 'Finnegans Wake.'* Austin: University of Texas Press 1963.

– 'Nodality and Infra-Structure in *Finnegans Wake.*' *JJQ* 16, Fall 1978, 135–49.

– *The 'Wake' in Transit.* Ithaca, London: Cornell University Press 1990.

Herr, Cheryl. *Joyce's Anatomy of Culture.* Urbana, Chicago: University of Illinois Press 1986.

Herring, Phillip F. *Joyce's Uncertainty Principle.* Princeton NJ: Princeton University Press 1987.

Hofheinz, Thomas. '"Group drinkards maaks grope thinkards": Narrative in the "Norwegian Captain" Episode of *Finnegans Wake.*' *JJQ* 29, no. 3, Spring 1992, 643–58.

Huizinga, J. *The Waning of the Middle Ages.* New York: Doubleday (Anchor) 1954.

Jaeger, Johann, and Ulrich von Hutten. *Epistolae Obscurorum Virorum: The Latin Text with an English Rendering, Notes, and Historical Introduction by Francis Griffin Stokes.* London: Chatto & Windus 1925.

The James Joyce Archive. General ed. Michael Groden. 63 vols. New York, London: Garland. The volumes on *Finnegans Wake* were published 1977–8: vol. 44, *'Finnegans Wake': Book I, Chapter 1. A Facsimile of Drafts, Typescripts, and Proofs;* vol. 45, *'Finnegans Wake': Book I, Chapters 2–3. A Facsimile of Drafts, Typescripts, and Proofs;* vol. 46, *'Finnegans Wake': Book I, Chapters 4–5. A Facsimile of Drafts, Typescripts, and Proofs;* vol. 51, *'Finnegans Wake': Book II, Chapter 1. A Facsimile of Drafts, Typescripts, and Proofs;* vol. 54, *'Finnegans Wake': Book II, Chapter 3. A Facsimile of Drafts, Typescripts, and Proofs, vol. 1;* vol. 55, *'Finnegans Wake': Book II, Chapter 3. A Facsimile of Drafts, Typescripts, and Proofs, vol. 2;* vol. 61, *'Finnegans Wake': Book III, Chapters 1–4. A Facsimile of 'transition' Pages;* vol. 62, *'Finnegans Wake': Book III. A Facsimile of the Galley Proofs.*

The James Joyce Quarterly. Tulsa OK: Univ. of Tulsa.

Jefferson, D.W. '*Tristram Shandy* and the Tradition of Learned Wit.' In *Essays in Criticism,* vol. 1. Oxford: Blackwell 1951, 225–48.

Joyce, James. *Anna Livia Plurabelle.* London: Faber and Faber 1930.

– *The Critical Writings of James Joyce,* ed. Ellsworth Mason and Richard Ellmann. New York: Viking 1959.

– *Finnegans Wake.* London: Faber and Faber; New York: Viking 1939. Subsequent printings incorporate the author's corrections made after publication of the first (and only) edition.

– *James Joyce's Scribbledehobble: The Ur-Workbook for 'Finnegans Wake,'* ed. Thomas E. Connolly. Evanston IL: Northwestern University Press 1961.
– *Letters of James Joyce*, ed. Stuart Gilbert. New York: Viking Press 1957. Reissued with corrections 1966, as vol. 1 of 3 (see next entry).
– *Letters of James Joyce*. vols. 2 and 3, ed. Richard Ellmann. New York: Viking 1966.
– *The Mime of Mick, Nick and the Maggies*. The Hague: Sevire Press, n.d. Also published in *transition* 22, February 1933.
– *Ulysses*. New York: Random House (Modern Library) 1961. Rpt. as *Ulysses: The Corrected Text*, ed. Hans Walter Gabler with Wolfhard Steppe and Claus Melchior. New York: Random House 1986.
Kenner, Hugh. *Dublin's Joyce*. Bloomington: Indiana University Press 1956.
Khayyam, Omar. *Rubaiyat*: trans. Edward Fitzgerald. 4th ed. New York: Crowell, n.d.
– *Fitzgerald's Rubaiyat*. Centennial edition, ed. Carl J. Weber. Waterville ME: Colby College Press 1959.
Kirk, Eugene P. *Menippean Satire: An Annotated Catalogue of Texts and Criticism*. New York, London: Garland 1980.
Korkowski, Eugene P. 'Menippus and His Imitators: A Conspectus, up to Sterne, for a Misunderstood Genre.' Diss. University of California, San Diego 1973.
Lanham, Richard A. *The Electronic Word: Democracy, Technology, and the Arts*. Chicago, London: University of Chicago Press 1993.
– *'Tristram Shandy': The Games of Pleasure*. Los Angeles, London: University of California Press 1973.
L'Estrange, Roger. *Los Sueños [The Visions]. Translated by Roger L'Estrange*, ed. J.M. Cohen. Carbondale: Southern Illinois University Press 1963. Translation of *Los Sueños* (1627 and later) by Gomez Francisco de Quevedo y Villegas (known as Quevedo).
Lewis, P. Wyndham. *Men without Art* (1934). Rpt. New York: Russell & Russell 1964.
– *One-Way Song*, with Foreword by T.S. Eliot. London: Faber and Faber 1933. Rpt. London: Methuen 1960.
– *Time and Western Man*. London: Chatto & Windus 1927. Rpt. Boston: Beacon Press 1957.
– *Wyndham Lewis on Art: Collected Writings 1913–1956*, ed. Walter Michel and C.J. Fox. New York: Funk & Wagnall 1969.
– *Wyndham Lewis the Artist: From Blast to Burlington House*. London: Laidlaw and Laidlaw 1939.
Lipari, Angelo. *The Dolce Stil Novo according to Lorenzo Da' Medici*. New Haven CT: Yale University Press 1936.
Lubac, Henri de, S.J. *Exégèse médiévale: Les quatre sens de l'Ecriture*. 4 vols. Paris: Aubier 1959–64.

Lucian. *The Works of Lucian,* ed. and trans. A.M. Harmon, K. Kilburn, and R.D. MacLeod. 8 vols. Loeb Classical Library. Cambridge MA: Harvard University Press; London: Heinemann 1913–61.

MacCabe, Colin. *James Joyce and the Revolution of the Word.* London, Basingstoke: Macmillan 1978.

MacManus, Seumas. *The Story of the Irish Race.* New York: Devin-Adair 1921, 1970.

Maspero, G. 'La Pyramide de Pepi II.' *Receuil de Travaux,* t. xii (Paris 1892) and t. x (Paris 1888).

McCarthy, Patrick A. 'The Last Epistle of *Finnegans Wake.*' *JJQ* 27, no. 4, Summer 1990, 725–33.

– *The Riddles of 'Finnegans Wake.'* Cranbury NJ, London, Toronto: Associated University Presses 1980.

McHugh, Roland. *Annotations to 'Finnegans Wake.'* Baltimore, London: Johns Hopkins University Press 1980. Rev. ed. 1991.

– *The 'Finnegans Wake' Experience.* Dublin: Irish Academic Press 1981.

– *The Sigla of 'Finnegans Wake.'* London: Edward Arnold 1976.

McLuhan, Eric. 'The Rhetorical Structure of *Finnegans Wake.*' *JJQ* 11, no. 4, Summer 1974, 394–404.

McLuhan, Eric, and Marshall McLuhan. *Laws of Media: The New Science.* Toronto: University of Toronto Press 1988.

McLuhan, H.M. *The Gutenberg Galaxy: The Making of Typographic Man.* Toronto: University of Toronto Press 1962.

– 'James Joyce: Trivial and Quadrivial,' *Thought: Fordham University Quarterly* 28, no. 108, Spring 1953.

McLuhan, H.M., and Quentin Fiore. *War and Peace in the Global Village: An Inventory of Some of the Current Spastic Situations That Could Be Eliminated by More Feedforward.* Coordinated by Jerome Agel. New York, London, Toronto: Bantam Books 1968.

McLuhan, H.M., and Barrington Nevitt. *Take Today: The Executive as Drop-Out.* Don Mills ON: Longman Canada 1972.

Mercier, Vivian. *The Irish Comic Tradition.* Oxford: Clarendon Press 1962.

Mierlo, Wim Van. 'Traffic in Transit: Some Spatio-Temporal Elements of *Finnegans Wake.*' In *'Finnegans Wake' 'teems of times,'* ed. Andrew Triep. *European Joyce Studies* 4, ed. Fritz Zenn and Christine van Boheemen. Amsterdam/Atlanta GA: Editions Rodopi B.V. 1994, 95–105.

Mink, Louis O. *A 'Finnegans Wake' Gazetteer.* Bloomington, London: Indiana University Press 1978.

Myers, Peter. *The Sound of 'Finnegans Wake.'* Houndmills, Basingstoke, Hampshire, London: Macmillan 1992.

Noon, W.T., S.J. *Joyce and Aquinas*. New Haven: Yale University Press 1957.

Norris, Margot. *The Decentered Universe of 'Finnegans Wake': A Structuralist Analysis*. Baltimore, London: Johns Hopkins University Press 1974, 1976.

O'Hehir, Brendan. *A Gaelic Lexicon for 'Finnegans Wake.'* Berkeley, Los Angeles: University of California Press 1967.

O'Hehir, Brendan, and John M. Dillon. *A Classical Lexicon for 'Finnegans Wake': A Glossary of the Greek and Latin in the Major Works of Joyce*. Berkeley, Los Angeles, London: University of California Press 1977.

Orkin, Mark M. *The Great Stork Derby*. Markham ON: General Publishing 1981. Rpt. Paperjacks 1982.

Otte, George. 'Time and Space (with the Emphasis on the Conjunction): Joyce's Response to Lewis,' *JJQ* 22, Spring 1985, 297–306.

The Oxford Companion to the Theatre, ed. Phyllis Hartnoll. 2nd. ed. London, New York, Toronto: Oxford University Press 1957.

Parr, Mary. *James Joyce: The Poetry of Conscience*. Milwaukee WI: Inland Press 1961.

Partridge, Eric. *A Dictionary of the Underworld*. London: Routledge and Kegan Paul 1949–50.

Paulson, Ronald. *Theme and Structure in Swift's 'Tale of a Tub.'* New Haven CT: Yale University Press 1960.

Payne, F. Anne. *Chaucer and Menippean Satire*. Madison, University of Wisconsin Press 1981.

Petronius: The Satyricon and the Fragments. Translated with an Introduction by J.P. Sullivan. Penguin Books 1965. Revised 1969. Rpt. 1971, 1972.

Pinker, Steven. *The Language Instinct: How the Mind Creates Language*. New York: Morrow 1994.

Power, Arthur. *Conversations with James Joyce*, ed. Clive Hart. Dublin: Cahill; London: Millington 1974.

Price, Martin. *Swift's Rhetorical Art: A Study in Structure and Meaning*. Hamden, London: Archon; New Haven CT: Yale University Press 1963.

– *To the Palace of Wisdom: Studies in Order and Energy from Dryden to Blake*. Garden City NY: Doubleday 1964.

Purdy, Strother B. 'Mind Your Genderous: Toward a *Wake* Grammar.' In *New Light on James Joyce, from the Dublin Symposium*. Bloomington, London: Indiana University Press 1972, 46–78.

– 'Vico's Verum-Factum and the Status of the Object in "Finnegans Wake."' *JJQ* 26, no. 3, Spring 1989, 367–78.

Quintilian. *Institutio Oratoria*, trans. H.E. Butler. 4 vols. Loeb Classical Library. Cambridge MA: Harvard University Press; London: Heinemann 1920–2. Rpt. 1963.

Rabelais, François. *Gargantua and Pantagruel*, trans. Jacques Le Clercq. New York: Modern Library 1944.

Riquelme, John Paul. *Teller and Tale in Joyce's Fiction: Oscillating Perspectives.* Baltimore MD: Johns Hopkins University Press 1983.

Rooke, Leon. *Shakespeare's Dog.* Toronto: Stoddart 1981, 1983.

Rose, Danis, and John O'Hanlon. *Understanding 'Finnegans Wake': A Guide to the Narrative of James Joyce's Masterpiece.* New York, London: Garland 1982.

Russell, Bertrand. *A History of Western Philosophy.* New York: Simon and Schuster 1945. Rpt. 1964.

Sailer, Susan Shaw. *On the Void of to Be: Incoherence and Trope in 'Finnegans Wake.'* Ann Arbor: University of Michigan Press 1993.

Saintsbury, George. *The Earlier Renaissance.* Edinburgh: Blackwood; New York: Scribner 1901.

La Satyre Menippée, ou La Vertu du Catholicon, selon l'édition princeps de 1594. Anonymous: various hands. Ed. M.C. Read. Paris: Flammarion 1926. One translation is *A Pleasaunt Satyre or poesie, A Satyre Menippized.* London: Ortwin 1595. STC 15489, AA Carton 263. Another: *Englande's Bright Honour: Shining through the dark Disgrace of Spaines Catholicon.* London: Ortwin 1602. STC 15490, AA Carton 842.

Schaffer, Talia. 'Letters to Biddy: About That Original Hen.' *JJQ* 29, no. 3, Spring 1992, 623–42.

Senn, Fritz. *Joyce's Dislocutions: Essays on Reading as Translation,* ed. John Paul Riquelme. Baltimore, London: Johns Hopkins University Press 1984.

– 'A Note on Burlesque Bloom.' *JJQ* 32, no. 3/4, Spring/Summer 1995, 728–36.

Senn, Fritz, and S. Purdy, eds. 'Mind Your Genderous: Toward a *Wake* Grammar.' In *New Light on James Joyce, from the Dublin Symposium.* Bloomington, London: Indiana University Press 1972, 46–78.

Smidt, Kristian. *James Joyce and the Cultic Use of Fiction.* Oslo: Akademisk Forlag; Oxford: Blackwell 1955.

Solomon, Margaret C. *Eternal Geomater.* Carbondale: Southern Illinois University Press 1969.

Steiner, George. *After Babel.* London, New York, Toronto: Oxford University Press 1975.

Stephens, James. *Letters of James Stephens,* ed. R.I. Finneran. New York: Macmillan 1974.

Sullivan, Sir Edward. *The Book of Kells.* London, Paris, New York: Studio Press. 2nd ed. 1920.

Swartzlander, Susan. 'Multiple Meaning and Misunderstanding: The Mistrial of Festy King.' *JJQ* 23, no. 4, Summer 1986, 465–76.

Swift, Jonathan. *A Tale of a Tub, To Which Is Added An Account of a Battel between the Ancient and Modern Books in St James's Library, and A Discourse concerning the Mechanical Operation of the Spirit in a Letter to a Friend. A Fragment.* 5th ed. Facsimile rpt. Menston YKS: Scolar Press n.d.

– *Works of the Rev. Jonathan Swift, D.D.*, Thomas Sheridan; rev. and corr. John Nichols. 19 vols. London: n.p. 1808.

Theall, Donald F. 'The Hieroglyphs of Engined Egypsians: Machines, Media, and Modes of Communication in *Finnegans Wake.*' In *Joyce Studies Annual, 1991*, ed. Thomas F. Staley. Austin: University of Texas Press 1991, 129–52.

Tindall, W.Y. *James Joyce: His Way of Interpreting the Modern World.* New York, London: Scribner's 1950.

– *A Reader's Guide to 'Finnegans Wake.'* London: Thames and Hudson; New York: Farrar, Straus & Giroux 1969.

Tuve, Rosemond. *Elizabethan and Metaphysical Imagery.* Chicago: University of Chicago Press 1947.

Vanderham, Paul. 'Ezra Pound's Censorship of *Ulysses.*' *JJQ* 32, no. 3/4, Spring/ Summer 1995, 583–95.

Varro, Marcus Terentius. *De Lingua Latina (On the Latin Language)*, trans. R.G. Kent. 2 vols. Loeb Classical Library. Cambridge MA: Harvard University Press; London: Heinemann 1938. Rev. ed. 1958.

– *Saturarum Menippearum reliquiae: Recensuit, prolegomena scripsit, appendicem adjecit Alexander Reise.* Lipsia: Teubner 1865. Rpt. Hildesheim: Olms 1971. The only entire translation thus far is *Varro's Menippean Satires*, trans. Charles Marston Lee. Diss. University of Pittsburgh 1937.

Verene, Donald Phillip. *Vico's Science of the Imagination.* Ithaca NY, London: Cornell University Press 1981.

Vico, Giambattista. *La Scienza nuova*, ed. Paolo Rossi. Milano: Rizzoli 1963.

– *The New Science.* trans. T.G. Bergin and M.H. Fisch. Ithaca NY: Cornell University Press 1948.

Vico and Joyce, ed. Donald Phillip Verene. New York: State University of New York Press 1987.

A Wake Newslitter. Colchester: University of Essex.

Wales, Katie. *The Language of James Joyce.* New York: St Martin's; London: Macmillan Education 1992.

Wiggin, L.A. 'The First Thunderbolt.' In *James Joyce Review*, 3, nos. 1–2, 1959.

Wilson, Edmund. *Letters on Literature and Politics 1912–1972*, ed. Elena Wilson. New York: Farrar, Straus and Giroux 1977.

Yates, Frances A. *The Art of Memory.* London: Routledge & Kegan Paul 1966.

Index

Eliot), 30; and the blind seer, 29;
bodily and exegetical, 23–5, 27–8, 96,
102–3, 117, 120; of eye and ear, in
Ulysses, 24–5; of eye, ear, nose, and
throat, 96; in *Finnegans Wake*, 30;
and reading *Finnegans Wake*, 10, 32,
273–4.n.6; and technology (Vico),
28–9, 118
shock. *See* jolt/shock.
sigla: □, 19; �, 77, 122, 289; △ and ⊏,
77; Λ, 77, 116, 192, 194, 315n.2; ⊣,
77, 305n.19; Ш, 155, 310n.5; +, 205
Smidt, Kristian, 317n.14, 321n.11
Solomon, Margaret C., 290n.2
spectrum/rainbow, 47, 67, 96, 197, 216
Steiner, George, 289–90n.2
Stephen Hero, 21
Stephens, James, 277n.16
Sterne, Laurence, x, 11; menippism and,
301n.6; and rhetorical characteriza-
tion in *Tristram Shandy*, 12, 303n.11
Stoics, 9
stork derby. *See* Orkin, Mark.
Strabo, 3
stuttering, 44, 81, 155, 200–1
Swift, Jonathan, x, 3, 11, 12–13, 19, 64,
116, 312n.12

*Thousand and One Nights, The. See
Arabian Nights, The*
thunders, x; as constitutive utterance
(logos), 237; and development
throughout writing of *FW*, 306n.5; as
digression, 152, 238; as farrago, 238;
function of, x, 37–8; and 100-letter
length, 245; and lightning (thunder
2), 67; and pattern of action in *FW*,
41; as speech of Nature, 288n.4; as
spoken by language itself, 33; as
statements without syntax, x, 37; and

The Thousand and One Nights, 246,
257; as two sets of five, 38, 137, 260,
263, 265. *See also* minor rumbles.
thunder 1: Arabic in, 38, 48, 262; composition of, 243; the Fall in, 44, 47;
fallout of, 39; images of: frontispiece,
42, 46; topics of, x, 43, 261
thunder 2: clothing as weaponry in, 56,
63, 65, 136, 293n.13, 307n.8; composition of, 244; fallout of, 67–9; fragmentation in, 67; images: 58, 66; and
manuscript culture, 59; and PQ
themes, x, 61, 262, *see also*
Prankquean; and rain, 57, 63; revision
of, 246–8; and the Two Books (q.v.),
60–1
thunder 3: fallout of, 86–7; HCE as civilized man in, 78, 262; HCE's disease
in, 82; HCE as ear dominated by eye
in, 83; identity quest (Parsifal) in, 78,
80, 82; images: 76, 84; revision of,
246, 248; 'royal divorce' (dissociation
of sensibility) in, 78, 83, 261; themes
in, 80–2, 86
thunder 4: the court in, 95; fallout of,
103; the Four in, 95; four senses (eye,
ear, nose, throat) in, 4, 96, 102–3;
images: 94, 100; prostitution/disease/
whores' race in, 95–8; railroad/Eire-
ann-horse race in, 95, 98–101; revision of, 244; roads in, 95; spectrum in,
96; themes in, x, 94–5, 262
thunder 5: Belinda as, reproductive
matriarch in, 115, 117, 119, 125–6;
Humpty Dumpty in, 19, 44, 47, 80,
120, 123, 175, 261–2, 264; identity
quest in, 123; images: 112, 121,
246; the learned critics in, 111,
113, 115, 118, 124; the photo and,
115, 122–3; printing press in, 120;